The Jewish Discovery of Islam

The Jewish Discovery of Islam

STUDIES IN HONOR OF BERNARD LEWIS

edited by
Martin Kramer

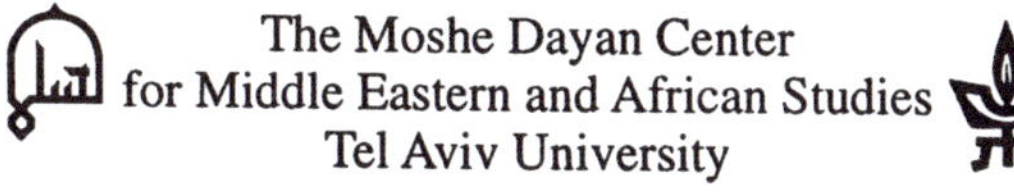

The Moshe Dayan Center
for Middle Eastern and African Studies
Tel Aviv University

TEL AVIV

First published in 1999 in Israel by
The Moshe Dayan Center for Middle Eastern and African Studies
Tel Aviv University
Tel Aviv 69978, Israel
dayancen@ccsg.tau.ac.il
www.dayan.org

ISBN 965-224-040-0 (hardback)
ISBN 965-224-038-9 (paperback)

Publication of this book has been made possible by a grant from the Lucius N. Littauer Foundation.

Cover illustration: The Great Synagogue (const. 1854–59), Dohány Street, Budapest, Hungary, photograph by the late Gábor Hegyi, 1982. Beth Hatefutsoth, Tel Aviv, courtesy of the Hegyi family.

Cover design: Ruth Beth-Or
Production: Elena Lesnick

Printed in Israel
on acid-free paper
by A.R.T. Offset Services Ltd., Tel Aviv

Contents

Preface

This volume brings together the presentations made at a conference entitled "The Jewish Discovery of Islam," and convened at Tel Aviv University in June 1996 in celebration of Bernard Lewis on his eightieth birthday. Participants were asked to take his famous article, "The Pro-Islamic Jews," as a point of departure. In that article, Lewis underlined the prominent role played by Jews in advancing modern Europe's understanding of Islam, Islamic history, and Muslim societies. According to Lewis, the similarities between Hebrew and Arabic, the parallels between two faiths grounded in law, and the relative tolerance of Muslim rule toward Jews, allowed many Jewish scholars to approach Islam with an understanding and sympathy then uncommon in Europe.

The conference, as its title suggests, went beyond Lewis's observation, to ask this question: Was there a "Jewish discovery of Islam," distinct from Europe's discovery? Does it make sense to assess Jewish travellers, writers, and scholars—some of them only nominally Jewish—outside the broad context of European intellectual history and orientalism? And is there an alternative context, some unifying characteristic to the approach of these Jewish "discoverers"? Several possible answers to each of these questions are suggested by a reading of the unique collection of studies assembled in this volume.

From the task of *editing* the collection, an answer has emerged. No appreciation of Islamic studies is complete without some appreciation of the special character of the contribution made by Jews. Most obviously, many Jews approached Islam in ways inspired by their understanding of Judaism, and one basic feature of the Jewish discovery was the drawing of analogies between Judaism and Islam. But there also was an ideological dimension to their contribution.

Jews fascinated by Islam were formed through participation in Europe's scholarly, political, and intellectual debates. But they were also formed by an urgent debate over the past, present, and future of the Jews—a debate fueled by the persistence of anti-Semitism, even its resurgence. Europe still vacillated over whether the Jews belonged to Europe or the East, whether they were compatriots or foreigners, whether they were a race apart or an assimilable minority. Every Jew hoped to see Europe grow tolerant of difference and regard its civilization as the product of a symbiosis with other civilizations. The thread that runs through the contribution of Jewish scholars of Islam is the denial of a dichotomy between East and West. The Jewish discovery of Islam was not distinct from Europe's; it was an inseparable part of it. But it was overwhelming biased against "Orientalism" as an ideology of difference and supremacy.

This book is a tribute to Bernard Lewis, who in many ways personifies its theme. It is more than an offering in recognition of his already widely acclaimed erudition and scholarship. Lewis has been a vital link between Israel and that broad Western tradition of scholarship of which he himself is the foremost exemplar. The halls of Israel's universities are home to many of his students, from his years of teaching in London and Princeton. More than twenty years ago, he chose Tel Aviv University as the place to invest his energies and affections. For some years now, he has been what he calls a "hardy perennial" at Tel Aviv University, visiting during the winter months, lecturing at the university, and meeting with students. The debt owed by us to Bernard Lewis is large and continues to grow. This volume, and the conference behind it, are grateful acknowledgments of all that he has done and still does for scholarship on this shore.

The conference was the work of three sponsors: the Moshe Dayan Center for Middle Eastern and African Studies at Tel Aviv University, which I direct; the Diaspora Research Institute, at the time directed by Minna Rozen; and the Mortimer and Raymond Sackler Institute of Advanced Studies, at the time directed by Yuval Ne'eman. I wish to thank Professors Rozen and Ne'eman for their close cooperation and shared sponsorship. At the Moshe Dayan Center, I would like to single out my assistant, Amira Margalith, for the vital assistance she extended to me on this (and every) project. The conference was made possible by the support of the following generous friends: the late Raphael Recanati, Mortimer and Raymond Sackler, Yad Avi Ha-Yishuv, the Kalman Lassner Lectureship, and the late Henry Ergas.

Martin Kramer

Introduction

Martin Kramer

The European exploration, study, and representation of Islam are beginning to find their historians. The "Orientalism" debate, begun in earnest twenty years ago, provided a stimulus for research in all these areas—a research that has gradually edged beyond polemics. The work of European explorers, travellers, and writers from the Renaissance onward is under reexamination. Orientalist art is receiving its due. So too is the history of modern scholarship—the role of individuals and institutions in the great centers of European academe. And at some point, this question will have to be answered: Did Jews make a distinct contribution to the Western discovery of Islam?

Bernard Lewis first posed the question thirty years ago, in an article entitled "The Pro-Islamic Jews."

> In the development of Islamic studies in European and, later, American universities, Jews, and in particular Jews of Orthodox background and education, play an altogether disproportionate role....The role of these scholars in the development of every aspect of Islamic studies has been immense—not only in the advancement of scholarship but also in the enrichment of the Western view of Oriental religion, literature, and history, by the substitution of knowledge and understanding for prejudice and ignorance.[1]

Elsewhere Lewis writes more explicitly about the nature of this contribution:

> A major accession of strength resulted from the emancipation of Jews in central and western Europe and their consequent entry into the universities. Jewish scholars brought up in the Jewish religion and trained in the Hebrew language found Islam and Arabic far easier to understand than did their Christian colleagues, and were, moreover, even less affected by nostalgia for the Crusades, preoccupation with imperial policy, or the desire to convert the "heathen." Jewish scholars like Gustav Weil, Ignaz Goldziher, and others played a key role in the development of an objective, nonpolemical, and positive evaluation of Islamic civilization.[2]

Elsewhere Lewis goes still further: "Jewish scholars were among the first who attempted to present Islam to European readers as Muslims themselves see it and to stress, to recognize, and indeed sometimes to romanticize the merits and achievements of Muslim civilization in its great days."[3]

No other general survey of the development of the Western understanding of Islam makes a similar statement. Edward Said, in *Orientalism,* made no reference at all to the emergence or role of Jewish scholars.[4] Maxime Rodinson, in his essay on "Western Views of the Muslim World," omitted any reference to a contribution by Jews as such, and made no mention at all of the most important Jewish interpreter of Islam, Ignaz Goldziher.[5] Albert Hourani, in his articles "Islam and the Philosophers of History" and "Islam in European Thought," wrote nothing specific about the role of Jews in Islamic studies, although he stressed the supreme importance of Goldziher on both occasions, and recognized the link between his Jewish formation and his understanding of Islam.[6] Lewis thus stands alone in his explicit assessment of the crucial role of Jews in the emergence of a detached, even sympathetic understanding of Islam in Europe.

This book seeks to pose the questions once again, in a more insistent way. Was there a Jewish discovery of Islam, distinct from Europe's? Did the culture of central and western European Jewry provide the foundations for a more accurate and sometimes more favorable assessment of Islam than the general culture of Europe? Is there any common feature in the approach of these persons of Jewish background (who included practicing Jews, lapsed Jews, and even a few converts to Christianity and Islam)?

A comprehensive list of Jewish travellers, writers and scholars who contributed to Europe's understanding of Islam and the Middle East would fill pages. (Such lists appear in the articles "Travellers" and "Orientalists" in the *Encyclopaedia Judaica,* which also has entries on all the major figures.) An integrated assessment of their influence at all levels would make for a complex book—a combination of European, Jewish, and Islamic history, and the history of every scholarly discipline and creative genre as it encountered Islam and Muslims. This collected volume is more selective and less integrated, focusing on figures who may be said to represent larger trends in exploration, literature, and scholarship.

Yet even these disparate studies suggest some possible answers. Jews found themselves in a Europe constructed upon a series of evolving dichotomies: Christendom and Islam, Europe and Asia, West and East, Aryan and Semite. The Jews posed a challenge to these dichotomies on practically every level. At first, their role was passive, as others debated their proper classification. By the nineteenth century, Jews had entered the debate, questioning not just their classification, but the very validity of the dichotomies. Such dichotomies were regarded as obstacles to assimilation, which remained the dominant project of central and western European Jewry from the French Revolution to the Holocaust.

In pursuit of this project, Jews tended to differ from other Europeans in their response to Islam, and the ways in which they represented it. In the Middle Ages, Islam excited only fear and loathing in Europe, fed by Muslim conquests on both ends of the continent. With the retreat of Muslim power and European imperial expansion into the lands of Islam, fear yielded to contempt. But the spirit of the Enlightenment and the rise of romanticism introduced much more variety in Europe's responses to Islam. These began to include curiosity, fascination, admiration, and scholarly study. European thinkers came to differ widely in their understanding of Islam, as a religious system and a social order.

Europe's Jews stood almost entirely on one side of this debate. To be sure, Jews also differed in their attitudes to Islam, as this volume demonstrates. But in the aggregate, their approaches rested upon a heightened empathy and sympathy for Islam, conveyed to the rest of Europe through literature, exploration, and scholarship. And the common rationale, reduced to a sentence, was this: a Europe respectful of Islam and Muslims was more likely to show respect for Judaism and Jews.

This introduction follows some of the main lines in the Jewish discovery of Islam, as it unfolded in Europe from the early nineteenth century through the middle of the twentieth. It does not pretend to be an exhaustive catalogue of all those involved in this discovery. Individuals and their works are mentioned as points of ready reference, in a process of discovery which involved hundreds of individuals and thousands of creative works, from books to plays, from travelogues to catalogues. From the 1920s, part of this work of discovery was transferred from Europe to Palestine, and the earliest stages of this transfer are also considered. The Holocaust and the creation of Israel closed one phase and opened another, and they form the outer boundary of this introduction. To maintain that boundary, no one born after 1920 is mentioned, and there is no discussion of the role of Jews in America as interpreters of Islam.

The Romantic Impulse

Romanticism toward the Muslim world, which swayed the poets of Europe in the first third of the nineteenth century, found an echo among Europe's Jews. In myriad ways, they sought to emphasize Islam's splendor, as a strategy to remind Europe of the multiple origins of its own civilization, and its debt to Islam and Judaism. This meant a deliberate effort to associate Jews with those periods, places, and elements in Islamic civilization most admired by Europe. The message was straightforward: Jews had helped to bring the civilization of medieval Islam to its apex. Given the chance, they could do the same for the civilization of modern Europe. This interpretation of Islam, emphasizing its achievements and tolerance, had nothing in common with "Orientalism" as ideology. Its purpose was to facilitate Europe's assimilation of Jews.

The romantic enthusiasm for high Islam at its apex was strongest among the German-speaking Jews of central Europe. It manifested itself most famously in the work of the poet and essayist Heinrich Heine (1797–1856).[7] Heine, like Victor Hugo, never set foot in the East, but like Hugo he found it ideal space for his imagination. As a university student in Bonn and Göttingen, he read widely in the then-available translations of Arabic and Persian classics.[8] His tragedy *Almansor* (published in 1823, later supplemented by a poem of the same name) is set in a dilapidated Alhambra, and deals with the adjustment of Muslims to the

Christianization of Spain in the sixteenth century. Nearly every literary analysis of the play and the poem has read them as allegories to the predicament of nineteenth-century German Jewry.

But *Almansor* also displays a profound empathy for the Muslims themselves, about whom Heine troubled to learn a great deal. Its blunt jabs at proselytizing Christianity led audiences (especially in the Catholic Rhineland) to understand *Almansor* as an anti-Christian diatribe, and it caused a scandal. (A typical passage: "On the tower where the muezzin called to prayer there is now the melancholy tolling of church bells. On the steps where the faithful sang the words of the Prophet, tonsured monks are acting out their lugubrious charades.")[9] The play, incidentally, includes one of Heine's most quoted lines, in an exchange between the eponymous hero Almansor and the servant Hassan:

ALMANSOR: We heard that Ximenes the Terrible
in Granada, in the middle of the market-place
—my tongue refuses to say it!—cast the Koran
into the flames of a burning pyre!

HASSAN: That was only a prelude; where they burn books
they will, in the end, burn human beings too.[10]

Heine bought what he called his *entrée billet* to Europe in 1825, with his baptism. But he could well have subscribed to the words he put in the mouth of Almansor: "For all my hat and coat I have remained a Muslim: I wear my turban here, in my heart."[11]

As the nineteenth century progressed, German-speaking Jews actively sought to be associated with the legacy of Islam, and to bask in its reflected glory. In doing so, they showed an acute awareness of the favored place occupied by Islam in the German collective consciousness. The Tunisian historian Hichem Djaït writes of how "the German-speaking world, badly fragmented, lacking a concerted diplomacy...did not experience the continual trafficking, the struggles, and the permanent contacts that France, Spain, Italy, and England had with Islam in the Mediterranean basin or Asia." As a result, Islam for Germans evoked "neither intimacy nor hostility but a positive inclination, a favorable prejudice."[12]

The tangible evidence for the Jewish appreciation of this favorable prejudice may be seen in mid-nineteenth-century urban synagogue architecture in the "Moorish" style. Minarets and domes rose above the skylines of Leipzig, Frankfurt, Berlin, and Cologne. The style spread eastward to Budapest and St. Petersburg, southward to Florence, and westward to New York, Philadelphia, and Cincinnati.[13] In some of these synagogues, opined one contemporary Jewish critic, "the crescent alone is wanting at the summit."[14] Certainly one factor in this choice was a desire to avoid explicitly Christian styles; another was the Moorish style's freedom from figural ornamentation. But the splendor of Islamic architecture deployed in a synagogue sent a subliminal message. Jews had shared in the genius of Islamic civilization, and they could provide cultural leaven for a new and open Euro-American civilization, based upon a shared aesthetic and transcending religious differences.[15]

In France, the work of associating the Jews with the romantic Orient did not have to be done by Jews themselves; it was done for them by the orientalist painters. The great nineteenth-century painters included no Jews, but in Morocco and Algeria, which the artists much favored, they often chose local Jews as subjects, especially for domestic scenes and whenever Muslims were unapproachable. In the words of one art historian: "In North Africa, as [Eugène] Delacroix [1798–1863], [Théodore] Chassériau [1819–56], and [Alfred] Dehondencq [1822–82] had found, it was only in Jewish houses that artists could get an idea of Oriental life. The same was true of the Levant."[16] The romantic representations of Jews in the work of the French orientalist painters were almost wholly sympathetic and admiring.[17] The exhibition of such works, at the Salon in Paris and elsewhere, reminded Europeans of the placement of Jews in Islamic civilization, and the role of Mediterranean Jews as mediators between Europe and Islam.

In English letters, Jewish orientalism manifested itself in the literary works of Benjamin Disraeli (1804–81), the subject of an essay by Minna Rozen in this volume. Disraeli was born to Jewish parents, but his father had him baptized at the age of thirteen. His conversion opened doors that otherwise would have been closed to the ambitious young man. But his physical appearance proclaimed him a foreigner, in an England preoccupied with pedigree. Painfully aware of the ways his Jewish origins could be used against him, he sought to turn them to advantage by associating the Jews with the noble Arabs of the desert and the refined Arabs of Spain—both the focus of a burgeoning English romanticism.[18] Disraeli worked to achieve this purpose through his novels. In *Tancred* (1847), the reader learned that the Arabs of the desert were "Jews upon horseback," and that Jews were "Mosaic Arabs," bound by ties of race to

"Mohammedan Arabs." In *Coningsby* (1844), the reader learned that in the "unrivalled civilization" of Muslim Spain,

> the children of Ishmael rewarded the children of Israel with equal rights and privileges with themselves. During these halcyon centuries, it is difficult to distinguish the followers of Moses from the votary of Mahomet. Both alike built palaces, gardens, and fountains; filled equally the highest offices of the state, competed in an extensive and enlightened commerce, and rivalled each other in renowned universities.[19]

By linking himself with that East most romanticized by the English, Disraeli sought to appear as heir to its store of wisdom, which he would put at the service of England's new power.

Disraeli moved from literature to politics after the decline of romantic orientalism, and it became the turn of his opponents to associate him with the Orient, in a malevolent way. Lord Cromer (1841–1917)—his own claim to wisdom resting upon years of administration in India and Egypt—offered this retrospective on Disraeli: "No one who has lived much in the East can... fail to be struck with the fact that Disraeli was a thorough Oriental." As evidence for this categorization, he cited Disraeli's

> taste for tawdry finery, the habit of enveloping in mystery matters as to which there was nothing to conceal, the love of intrigue...the luxuriance of the imaginative faculties, the strong addiction to plausible generalities set forth in florid language... all these features, in a character which is perhaps not quite so complex as is often supposed, hail from the East.[20]

Any English reader would know that by "Oriental," Cromer did not mean the noble desert Arabs or the cultivators of Andalusian gardens. He was making of Disraeli an Egyptian effendi or an Indian nawab—those dissembling Oriental gentlemen whom Cromer professed to know so well.

For Europe's Jews, there seemed no reason to think twice about identification with the caliphate of Baghdad, the glories of Muslim Spain, and the landscapes of Morocco—all the subjects of admiration by Europe's romantics. But the efforts of Jews to associate themselves with the Islamic Orient, even when successful, had mixed results, if only because that Islamic Orient evoked a very wide range of associations in Europe, including dismissive contempt. The fanatically nationalist Prussian state historiographer Heinrich von Treitschke (1834–96) did not intend a compliment when he wrote in 1879 that "there will always be

Jews who are nothing but German-speaking Orientals."[21] As worldly romanticism gave way to racial nationalism in Europe, Jewish identification with the Orient became less of an asset, and played into the hands of growing numbers of anti-Semites.

The Jewish Explorers

Literary exploration was supplemented by geographic exploration. Travel to remote places was one of the great avenues of social mobility in the nineteenth century, and provided a high platform for self-expression. While Indian and Mediterranean Islam fell increasingly under the influence and direct control of Europe, other Muslim regions had yet to be "explored"—that is, visited and documented by Europeans. During the nineteenth century, several European Jewish travellers traversed the lesser-known lands of Islam.[22] But two men gained particular fame for their accounts of travels across Arabia and Central Asia, both formidable frontiers of nineteenth-century exploration.

William Gifford Palgrave (1826–88), born in London, was not a Jew by any conventional definition. But he had a Jewish background. His father, Francis Ephraim Cohen, converted to Anglicanism before his church marriage, and emerged transformed as Sir Francis Palgrave (1788–1861), distinguished author of *The Rise and Progress of the English Commonwealth* (1832) and founder of the Public Record Office. His second son, William Gifford, was left with the thinnest residue of Jewish identity, which apparently included a smattering of Hebrew. After studies at Oxford and a stint of service with the Indian army, "Giffy" not only became a Catholic, but joined the Society of Jesus, and was ordained a priest. He arrived in Lebanon in 1855, where he preached the gospel in Arabic—and, without explanation, reverted to the name Cohen. Palgrave had no interest in Judaism, but he increasingly harked back to his Jewish origins, as part of his growing preoccupation with race and nationality.

In 1862, Palgrave secured funding from Napoleon III (r. 1852–70) for a mission to the deepest parts of Wahhabi Arabia, with the purpose of exploring possibilities for a Franco-Arab alliance. He disguised himself as a Syrian Christian doctor ("Seleem Abou Mahmood-el-Eys"), and it is possible that he also pretended to be a Muslim on occasion in Najd. Nothing came of his political scheme, but Palgrave did write an account of his travels, his *Narrative of a Year's Journey through Central and*

Eastern Arabia, 1862–1863 (1865). This book had an immense influence, and not just as a (controversial) travelogue of Arabia. As Benjamin Braude shows in his essay for this volume, Palgrave contributed to the later British conviction that the Arabs were a noble people—"the Englishmen of the East"—entitled to independence from Ottoman rule. Yet it must be conceded that the relationship of Palgrave's Jewish origins to his own ideas about the Arabs must remain a matter of speculation, since all his references to those origins are so oblique.

A clearer picture emerges in the case of an explorer with much firmer Jewish moorings: Arminius Vámbéry (1832–1913). Vámbéry was born into an impoverished Jewish family in Slovakia, then part of the Habsburg Empire. "Hershel" spent his first years in the traditional *heder,* where he acquired a command of the Hebrew Bible and Talmud. But he soon distanced himself from belief, and in his later studies (pursued intermittently in Christian denominational schools) he demonstrated a talent for languages. He became an itinerant tutor, and began to teach himself Arabic and Turkish, while dreaming of adventure in the East. In 1857 he left for Istanbul, where he worked as a tutor in better Turkish households, and where doors finally began to open. In 1863, disguised as a dervish ("Rashid Effendi"), he visited Khiva, Bukhara, Samarkand, and Herat. His account of this journey, *Travels and Adventures in Central Asia* (1864), made him internationally famous, especially in Britain where interest in Central Asia ran high. He then appeared to have converted to Protestantism, in order that he might teach Oriental languages at the University of Pest. One of his first students was the young Ignaz Goldziher. His subsequent career included philological research and political advocacy, marked by a combination of Russophobia and Anglophilia.

Vámbéry's motives were always mixed. From poor and humble origins, he remained obsessed with money and station throughout life. He was not free of prejudice, and he often wrote sardonically about the customs and beliefs he encountered in the East. But he had a fundamental sympathy for Muslim peoples. "We alone, we think, have the right to be mighty and free, and the rest of humanity must be subject to us and never taste the golden fruits of liberty," he wrote after the Young Turk revolution. But Europeans "tend to forget that constitutional government is by no means a new thing in Islam, for anything more democratic than the doctrine of the Arab Prophet it would be difficult to find in any other religion."[23] As Jacob M. Landau suggests in his essay in this volume,

Vámbéry's Jewish origins may have been at the root of his sympathy for the oppressed—a sympathy he extended not just to Muslim peoples, but to the Jews themselves. It was Vámbéry who arranged the 1901 meeting between the Zionist leader Theodor Herzl (1860–1904) and the Ottoman Sultan Abdülhamid II (r. 1876–1909).

The First Scholars

Academe put up the most formidable barriers to Jewish participation—barriers which stood well into the nineteenth century. Before the emancipation of Europe's Jews, learned Christians did not regard them as credible authorities in matters of faith—even the false faith of Islam. Such credibility was inseparable from an adherence to the true Christian faith, and information about Islam had to be embedded in an affirmation of Christianity's truth and Islam's falsehood. Even in the Enlightenment, Arabic studies remained a handmaiden of theology, and in most cases served as an adjunct to the Hebrew and biblical studies of Christian theologians. The theological connection formed an insurmountable barrier to the emergence of Jewish academic authorities on Islam in Europe.

Three developments combined to break down the barrier and afford Jews a role in the rapid expansion of the European scholarly exploration of Islam. The first was the Haskala, the Jewish Enlightenment: Jewish scholars began to take an interest in secular history, and the place of Jewish narratives within that history. The second development was the Jewish emancipation: Jews gradually won admission to secular academic institutions, as students and professors. The third development was Europe's secularization: Europeans increasingly sought an understanding of Islam and the Muslims freed from Christian theological dogma.

In the nineteenth century, the scope of Jewish scholarship expanded. No longer limited to traditional study of the law, it came to embrace the origins and history of the Jews, and of the peoples with which they had interacted. The new "science" of Jewish studies, emphasizing history and philology, focused also upon the history of Jews under Islam. Many European Jewish scholars first acquired Arabic and Judeo-Arabic as a basic tool for the study of medieval Jewish philosophy and history. Jewish cultural history could not be researched and written without this tool, and while Jews learned Arabic alongside non-Jews in universities, they usually did so with the different intent of studying Jewish sources. Two of the pioneers in this field were Solomon Munk (1805–67) and Moritz Steinschneider (1816–1907).[24]

Only a minority applied these linguistic tools to the study of Islam, usually in the first instance to Jewish-Muslim relations and Jewish elements in Islam. The theme of Islam's debt to Judaism would be a recurrent one in the Jewish study of Islam, precisely because Jewish scholarship, following Hegel, had settled upon monotheism as the great contribution of the Jews to world civilization. In 1833, Abraham Geiger (1810–74), a brilliant young rabbi from Frankfurt, published a book entitled *Was hat Mohammed aus dem Judenthume aufgenommen?,* analyzing the Prophet Muhammad's adaptations from Judaism. (The original Latin thesis was written for a competition at the University of Bonn, where it took the prize.) Geiger's adept handling of the sources and his careful analysis won him widespread praise among the handful of scholars then devoted to the academic study of Islam.

As Jacob Lassner points out in his study for this collection, Geiger overstated the case for Islam's borrowing from Judaism. But the book has rightly been called the dawn of historical research on Islam, and Geiger's approach to the relationship of Islam to other religions retained its validity for a century. No less important, it introduced a tone of respect into the study of Islam—so much so that Geiger came under some criticism from Christian colleagues, particularly for assuming the sincerity of the Muslim prophet. Muhammad, he wrote, "seems to have been a genuine enthusiast who was himself convinced of his divine mission." His conclusion: "The harsh judgment generally passed upon him [by Europeans] is unjustifiable."[25] This caused something of a stir, and in an otherwise favorable review of Geiger's book, the French scholar Antoine-Isaac Silvestre de Sacy (1758–1838), founder of modern Arabic studies, felt compelled to insist that Muhammad was a "skilled imposter."[26]

Geiger, however, was not destined to become a historian of Islam. He applied his immense talents to building the intellectual foundations of Reform Judaism, applying the same source-critical techniques to Jewish origins. Nonetheless, Geiger remained a partisan of Islam, especially in comparing the experience of Jews under Islam and Christianity. In 1865, he contrasted Islam, which "always left itself favorable to the cultivation of science and philosophy, with a Christian Church that increasingly nourished a repugnance of science and reason."[27] This was a clear voice of dissent in a Europe where Islam continued to be regarded as inimical to science and reason.

Only a handful of Jewish scholars, formed in the "science of Judaism," went still further, and devoted themselves fully to Islamic studies. A German Jewish contemporary of Geiger's was the first to do so. Gustav Weil (1808–89) was born in Sulzburg, Baden, to a rabbinical family. Like his forebears, he was to have been a rabbi, and he studied Talmud under his grandfather in Metz. But he abandoned this at the first opportunity, entering the University of Heidelberg at the age of twenty. There he studied philology and history, as well as Arabic. In 1830 he went to Paris to study under Silvestre de Sacy, and from there he accompanied the French forces which occupied Algeria, as a correspondent for an Augsburg newspaper. In 1831 he proceeded to Cairo, where he spent more than four years teaching French at the new Egyptian medical school established by Muhammad 'Alī Pasha (r. 1805–49) and run by the French physician Antoine Barthélémy Clot-Bey (1799–1867). In Egypt he perfected his Arabic and acquired Turkish and Persian. After some months in Istanbul, he returned to the University of Heidelberg, where he served as a librarian for almost twenty-five years. He was appointed a professor in 1861.

In 1843, Weil published a life of Muhammad entitled *Mohammed der Prophet.* Lewis describes this work as the first Western biography of Muhammad "that was free from prejudice and polemic, based on a profound yet critical knowledge of the Arabic sources, and informed by a sympathetic understanding of Muslim belief and piety. For the first time, he gave the European reader an opportunity to see Muhammad as the Muslims saw him, and thus to achieve a fuller appreciation of his place in human history."[28] Weil achieved this through an exacting and exhausting use of manuscripts then available in Europe.

Although trained in philology, Weil came to regard himself as a historian of Islam, who took his inspiration from Leopold von Ranke (1795–1886). The Rankean influence was most notable in Weil's five-volume *Geschichte der Chalifen* (1846–62). A contemporary French scholar described this work as "the first complete history of the caliphate, written according to the demands of European criticism and composed from the original sources... the authors are controlled by each other, the facts discussed and the authorities cited."[29] Weil reproduced the narrative style of his Arabic sources, resulting in an account that was neither dramatic nor analytical—a critic once described it unkindly as *ledern,* dull. But Weil's work nonetheless represented an advance in its dispassion and detachment.

Another Jewish scholar, Hartwig Derenbourg (1844–1908), achieved something similar in making possible a more sympathetic understanding of the Muslim view of the Crusades. The Paris-born Derenbourg, son of a specialist in Judeo-Arabic and Hebrew, studied Arabic in Leipzig. He then taught it in Paris, and in 1885 was appointed to the new chair of Islamic studies at the École des langues orientales. In 1880, while cataloguing Arabic manuscripts in the library of the Escorial, he discovered the autobiography of Usāma ibn Munqidh, a twelfth-century writer and diplomat from Syria, who left a vivid and very human account of Muslim life at the time of the Crusades. Derenbourg published the text in 1886, and a French translation in 1889. Derenbourg also would be remembered for the direction he gave to one of his last students, Louis Massignon (1883–1962). In 1907, Massignon read Muslim mystical texts with Derenbourg, who encouraged him to take up the tenth-century mystic Ḥallāj as his thesis subject. Derenbourg died before the thesis was completed, and Massignon dedicated his *thèse complémentaire,* a lexicon of Muslim mysticism, to Derenbourg's memory.[30]

The Great Goldziher

By the middle of the nineteenth century, research had replaced romance, philology had replaced poetry, and the new authorities on the East became preoccupied with establishing "scientific" hierarchies and categories. The idea that the Jews were Semites owed its origins to philologists, concerned to establish the genealogy of languages. Jews and Muslims came together under this Semitic rubric—benignly, as speakers of cognate languages, Hebrew and Arabic; condescendingly, as peoples limited in their cultural development and mental processes by the languages of their expression; and, ominously, as members of an inferior racial category. The passage from the benign to the condescending is usually associated with two comparative philologists, Ernest Renan (1823–92) in France, and Theodor Nöldeke (1836–1930) in Germany. Both had disparaging things to say about Semitic cultures—Renan, from a belief in the supremacy of Indo-European peoples; Nöldeke, from a veneration of Graeco-Roman antiquity.

Yet in the schema of both Renan and Nöldeke, the Jews of Europe had escaped the Semitic bind. Renan held that "race" was determined not by blood, but by language, religion, laws, and customs. A Muslim

Turk, in his estimate, was "today more a true Semite than the Jew who has become French, or to be more exact, European."[31] Theodor Nöldeke, writing on "Some Characteristics of the Semitic Race," reached essentially the same conclusion:

> In drawing the character of the Semites, the historian must guard against taking the Jews of Europe as pure representatives of the race. These have maintained many features of their primitive type with remarkable tenacity, but they have become Europeans all the same; and, moreover, many peculiarities by which they are marked are not so much of old Semitic origin as the result of the special history of the Jews, and in particular of continued oppression, and of that long isolation from other peoples, which was partly their own choice and partly imposed on them.[32]

If this were so, then Jewish scholars were not to be regarded as Semitic specimens, but as fellow Europeans, who could participate as intellectual equals in Europe's discovery of Islam. And so even as Nöldeke made disparaging remarks about Eastern peoples and Semitic cultures, he could hail a Jew, Ignaz Goldziher (1850–1921), for his brilliant insights into Islam.

Goldziher produced nineteenth-century Europe's great breakthrough in Islamic studies. Born in the Hungarian town of Székesfehérvár, son of a leather merchant, he received a rigorous schooling in the Hebrew Bible and Talmud from an early age. He completed his philological studies in Leipzig in 1870, and then undertook further travels in Europe and the East. But he could not secure a professorship at the University of Budapest on his return, and from 1876 he made his living as secretary of the Reform (Neolog) Jewish community in the city.

His two-volume *Muhammedanische Studien* (1888–89) overturned the world of orientalist scholarship, not just by its sheer virtuosity, but by its guiding notion that Islam was a faith in constant evolution. Goldziher's interests ranged widely, from the development of Muslim sects to Arabic poetry. But his best-known contribution lay in his study of Islam's oral tradition, the *ḥadīth,* and his realization that it must be regarded not as a record of the Prophet Muhammad's deeds and sayings, but as window on the first centuries of Islam. Bernát Heller (1871–1943), Goldziher's closest student, wrote of his teacher that

> [Goldziher] was able to grasp the depth and breadth of Islam because he had a deep understanding of Judaism. The distinction between the

> Koran and the Sunna became so clear to him because he grew up in the respect of written and oral teachings. He distinguished between *halachah* and *haggadah* in the Jewish tradition just as he did between the standards of the law and the ethical narrative and eschatological tenets within the *ḥadīth.*[33]

This assessment has been criticized for implying "that the secret of [Goldziher's] academic achievement... must be something mysteriously Jewish," whereas "several of Goldziher's contemporaries (mostly the bearers of the 'white man's burden') recognized this duality within Islam and the special sanctioning of the social practice without much knowledge of the Talmud. The cleverest of all was C. Snouck Hurgronje."[34] The criticism simultaneously succeeds in making the point and missing it. The Dutch Islamicist Snouck Hurgronje (1857–1936) reached his understanding of this "duality" through extensive travel in Muslim lands and years of service as a colonial administrator in the Dutch East Indies. He also drew upon the inspiration of Goldziher himself (to whom, wrote Snouck Hurgronje, "in defining the direction of my studies, I owe more than to anyone else.")[35]

Goldziher, in contrast, did not need to be positioned in a Muslim land by an imperial power to achieve his insight. As a young man of twenty-three, he did spend a *Wanderjahre* in Egypt, Palestine, and Syria, but he never again stopped for more than a few days in a Muslim land. How was it that Goldziher achieved such an intimate understanding of Islam, without sustained contact with its living expression? There was the fact of his genius. But his understanding of Islam was mediated by his intimate familiarity with another religion of law, in constant tension with actual practice, and formulated in a Semitic language: Judaism.[36]

Goldziher regarded Judaism and Islam as kindred faiths. Islam originated as a "Judaized Meccan cult," but evolved into "the only religion which, even in its doctrinal and official formulation, can satisfy philosophical minds. My ideal was to elevate Judaism to a similar rational level."[37] During his stay in Damascus, Goldziher's assimilation of the two faiths reached a point where "I became inwardly convinced that I myself was a Muslim." In Cairo he even prayed as a Muslim: "In the midst of the thousands of the pious, I rubbed my forehead against the floor of the mosque. Never in my life was I more devout, more truly devout, than on that exalted Friday."[38] He nevertheless remained a committed Jew, convinced that a reformed Judaism, salvaged from rabbinic obscurantism, could attain Islam's degree of rationality without sacrificing its spirituality. During his career, he continued to produce studies on Jewish themes, of a kind that followed the path pioneered by Geiger before him.

In his politics, Goldziher supported the movement of Islamic revival and sympathized with resistance to Western imperialism. The diary of his youthful travels is replete with expressions of indignation over Europe's intrusion in the East: "Europe has spoiled everything healthy and tanned the honest Arab skins morally to death after French example!"[39] During his stay in Cairo, where he became the first European admitted to studies at the Azhar mosque-university, "I spoke out against European domination in the bazaar....I spoke about theories of the new local Muslim culture and its development as an antidote to the epidemic of European domination."[40] Goldziher also formed a fast friendship with Jamāl al-Dīn al-Afghānī (1839–97), who was then in Egypt preaching against the country's subordination to foreigners. His anti-imperialism found little outlet after his return to Budapest—Austro-Hungary had no colonial possessions in Muslim lands—but he later expressed sympathy for the 'Urābī uprising in Egypt, and remained an unwavering believer in the project of Islamic reformism.

The mid-nineteenth century saw the completion of the formal emancipation of Hungary's Jews, most of whom registered their nationality as Hungarian. Like many Jewish intellectuals, Goldziher became a fervent Hungarian nationalist, which destined him to remain on the margins of learned Europe. He was offered positions at the University of Heidelberg and Cambridge University during the 1890s. But Goldziher, for reasons personal and patriotic, would not leave Budapest, and so did not assume a university chair until 1905. Neither was Goldziher a Zionist: freedom for the Jews had to come through affiliation with Europe, not separation. In a letter of 1889, he wrote: "Jewishness is a religious term and not an ethnographical one. As regards my nationality I am a Transdanubian, and by religion a Jew. When I headed [back] for Hungary from Jerusalem [after his *Wanderjahre*] I felt I was coming home."[41] In 1920, Goldziher's schoolmate from Budapest, the Zionist leader Max Nordau (1849–1923), urged him to join the planned university in Jerusalem —the future Hebrew University. Goldziher replied: "Parting with the [Hungarian] fatherland at this time would be like demanding a heavy sacrifice from a patriotic point of view."[42] He declined the offer.

In this collection, Lawrence I. Conrad considers Goldziher's critique of Renan. Goldziher was an incisive critic of Renan's theories about the limits of the Semitic mind, and Goldziher's deflation of Renan laid the groundwork for the subsequent development of Islamic studies. Ultimately, Goldziher, not Renan, exercised a predominant influence on the new field. (Unwary readers of Said's *Orientalism,* in which Renan looms large and Goldziher has gone missing, are all too liable to conclude the opposite.) Goldziher's enduring work, according to Albert Hourani, "created a kind of orthodoxy which has retained its power until our own time."[43] "Our view of Islam and Islamic culture until today is very largely that which Goldziher laid down."[44] Goldziher's paradigm has persisted for reasons best explained by Jaroslav Stetkevych:

> [Goldziher] is emerging more and more as quite a solitary survivor of another age, looming higher the lonelier he stands. From among all the nineteenth-century philologists he is the one still capable of informing us and surprising us by being ahead of us in much of what we are doing or of what remains to be done....he figures among the pioneers of a meaningful integration of literary studies into cultural anthropology....At his best, he ceased practising the rites of Orientalism and participated in a cultural-interpretative enterprise of broad, contemporary validity.[45]

German-Jewish Preeminence

From the turn of the century, universities across Europe opened their doors to Jewish scholars of Islam, especially in Germany, where the new Jewish scholarship already included the study of Arabic and Islam. Yet precisely in this heart of Europe, anti-Semitism was evolving into a fatal racism. It would strike the universities early and in full force, so that at crucial points in their careers, many of these scholars would become migrants and refugees. Some of them are the subjects of studies in this collection—an arbitrary selection from a distinguished list of displaced orientalists. If they may be said to have shared one thing, it would have been an admiration for high Islam, confirmed by the turning of much of Europe against its Jews.

Where does one begin? Perhaps with Josef Horovitz (1874–1931), born in Lauenburg, Germany, and son of a prominent Orthodox rabbi. Horovitz studied at the University of Berlin, where he also began to teach. He also travelled through Turkey, Egypt, Palestine, and Syria, on commission to find Arabic manuscripts. From 1907 to 1914, he lived in India, where he taught Arabic at the Muhammadan Anglo-Oriental College in Aligarh, the modernist school established by Sayyid Aḥmad Khān in 1875. In 1914, he was appointed to teach Semitic languages at the University of Frankfurt. His range included early Islamic history, early Arabic poetry, Qur'anic studies, and Islam in India. In this collection, the late Hava Lazarus-Yafeh examines Horovitz's long-distance role as first director *(in absentia)* of the School of Oriental Studies at the new Hebrew University. He was not a fervent Zionist, and his political sympathies lay with Brit Shalom, the intellectual movement (comprised largely of German Jews) that abjured a Jewish state. Nevertheless, he gave crucial scholarly legitimacy to the fledgling enterprise in Jerusalem, which would provide a haven for so many of the Jewish refugee scholars from Nazi Germany.

Or one might begin with Max Meyerhof (1874–1945) born in Hildesheim, Germany. Trained as an ophthalmologist, he went to Egypt in 1903, where he served as chief of the Khedivial Ophthalmic Clinic. In 1914 he returned to Germany to serve as a military medical officer, and then practiced for a while. But he returned to Cairo in 1923 and remained there for the rest of his life, practicing medicine by day, and investigating the history of medieval Arab medicine and science by night. Meyerhof was also famous for his organization of medical care for Egypt's poor, for which he was much honored by medical societies.

Or one might well begin with the archeologist and art historian Ernst Herzfeld (1879–1948). Born in Celle, Germany, he conducted a sensational excavation at Samarra in Iraq, from 1910 to 1913. The discoveries in this early Abbasid capital put him at the forefront of the new field of Islamic art, and in 1920 he was made professor at the University of Berlin. The art historian Oleg Grabar has called Herzfeld "the most versatile of the small group of scholars who, at the turn of the century, set the study of Islamic art on a more or less scientific basis." He was the first to address the question of the uniqueness and originality of Islamic art, and "he was much in advance of his time and of the knowledge available to it. Because of his involvement in the exciting arguments of the newly developed art historical schools in Vienna, he was conscious, especially in his earlier works, of the importance of theoretical and abstract considerations in dealing with the problems of early Islamic art."[46] After the First World War, Herzfeld focused on pre-Islamic Persia; in 1935, he left Nazi Germany and was appointed to the Institute for Advanced Study in Princeton.

Or perhaps one might begin with Gotthold Weil (1882–1960), born in Berlin, founder of the oriental department of the Prussian State Library in that city, professor of Jewish history and literature at the University of Berlin from 1920, and successor to Horovitz as professor of Semitic languages at the University of Frankfurt from 1931 until the Nazis dismissed him three years later. (Following Horovitz, he headed the School of Oriental Studies in Jerusalem *in absentia.*) In 1935 he emigrated to Palestine, and was named head of the National and University Library in Jerusalem. Weil's field was Arabic grammar and prosology, but his contact with Tatar prisoners-of-war in the First World War stimulated an interest in Turkish studies, a field in which he held a chair at the Hebrew University.

Or perhaps a point of departure might be Richard Walzer (1900–75) born in Berlin, who specialized in Islamic philosophy, and who sought the continuity of Greek tradition in the Islamic world, demonstrated by the preservation of lost Greek materials in Arabic philosophical texts. In 1933 he left Nazi Germany for the University of Rome, and then in 1938 relocated again to Oxford. Albert Hourani has attested to Walzer's influence there:

> He and his wife Sofie had a kind of salon in which, among Biedermeier furniture and with the lovely Monet inherited from her parents looking down at us from the wall, we would meet colleagues and visiting scholars, and where books were discussed and a kind of stock exchange of scholarly reputations was held. Richard taught me the importance of scholarly traditions: the way in which scholarship was passed from one generation to another by a kind of apostolic succession, a chain of witnesses (a *silsila,* to give it its Arabic name). He also told me much about the central tradition of Islamic scholarship in Europe, that expressed in German.[47]

Or perhaps once might commence with the Frankfurt-born Richard Ettinghausen (1906–79). After completing his doctorate in Islamic studies in Frankfurt, Ettinghausen came to the United States in 1934, in the first instance to the Institute for Advanced Study, and ultimately to the Institute of Fine Arts at New York University. Ettinghausen had a far-ranging expertise in all aspects of Islamic art, but specialized in Islamic painting—Arab, Turkish, Persian, and Indian. He was famously active in the museum world, doing much to place Islamic art before the American public through exhibitions. He served as a head curator of the Freer

Gallery of Art at the Smithsonian, and as the consultative chairman of the Department of Islamic Art at the Metropolitan Museum of Art, directing its permanent installation. His ties to Israel found expression in his avid promotion of the establishment of a museum for Islamic art in Jerusalem.

One could well conclude with the youngest of them all, Franz Rosenthal (b. 1914). Born in Berlin, where his early work focused on Aramaic studies, Rosenthal fled Germany in 1938, arriving in the United States in 1940. In 1943 he was naturalized, and he spent two years in army intelligence. In 1956, after teaching in Cincinnati and Philadelphia, he commenced a thirty-year career at Yale University. Rosenthal excelled in Muslim intellectual history, and especially thc development of early and classical Muslim scholarship and historiography. He gained his widest renown for his fully annotated three-volume translation of Ibn Khaldūn's *Muqaddima.*

These (and other) German-Jewish scholars viewed the study of Islam as the perfect point of intersection of classical and Jewish studies. They were drawn to "golden ages" and those achievements of Islamic civilization which had universal significance, and which demonstrated Islam's tolerance of difference. They worked from the assumption that Islam arose in part upon Jewish foundations, and emphasized that it had provided the civilizational framework for a period of Jewish achievement since paralleled only by the present age. They also were fascinated by the role of this Judeo-Islamic civilization in the preservation and transmission of Greek philosophy and science. Needless to say, these Jewish scholars remained completely aloof from the efforts to mobilize German orientalism for political purposes, and they stood at the forefront of the intellectual struggle against the increasing ethnocentrism of the German academy.

Jews were forced out of the universities very early in the Nazi reign, so that nearly all of the Jewish orientalists managed to leave Germany.[48] Former colleagues who were Nazi sympathizers then wrote the Jews completely out of the history of German oriental studies. Hans Heinrich Schaeder (1896–1957), professor at the University of Berlin, was an authority on Islamic mysticism, the Persian poet Ḥāfiẓ, the orientalism of Goethe, Iranian Manichaeism, and much else. He was also the effective spokesman of German orientalism throughout the Nazi period. Schaeder's colleagues and students included many Jews. But it was Schaeder who, in 1940, published a remarkable historical summary of the development of German oriental studies which managed to avoid mention of a single Jewish scholar.[49]

The excision of Jews from the past record was not nearly as consequential as their absence from the subsequent development of Islamic studies in Germany. Not a single Jewish orientalist returned to Germany after the war. "The tradition of Islamic studies in Germany suffered irreplaceable losses in this period," relates a recent German account of postwar scholarship, "because most of the younger scholars who worked in the field had to leave the country. Their emigration has seriously and for at least two generations weakened the potential of the German tradition of Islamwissenschaft."[50]

The greatest wartime loss to Jewish scholarship on Islam was the death by suicide of Paul Kraus (1904–44). Kraus, who was born and raised in Prague, accumulated superlatives over a short but brilliant career. After Goldziher, opined one Jewish colleague, "there has not been a scholar like Kraus in this field who combined so many signs of scholarly genius."[51] An Egyptian colleague said that he inspired "awe." After preparation in ancient Semitics at the University of Berlin (where he studied under Schaeder), Kraus became fascinated by the history of Islamic sciences, and seemed destined for fame at an institute established precisely for this field in Berlin. But the rise of the Nazis in 1933 compelled a move, and he managed to secure a scholarship in Paris with the help of Louis Massignon. There he and Massignon began an intensive cooperation, preparing the pericopes of Ḥallāj for publication.

The relationship between Massignon and Kraus was complex and asymmetrical, and remains difficult to put in focus. As Joel L. Kraemer demonstrates in his study for this collection, the two men were complementary opposites. Had Kraus remained in Paris, he might have opened an entirely different line of intellectual succession to Massignon, far from the spirit of Catholic penitence. But he was not a French national, and in 1936 he was informed that he could not be employed in France any longer. The Hebrew University made Kraus an offer at that time, but he had spent time in Palestine some years earlier, and found it an inhospitable place. He preferred an offer, arranged for him by Massignon, at the Egyptian (later Cairo) University, where he became a protégé of the Egyptian critic and scholar Ṭāhā Ḥusayn (1889–1973).

Kraus spent eight years in Cairo. He had a masterly command of Arabic, in which he lectured and sometimes wrote, and a passion for the study of Islamic civilization in all its aspects. Yet in Cairo, his spirit was eroded by the spectre of a possible German invasion, the death of his wife, fear for his academic reputation, and Egyptian nationalist resentment against foreigners in the university. He had come from a world which had gone dark, and whose darkness continued to pursue him. In 1944, after a change of government in Egypt, Kraus was told he would be dismissed from his post. He returned to his flat and hanged himself. Kraus, for all the complexity of his motives, must be numbered among the casualties of war.

The fate of Kraus raises the question of solidarity: the extent to which Jewish scholars were protected or assisted by their colleagues outside Germany. There is much lore about the many German-Jewish scholars of Islam who reached safe haven in America and Britain through the help of colleagues. France, however, represented a more complex instance, personified by towering figure of French orientalism, Massignon. In December 1933, Massignon wrote this to a French diplomat in Cairo: "For myself, as one who has personally rescued one of the academic victims of the Hitlerite regime [Kraus], I am certain that we in France must resist every demand to increase the percentage of Jews among us, if we want to avoid a crisis as violent as that of our neighbors." In the same letter, he took a dim view of the arrival of Jewish scholars in Turkey. (The Turkish government in 1933 invited some thirty German refugee professors, many of them Jewish, to assist in the reorganization of the University of Istanbul.) "There is evidently a very strange international role that is being played presently in the world by a Jewish elite," wrote Massignon. "The massive injection of German scholars of Jewish origin, to which Turkey has consented (the University of Istanbul) is rather revealing of this action. I hope we can spare Syria an immigration of the same kind, which would precipitate catastrophes."[52] And, of course, neither did he want the German-Jewish scholars in Palestine: in 1939, he lamented that at the Hebrew University, "instead of Oriental Sephardim speaking Arabic, there are these Germanized Ashkenazim."[53]

This was the same Massignon who was guided to the subject of his life's great work by his Jewish teacher, Derenbourg; who acknowledged the crucial encouragement he received from a Jewish mentor, Goldziher; and who depended in his later work upon the labors of a Jewish student, Kraus. Yet as the 1930s unfolded, Massignon showed a growing hostility to Jewish refugees, experiencing what he himself would describe as his "crisis of anti-Semitism." This has been documented in detail by Massignon's most recent biographers, who conclude that "in his episodic reactions to the Jewish question in France, Massignon was incontestably the prisoner of a time and a place in which anti-Semitism had become banal."[54] Massignon's views were an intimation of just how saturated with anti-Semitism continental Europe's intellectual classes had become, and how certain it was that the continent would lose its privileged place as the center of great Jewish achievement in the field of Islamic studies.

Lay Orientalists

Scholarship was not the only medium of expression for the Jewish fascination with Islam. Jewish artists and writers also explored Islam for wider audiences, with an emphasis upon its superiority over a satiated, materialistic, or intolerant Europe.

Jews played no role at all in the nineteenth-century emergence of orientalism as a genre of art. Europe's Jews hailed from those parts of the continent most remote from the Muslim world, and they came late to the traditions that informed orientalist art. By the turn of the century, however, a few Jewish artists began to draw upon orientalist themes, as they came into contact with the living East and orientalist art. Perhaps the most internationally famous was Léon Bakst (1866–1924). Born Lev Samoilovich Rosenberg in Grodno, Belorussia, he was raised in St. Petersburg, where he enrolled the Academy of Arts. Bakst did not conceal his Jewish origins; indeed, he announced his Jewishness to every acquaintance, sometimes as a provocation. (He was expelled from the academy for a canvas that portrayed a bereaved Mary as an old hag, "whilst the mourning band of Disciples gesticulated and shook like the congregation of a Lithuanian ghetto synagogue.")[55]

Bakst left St. Petersburg for Paris, and there he studied under the most famous of the late-nineteenth-century orientalist painters, Jean-Léon Gérôme (1824–1904). But ultimately, Bakst became famous not for his painting, but for his inspired work in stage and costume design for the ballet, and above all the Ballets Russes, which took Paris and London by storm just before the First World War. The Ballets Russes pushed well beyond the outer limits of Victorian taste, by their excursions into sexuality and violence. Bakst had visited Istanbul, Algiers, Tunis, Crete, and the Caucasus, and oriental settings became his trademark: ancient Egypt in the case of the ballet *Cleopatra,* Near Eastern antiquity in the instance of *Salomé,* and then his greatest triumph, the 1910 ballet *Schéhèrazade,* based upon a story from *A Thousand and One Nights*. An admirer later described Bakst as "the Delacroix of the costume." Bakst's was a highly erotic orientalism, itself a precursor to the liberation of sexuality which would distinguish the twentieth century from its predecessor.

Some of Bakst's critics, and some biographers, located the source of his orientalism in his Jewish background. As one put it, "stimulated by a sort of atavistic instinct, having its roots, undoubtedly, in his Semitic origins, Bakst inhaled with delight all the emanations of the Oriental spirit." During Bakst's travels, claimed another critic, "the call of the Asiatic was indistinctly awakened in this Occidental Jew."[56] Bakst probably owed as much to his immersion in the traditions of Russian and French orientalism. But he certainly enjoyed presenting himself as a living embodiment of the East, and in a "Who's Who" entry which he provided, he even concocted for himself a bogus Sephardic lineage, stretching back to King David.

While the Islamic East could be admired for its sensuality, it could just as readily be admired for its austerity. This approach characterized the work of the prolific dramatist Friedrich Wolf (1888–1953), specifically his play *Mohammed*.[57] Wolf, born in Neuwied, Germany, rebelled against all convention as a young man, and in 1913 renounced Judaism without taking up another faith. During the First World War he served in Flanders as a physician, but declared himself a conscientious objector and was sent to a sanatorium. After the war, he became a communist, practiced homeopathic medicine, organized free medical service for the poor, and wrote many plays, the most famous of which, *Professor Mamlock* (1933), warned of impending disaster in Germany. He fought briefly in the Spanish Civil War, then took refuge in France, and spent the Second World War in Moscow. After the war, he settled in East Berlin, and he served for two years as East German ambassador to Poland. His son was the famous East German spymaster, Markus Wolf (b. 1923).

In 1917, Wolf wrote his first play, *Mohammed,* at the battlefront in Flanders, where he had a German translation of the Qur'an in his possession. "I find hope in Mohammed," he wrote to his mother from the trenches, "bone from my bone, and flesh from my flesh." The play follows Muhammad from his youth through the *hijra,* the departure from Mecca to Medina. Wolf presents the Prophet as a great champion of social justice and fervent advocate of non-violence, who distributes his wealth and frees his slaves. The Meccan oligarchy organizes against him, but he repels them by non-violent tactics, never raising a fist, until he finally chooses to migrate with his followers. Wolf's Muhammad repudiates crass materialism in this exchange with the wealthy of Mecca:

> MUHAMMAD (RESOLUTELY): ...you already have too much and yet you reach for more; you hunt down the smallest advantage, cleverness becomes cunning, cunning becomes spite, power becomes violence, violence becomes rape, feuds start, blood flows, clans kill one another, and the race for more finally ends in the grave of nothingness.
>
> ABU JAHL: The bleating of a lamb! A strong people needs land and power—just as the body needs nourishment—or else it suffers from need.
>
> MUHAMMAD (FIERY): Need! How would you know what we are suffering from? The despair of the people is the despair of the heart! Do not imagine you can subdue the people with land and bread, with swords and gold! One measures a people not by how much power and how many possessions it needs, but by how little it needs to be great![58]

Wolf wrote these words in the midst of Europe's self-immolation, which he saw as the wage of greed. The play sought to turn Europe's prejudice against Islam on its head, holding up the Prophet Muhammad as an exemplar of non-violence to a Europe seemingly bent upon its own destruction. (To do so, the play had to end at the *hijra,* before Muhammad's confrontation with the Jews of Medina, and before his emergence as a conqueror in battle.) The play was published in 1924, and excited interest among some Muslims, who wrote to Wolf expressing hope that it might be performed. But it never reached the stage, and by then Wolf had made a different commitment, not to Islam but to communism. Still, he continued to revise the play almost up to his death.

Another Jew drew a different conclusion, based upon a similar reading of the Qur'an. Leopold Weiss (1900–92) was born in Austrian-ruled Lemberg (now Lvov, in Ukraine) and raised in Vienna. Although he received a traditional education, Weiss turned away from Judaism, and at the age of twenty went to Berlin to pursue a career as a writer and journalist. On a visit to Palestine in 1922, he became persuaded of the injustice of Zionism, and joined the prestigious *Frankfurter Zeitung* as a stringer. The newspaper later commissioned him to travel across the Middle East and produce a book.

But in 1926, after his return to Germany, Weiss converted to Islam. On a Berlin subway, he noticed "an expression of hidden suffering" upon the faces of the "well-dressed and well-fed" passengers. They suffered because they were "without any goal beyond the desire to raise their own 'standard of living', without any hopes other than having more material amenities, more gadgets, and perhaps more power." At home, his eye fell upon an open Qur'an he had been reading, to this verse: "You are obsessed by greed for more and more / Until you go down to your graves."[59] All doubt in the Qur'an as a revealed book vanished, and he converted to Islam. Weiss, like Wolf, thought Islam averse to materialism, and it is telling that Weiss in 1926 should have fixed on precisely the same verse in the Qur'an (102) that Wolf puts in the mouth of Muhammad in his play published in 1924: "you already have too much and yet you reach for more... and the race for more finally ends in the grave of nothingness." This idea of Islam as a spiritual antidote to Western materialism seems to have had a particular appeal to Jewish seekers who felt that their own faith failed to strike a balance in its encounter with capitalism.

Weiss took the name Muhammad Asad and departed for Saudi Arabia, where he lived as a Muslim and married an Arab woman (a union that produced Talal Asad, the noted anthropologist). He became an adviser to Ibn Saud, and wrote Arabia-bylined stories for German-language newspapers. In 1932, he broke with the Saudi monarch and left for India, where he emerged as an Islamic thinker. In 1952, Pakistan appointed Asad to its mission at the United Nations in New York, and in 1954 he published an immensely popular account of his travels and life, entitled *The Road to Mecca.* In his later years, he lived mostly in the West, and published a modernist translation of the Qur'an.

Asad believed that, in embracing Islam, he was actually continuing the tradition of Abraham, that the Arabian sky was "my sky," the same sky that "vaulted over the long trek of my ancestors, those wandering herdsmen-warriors"—"that small beduin tribe of Hebrews."[60] While this was hardly a new idea, Asad's conclusion—conversion to Islam—did go far beyond the literary and scholarly expressions of "Semitic" solidarity made by other Jews. Still, in his idealization of Islam, Asad did not depart from the path followed by earlier Jewish romantics and orientalists. As I suggest in my article for this collection, his attempt to make the Qur'an speak to modern minds incorporated those very ideals that drove the reform of Judaism. Indeed, it was precisely this resemblance that made his project so suspect in the eyes of many Muslims.

The Palestine Option

In the first half of this century, several hundred thousands of European Jews settled and remained in Palestine, where they came into sustained contact with the religion, languages, and peoples of Islam. This process of discovery constituted an important chapter in the history of modern Zionism, but it came too late to have much of an impact upon Europe. For example, the Zionist encounter with the scenery and Arab inhabitants of Palestine produced a brief flowering of orientalist painting in the 1920s. But by the time European-born Jewish artists painted orientalist canvases, orientalism as a genre had waned in Europe. Their works never reached European galleries and never entered the Western canon.[61]

But Jewish scholarship on Islam, transplanted to Palestine, did have a continuing impact, drawing as it did upon a century-long tradition. The founding in 1925 of the Hebrew University in Jerusalem, in large part a project of German-speaking Jews, exercised a strong attraction upon a younger generation of scholars, influenced already in their teens by organized political Zionism, the Balfour Declaration, and anti-Semitism. The late Hava Lazarus-Yafeh, in her essay for this volume, sketches some of the figures who established the study of Islam in Jewish Palestine. Mention has been made of Josef Horovitz and Gotthold Weil, the first two directors of the School of Oriental Studies at the Hebrew University. These were men of an older generation, educated, tenured, and rooted in the universities of Frankfurt and Berlin. It is doubtful they would have ever relocated to Jerusalem of their own free wills. (Horovitz never did, Weil came only after the Nazis dismissed him from his post.)

But their immense influence was sufficient to set the Hebrew University on a trajectory determined by the priorities of German Jewish scholarship on Islam, with its emphasis on philology and the history of classical periods. In their own way, they regarded this as a practical choice. Horovitz, who had taught for years in a Muslim institution in India, wanted the new School of Oriental Studies to be respected in Muslim lands. The large projects he launched, such as the concordance of early Arabic poetry, were meant to stand up to exacting orientalist standards, but also to win Arab admiration.

In the conditions that prevailed in the 1930s, these emphases seemed like luxuries to some outside observers. A 1934 report by an external committee of inquiry, submitted to the board of governors of the university, related that the School of Oriental Studies "has been and still is criticized by many," because it had "no other object in view than to give the students a picture of Moslem civilization of the past." This would not do: Jewish Palestine

> is surrounded on all sides by the Moslem world, a thorough knowledge of which is of the greatest importance for the economic and political development of the country. For this purpose it is not the study of pre-Islamic poetry nor the study of old Arab historians that matters, but the study of the living Islamic world. Its geography, dialectology, and commerce are far more important to the Palestinian Jew than Islamic art and archeology. In short, the School of Oriental Studies should be modeled on similar schools in Paris, Berlin, and London, in which the student is made to know the living and not only the dead Orient.[62]

The committee dismissed the notion that the emphasis on classical Arabic and Islam would win Muslim admiration: "It is now quite evident that no Arab will change his political views on the Jewish question because of the preparation by the Hebrew University of a Concordance of Ancient Arabic Poetry." The School, concluded the committee, should "begin the kind of practical work that is expected from a school of this kind."[63]

Yet this view never prevailed. In the midst of the dispersal from Europe, immigrant Jews sought to duplicate in Palestine the conditions under which they had thrived—whether they were ultra-Orthodox Ostjuden departed from their talmudic academies, or worldly academics departed from the universities of Mitteleuropa. Chains of scholarly transmission continued to transmit. Scholarly agendas fixed in *fin-de-siècle* Berlin and Frankfurt could not simply be abandoned, and they survived intact in the new centers of scholarship in Palestine, later Israel. Even the exacerbation of conflict with the Arabs did not alter these priorities.

Leo Ary Mayer (1895–1959) was the decisive figure in perpetuating this tradition—and deflecting criticisms of it. Mayer, born in Stanislav (in Austrian Poland), came from a strongly Zionist background, and he settled in Palestine in 1921, after completing his studies at the University of Vienna. His field was Islamic art and archeology, and he worked for the department of antiquities before joining the fledgling Hebrew University in 1925, the very year of its establishment. At the new university, the personable Mayer became a mandarin. He was the first local director of the School of Oriental Studies, which he guided from 1935 to 1949, while at the same time serving terms as dean and rector. In Palestine, Mayer had endless opportunities to explore the many facets of Islamic art, and embarked on a project to recover the identities of the great anonymous artisans of Islam, producing studies on architects, astrolabists, wood-carvers, metal-workers, and sword-cutlers. He was best known for two works, *Saracenic Heraldry* (1933) and *Mamluk Costume* (1952). A museum of Islamic art in Jerusalem—itself an unabashed statement of admiration for the high civilization of Islam—today bears Mayer's name.

Under the impetus of Horovitz's plan and the protection of Mayer, the Hebrew University perpetuated central European traditions in philology and Islamwissenschaft. In her essay, Lazarus-Yafeh emphasizes the role of David Hartwig (Zvi) Baneth (1893–1973), the son of a noted talmudist, in establishing exacting standards in both fields. Baneth, who was raised in Berlin and educated there and in Frankfurt, came to Palestine in 1924. He began teaching in the School of Oriental Studies two years later, and continued to do so for forty years, essentially following the Frankfurt curriculum. Baneth, who was famously self-effacing and equally demanding, published little in his field (Jewish thought expressed in Arabic), but played a decisive role in transplanting the rigorous standards of central European scholarship to Jerusalem. Thanks to Baneth and others, the study of early and classical Islam, with an emphasis upon philology, philosophy, religion, and art, became a hallmark of the Jerusalem school. The scholars in this field, listed by Lazarus-Yafeh, enjoyed formidable reputations for their exacting scholarship, and put the Hebrew University in the first rank of Islamic studies.

Among the many scholars produced in Jerusalem, one carried its reputation far afield: Hungarian-born Samuel Stern (1920–69). Educated in a Benedictine school and a rabbinical seminary, Stern began to teach himself Arabic at the age of sixteen. In 1939, when war broke out, his mother sent him to Jerusalem, sparing him the grim fate which befell her and Budapest Jewry. At the Hebrew University, his star shined. ("Stern had no need to be taught anything anymore," recalled Baneth.) But the war of 1948 disrupted the university, and Stern, an asthmatic, could not be mobilized. He left for Oxford, where he prepared his doctorate under Sir Hamilton Gibb (1895–1971), and there he remained for the rest of his career.

Stern's interests ranged widely, from medieval poetry (in Arabic, Spanish, and Hebrew) to the dissident sects of Islam, via diplomatics and numismatics. Shulamit Sela, in her article for this collection, relates how Stern combined his Islamic and Jewish interests, and how he used Jewish sources, including the Geniza, to illuminate aspects of medieval Islamic history. Stern wished in the early 1950s to return to the Hebrew University, but no place could be found for him. Later, after he established himself in Oxford, he declined an offer from Jerusalem. Stern died young in 1969, his work uncompleted. His colleague Albert Hourani wrote in a eulogy that he came to Oxford as a stranger, and "he remained a stranger, not quite at home in the world."[64] In fact, he had a strong attachment to Jerusalem, and he bequeathed his house and library to the Hebrew University.

New Emphases in Jerusalem

Another approach also flourished in Jerusalem, which was prompted by a deepening interest in the evolution of Muslim societies. This interest in Islamic history as something larger than language, religion, and art took its first strides forward in the work of Shlomo Dov Goitein (1900–85). Goitein was born in Burgkunstadt, Germany, and studied under Horovitz in Frankfurt. He emigrated to Palestine in 1923, and in 1928 joined the faculty of the Hebrew University, where he taught until 1957. His early work dealt with Islamic religious institutions and Muslim history. In recalling this phase of Goitein's career, Lazarus-Yafeh points to his abiding interest in the religious manifestations of Islam, and their relationship to Judaism—the kind of concerns typical of his teachers in Germany and his colleagues in Jerusalem. Goitein himself remained a practicing Jew throughout his life.

But he broke completely new ground in his monumental work on the Geniza documents—research and writing largely undertaken after he left for the United States in 1957. R. Stephen Humphreys has suggested the importance of the Geniza (the documentary storehouse of the Jewish community of medieval Cairo): the study of Jewish history in medieval Islam "can yield social history of a depth which we cannot achieve for any other group, even the highly articulate and vastly larger Muslim majority." But because of the Jewish milieu in which these documents were created, notes Humphreys, "it helps to have been brought up in an observant Jewish home and to have had some training in rabbinics." Goitein was the perfect match for Geniza research, and in the five volumes of *A Mediterranean Society* (1967–88), he laid the foundations for a revolution in the social and economic history of Islam in the Middle

Ages—an achievement Humphreys calls "one of the most impressive and moving in the history of our field."[65] The Geniza documents continue to yield new insights, and are likely to remain at the epicenter of research on the social and economic history of the Muslim Middle Ages.

The Jerusalem school also led breakthroughs in the social and economic history of other periods. David Ayalon (Neustadt) (1914–98) personified the successful transplantation of the European tradition to Palestine. Born in Haifa, he was educated entirely at the Hebrew University (apart from one year spent at the American University of Beirut). He worked for a time for the Political Department of the Jewish Agency, and served in the British army during the Second World War. In 1947 he published (with Pessah Shinar) an Arabic-Hebrew dictionary which has maintained its preeminence to this day. In 1950, Ayalon joined the faculty of the Hebrew University, and began to center his research on the Mamluks of Egypt. His work was the first to elucidate the social underpinnings of the institution of military slavery, without which no understanding of late medieval Muslim history is possible.

The economic history of this same period was explored by Eliyahu Ashtor (Eduard Strauss) (1914–84). Born in Vienna, Strauss came from a strongly Zionist background, and at the age of nineteen he published an ardent defense of Zionism against its Marxist critics. Strauss took his doctorate at the University of Vienna in 1936, and would have been ordained a rabbi had the Nazi annexation of Austria in 1938 not cut short his studies. He came to Palestine that year and became keeper of oriental books at the National and University Library. In 1955, Ashtor joined the faculty, and later published what became the standard history of the Jews of Muslim Spain, before taking up the economic and social history of the Muslim Middle Ages. In this work, Ashtor made extensive use of Geniza materials, combined with Arabic chronicles and European trade records. In doing so, he was critical of "the Orientalists themselves [who], with few exceptions, have always been interested in the spiritual life of the Moslems, in Islam and in Arabic literature. So many texts which indeed refer to social and economic life have been overlooked or misunderstood." It was his purpose to show that the Muslim East in the Middle Ages was "not at all a static, unchanging society," and that "the bourgeois played a great role in political history and that there were strong revolutionary movements."[66]

The new emphasis on social history also characterized the career of Gabriel Baer (1919–82). Born in Berlin, Baer escaped to Haifa in 1933.

He studied at the American University of Beirut and the Hebrew University, where he prepared under Goitein. In 1954, he joined the faculty of the Hebrew University, specializing in nineteenth-century social history, with an emphasis on Egypt. Baer did pioneering work on the history of guilds, landownership, and urban-rural relations, challenging entrenched myths. He died in the midst of an ambitious project on Muslim endowments. A German scholar has described him as a rebel against scholarly convention:

> His studies of specific social institutions within history contributed greatly to demolish the traditional orientalist view of an "Islamic" or "Arab" or "Middle Eastern" society as a uniform and static phenomenon. These facile generalizations of an "Islamic" mode of thought or behavior were unacceptable to him. In his opinion, the term "Islamic city," for instance, could not account for the great differences and creative variations over space and time which could be observed for the city in the area.[67]

Yet Baer "refused to replace the simplistic traditional orientalist approach with the fashionable but often facile theories and models of more recent origin."[68]

The same could be said of the entire Jerusalem school of social and economic history. Its practitioners sought to expand the perimeters of history, to widen the lens to include the breadth of society. But they were reluctant to trade tested tools for untested theories. The solidity and density of their work established standards of evidence and explanation which have not been superseded.

As late as 1948, the entire Jewish community of the country numbered only half a million, a narrow base to sustain the importation of so much specialized scholarship. The war of 1948 and the years of austerity and isolation which followed it were difficult ones at the Hebrew University. The campus on Mt. Scopus became inaccessible, conditions were far from ideal, and academic positions were few compared to the number of immigrant scholars. Jewish scholars who once freely traversed the region became Israeli scholars, isolated from sustained contact with Arab-Muslim colleagues, important archives and libraries.

Given these circumstances, the successful transfer of the Jewish tradition of scholarship on Islam to Palestine and Israel must be regarded as a signal achievement. The Hebrew University built directly upon the hugely influential legacies of central European Islamwissenschaft. And despite the difficulties, contact with the living East made for a diversification, which carried scholarship beyond the study of Islam as religion, to include the study of the social and economic history of Muslim peoples, and even the realities of contemporary Islam. In many of these areas, the Jerusalem school and its offshoots in newer Israeli universities not only held their own, but helped to define the evolving international research agenda as oriental studies gave way to the disciplines.

The Continental Remnant

The Jewish tradition of Islamic studies in central Europe, especially in Germany, generated immense energy at its height, and continued to do so after its displacement to Palestine, the United States, and Britain. The permanent departure of these scholars left a void in the heart of Europe. Yet Jews also occupied a significant place in the French and Italian traditions of Islamic studies. Jewish Islamicists from France and Italy knew less of the efforts to reconcile Judaism and modernity than did their German Jewish counterparts, many of whom had rabbinical training. They tended to be more assimilated, less grounded in the Jewish tradition, less interested in the comparison of Islam and Judaism, and more influenced by Europe's reigning ideologies. Like their German Jewish counterparts, they were displaced by the war, but unlike them, they returned afterwards to the same universities, where they continued to exercise a profound influence on Islamic studies.

Giorgio Levi Della Vida (1886–1967) was born in the Piedmont of Italy, to a highly assimilated family of mixed Italian and Spanish origin. "For two generations," he testified,

> my family had detached itself from the practice of the Jewish religion. Brought up without any religious indoctrination, supposedly substituted by the vague theism of my mother and by the religion of duty and humanism of my father, one day I found within and around myself a great void which needed to be filled. Two ways were open to me: the return to the ancestral faith, of which I perceived the august majesty and which my family had put aside without formally denying it; or the resolute entry into the fold of the Catholic Church, which attracted me by its harmonious and solid doctrinal structure and by the very strong emotional charge of its cult.[69]

But Levi Della Vida opened a third way: the comparative study of religion and Semitic languages, a labor which provided a measure of spiritual sustenance. He prepared himself by assisting Prince Leone Caetani (1869–1935) in the monumental translation project, the *Annali dell'Islam.* Such preparation enabled him in 1914 to secure the chair of Arabic at the University of Naples, and in 1920 he occupied the chair of Hebrew and comparative Semitic languages at the University of Rome. Yet Levi Della Vida's horizons were much broader than philology. He synthesized many disciplines in his work, and he criticized orientalists who "do not see nor hear anything outside the closed and arid field of their erudite researches." He also showed political courage. At the end of 1931, Levi Della Vida was one of twelve lecturers, out of 1,225 university faculty, who refused to take the oath of allegiance to the Fascist regime—this, at a time when most Italian intellectuals, Jews among them, supported Fascism. His principled stand cost him his professorship. In 1939, he relocated to the University of Pennsylvania, where he taught until his reinstatement in Rome in 1948.

Evariste Lévi-Provençal (1894–1956) completely obscured his Jewish antecedents, although he earned his fame for his work on Islamic Spain, the very font of Jewish romanticism. Born in Algeria, Lévi-Provençal remained extremely reticent about his origins. He made a point of noting his military service to France in the First World War (he was wounded in the Dardanelles in 1917), his years of teaching and research in Rabat (he joined the Institut des hautes études marocaines in 1922), and his chair at the University of Algiers (occupied from 1935). But he was careful never to hint at his Jewish origins. Was this due to his thorough assimilation, or to the pervasiveness in France of the "banal" anti-Semitism personified by Massignon? Lévi-Provençal certainly fell victim to the latter: Vichy racial laws unseated him from his Algiers chair. It was during his "enforced leisure" that he began his three-volume *Histoire de l'Espagne musulmane* (1944–53), a synthesis that superseded its predecessors and has yet to be superseded.

As David Wasserstein notes in his essay for this volume, Lévi-Provençal seemed to avert his gaze deliberately from the crucial contribution of Jews to the life of Islamic Spain, and made no use of very rich Jewish sources. The reasons may have been technical. (Lévi-Provençal apparently knew no Hebrew, and had no background in Jewish studies.) Or they may have run deeper. The Jewish absence leaves Lévi-Provençal's history of Muslim Spain an unreservedly French history, just as he gave himself an unreservedly French biography, culminating in service as an officer in the ranks of Free France. After the war, he relocated to Paris, where he became professor at the Sorbonne and the director of two institutes, for Islamic studies and the contemporary Middle East. But loyal as he was to France, he did not confuse France with French empire. In Paris, Lévi-Provençal became a critic of attempts to reestablish France's damaged standing in North Africa by force, and was later an active member of the liberal Comité France-Maghreb.

Robert Brunschvig (1901–90) shared some of these scholarly commitments, but had much firmer Jewish moorings. Born in Bordeaux, he arrived in Tunis in 1922, where he taught French at a *lycée* for eight years. There he became interested in history, and he gained an appointment as professor in Muslim civilization at the University of Algiers in 1932. Brunschvig was also an avowed and charismatic Zionist, of the revisionist school of Jabotinsky, and a community activist who organized a parallel educational system for 20,000 Jewish children driven out of Algeria's schools by the Vichy regime. (Brunschvig likewise was dismissed from the university.) After the war, he taught at the University of Bordeaux, and from 1955 to his retirement in 1968, at the Sorbonne, where he also headed the Institut d'études islamiques. Brunschvig specialized in North African Islam in the medieval period and the history of Islamic law, and became best known for his exemplary two-volume history of the Ḥafṣid dynasty, *La Berbérie orientale sous le Ḥafsides* (1940–47). His work on North Africa, in contrast to Lévi-Provençal's on Muslim Spain, included very dense accounts of Jewish life, based in part upon a close reading of rabbinic responsa.

Claude Cahen (1909–91) concentrated upon the Muslim East. Born in Paris, he received his *diplôme* in Arabic from the École des langues orientales in Paris in 1931, and undertook a research trip to Turkey in 1936 which set his scholarly agenda. After the war, Cahen taught at the University of Strasbourg, where he founded the first journal devoted to the social and economic history of the East. In 1959, he went to the Sorbonne, where he taught for twenty years. Cahen specialized in the economy of the medieval Muslim world, with an emphasis on Anatolia and the Levant. Hourani has described Cahen's work as "perhaps the most systematic attempt to apply mature sociological concepts to the realities of Islamic society."[70] In doing so, he created an alternative to the heavy emphasis on religion and theology in French Islamic studies, itself the legacy of Massignon.

Cahen was more than ambivalent about his origins. An avowed communist, he once told a colleague outright that "I am not a Jew." In a document from the war years only recently published, he took a different tack: "I am [a Jew], it is a fact. I draw no pride or shame from it, I see it neither as a sign of a providential designation, nor as an outcome of my own will...Nothing in my education or associations has prepared me to declare myself a member any group other than humanity or France, or a professional community, an ideal, an action—the many forms of acceptable solidarity." He disliked

> encountering people who, due only to an accident of birth, treat you as someone who shares ideas and communal sentiments with them, who shares in their interests...in a word, members of a kind of conspiracy that positions you against the rest of humanity or the nation. It is still more disagreeable when circumstances make it impossible to disavow this solidarity without effectively breaking that other tie, so noble and consensual, which must bind us to any category of people who suffer.[71]

Maxime Rodinson (b. 1915) had similar ideological commitments, although he struck a different balance between history and politics. Rodinson was born to Russian immigrant parents in an impoverished working-class neighborhood of Paris. He grew up in a home and surroundings that were fervently communist and Stalinist, "de-Judaized," and anti-Zionist. In 1932 he entered the École des langues orientales to prepare for a career as a diplomat-interpreter, and there took up the study of Arabic. Later he decided to prepare a thesis in comparative Semitics. Rodinson had none of the advantages brought to this field by other Jewish students. He was "initially quite ignorant of the Jewish religion," and his parents "were dismayed when they saw me learning Hebrew. For them, Hebrew was the language of the rabbis, and when they saw I was copying Hebrew letters they said, 'Look how he has tumbled into such foolishness.'"[72] (His parents both perished in Auschwitz in 1943.) Rodinson spent the wars years in Lebanon (in Sidon and then in Beirut), before becoming a librarian at the Bibliothèque nationale in Paris in 1948. In 1955, he began to teach at the École pratique des hautes études. Rodinson joined the French communist party in 1937; he left it in 1958.

Rodinson's seven years in Lebanon drew him to the study of the Muslim world. His work combined sociological and Marxist theorizing in an accessible (and polemical) style. Rodinson became best known for his 1961 biography of Muhammad ("probably in an unconscious fashion, I compared him to Stalin"),[73] a work of deep empathy setting the Prophet within a social context, but one resented by many Muslims because of its atheistic premises. In his *Islam et le capitalisme* (1966), Rodinson took issue with the view, widespread in Europe, that Islam hindered the development of capitalism and thus explained the underdevelopment of the Muslim world. At the same time, he did not accept the apologetic Muslim view of Islam as egalitarian. Islam was a completely neutral element, overridden by social factors—a position in accord with his theoretical premises. He credited his Marxism with "opening my eyes and making me understand and say that the world of Islam was subject to the same laws and tendencies as the rest of the human race."[74]

Like other Jewish Marxists (and, indeed, Marx himself), Rodinson judged the Jews by another standard: "I confess a repugnance for Jewish nationalism (common among very many Jews of my generation) even stronger than the repugnance I feel for other nationalisms, as strong as it is."[75] Rodinson was an avowed anti-Zionist, whose views resembled Cahen's. But unlike Cahen, he published his positions repeatedly, especially after 1967, in articles and books. Rodinson regarded Judaism as a personal choice (which he rejected: "I have always had a greater repugnance for Jewish ritual than for any other"),[76] and he saw Israel as a colonial project, which could only be implemented through the wrongful displacement of Palestinian Arabs. But in later years he concluded that Israel's Jewish inhabitants, under changed historical circumstances, had become "a new nationality with a culture of its own," and that Israel rested on international legality, hence the necessity for a mutual reconciliation. Rodinson's political engagements were never far beneath the surface of his scholarship. He once compared himself to the controversial philosopher Levi ben Gershom (1288–1344), who saw his struggles over ideas as "wars for God."[77] This was a far cry from the traditional scholarly detachment from politics, but the dislocations of twentieth-century Europe, from the Holocaust to decolonization, made such detachment difficult to maintain or justify.

These changes also eliminated continental Europe as a center of Jewish accomplishment in Islamic studies. The Italian and French Jewish scholars who embarked on their careers before the war finished them in Europe. But Jews then disappeared from the field. Not only were there far fewer Jewish academics in Europe, there were far more Muslims, and these would come to play the more significant role in the years following the war.

The End of Mystique

Most Jews drew very different conclusions from the Holocaust and the creation of Israel than those drawn by Rodinson. For many Jewish scholars of Islam, the experiences of the war put in question the spirit which had underpinned favorable European Jewish approaches to Islam. "The [Arab] masses preponderantly favored a German victory," acknowledges the Tunisian historian Hichem Djaït, "through which they hoped to be freed from colonialist rule. Beyond that, Nazism fueled the anti-Semitism that undeniably smoldered among the common people—who had no idea of the scope of Nazi persecution or of the dreadful atrocities being committed in Europe."[78] Muslim anti-Semitism cast into doubt the very premises of a Jewish scholarly tradition that had presented Islam to Europe as a model of tolerance, especially toward Jews. Outbreaks of violence against the ancient Jewish communities of Muslim lands eventually led to their emigration and sometimes their outright expulsion. Arab opposition to Israel in the early years often employed anti-Semitic motifs, as did the Soviet effort to delegitimize Israel as racist. All of these revolutions in the Jewish condition fundamentally altered the vantage point from which many Jewish scholars viewed the Arab and Muslim worlds. Bernard Lewis (b. 1916) came to personify the post-war shift from a sympathetic to a critical posture.

Lewis was born to middle-class Jewish immigrant parents in London, and he began to study law. But he became captivated by history, which he studied at the University of London. As a youth, Lewis received a solid training in Hebrew, in which he composed both prose and poetry. Hebrew thus became his gateway to Arabic, and he later allowed that his own Jewish education made it easier for him to understand Islam, and even sympathize with its premises.[79] There were those who attributed his aptitude to his origins, as did Sir Cyril Philips (b. 1912), a pillar of the School of Oriental and African Studies at the University of London:

> Capitalizing on the initial advantage of a Jewish background and knowledge of Hebrew, [Lewis] had gone on to achieve a first-class and higher degree in the history of the Near East and also an enviable command of Arabic and Turkish; and his abilities and qualifications were so obviously outstanding that I sought the earliest opportunity to get him established beside me with the rank of professor.[80]

This was 1945, by which time Lewis had been through Syria on research, done a year in Paris under Massignon, received his doctorate, and spent the war years in intelligence work. He remained at the School of Oriental and African Studies until 1974, during which time he became the most influential post-war historian of Islam and the Middle East.

While Lewis possessed all the tools of orientalist scholarship, he was a historian by training and discipline, intimately familiar with new trends in historical writing. Along with Cahen, he was one of the first historians to apply new approaches in economic and social history to the Islamic world. While a student in Paris, Lewis had a brief encounter with the Annales school, which inspired an early and influential article on guilds in Islamic history. He subsequently refused the straightjacket of any overarching theory, and especially Marxism, which he regarded as particularly unsuited to an understanding of the Middle East. But his studies of dissident Muslim sects, slaves, and Jews in Muslim societies broke new ground by expanding the scope of history beyond the palace and the mosque.

Lewis's early work centered upon medieval Arab-Islamic history, especially in what is now Syria. However, after the creation of Israel, it became difficult for Jewish scholars to conduct archival and field research in many of the eastern Arab countries. Lewis turned his efforts to the study of these Arab lands through Ottoman archives available in Istanbul, and to the study of the Ottoman empire itself. His great classic, *The Emergence of Modern Turkey* (1961), examined the history of modernizing reform not through European diplomacy of the "Eastern Question," but through the eyes of the Ottoman reformers themselves. Lewis relied almost entirely on Turkish sources, and his history from within became a model for many other studies of nineteenth-century reform in the Middle East. It also signaled his own deepening interest in the history of ideas and attitudes in Islam's relationship to the West.

While Lewis's work demonstrated a remarkable capacity for empathy across time and place, he stood firm against the growing ideological third worldism of Western intellectuals and scholars. Lewis had an unshakable liberal commitment to democracy and its dissemination. With the onset of the cold war, he became alarmed by the expansion of Soviet influence in the Middle East, and the erosion in the Arab lands of the last vestiges of liberalism by strident anti-Western nationalism. In these years, he wrote, "the choices before us still retained something of the clarity, even the starkness, which they had kept through the war years and which they have subsequently lost."[81] Certainly the choices made by Israel and Turkey—in favor of democracy and Western alliances—were his own moral preferences, and led to his growing identification with both countries, where he came to enjoy a broad influence.

In 1974, Lewis relocated to Princeton University and the Institute for Advanced Study, precisely at a time when orientalism as a branch of scholarship came under a combined attack by Arab-Muslim nationalists and Western post-modernists. These argued that the modern study of Islam in the West had evolved as a tool of imperialist domination, and that the West's pursuit of knowledge had conspired with its pursuit of power. Orientalism, effectively a form of racism, had misrepresented Islam as static, irrational, and in permanent opposition to the West. Lewis, whose own work was maligned in the campaign, offered a vigorous refutation. The development of orientalism, he argued, had to be understood as a facet of Europe's humanism, which arose independently of, and sometimes in opposition to, imperial interests. It was precisely the orientalists who broke the grip of medieval prejudice against Islam, and who diversified the representation of Islam in the West. Lewis also rejected the view that only Muslims, Arabs, or their political sympathizers could write the region's history: he called this "intellectual protectionism." A combination of curiosity, empathy, competence, and self-awareness was the only prerequisite for the writing of "other people's history."

The orientalism debate developed, in part, as a consequence of the large-scale entry of Arabs and Muslims into institutions of Middle Eastern and Islamic studies in the West. These now staked a claim to that "initial advantage" of intimacy with Islamic culture and the languages of its expression formerly claimed by Jews in the West. Yet no one could displace Lewis as preeminent interpreter of Islam, for his stature rested upon his elegant syntheses for general audiences, which were translated into over twenty languages, and which made his name synonymous with Islamic history for educated publics in the West. Neither could any scholar match what Humphreys calls "the extraordinary range of [Lewis's] scholarship, his capacity to command the totality of Islamic and Middle Eastern history from Muhammad down to the present day. This is not merely a matter of erudition; rather, it reflects an almost unparalleled ability to fit things together into a detailed and comprehensive synthesis. In this regard, it is hard to imagine that Lewis will have any true successors."[82]

A Jewish Contribution?

With Lewis, a chapter closed not only in the development of the Western understanding of Islam, but also in the role of Jews as interpreters of Islam in the West. Europe began that chapter as the prime center for the processing of Western (and Jewish) knowledge of Islam. Jews were the first to disappear from the field in Europe, but others followed, driven out by totalitarian rule. After mid-century, many more of Europe's leading scholars moved to America. From Cambridge to California, America's institutions imported Europeans, and the center of gravity of the Western understanding of Islam crossed the Atlantic.

The past was now forgotten. Nikki Keddie has pointed to the absence of a sense for the ways knowledge accumulates over time, as a succession of contributions:

> [T]he giants of the recent past tend to be largely forgotten as soon as they are dead if not before, especially if what they have written isn't what is now considered fashionable or central. There is also an optical illusion, in the sense that much of what these people have contributed is not recognized because it has entered so much into the field that people do not realize how novel a contribution it was. They are criticized when they are in error, but their achievements are forgotten. So Middle Eastern history has become a field without its own history.[83]

It has been easiest to forget many of the Jewish "discoverers" of Islam, especially those who wrote in German or lost crucial parts of their careers to war and wandering. Many of their names are no longer recognized, many of their writings are no longer read.

Yet an identifiable legacy was left by these Jewish "discoverers." They contributed to Europe's initial willingness to reevaluate Islam in an objective and even positive light. The Enlightenment in Europe had not banished ignorance of Islam or the tendency to denigrate it, both a legacy of medieval Christian prejudice. One historian of Western scholarship has written that "if we take a closer look at the many studies of Islam written between 1650 and, say, 1830, we see that prejudice, rather than disappearing, was usually only being modified or shifting from one object to another."[84] It was Geiger's essay of 1833 that broke with this prejudice, and Goldziher's subsequent work which consolidated the new approach. Time after time, for over a century, Jews were among the first to arrive at insights that would serve as the basis for a modern and objective appreciation of Islam. This would have happened without the Jews; it happened earlier because of them.

They were motivated, for the most part, not by the kind of Islamophilia that found adherents on Europe's cultural margins, and which was always suspect for its association with radicals and dilettantes. The Jews, on the contrary, hoped to assume their place in Europe's cultural centers, in its great universities, newspapers, and theatres. They began their discovery of Islam at a time and place in the nineteenth century when some form of assimilation still represented their preferred option. Under these conditions, the favorable portrayal of the Jews under Islam, and the sympathetic study of Islam itself, served a purpose. They demonstrated the leavening role of Jews in the civilization of Islam in a past age when Islam had changed the world, and suggested that Jews could play that role for modern Europe.

The work of Jewish orientalists—liberals and Marxists, Zionists and assimilationists, believers and atheists—subverted the idea that East and West were polar opposites. Much of Europe debated whether the Jews belonged to one or the other; Jews replied that the question itself lacked validity. The work of Jewish orientalists at every turn challenged the tendency to interpret Islam or Judaism *sui generis,* and their message was remarkably uniform: Islamic history (like Jewish history) can be subjected to the same analytical tools as Europe's; Europe's civilization rests also on Islamic (and Jewish) foundations; Islam (like Judaism) is no anachronism, but undergoes constant adaptation, and would accomodate even European modernity. Jews urged European respect for peoples bearing cultures of extra-European origin, precisely because the Jews were the most vulnerable of these peoples, residing as they did in the very center of Europe.

Paradoxically, while Europe gradually assimilated this approach to Islam, it often declined to assimilate its Jewish bearers. Anti-Semitism in central Europe, and its manifestations in eastern and western Europe, undermined the project of Jewish assimilation. Jews were chased from the universities, then from the continent, as a prelude to the "final solution." Yet their contribution to the understanding of Islam could not be erased from consciousness of Europe, even where their very names were excised from bibliographies. Goldziher's influence on Islamic studies remained as profound as Durkheim's on sociology and Freud's on psychology. And the respect for Islam which Jews had done so much to disseminate not only survived in Europe, but served as the basis for Europe's tolerance of Muslim minorities after the war. The mosque-like synagogues erected by Jewish communities in the nineteenth century prepared Europe to accept the real mosques which Muslim communities erected across the continent in the twentieth. Indeed, in the absence of Jews, Muslim migrants became primary beneficiaries of the regret felt by new European elites for Europe's failing of the Jews.

The history of Europe's discovery of Islam is being written piecemeal—a chapter here, an article there. Eventually this work will be synthesized, and the relative significance of the Jewish contribution—and indeed, the very idea of such a contribution—will have to be weighed carefully. The question has been posed. It may prove difficult to answer. To judge from the articles that follow, it will be impossible to ignore.

Notes

1. Bernard Lewis, "The Pro-Islamic Jews," in his *Islam in History: Ideas, People, and Events in the Middle East,* new rev. ed. (Chicago: Open Court, 1993), 142, 144.
2. Bernard Lewis, "The State of Middle Eastern Studies," *American Scholar* 48, no. 3 (summer 1979): 369–70.
3. Bernard Lewis, "The Study of Islam," in his *Islam in History,* 12.
4. Edward Said, *Orientalism* (New York: Pantheon, 1978).
5. Maxime Rodinson, "Western Views of the Muslim World," in his *Europe and the Mystique of Islam,* trans. Roger Veinus (Seattle: University of Washington Press, 1987), 3–82.
6. Albert Hourani, "Islam and the Philosophers of History," in his *Europe and the Middle East* (Berkeley: University of California Press, 1980), 19–73 (on Goldziher, 51–53); idem, "Islam in European Thought," in his *Islam in European Thought* (Cambridge: Cambridge University Press, 1991), 7–60 (on Goldziher, 36–41). "Edward [Said] totally ignores the German tradition and philosophy of history which was the central tradition of the orientalists," said Hourani in an interview. "Therefore among others he has ignored Goldziher." *Approaches to the History of the Middle East: Interviews with Leading Middle East Historians,* ed. Nancy Elizabeth Gallagher (London: Ithaca Press, 1994), 43.
7. On Heine's orientalism, see Mounir Fendri, *Halbmond, Kreuz und Schibboleth: Heinrich Heine und der islamische Orient* (Hamburg: Heinrich Heine Verlag, 1980); and Christiane Barbara Pfeifer, *Heine und der islamische Orient,* Mizan, vol. 1 (Wiesbaden: O. Harrassowitz, 1990).

8. On Heine's reading in orientalist sources, see *Heinrich Heine. Säkularausgabe,* vol. 4K (Kommentar) (Berlin: Akademie-Verlag, 1996), 21–46.
9. Ibid., vol. 1 (Gedichte, 1812–1827) (Berlin: Akademie-Verlag, 1979), 140. (The lines are from the poem.).
10. Ibid., vol. 4 (Tragödien, Frühe Prosa, 1820–1831) (Berlin: Akademie-Verlag, 1981), 15.
11. Ibid., 11.
12. Hichem Djaït, "Islam and German Thought," in his *Europe and Islam,* trans. Peter Heinegg (Berkeley: University of California Press, 1985), 75.
13. For an extensive survey, see Hannelore Kunzl, *Islamische Stilelemente im Synagogenbau des 19. undfruhen 20. Jahrhunderts,* Judentum und Umwelt, vol. 9 (Frankfurt: P. Lang, 1984).
14. Albert Rosengarten, *A Handbook of Architectural Styles,* trans. W. Collett-Sandars (London: Chatto and Windus, 1878), 485 (originally published in 1857). Rosengarten was the first modern architect of Jewish birth in Germany, and a critic of the "Moorish" style, which he thought lacked the "elevating effect" of the Romanesque and Gothic styles.
15. Cf. John Sweetman, *The Oriental Obsession: Islamic Inspiration in British and American Art and Architecture 1500–1920* (Cambridge: Cambridge University Press, 1988). Sweetman (287 n.13) points to the role of synagogues in familiarizing Europe with Islamic architectural forms. But he attributes use of these forms to an "urgent Zionism which sought to draw attention to Palestine as the true home of the Jews....the interesting fact remains the choice, by Jews disenchanted with Europe, of Islamic dome and minaret-forms." He also writes (236) that in adopting these architectural forms, "the Jews sought to give expression to their sense of alienation in Europe." This interpretation misses the mark. The Moorish style was most popular with the most assimilationist and anti-Zionist segments of European (and American) Jewry. Another verdict on one of the most famous Moorish synagogues in Europe, the Oranienburgerstrasse synagogue in Berlin, is applicable to the style as a whole: it "revealed the taste for Reform and modernity and cultural assimilation," and expressed "optimism and confidence." Carol Herselle Krinsky, *Synagogues of Europe: Architecture, History, Meaning* (Cambridge, Mass.: MIT Press, 1985), 270.
16. Philippe Jullian, *The Orientalists: European Painters of Eastern Scenes* (Oxford: Phaidon, 1977), 146. These painters represented Jewish life in their work, but Jewish women also served as models substituting for Muslims: "Access to Muslim households and harems was notoriously difficult through the [nineteenth] century, and even in the 1880s Renoir complained of the difficulty of finding suitable models. In general, artists drew their subjects from the local Jewish population." *The Orientalists: Delacroix to Matisse,* ed. Mary Anne Stevens (London: Royal Academy of Arts, 1984), 177.

17. The famous landmarks: Delacroix's *Noce juive* (c. 1837–41, Louvre) and *Musiciens juifs de Mogador* (1847, Louvre); Chassériau's *Le Jour de Sabbat dans le quartier juif à Constantine* (c. 1847, lost to fire); and Dehondencq's *Mariée juive au Maroc* (c. 1870, Musée de Reims).
18. For Arabia, Spain, and English romanticism, see Kathryn Tidrick, *Heart-Beguiling Araby: The English Romance with Arabia,* rev. ed. (London: I.B. Tauris, 1989), 32–53; and the exhibition catalogue *The Romantic Image of the Legacy of Al-Andalus* (Granada: Presidential Committee of the Legacy of Al-Andalus, 1995), 30–44.
19. Benjamin Disraeli, *Coningsby or the New Generation* (London: The Bodley Head, 1927), 289. (The passage appears in book 4, chapter 10.)
20. Lord Cromer (Evelyn Baring) quoted by Anthony S. Wohl, "'Dizzi-Ben-Dizzi': Disraeli as Alien," *Journal of British Studies* 34, no. 3 (July 1995): 397.
21. Quoted by Paul Mendes-Flohr, "Fin de Siècle Orientalism, the Ostjuden, and the Aesthetics of Jewish Self-Affirmation," in his *Divided Passions: Jewish Intellectuals and the Experience of Modernity* (Detroit: Wayne State University Press, 1990), 81.
22. They included David D'Beth Hillel (d. 1846), who spent a year in Baghdad, visited the Shi'ite shrine cities of Najaf and Karbala, and wrote a unique account of dissident sects of western Persia; Israel Joseph Benjamin (1818–64), who traversed Syria, Iraq, Persia, and Afghanistan, then crossed all of North Africa, and published an account; Jacob Eduard Polak (1820–91), physician to Shah Nāṣir al-Dīn (r. 1848–96); and Hermann Burchardt (1857–1909), photographer and ethnologist, who died at the hands of marauders between San'a and Mecca.
23. Arminius Vámbéry, "The Future of Constitutional Turkey," *The Nineteenth Century and After* (March 1909): 361–62.
24. Steinschneider's work did have an impact on Islamic studies; see Franz Rosenthal, "Steinschneider's Contribution to the Study of Muslim Civilization," *Proceedings of the American Academy of Jewish Research* 27 (1958): 67–81.
25. Quoted by Lassner, 107 below.
26. Ibid.
27. Ibid., 106.
28. Lewis, "Pro-Islamic Jews," 142.
29. Jules Mohl, quoted by D.M. Dunlop, "Some Remarks on Weil's History of the Caliphs," in *Historians of the Middle East,* eds. Bernard Lewis and P.M. Holt (London: Oxford University Press, 1962), 320.
30. Mary Louis Gude, *Louis Massignon: The Crucible of Compassion* (Notre Dame: University of Notre Dame Press, 1996), 17–18, 251 n. 44.
31. Quoted by Daniel Rivet, "Les délices de l'ailleurs," *Télérama hors-série: Delacroix* (September 1994): 44.

32. Theodor Nöldeke quoted by Bernard Lewis, *Semites and Anti-Semites* (London: Weidenfeld and Nicolson, 1986), 45–46.
33. Quoted by Róbert Simon, *Ignác Goldziher: His Life and Scholarship as Reflected in his Works and Correspondence* (Budapest and Leiden: Library of the Hungarian Academy of Sciences and Brill, 1986), 20.
34. Ibid.
35. Quoted in *Scholarship and Friendship in Early Islamwissenschaft: The Letters of C. Snouck Hurgronje to I. Goldziher,* ed. P.Sj. van Koningsveld (Leiden: Rijksuniversiteit Leiden, 1985), xiv.
36. Cf. Jean-Jacques Waardenburg, *L'Islam dans le miroir de l'occident,* 3d rev. ed. (Paris and the Hague: Mouton, 1962), 266.
37. Raphel Patai, *Ignaz Goldziher and His Oriental Diary* (Detroit: Wayne State University Press, 1987), 20.
38. Ibid., 28.
39. Ibid., 144.
40. Quoted by Simon, *Ignác Goldziher,* 44.
41. Quoted by Simon, ibid., 61.
42. Quoted by Simon, ibid., 60. After Goldziher's death, the new Hebrew University purchased his library of 6,000 books and transferred it to Jerusalem.
43. Hourani, *Islam in European Thought,* 2.
44. Interview with Hourani, in *Approaches to the History of the Middle East,* 42.
45. Jaroslav Stetkevych, "Arabic Poetry and Assorted Poetics," in *Islamic Studies: A Tradition and its Problems,* ed. Malcolm Kerr (Malibu, Calif.: Undena, 1980), 120–22.
46. Oleg Grabar, *The Formation of Islamic Art,* rev. ed. (New Haven: Yale University Press, 1987), 12–13.
47. Albert Hourani, "Patterns of the Past," in *Paths to the Middle East: Ten Scholars Look Back,* ed. Thomas Naff (Albany: State University of New York Press, 1993), 38.
48. The Iranologist Fritz Wolff (1880–1943) was an exception, and did perish. The Arabist Werner Caskel (1896–1970), although not Jewish by any other criterion, had a Jewish father. He was dismissed from the University of Greifswald in 1938, and narrowly avoided deportation. The Turcologist Franz Babinger (1891–1967) had a grandmother of Jewish birth. In 1934, *Der Stürmer* denounced him as racially tainted, and he left Germany.
49. Hans Heinrich Schaeder, "Deutsche Orientforschung," *Der Nahe Osten* (Berlin) 1 (1940): 129–34.
50. Baber Johansen, "Politics, Paradigms and the Progress of Oriental Studies: The German Oriental Society (Deutsche Morgenländische Gesellschaft) 1845–1989," *M.A.R.S.* (Paris), 4 (winter 1995): 88.
51. D.H. Baneth, quoted by Kraemer, 181 below.

52. Massignon (Paris) to Henri Gaillard (Cairo), 12 December 1933, in the archives of the French embassy in Cairo, Archives du MAE, Nantes, carton 74/14 ("Français islamisants"). For Jews and other Germans at the University of Istanbul, see Hort Wildmann, *Exil und Bildungshilfe: Die deutschsprachige akademische Emigration in die Turkei nach 1933* (Bern: Herbert Lang, 1973).
53. Massignon's letter to *Nouveaux Cahiers,* quoted by Christian Destremau and Jean Moncelon, *Louis Massignon* (Paris: Plon, 1994), 257.
54. Ibid., 258.
55. Charles Spencer, *Léon Bakst and the Ballets Russes,* rev. ed. (London: Academy Editions, 1995), 19.
56. Ibid., 77, quoting Louis Reau and André Levinson.
57. For Wolf and his play, see Donna K. Heizer, *Jewish-German Identity in the Orientalist Literature of Else Lasker-Schuler, Friedrich Wolf, and Franz Werfel* (Columbia, South Carolina: Camden House, 1996), 50–66.
58. Ibid., 58.
59. Muhammad Asad, *The Road to Mecca* (New York: Simon and Schuster, 1954), 309.
60. Ibid., 49.
61. For examples of the genre, see the exhibition catalogue *To the East: Orientalism in the Arts in Israel* (Jerusalem: Israel Museum, 1998).
62. Report of the Survey Committee of the Hebrew University of Jerusalem, 1934, quoted by Menahem Milson, "The Beginnings of Arabic and Islamic Studies at the Hebrew University of Jerusalem," *Judaism* 45 (1996): 175–76. The committee was headed by the British Jewish educator Sir Philip Hartog (1864–1947), who had been involved in the founding of the School of Oriental and African Studies in London, and who had served from 1920 to 1925 as the first vice chancellor of the University of Dacca in Bengal.
63. Ibid., 176.
64. Quoted by Sela, 264 below.
65. R. Stephen Humphreys, *Islamic History: A Framework for Inquiry* (Princeton: Princeton University Press, 1991), 262, 264, 268.
66. E. Ashtor, *A Social and Economic History of the Near East in the Middle Ages* (Berkeley: University of California Press, 1976), 7–8.
67. Thomas Philipp, "In Memoriam: Gabriel Baer 1919–1982," *Middle Eastern Studies* 19 (1983): 275–76.
68. Ibid.
69. Quoted by Dan V. Segre, "Patriotism and Faith: Giorgio Levi Della Vida," *Middle Eastern Lectures* 2 (1997): 96.
70. Hourani, "Islam and the Philosophers of History," 73.
71. "Claude Cahen: Histoire et engagement politique, entretien avec Maxime Rodinson," *Arabica* 43 (January 1996): 23, n. 21.

72. Interview with Rodinson, in *Approaches to the History of the Middle East,* 113.
73. Ibid., 119.
74. Maxime Rodinson, *Marxism and the Muslim World,* trans. Jean Matthews (New York: Monthly Review Press, 1981), 22.
75. Maxime Rodinson, *Cult, Ghetto, and State: The Persistence of the Jewish Question,* trans. Jon Rothschild (London: Al Saqi, 1983), 10.
76. "Entretien avec Maxime Rodinson," *M.A.R.S.* (Paris), 4 (winter 1995): 27.
77. "Un texte inédit de Maxime Rodinson sur Maxime Rodinson," in *La Cuisiner et le philosophe: Hommage à Maxime Rodinson,* ed. Jean-Pierre Digard (Paris: Maisonneuve et Larose, 1982), 22.
78. Djaït, "Islam and German Thought," 77–78.
79. Lewis describes his Jewish education in the preface to his *Alei Historia: Qovetz Mehqarim* (Jerusalem: Ben-Zvi Institute, 1988), 1–4.
80. Cyril Philips, *Beyond the Ivory Tower* (London: The Radcliffe Press, 1995), 158.
81. Bernard Lewis, "Modern Turkey Revisited," *Humanities* 11, no. 3 (May–June 1990): 12
82. R. Stephen Humphreys, "Bernard Lewis: An Appreciation," *Humanities* 11, no. 3 (May–June 1990): 19.
83. Interview with Nikki Keddie, *Appoaches to the History of the Middle East,* 145–46. She mentions the "true early giant" Goldziher as one who goes unmentioned.
84. Alastair Hamilton, "Western Attitudes to Islam in the Enlightenment," *Middle Eastern Lectures* 3 (1999): 69.

1

Pedigree Remembered, Reconstructed, Invented: Benjamin Disraeli between East and West

Minna Rozen

In the summer of 1877, William Gladstone (1809–98)—never a great admirer of Benjamin Disraeli—offered this assessment of his character in a private letter: "Though he has been baptized, his Jew feelings are the most radical and the most real, and so far respectable, portion of his profoundly falsified nature."[1] A year later, after the signing of the Treaty of Berlin, Otto von Bismarck's astonished pronouncement was on everyone's lips: "Der alte Jude, das ist der Mann!"[2] Indeed, despite Disraeli's conversion, and even at the height of his career, his Jewish origins were never forgotten—not in England and not abroad, not by supporters and not by opponents.[3] Disraeli himself did not forget them either. But what is meant when we say "he did not forget"?

Recalling the origins of Benjamin Disraeli (1804–81) is a complex task that entails constructing, or reconstructing, his lineage, personal history, and way of remembering. For Benjamin Disraeli had at least three "pedigrees." The first can be documented through the historian's usual tools of the trade. In other words, it is the one closest to verifiable fact. The second is the fictitious pedigree that Disraeli himself presented as his own. Since it was fabricated, this lineage has a history of its own, with its own stages of development. It is not a static, finished version of his genealogy but rather a picture in motion, more reminiscent of a film.

Disraeli's third pedigree is no less imaginary than the second, but it is utterly different from it both in substance and function. Whereas the second lineage had some connection with reality, and was intended for "daily use," the third is totally imaginary; it represents the element of Disraeli's historical and spiritual memory. This lineage served Disraeli, first and foremost, as an inner beacon that lit his way through life. This third pedigree is also a dynamic one, with its own internal history and stages of creation and evolution.

The historical elements of Disraeli's lineage, when viewed as a totality, may provide us with a deeper understanding of the link between his own past and the world view underlying his policies with regard to the East. In a broader context, such a discussion may shed some light on the nature of memory in general.

The Father's Choices

Benjamin Disraeli did not convert out of a personal decision. He was baptized into the Anglican Church in 1817 at the age of thirteen, together with his brothers and sisters, on the initiative of his father, Isaac D'Israeli (1766–1848).[4] The reasons for the father's action are not entirely clear, but they can be summarized as an expression of his own desire not to continue on the path open to a normative Jew in the England of his time, although he had no other religious preference.

Thus he left the Bevis Marks synagogue at precisely the point when he would have been obliged to make the necessary preparations for his son's transition into manhood in the eyes of Jewish law, with responsibility for his actions and his transgressions.[5] While he himself led the life of a "Jew without a synagogue," it would seem that he did not view this as an adequate solution for his children. The Anglican Church, in his eyes, offered the answer to the social problems and questions of affiliation that would confront them if he left them in the status that he had chosen for himself.[6]

Isaac D'Israeli himself never converted. He was the ultimate Spinozist in his religious philosophy, and a "Jew without a synagogue" in his actions.[7] In both thought and deed, there was not a great deal separating him from the generations of "New Christians" who made their way to

Italy, the Netherlands, France, and England in the seventeenth and eighteenth centuries. There they found that they had to forge their own brand of Judaism, since there was no connection between the faith of their fathers, as they had imagined it in the countries of their persecution, and what Judaism turned out to be in those parts of the world where Jews were permitted to observe their religion unhampered.[8]

Although Benjamin Disraeli, like his father, did not fit the pattern of the normative Jewish believer, he differed from his father in his tremendous ambition. The clash between his modest origins and his lofty ambitions led to his invention of fictitious pedigrees and the emergence of a man altogether different from D'Israeli the father, both in actions and in attitude toward the origins and the role of the Jewish people.

Lineage A: The Established Pedigree

The following are the facts relating to Benjamin Disraeli's background that can be verified:

Benjamin D'Israeli the elder (1730–1816), the grandfather of the statesman, was a hatmaker who moved to London from Italy in 1748 at the age of eighteen. The earliest known link on the family tree is that of Benjamin Disraeli's great-grandfather, Yitzhak D'Israeli, from the small town of Cento, near Ferrara.[9] The origins of the name "Israeli" or "Israel" can be traced back as far as the tenth century.[10] The name was very popular among the "New Christians," who returned to Judaism after several generations as practicing Christians. In cases where they did not know the original Hebrew family name, but had a family tradition that they were not a Cohen or a Levi, some of them simply adopted the name "Israel." Families with this name are recorded in 1546 in Salonika,[11] in 1613 in Venice,[12] 1624 in Jerusalem,[13] and later in Livorno, Rhodes, Ancona, and Alexandria.[14]

Disraeli's family, then, may be assumed to have a Spanish-Portuguese origin. They reached a "place of Judaism" in the late sixteenth or early seventeenth century, and wandered the eastern parts of the Mediterranean until Benjamin D'Israeli the elder decided to try his luck in London. He ultimately left a sizeable inheritance to Isaac D'Israeli that enabled him to dabble in literature without having to work a day in his life.[15]

The lineage of the mother of Benjamin Disraeli's grandfather, Henrietta, is much clearer. She came from an ancient Italian family, di Rossi, that claimed to trace its roots to one of the four families that the Emperor Titus brought back with him from Jerusalem after the destruction of the Temple.[16] Ironically, Disraeli was unaware of this myth, and so made no use of it. Disraeli's paternal grandmother was Sarah Syprut (née Gabbai Villa-Real) (1742/3–1825). The Gabbai Villa-Reals were a well-to-do Portuguese family of merchants from Livorno that had branches in every place where there was a profit to be made from trade.[17]

Thus far we have presented the ascertained facts regarding the father's side of the family, which served as the basis for Disraeli's fictitious pedigree. Disraeli never made use of the family history of his mother, Maria D'Israeli (1775–1847), despite the fact that her lineage was a good deal clearer than that of his father. This may be due to an estrangement between mother and son,[18] although another possible explanation is the lesser importance that Disraeli attached to his mother's family tree. Be that as it may, she came from an Ashkenazic family by the name of Basevi (actually "Bashevis" in Yiddish , meaning "belonging to Batsheva"). Her mother was Rebecca Rieti of the ancient Italian-Jewish family of that name, and her grandmother belonged to the Aboab Cardoso family which had settled in England as far back as the late seventeenth century. The Aboab Cardoso family claimed a connection with the rabbinic sage Yitzhak Aboab of Castille, who led his congregation to Portugal at the time of the expulsion.[19] Whether or not this is true, this branch of the family could have provided Disraeli with a history of four generations in England, at a time when his opponents claimed he had only one generation in England behind him. However, he never made explicit reference to this information.

These are the facts that are verifiable, to a greater or lesser extent.[20]

Lineage B: The Fictitious Pedigree

Disraeli presented his fictitious pedigree, in its virtually completed form, in 1849 in the introduction to a collection of his father's writings. Its resemblance to seventeenth- and eighteenth-century *halakhic* works is inescapable. Books published by the children or relatives of the author, or even by strangers, always contained an introduction with a detailed description of the author's lineage.[21] This is exactly what Disraeli did.

His version was an approximation of reality. In this account, Disraeli's family left Spain during the expulsion and settled in Venice where they "dropped their Gothic surname and, grateful to the God of Jacob who had sustained them through unprecedented trials and guarded them through unheard of perils, they assumed the name of Disraeli, a name never borne before or since by any other family in order that their race might be forever recognized." In Venice, they flourished "as merchants for more than two centuries under the protection of the lion of St. Mark." Then, towards the middle of the eighteenth century, his great-grandfather sent the younger of his two sons, Benjamin, to England "where the dynasty seemed at length established through the recent failure of Prince Charles Edward and where public opinion appeared definitively adverse to the persecution of creed and conscience." The other son, so Disraeli alleged, remained in Venice as a banker and became a friend of Sir Horace Mann (1701–86), the British envoy in Florence.[22]

The voluminous correspondence of Sir Horace Mann offers no indication of any ties to the Disraeli family, and the only Disraelis with a genuine connection to the family who settled in Venice were the two sisters of his grandfather, who moved there at an advanced age and founded a school for girls. It is interesting to note that when Disraeli visited Venice in 1826, his relatives were still living there, but there is no mention in his letters of any attempt on his part to seek them out. In other words, he considered his true lineage unworthy of any investment of his time, not to mention the fact that it stood in the way of his attempts to reshape his past into a form more to his liking.[23]

Another link in the fabrication of Disraeli's past grew out of his encounter with a woman by the name of Sarah Brydges Williams, also known as Sarah Mendez da Costa. She was about seventy years old when she met Disraeli in 1851. Their relationship was a multi-faceted one. Disraeli was deeply in debt throughout most of his life, a fact of which Sarah was unaware. She was a childless widow, fabulously wealthy, who gave Disraeli to understand that she would leave him her worldly goods, which she ultimately did.

The most interesting aspect of the ties between them was Sarah's belief that, being descended from the Mendez da Costa family and, through them, the Lara family, she was also connected to the Spanish Lara dynasty. Disraeli also believed that there was a link between his own family and the Lara clan. His father's first wife, Rebecca Furtado, was the sister-in-law of the wealthy banker Francisco Aaron Nuñez de Lara, and the mother-in-law of his son Aaron Lara. It would appear that there were no blood ties between the two families, but Disraeli took pleasure in believing that there were. Sarah Mendez da Costa saw Disraeli as representing the future, and was immensely proud of him; at the same time, she also cultivated in him an awareness of his "noble ancestry." Matters reached such a point that in 1859, Disraeli pressed the ambassadors of Spain and Portugal to locate the family crests of the Mendez da Costa and Lara dynasties, partly to placate Sarah but also because the entire enterprise substantiated what he had always wished to believe about himself: that he stemmed from nobility.[24]

Lineage C: The Pedigree in Spirit

Disraeli was motivated by an urgent desire to reach great heights. In a society where a good pedigree, preferably accompanied by an income to match, was the usual prerequisite for glory, he tried to achieve it by two other routes: literature and politics. In different ways, these two paths reflected a colossal arrogance on his part. Disraeli might not have been a literary genius, but he was, without question, a gifted artist in his use of the English language—the language of a people that viewed him as alien. Partly through his mastery of language, he ultimately became one of Britain's greatest prime ministers.

But even the political route, which eventually brought Disraeli the renown he sought, was extremely difficult to follow without the right pedigree. Disraeli's problem was that, even if he had wished to do so, he could not pretend to be anything other than what he was: his black curls, his hooked nose practically shouted: "I am a foreigner, I am a Jew."

The only way to stay the path to glory was to prove that this same foreign ancestry, which so many found repulsive, was superior to the pedigree of the society whose heights Disraeli wished to scale. This need is also the reason why Disraeli did not do the first thing that any apostate who wishes to assimilate into larger society would do: he did not change his name. And his name, along with his appearance, loudly proclaimed: "I stem from the Israelites," i.e. the Jews.

Proving his nobility was therefore a basic element of Disraeli's inner being and his personality. It should be recalled that one's lineage was a central value not only of the society in which Disraeli sought fame. In Spanish-Jewish society, as in Iberian society in general, lineage was a central—if not a supreme—value. The "New Christians" maintained lengthy genealogical charts in order to prove that their blood had not been tainted by that of the "old Christians" and that they were in fact proper Jews, while the Spanish and Portuguese kept similar records to prove the purity of their own blood—*limpieza de sangre.* A long and verifiable family tree was part of the *honra,* the honor, of the Spanish male, such that it is not hard to comprehend the cultural and historical memory that shaped Disraeli's preoccupation and motivated his actions.[25]

The most compelling expression of the impact of this historical memory on Disraeli's personality is the lineage that I have termed his "spiritual pedigree"—the beacon that illuminated his way. It has no connection with reality. Yet it expresses various strata of Disraeli's personality and his perception of his origins. This lineage appears throughout his literary works.

All of Disraeli's biographers have made use of his novels as a historical source, especially since, in most of these works, he described the society in which he lived. Moreover, the protagonists were often drawn from Disraeli's daily life. His biographers, whether sympathetic or critical, have detected in these novels an attempt to refine and polish the image of the Jewish people. Some see in them a simple identification with Disraeli's true origins, while others point to a connection between the glorification of his roots and the constant struggle that Disraeli was compelled to wage against the anti-Semitism of British society.[26] Yet none have delved into the gradual evolution of the imaginary spiritual lineage that Disraeli constructed for himself in his novels. At most, his biographers have attempted to identify obvious historical figures in specific literary characters.[27] The failure to grasp the full significance of this genealogy has prevented Disraeli's biographers from fully understanding his perspective regarding relations between East and West—expressed long before Disraeli had the power to affect the fate of peoples and nations.

Between Literature and Autobiography

It is no accident that the first two works important for this purpose began to take shape in Cairo at the end of Disraeli's journey to the Levant in 1831.[28] The work *Contarini Fleming* is described by Disraeli as "a development of my poetic character," and the subtitle itself defines the book as a psychological romance. The book is written in the first person, and in certain ways is an autobiography of Disraeli, a sort of "Disraeli as a young man."

The autobiographical aspect of this work consists of two elements: a fictitious component in which symbols and surrogates take the place of the protagonist and his family, and their true ancestry; and a documentary component which recounts, almost in the style of a travelogue, the story of Disraeli's journey from England, by way of Spain, to Italy, Greece, Turkey, Syria, Palestine, and Egypt. At the same time, through the symbols he employs, Disraeli presents the central conflicts of his existence. Already in the title of the work, Disraeli offers his own view of his character: to borrow from the world of flora, he sees himself as a north European graft onto a Mediterranean shoot. Contarini is the name of the patrician Venetian family to which the protagonist's mother belongs, and Fleming is the family name of his father, a north European nobleman. Contarini Fleming is the product of this grafting, a descendant of nobility who harbors elements of both East and West engaged in a perpetual inner struggle.

The father of young Contarini Fleming tells his son that he will one day be prime minister. Like Disraeli, Contarini abandons his original faith, but in this case for Catholicism, and sets out on his "odyssey of initiation" through the East. Disraeli's poetic novel reflects his own view of himself in 1831, at the age of twenty-eight—a young man struggling with questions of national, religious, and cultural identity. His culture is British, but beneath the surface are distant, alien elements from which he cannot bring himself to sever all ties. How convenient it would be if, like Contarini Fleming, he were descended on one side from European or British nobility! But this is only a poetic history—and he knows it—so he creates for himself a different nobility.[29]

Concurrent with *Contarini Fleming,* Disraeli began to write a historical novel entitled *Alroy.* Relying heavily on literary license, he described the revolt and eventual fall of the false messiah, David Alroy, who was active in the northeastern Caucasus, Iran, and Iraq in the twelfth century. Disraeli referred to this novel as portraying his "ideal ambition." This particular work has baffled most of Disraeli's biographers, who have had difficulty explaining the nature of this ambition. And what benefit did Disraeli foresee for himself—a young man pursuing a political career in Britain—in writing a fictional, highly emotional work describing the heroic but unsuccessful struggle of a Jewish leader, a descendant of King David, to achieve political redemption for the Jewish people?[30]

In the words of David Alroy:

> You ask me what I wish: my answer is, a national existence, which we have not. You ask me what I wish: my answer is the Land of Promise. You ask me what I wish: my answer is, Jerusalem. You ask me what I wish: my answer is, the Temple, all we forfeited, all we have yearned after, all for which we have fought, our beauteous country, our holy creed, our simple manners, and our ancient customs.[31]

David Alroy appraises the past and present of the Jewish people:

> There was a glorious prime when Israel stood aloof from other nations, a fair and holy thing that God had hallowed. We were then a chosen family.... We shunned the stranger as an unclean thing that must defile our solitary sanctity, and keeping to ourselves and to our God, our lives flowed on in one great solemn tide of deep religion, making the meanest of our multitude feel greater than the kings of other lands.... It was a glorious time. I thought it had returned, but I awake from this, as other dreams.[32]

The question not posed by Disraeli's biographers is this: How did *Contarini Fleming* and *Alroy* spring from the author's pen at the same time?

The answer, to my mind, lies in Disraeli's experiences on his Levantine odyssey. There is no doubt that the entire journey, and especially the trek through the Holy Land and the few days he spent in Jerusalem, left a profound impression on Disraeli. In this sense, it was unquestionably a classic journey of initiation. The literary outburst at the end of the journey was a releasing of his emotional tension, and the two novels are Disraeli's literary expression of the two sides of his personality.

The first novel, *Contarini Fleming,* said: "This is me, this is what I do, this is what I am going to do in future. I am an Englishman. I have foreign roots, but do not be mistaken: I am of noble blood like you, and I will be a great statesman." *Contarini Fleming,* for all its fictitious nature, represents reality. *Alroy,* in contrast, is the unattainable ideal: "This is what I would have liked to be, this is what I should have done. I would like to have been a courageous leader possessed of supernatural powers, who brings redemption to his people, the people of Israel." But in *Alroy,* even more than in *Contarini Fleming,* the message is unmistakable:

"Know that my lineage is more ancient and more noble than any you can imagine."

The title that Disraeli confers upon Alroy, namely "the prince of captivity," has significance beyond that of a mere translation of the Hebrew term *rosh ha-golah.* It expresses the sharp dichotomy between nobility and captivity—a dichotomy which is a recurring theme in Disraeli's perception of himself. He was born to rule, but his hands are shackled by invisible chains. Did Disraeli not realize the likely damage to his political career from a work on the political independence of the Jewish people, in a country where a Jew was not even permitted to sit as a member of Parliament? The answer is simple: Disraeli would have encountered these same obstacles even had he not written this book (and his later works). Instead of avoiding the issue, he seized the bull by the horns, so to speak, and offered this response to those who would denigrate his origins: "I come from an ancient, distinguished people, superior to yours. I would like to act on behalf of my people, but this is not possible. In truth, you should consider yourselves fortunate that I strive to act on behalf of *your* people."

Disraeli continued to develop his fictitious lineage and his personal identity in the political novel *Coningsby,* published in 1844. The novel sprang from his struggle with the then-prime minister of England, Sir Robert Peel (1788–1850). Peel did not recognize Disraeli's abilities and hampered his advancement. A disappointed Disraeli founded the Young England opposition, operating within the Tory party, and sat down to write *Coningsby* to explain his political ideology. *Coningsby* therefore is meant to represent political reality. But embedded in the novel once again is his idealized ambition, this time not in the form of David Alroy, the twelfth-century hero, but in a later incarnation: Sidonia, the ideal Jewish leader of the mid-nineteenth century. The true hero of *Coningsby* is not Coningsby at all but Sidonia. Sidonia, like Alroy, is Disraeli's alter-ego, two links in the fictitious family tree that shapes his inner world.

All of Disraeli's biographers have identified Sidonia with Rothschild. Blake, as well as Monypenny, Buckle, and Ridley speculate as to Disraeli's true intent, and describe Sidonia as a combination of Rothschild and Disraeli.[33] The truth is that Sidonia is much more than Nathaniel Meyer Rothschild (1777–1836) or Lionel Nathan de Rothschild (1808–79). He also contains elements of Moses Montefiore (1784–1862), and readers of *Original Letters from India, 1779–1815* by Eliza Fai, will also find in Sidonia traces of Señor Franco of Livorno.[34] None of Disraeli's biographers offers much in the way of an analysis of the character of Sidonia beyond the statement that he is an enigmatic figure. And none attempts to pursue the significance of the strong similarity between Disraeli and Sidonia.

The enigma embodied in Sidonia's character stems from the superhuman qualities with which Disraeli endows him.[35] Sidonia is a Jewish businessman of Sephardic origin, amazingly well-educated and highly knowledgeable in the mysteries of international politics, including those of Britain. His wealth is legendary and he has branches and agents in every corner of the globe. He knows all the world's leaders personally, and they know and respect him. Disraeli places in Sidonia's mouth his own political and social commentary and perceptions—the same perceptions that will guide his own actions in future.

But there is a flaw in Sidonia's personality: he is unfeeling. He is unfeeling in the sense that he experiences neither the agony nor the ecstasy of love. This flaw deprives him of one of the most wondrous expressions of the human condition. Yet it makes him freer and stronger than most other men. It should be noted here that Sidonia is not the equivalent of the actual Disraeli; Sidonia, like Alroy, is what Disraeli would wish to be. He would wish to be powerful, all-knowing, and capable of absolute control over his emotions, but this does not mean that he is. Disraeli, it should be stated here, did not marry for love.

Disraeli constructs a family tree for Sidonia. He was born in Aragon to a noble family of "New Christians" who provided the Spanish nation with statesmen, members of the church hierarchy such as the archbishop of Toledo, and even one grand inquisitor. They always remained secretly loyal to their Jewish faith, and many were burned at the stake for this sin. And so things continued until the youngest Sidonia decided to leave the Iberian peninsula and settle in London. In the description of Sidonia's lineage, we again encounter the element of the prince in captivity, the nobleman trapped behind a mask, forced to dissimulate, shackled by invisible chains.

In his description of Sidonia's family tree, Disraeli for the first time addresses his relationship with the world of Islam. The genealogy is traced backward from the present; thus, after establishing the noble ancestry of the Sidonia family, who stem from the "New Christians," he shifts his attentions to an ancient link in their history. Where did the family live originally, before coming to the Iberian peninsula? They came from the Middle East by way of North Africa and settled in Iberia long before its conquest by the Arabs. It is at this juncture that Disraeli expresses, perhaps for the first time, his concept of the origins of the Jewish people. He imparts this view through an "objective" description of the migration of the Jews around the Mediterranean basin, placing it in the mouth of Sidonia for good measure. The Jews are Mosaic Arabs, while the Muslims are Mohammedan Arabs. Race is all-important—and Jews and Muslims are of the same race.

Disraeli then offers his own history of the Iberian peninsula. The amazing success of the Mosaic Arabs aroused the envy and hatred of the Visigoths, who initiated a brutal persecution against them. The Mosaic Arabs turned for help to the Mohammedan Arabs, who had already established themselves across the Strait of Gibraltar. The sons of Ishmael (i.e., the Muslims) favored the sons of Israel (the Jews) with equal rights, and thus was launched the golden age of Spanish Jewry. When the situation was reversed with the Reconquista, the "Spanish Goths" still treated the Jews with courtesy and consideration, but the moment they had conquered the last Muslim stronghold, the fate of Spanish Jewry was sealed—along with the fate of Spain itself. It was the Muslims and the Jews who had provided Spain with its wealth and achievements, and these vanished without a trace upon their expulsion.

> Where is that tribunal that summoned Medina Sidonia and Cadiz to its dark inquisition? Where is Spain? Its fall, its unparalleled and its irremediable fall, is mainly to be attributed to the expulsion of that large portion of its subjects, the most industrious and intelligent, who traced their origin to the Mosaic and Mohammedan Arabs.[36]

The notion of a noble Arab desert nomad who is both Jewish and Muslim is a romantic version of the biblical Abraham. The figure of Abraham, forefather of Ishmael and Israel, was certainly familiar to Disraeli from his childhood. But the unique qualities with which Disraeli endows this noble savage were apparently a product of Disraeli's journeys through the East. The more Disraeli probed the question of relations between different religions, peoples, and races—and the fate of the Jewish people in particular—the more the notion evolved and solidified. In *Coningsby,* Disraeli outlines the basic features of this noble nomad, bringing him to the origins of the Sidonia dynasty: the Arabian desert, from which everything began.

> Sidonia was well aware that in the five great varieties into which Physiology has divided the human species—to wit, the Caucasian, the Mongolian, the Malayan, the American, the Ethiopian—the Arabian tribes rank in the first and superior class, together, among others, with the Saxon and the Greek. This fact alone is a source of great pride and satisfaction to the animal man. But Sidonia and his brethren could claim a distinction which the Saxon and the Greek and the rest of the Caucasian nations have forfeited. The Hebrew is an unmixed race. Doubtless, among the tribes who inhabit the bosom of the Desert, progenitors alike of the Mosaic and the Mohammedan Arabs, blood may be found as pure as that of the descendants of the Sheikh Abraham. But the Mosaic Arabs are the most ancient, if not the only, unmixed blood that dwells in cities. An unmixed race of a first-rate organisation are the aristocracy of Nature. Such excellence is a positive fact, not an imagination.[37]

This presentation of Sidonia's world view insinuates not only a certain criticism of British society regarding its view of Disraeli's origins, but also a debate with an unseen interlocutor, who, we are to imagine, asks Disraeli: "If you are so superior and wise and noble, why are you so downtrodden?" The question was at the core of Jewish-Christian polemic in Europe, and echoes of this debate are heard in Sidonia's thoughts on the future of the Jewish people. He sees the Jews' shortcomings, yet he is hopeful:

> In his comprehensive travels, Sidonia had visited and examined the Hebrew communities of the world. He had found, in general, the lower orders debased; the superior immersed in sordid pursuits; but he perceived that the intellectual development was not impaired. This gave him hope. He was persuaded that organisation would outlive persecution. When he reflected on what they had endured, it was only marvellous that the race had not disappeared. They had defied exile, massacre, spoliation, the degrading influence of the constant pursuit of gain, they had defied Time.[38]

Sidonia is therefore not merely another chronological stage in Disraeli's spiritual lineage; he also represents a certain ideological evolution. Whereas David Alroy sees no hope for the Jewish people, Sidonia does feel hopeful. He still does not express this hope explicitly, but he will do so shortly.

Tancred and the Peoples of the Desert

In 1847, Disraeli's novel *Tancred or the New Crusade* appeared. From a literary point of view, the novel is incomplete and even illogical. The plot unfolds in a certain direction only to be abruptly cut off without explanation. The reader is left dumbfounded at being cast adrift by the author. There were two possible explanations that might have occurred to the baffled reader of the time. The first: perhaps there would be a sequel. The book ends in a manner reminiscent of a serial, and some may well have expected a sequel—which, of course, never appeared.

But there is a second possible explanation, albeit one that the naïve reader of Disraeli's generation would have been hard-pressed to offer. Disraeli began his literary involvement as a means of achieving fame and glory, but most of his novels served as instruments for explaining himself or his views. The plot was only a means to this end. *Tancred* ends at precisely that moment when Disraeli has finished saying what he wished to say. Any additional development of the plot would have forced him to address its inherent contradictions.

Tancred is a parable dealing with Britain's role in the East, and, in particular, relations between East and West. In the course of the story, all the questions that were raised briefly in *Coningsby* are addressed in broader form: relations between religions, relations between peoples—Israel, Ishmael, and Albion; and relations between races—the peoples of the desert vis-à-vis the peoples of the woods.

Tancred is the wise, beloved, honest, naïve, emotional, and religious son of an ideal English noble family. He is the direct and predictable result of the proper British education that he has received. But surprisingly, upon completing his studies, he adamantly refuses to continue along the path that has been laid out for him, namely, a seat in Parliament, a brilliant political career, a "correct" marriage, and the perpetuation of the Montacute dynasty. He insists on following in the footsteps of his ancient ancestor Tancred, who participated in the First Crusade. He must understand "where it all began." Friends of the family are shocked. The young man's interest in the Holy Land appears obsessive. Lord Milford's remarks on the subject express the typical British attitude toward the East as seen from Disraeli's (mocking) point of view: "My brother was there in '39; he got leave after the bombardment of Acre, and he says there is absolutely no sport of any kind."[39]

But Tancred stands his ground, and his overprotective family arranges a meeting between him and Sidonia. Their intent is that Sidonia, by means of his vast connections throughout the Middle East, will help the son to make the journey, wind it up quickly, and return safe and sound to the "normalcy" of England. In *Tancred,* Disraeli continues to develop the character of Sidonia "the all-powerful," but places him in the background. Sidonia remains in England, where he serves Tancred—just as he served Coningsby—as moral compass and anchor.

Tancred personifies naïve, innocent England confronted with the charms and mysteries of the East. And the greatest mystery of all is the human race as embodied in the characters of Eva Besso and Fakredeen. Eva Besso is the beautiful daughter of a Jewish banker from Aleppo, Adam Besso, who maintains branches throughout the East, from Istanbul to Jerusalem. He is, of course, closely linked to Sidonia in London. Fakredeen is the son of the Emir Shihab, ruler of Lebanon, who was murdered during a revolt against the Ottoman Turks.[40] The infant Fakredeen was smuggled to the home of Adam Besso and raised as a brother to Eva. Eva's grandfather is a Jewish bedouin sheikh, king of the desert. He is the embodiment of the idealized bedouin of Jewish origins already portrayed in *Coningsby.* Eva, her father, and his family are a refined, urbane version of this ideal. While Eva and her family symbolize pride and honesty, Fakredeen represents the Muslim Levantine (Disraeli does not concern himself with the fine points) whose entire existence revolves around plots and schemes. From Disraeli's perspective, Eva and Fakredeen are two sides of one entity; what unites them is their shared origins in the Arabian desert.

The lives of these three characters symbolize the course of history in the East as Disraeli sees it. The East is the cradle of Western culture, of the three monotheistic religions, which, according to Disraeli, are actually one religion first revealed to the desert tribes at Mount Sinai. In his view, the Jews and the Muslims are the original and far superior races, both believing in the one God of Sinai.[41] Christian Europe (and, by extension, England) cannot rule the East; this is not its historic role. And if it tries to do so, it will fail, just as Tancred's ancestor, the original Crusader, failed. Disraeli is uncertain who will rule Jerusalem, but it will most assuredly not be Europe or England:

> Jerusalem, it cannot be doubted, will ever remain the appanage either of Israel or of Ishmael; and if, in the course of those great vicissitudes which

> are no doubt impending for the East, there be any attempt to place upon the throne of David a prince of the House of Coburg or Deuxponts, the same fate will doubtless await him as, with all their brilliant qualities and all the sympathy of Europe, was the final doom of the Godfreys, the Baldwins, and the Lusignans.[42]

And so what role should England play in the East? A somewhat muddied one, as a "supreme power" that can bridge the numerous contradictions among the different elements in the region.

Early in the novel, Fakredeen attempts to make use of the money and influence of Besso, and the power of England (via Tancred), to unite all of Lebanon, Syria, and Palestine under his rule in an ideal state inhabited by Sunni and Shi'ite Muslims, Druze, Maronites, and Jews. If need be, the state would be under the aegis of the Sublime Porte. Minimally, he would settle for Lebanon and Syria alone. He is aware of the objective difficulties:

> "But you forget the religions," said Fakredeen. "I have so many religions to deal with. If my fellows were all Christians, or all Moslemin, or all Jews, or all Pagans, I grant you, something might be affected; the cross, the crescent, the ark, or an old stone, anything would do; I would plant it on the highest range in the centre of the country, and would carry Damascus and Aleppo both in one campaign; but I am debarred from this immense support; I could only preach nationality, and, as they all hate each other worse almost than they do the Turks, that would not be very inviting; nationality, without race as a plea, is like the smoke of this nargilly, a fragrant puff. Well, then, there remains only personal influence: ancient family, vast possessions, and traditionary power."[43]

Tancred has other beliefs. He sees no purpose in taking over the world in order to spread a certain dynasty; dynasties become tainted by outsiders, they break apart, they come to an end. Better to conquer the world in order to spread an idea, for ideas live forever. But to his great sorrow, he does not know what that one great idea is. The revelation that he awaits has yet to come, and he begins to suspect that the right place is not enough. A person must also be from the right race in order to merit such a revelation: one must be a Mohammedan Arab or a Mosaic Arab. But Fakredeen does not desist; he persuades Tancred that he has an idea, together with a new plan—this time, a master plan that will surely be successful:

> Let the queen of the English collect a great fleet, let her stow away all her treasure, bullion, gold plate, and precious arms; be accompanied by all her court and chief people, and transfer the seat of her empire from London to Delhi. There she will find an immense empire ready made, a first-rate army and a large revenue. In the meantime I will arrange with Mehemet Ali. He shall have Bagdad and Mesopotamia, and pour the Bedoueen cavalry into Persia. I will take care of Syria and Asia Minor... We will acknowledge the Empress of India as our suzerain, and secure for her the Levantine coast. If she like, she shall have Alexandria, as she now has Malta; it could be arranged. Your queen is young; she has an *avenir.* Aberdeen and Sir Peel will never give her this advice; their habits are formed. They are too old, too *ruses.*[44]

The Fate of the Jews

The future of the Jewish people as an independent entity is not entirely clear in this scenario. At the end of the novel, Tancred and Adam Besso finally meet at the latter's home in Damascus, and their conversation unfolds as follows:

> [Besso:] "My daughter tells me you are not uninterested in our people, which is the reason I ventured to ask you here."
> [Tancred:] "I cannot comprehend how a Christian can be uninterested in a people who have handed down to him immortal truths."
> [Besso:] "All the world is not as sensible of the obligation as yourself, noble traveller."
> [Tancred:] "But who is the world? Do you mean the inhabitants of Europe, which is a forest not yet cleared; or the inhabitants of Asia, which is a ruin about to tumble?"
> "The railroads will clear the forest," said Besso.
> "And what is to become of the ruin?" asked Tancred.
> [Besso:] "God will not forget His land."[45]

The question of the future of the Jewish people preoccupied Disraeli on more than just the literary level. In the England of the 1840s and 1850s, the notion of establishing a Jewish state in the Holy Land, under the aegis of Great Britain, was a popular topic of discussion. The rationale behind the various proposals was that such a state would help ensure stability in the East, and consolidate and safeguard British interests in the region. It should be noted that British statesmen were not the only ones to raise such proposals.[46] In the 1850s, London was home to a group of Italian political exiles who were active in the Risorgimento movement. These included Benedetto Musolino (1809–85) of Calabria, who in 1851 formulated a detailed plan to establish a Jewish state in Palestine under British protection. He was seeking a way to present his plan before the British government during the period when Disraeli served as a member of the Opposition.

Coincidentally, the Disraelis' home in the tiny ghetto of Cento adjoined the home of the Carpi family. Leone Carpi (1815–98), a Risorgimento activist, was one of the Italian political exiles residing in London in 1851, and even had occasion to meet Disraeli. It is unclear whether Musolino and Disraeli ever met, or if Disraeli ever actually saw Musolino's plan; but it is not hard to imagine that the "Italian connection" played a role in bringing the plan to Disraeli's attention.[47] In any event, the idea of a Jewish political renaissance, much like the notion of an Italian resurgence, was being bandied about at the time. Disraeli's attitude might therefore best be viewed within the intellectual context of these contemporary circles.

The memoirs of Edward Henry Stanley (1826–93; son of Britain's prime minister, Lord Stanley) provide a fascinating glimpse into Disraeli's state of mind shortly after the publication of *Tancred* and at about the same time as Musolino was active in London. There, Stanley describes the lengthy conversations he had with Disraeli as the two would stroll along together (walking being the only physical activity that Disraeli enjoyed). During these walks, Disraeli spoke of two subjects: politics and the origin of the various religions. He believed that as the human race became more educated, religion would no longer fulfill any function. On one especially cold winter's day, he held forth in all seriousness on the return of the Jewish people to its land. Oblivious to the frigid weather, Disraeli stopped to sketch the details of his plan in the dirt:

> The land might be bought from Turkey. Money would be forthcoming: the Rothschilds and leading Hebrew capitalists would all help. The Turkish empire was falling into ruin; the Turkish government would do anything for money. All that was necessary was to establish colonies, with rights over the soil, and security from ill treatment. The question of nationality might wait until these had taken hold. He added that these ideas were extensively entertained among the Jewish nation. A man who should carry them out would be the next Messiah, the true Saviour of

> his people. He saw only one obstacle arising from the existence of two races among the Hebrews, of whom one, those who settled along the shores of the Mediterranean, look down on the other, refusing even to associate with them. "Sephardim," I think he called the superior.[48]

Stanley wrote that he had never seen Disraeli so animated as during that walk in the cold air at the estate of Lord Carrington. The reference to the question of nationality during this conversation indicates that Disraeli was not blind to the political significance of the Jewish people's return to its land, nor to the potential conflict that this entailed. But in reality, as in *Tancred,* he offered no clear solution. And just as, in reality, he preferred to defer a solution to the future, on the literary level he proposed a solution that "glossed over" the historical facts in much the same way he had brushed off details when constructing his personal lineage.

Disraeli continued to pursue the dreams expressed in *Alroy* not only in his vision of a Jewish state but in his concept of the superior nature of the Jewish race. As time went on, this notion of supremacy, entwined with an overall theory of race and bloodlines as the basis of human history and fate, became almost an *idée fixe,* which he developed both in his writing and in private conversations. The refining of this concept—absurd as it may seem—and its extension to theoretical extremes, were an outlet for the never-ending frustration experienced by Disraeli on two levels: one, his personal humiliation throughout his career, as a result of his Jewish ancestry; the other, his inability to achieve any change in the actual status of his people.[49]

In all fairness to Disraeli, one cannot omit mention of the fact that at the most critical juncture of his career—when he numbered among a select group of individuals who held the fate of both Europe and the Middle East in their hands—he sought to do something for his own people as well. He planned to bring before the Congress of Berlin a proposal for the establishment of a Jewish state in Palestine under British protection. As a first step, the plan was published anonymously in Vienna in 1877, under the title *Die jüdische Frage in der orientalischen Frage.* According to Johann Freiherr von Chlumecky (the Austrian statesman who translated the booklet from English to German at the request of the British Embassy in Vienna), Otto von Bismarck and the foreign minister of Austria, Count Julius von Andrássy (1823–90), were opposed to any move in this direction. Bismarck in particular argued that any discussion of the matter would provoke a huge political scandal in Germany.

The Congress of Berlin was intended to correct what Great Britain saw as an untenable agreement: the Treaty of San Stefano, concluded in 1877 following the Russo-Turkish War. The pact placed Russia in a superior position with regard to the other European powers, which were now attempting to seize as great a slice as possible of the crumbling Ottoman Empire. Disraeli's mission was to achieve one of the following: either rein in the appetites of the Great Powers, including Russia, or improve Britain's own position in the struggle for control over the Middle East.

The first option was considered preferable, as the second one meant the dissolution of the Ottoman Empire and the possibility of war. A dispute with Austria and Germany even before the opening of the congress would not have furthered Disraeli's agenda. So he shelved his plan: according to Baron Chlumecky's account to Leo von Bilinski (1846–1922; later, finance minister of Austria), Disraeli ordered that the booklet be destroyed. But not all copies of the work were done away with. One of them was preserved—together with other important documents relating to the history of Zionism—in the personal archives of Leo von Bilinski. Only thus has this record of Disraeli's only attempt to turn his idealized spiritual autobiography into reality come down to posterity.[50]

The ideas expressed in this booklet are much more prosaic than those expressed in Disraeli's novels. The booklet opens with the statement that the days of "the Sick Man on the Bosphorus" are numbered, and his estates are destined to turn into new national states. It proceeds to argue the right of the Jewish people to such a state. But the Jews, dispersed among other nations for so many centuries, have lost the qualities needed to found and maintain an independent state. The author therefore suggested a period of "political apprenticeship" for the Jewish state, which would be placed under the control of one of the European powers.

> The Jews, out of love for their ancient motherland, and with the whole-hearted certainty that they may expect only justice and freedom under this Power, shall come from all the countries and settle there and found colonies. Would not it be reasonable to expect that after fifty years, there will arise there a Jewish people of millions, speaking one language, the language of the state which protects them; a people imbued with one spirit, a spirit typical of it; a people capable of self-government and independent self-management?... Our generation should be satisfied with ploughing the soil and sowing the seed. The grandchildren shall harvest.[51]

Which of Europe's powers was suited to the purpose, if not England? The last part of the booklet echoes both Disraeli's conversation with Stanley, and the syncretistic ideas expressed in *Tancred:*

> This enterprise needs strong support from beginning to end! Each and every man from Israel who has the talents and the means, should bring his contribution to the temple of Jewish nationality. Thank God, there are still people rich in talent and money to be found in Israel. Both should shoulder the great enterprise together. Right at the outset, it would need a great practical talent, to get the enterprise off to a good start and protect it from its adversaries; but also afterwards, when the time will come to found committees to support settlement, a great know-how will be needed. Then will come the turn of the plentiful purses, small and large, which will always be open and will provide immense trusts, so that settlement will be vast, and its success speedy. Finally, it might not be redundant to add that this Jewish national revival is to be a national one, not a religious one. A Jewish state should be founded, but it should be a modern state, and not a state of the sons of Moses only. It is not that we would like the principles of the Mosaic religion to disappear from the world of Jewish beliefs and religious ideas. These principles were and are still today exalted and divine, and their role has not been exhausted in the history of human civilization. Nevertheless, as regards the Mosaic religion, the demands of the modern age should be taken into account. Therefore, the religious element should be detached from the state, in such a way that will prevent religion from encroaching upon the rights of the state.[52]

In demanding the separation of religion and state, Disraeli envisioned a state for the Jewish people in which "Mohammedan Arabs" as well as Christians—all the descendants of Judaism—would occupy their rightful place.

But in 1878, as in 1847, a Jewish state remained a distant vision. Disraeli might have been a dreamer, but he was also a pragmatic man of action who preferred solid ground to flights of fancy. For him, politics represented the art of the possible, and so his discarded his plan for a Jewish state.

Here ends this brief journey through the pathways of memory—and not only that memory subject to verification. Memory is not always a recollecting of what has happened; often it is a recalling of what one wished had happened, what one wants to remember. By such a process, a political world view may be shaped. Such an outlook is not necessarily the result of intellectual and pragmatic considerations. Memory, in the sense deployed here, plays a crucial role in its formation.

Disraeli's odyssey begins in the Arabian desert, circles the shores of the Mediterranean, shifts to England, and returns to the East. Traces of this odyssey are reflected in all of his actions, and in all of his quandaries. With the perspective of time, many of his writings appear almost prophetic. It was his good fortune to be able to realize some of these prophecies during his lifetime. Other issues with which he grappled remain as insoluble today as when he first engaged them.

Notes

1. Stanley Weintraub, *Disraeli: A Biography* (New York: Truman Talley Books and Dutton, 1993), 576–77.
2. Ibid., 598.
3. Disraeli's more recent biographers agree on this point to a greater or lesser extent. See ibid., xi–xii, 23–24, 113, 190–92, 196, 219–225, 247–48, 273, 276–77, 384, 426, 451, 453, 563–608; and Jane Ridley, *The Young Disraeli* (London: Sinclair-Stevenson, 1995), 22, 255–56, 342. The more conservative biographers are either reluctant to touch the subject or disregard it. See, for example, William Flavelle Monypenny and George Earle Buckle, *The Life of Benjamin Disraeli, Earl of Beaconsfield,* rev. ed., 2 vols. (London: John Murray, 1929). The word "anti-Semitism" does not appear. Compare with Robert Blake, *Disraeli* (London: Eyre and Spottiswoode, 1966), 10–11, 49–50, 81, 283–84.
4. Monypenny and Buckle, *Life,* 1:27; Blake, *Disraeli,* 10–11; Ridley, *Young Disraeli,* 19; Weintraub, *Disraeli,* 31–32.
5. The views concerning the reasons for Isaac D'Israeli's departure from the Bevis Marks synagogue differ. Monypenny and Buckle, *Life,* 1:26–27, attribute his decision to the pressure exerted on him by the elders of the synagogue to serve as a warden of the synagogue. So does Blake, *Disraeli,* 11, and Ridley, *Young Disraeli,* 18–19. Ridley, as well as Weintraub, *Disraeli,* 31, allude to the fact that if he would not have left the synagogue at that stage, he would have had to take some practical steps in preparation for Benjamin's upcoming bar mitzvah. It was one thing to lead the life of "a Jew without a synagogue" when one had no practical obligations; it was another matter when obligations became mandatory and one's deeds or omissions also affected the lives of one's children.
6. The choice of the Anglican Church was due to the influence of Isaac D'Israeli's friend, Mr. Sharon Turner; Monypenny and Buckle, *Life,* 1:27;

Blake, *Disraeli,* 11; Ridley, *Young Disraeli,* 19; Weintraub, *Disraeli,* 31–32. According to Weintraub, the first to be baptized were his younger brothers, on 11 July 1817, and only on 31 July of that year was he himself baptized. Sarah was baptized on 28 August. The gaps between the baptisms suggest that the decision to convert was not taken lightly.

7. For Isaac D'Israeli's spiritual world, see Ridley, *Young Disraeli,* 12–15, 18–19; Weintraub, *Disraeli,* 24–27.
8. On the molding of the "secular Jew" among the "New Christians" from the seventeenth century onwards, see especially Yirmiyahu Yovel, *Spinoza and Other Heretics,* 2 vols. (Princeton: Princeton University Press, 1989); Yosef Kaplan, *Mi-Natzrut le-Yahadut: Hayav u-fo'olo shel ha-anus Yitzhak Orobio de Castro* (Jerusalem: The Magnes Press, 1982); Richard H. Popkin, "Skepticism, Theology and the Scientific Revolution in the Seventeenth Century," in *Problems in the Philosophy of Science,* eds. Imre Lakatos and Alan Musgrave (Amsterdam: North-Holland Pub. Co., 1968), 1–28.
9. I am indebted to my teacher and friend, Prof. Daniel Carpi (whose family resided next to the D'Israeli family in Cento), for sharing with me a wealth of information about the D'Israeli family and the role of Disraeli in the history of Zionism.
10. Just a few examples: the physician-philosopher Isaac ben Solomon Israeli of Egypt (ca. 855–955); Israel Israeli of Toledo (d. 1317), who was a renowned Spanish Talmudist; and his brother, the famous astronomer Isaac ben Joseph Israeli.
11. See the tombstone of Istruga, daughter of Mosheh 'Ali and wife of Mosheh Ha-Israeli, in I. S. Emmanuel, *Matzvot Saloniqi* (Jerusalem: Ben Zvi Institute and Kiryat Sefer, 1963), 1:108–9. The inscription was written in a mixture of Hebrew and Ladino. The name "Ha-Israeli" is the exact equivalent of D'Israeli.
12. Daniel Carpi, "Benjamin Disraeli, la 'questione orientale' e un suo presunto progetto di costituire uno stato ebraico in Palestina," in *Gli Ebrei a Cento* (Cento: Comune di Cento, 1994), 80.
13. Here, the use of "Israel" as a family name is quite common. See, for example Elia Israel and Mosheh Israel, who were active in Jerusalem during this period; *Horvot Yerushalayim,* ed. Minna Rozen (Tel Aviv: Tel Aviv University, 1981), 55–56, 104, 106.
14. The Israel family of Jerusalem produced rabbis who served in all these communities. See Simon Marcus, *Toldot ha-Rabanim le-Mishpahat Yisra'el mi-Rodos* (Jerusalem: R. Mass, 1935).
15. See Weintraub, *Disraeli,* 19–21.
16. Ibid., 21.
17. Ibid., 22; McLeod, "Genealogy."
18. For the relations between Disraeli and his mother, Maria, see especially Ridley, *Young Disraeli,* 16–18.

19. Weintraub, *Disraeli,* 27–28; Ridley, *Young Disraeli,* 15.
20. Concerning Disraeli's ancestry, see also the detailed discussion in Cecil Roth, *Disraeli ha-Yehudi* (Tel Aviv, 1955), 9–25. For a detailed and documented family tree of the Disraelis, see J. McLeod, "Genealogy of the Disraeli Family," *Genealogists Magazine* 24, no. 8 (December 1993): 342–48.
21. By way of example, see Eli'ezer ben Nisim Ibn Shanji, *Sermons, Dat va-Din* (Istanbul, 1726); introduction by the author's son, Hayim Ibn Shanji.
22. See also Monypenny and Buckle, *Life,* 1:6–8; cf. Weintraub, *Disraeli,* 19–20, and Ridley, *Young Disraeli,* 10–12.
23. Weintraub, *Disraeli,* 73; Ridley, *Young Disraeli,* 56.
24. Monypenny and Buckle, *Life,* 1:1268–80; Weintraub, *Disraeli,* 307–10, 377–78; L. Wolf, "Mrs. Brydges-Williams and Benjamin Disraeli," *The Jewish Historical Society of England: Miscellanies* 1 (1925): xx–xxiii; McLeod, "Genealogy." It is noteworthy that the names of Spanish aristocratic families are commonly found among the "New Christians" and their descendants, because the converts frequently received the family name of the godfather (often a member of the Spanish aristocracy) at their baptism. What this indicates, of course, is the frequent lack of any blood ties between the "New Christian" family and the "old Christian" family of the same name.
25. Kaplan, *Mi-Natzrut le-Yahadut,* 151–52, 284–85.
26. On *Alroy,* see Monypenny and Buckle, *Life,* 1:197–204, who considers the novel a simple expression of Disraeli's hidden hopes for his people and for himself—hopes he was too practical to pursue: "With all his dreaminess, Disraeli's genius was far too practical to permit him to devote his life to the pursuit of a mere phantom; but it is probable that these early visions never wholly forsook him. They had a soil of genuine racial sentiment from which perennially to spring, and though it would be easy to exaggerate their significance, yet to know them is to get a glimpse into the inmost recesses of Disraeli's mind.... More than any of Disraeli's works, more even than *Tancred,* it reveals the Hebraic aspect of his many-sided nature." Blake, *Disraeli,* 38, does not elaborate at length on the significance of this novel. Ridley, *Young Disraeli,* 71, 125–27, stresses the meaning of *Alroy* as an effort to overcome Disraeli's Jewish inferiority complex. Weintraub, *Disraeli,* 111–14, also understands it as a step towards bolstering his self-esteem rather than the expression of a dream or hope. For *Contarini Fleming,* see Monypenny and Buckle, *Life,* 1:185–97; Blake, *Disraeli,* 13–17, 38, 50, 86; Ridley, *Young Disraeli,* 105; Weintraub, *Disraeli,* 20–21, 29–30, 36–40, 43, 63, 67–70, 79, 92, 96–97, 102–3, 105–6, 595. For *Coningsby,* see Monypenny and Buckle, *Life,* 1:560, 569, 581, 595–625, 628, 665–701, 817, 848; Blake, *Disraeli,* 16, 165–69, 190–218; Ridley, *Young Disraeli,* 265, 275–85; Weintraub, *Disraeli,* 93, 119, 154, 188, 242–43, 246, 269, 344, 362, 436, 502, 521, 531. For *Tancred* see Monypenny and Buckle, *Life,* 1:353–54, 561, 654, 848–95;

Blake, *Disraeli,* 194, 201–6, 214–16, 258–60, 284; Ridley, *Young Disraeli,* 316; Weintraub, *Disraeli,* 103, 106, 231, 280, 289, 307, 309, 362, 382, 481, 549, 568. We have addressed only those novels which are most relevant to the theme of this study. Regarding the entire subject, see also Roth, *Disraeli ha-Yehudi,* 80–88, esp. 82.

27. See n. 26 above and n. 34 below.
28. On the development and writing of *Alroy* and *Contarini Fleming* see Monypenny and Buckle, *Life,* 1:185–203; Weintraub, *Disraeli,* 110–113; Ridley, *Young Disraeli,* 105–27. The idea for *Alroy* came to Disraeli at his parents' mansion at Bradenham in the winter of 1829–30, at which time he made his first notes; Ridley, *Young Disraeli,* 71, 124–25; Monypenny and Buckle, *Life,* 1:125–26.
29. Blake, *Disraeli,* 59–60, was the first to fully appreciate the importance of Disraeli's trip to the East and its influence on the shaping of his political views. Ridley, *Young Disraeli,* 97, followed him.
30. See especially Monypenny and Buckle, *Life,* 1:199–201; Weintraub, *Disraeli,* 111–13.
31. *Alroy* (London: Peter Davis, 1927), 162.
32. Ibid.
33. Monypenny and Buckle, *Life,* 1:620; Blake, *Disraeli,* 202; Ridley, *Young Disraeli,* 264, 266–68, 279–83; Weintraub, *Disraeli,* 214–18, 264. Sidonia's character was used by several anti-Semitic authors as proof of the validity of *The Protocols of the Elders of Zion;* see Weintraub, *Disraeli,* 674.
34. Ridley, *Young Disraeli,* 68, 71, 91, 137, 156. See also W.J. Fischel, *Ha-Yehudim be-Hodu: Helkam be-Hayim ha-Kalkaliyim ve-ha-Mediniyim* (Jerusalem: Ben Zvi Institute, 1960), 116–19. Cecil Roth, who claimed that no one had as yet offered an explanation of the name (1951), suggested that one of the prototypes for Sidonia might have been Sir Solomon de Medina (ca. 1650–1730). De Medina was active in Britain's international trade during the War of the Spanish Succession. Roth also alludes to a possible connection with the name Medina-Sidonia, a famous Spanish aristocratic family (*Disraeli ha-Yehudi,* 87).
35. Sidonia's supernatural aspects are also noted by Ridley, *Young Disraeli,* 280, who attributes them to the notion of the "Wandering Jew."
36. Sidonia appears briefly in *Endymion* (first published in 1880), but the major aspects of his personality are developed in *Coningsby or the New Generation* (first published in 1844), and later on in *Tancred or the New Crusade* (first published in 1847). See *Coningsby* (London: Heron Books, 1968), 220–33; *Tancred* (London: Longmans, Green and Co., 1881), 118–26, 166. It is no accident that the letter of introduction which Sidonia gives to Tancred is addressed to Alonzo Lara (a Spanish monk at the Convent of Terra Santa in Jerusalem), Lara being the Spanish aristocratic family with which Disraeli

wished to associate himself (cf. above, n. 24). See also *Tancred,* 314–36. For the idea of the Mosaic Arabs and the Mohammedan Arabs, see *Tancred,* 253: "The Arabs are only Jews upon horseback."

37. *Coningsby,* 231–32.
38. Ibid., 232.
39. *Tancred,* 85.
40. Ibid., 196–222. Although the general framework of Middle Eastern politics described by Disraeli is accurate, he allows himself a great deal of literary license. The allusion here is to Emir Bashīr II of the Shihāb dynasty (1767–1850). For a historical survey of this period, see Moshe Ma'oz, *Ottoman Reform in Syria and Palestine, 1840–1861: The Impact of the Tanzimat on Politics and Society* (Oxford: Clarendon Press, 1968).
41. Although in *Tancred,* the superiority of the representatives of Judaism and Islam is very clear, it is obvious that Disraeli's ideas concerning the relationship between the various monotheistic religions underwent further development over the years. In *Lord George Bentinck* (London: Colburn and Co., 1852), 506–7, he presents Christianity as, simultaneously, an irresistible conquering force and the culmination of Judaism: "Has not Jesus conquered Europe and changed its name into Christendom? All countries that refuse the cross wither, while the whole of the new world is devoted to the Semitic principle and its most glorious offspring, the Jewish faith....Who can deny that Jesus of Nazareth the Incarnate Son of the Most High God is the eternal glory of the Jewish race?"
42. *Tancred,* 171; cf. 288–91.
43. Ibid., 258–59.
44. Ibid., 263.
45. Ibid., 393.
46. For the British movement for the establishment of a Jewish state in Palestine from the 1830s to the 1850s, see Frederick Stanley Rodkey, "Palmerston and the Rejuvenation of Turkey," *Journal of Modern History* 2 (1930): 214–16; Harold Temperley, *England and the Near East: The Crimea* (London: Longmans, 1936), 443–45; Charles K. Webster, *The Foreign Policy of Palmerston, 1830–1841,* 2 vols. (London: G. Bell, 1951), 2:760–63; N.M. Gelber, *Tokhnit ha-Medinah ha-Yehudit le-Lord Beaconsfield* (Tel Aviv: Z. Leinemann, 1947), 5–8; idem, *Zur Vorgeschichte des Zionismus* (Vienna: Phaidon-verlag, 1927), 1:133, 137, 141, 256; Mayir Vereté, "Ra'ayon Shivat Zion be-Mahshavah ha-Protestantit be-Angliah be-1799–1840," *Zion* 33, no. 3–4 (1968): 145–79; Menahem Kedem, "Tefisot ha-Ge'ulah shel 'Am Yisra'el be-Eretz Yisra'el ba-Eskhatologiah ha-Protestantit ha-Anglit be-Emtz'a ha-Me'ah ha-Yod-Tet," *Cathedra,* no. 19 (1981): 55–72; Yesha'yahu Friedman, "Tokhniot Britiyot le-Yishuv Yehudim be-Eretz Yisra'el be-shnot ha-Arbai'ym shel ha-Me'ah ha-Yod-Tet (1840–1850)," *Cathedra,* no. 56 (1990): 42–69.

47. Carpi, "Benjamin Disraeli," 79–92. See also Ferdinando Musolino, "Il sionismo e il suo vero precursore," *Calabria Rotary* (December 1976): 53–65. Interestingly, this same Musolino in 1883 had suggested to Sultan Abdülhamid II a plan of reform for the Ottoman Empire which did not include his Zionist ideas. See Jacob M. Landau, "Un projet de réformes dans l'empire ottoman en 1883," *Orient* 40 (1967): 147–67.
48. Quoted by Weintraub, *Disraeli,* 301–2. The same lines had caught the attention of Friedman, "Tokhniot," 68–69. However, Friedman was unaware of the fact that Disraeli was the author of the booklet *Die jüdische Frage in der orientalischen Frage* (see below), and concluded his article with the statement that Disraeli did not make an attempt to turn his dream into reality, since the opportunity to do so without rocking the status quo of world politics did not materialize in his lifetime. Strictly speaking, Friedman was right; however, the omission of the affair of *Die jüdische Frage* understates Disraeli's practical efforts.
49. See *Lord Bentinck,* 482–507; Roth, *Disraeli ha-Yehudi,* 88–106.
50. Gelber, *Tokhnit,* 9–111. See also idem, "She'elat ha-Yehudim li-fnei ha-Qongres ha-Berlinai be-Shnat 1878," *Zion* 8 (1943): 35–50; cf. Roth, *Disraeli ha-Yehudi,* 194–97. Roth doubts very much Disraeli's authorship of *Die jüdische Frage.* One of his arguments is that no mention of such an idea—or that Disraeli, Bismarck and Andrássy discussed it among themselves—appears anywhere in the vast documentation of the Congress or of the three men. The idea of Disraeli's reluctance to publish the booklet under his own name also seems to Roth absurd. In my opinion, neither argument is satisfactory. While the first can easily be explained away by the unequivocal rejection of the entire idea by Disraeli's interlocutors, the second point is even more readily explicable: Disraeli first initiated the publication of the booklet anonymously in order to test the political waters. When he realized, even before its distribution, that the idea had become unfeasible, he ordered the whole edition destroyed.
51. Gelber, *Tokhnit,* 11–13.
52. Ibid., 14–15.

2

'Jew' and Jesuit at the Origins of Arabism: William Gifford Palgrave

Benjamin Braude

During the nineteenth and early twentieth centuries, the dominant European view assumed that Arabs and Jews were racially so linked as to be brethren, natural allies who could easily come to a modus vivendi. Such an understanding was rooted in the omnipresent racism of the age, specifically the myth of Semitism, a concept which purported to explain and determine cultural values and political behavior. This myth had a decisive influence on British policy during and after the First World War—a policy which rested on the notion that Arab nationalism and Zionism were complementary, not contradictory. Such was the view of David George Hogarth, the mentor of T.E. Lawrence, who set in motion the wheels of the Arab Revolt in 1916. One source for Hogarth's understanding of the myth was the mysterious traveler, sometime-spy, sometime-Jew, sometime-Jesuit, William Gifford Palgrave (1826–88). The enigmatic Palgrave did not create the Semitic myth. But he constructed his own identity upon it, and then suggested to imaginative Englishmen how it might serve as the basis for a political program.

The Semitic Myth

For much of the nineteenth and early twentieth centuries, many Europeans, both Christians and Jews, assumed that there was a deep, abiding, and innate sympathy between Judaism and Islam as well as between Jews, Arabs, and Turks. This affinity was understood in a variety of terms, principally racial, but also, according to today's terminology, ethnic, linguistic, and religious.

The assumptions undergirding this supposed affinity were neither as long-established nor as long-lived as has been assumed. The linguistic pseudo-racial category of Semite had developed no earlier than the eighteenth century. While Christians in medieval Spain may have assumed a deep affiliation between Jews and Moors,[1] Jewish attitudes on this question were far more complex. Jews believed in the notion of a common Abrahamic ancestry with Ishmael, who came to be identified with the Arabs. But whether or not ties were better with Ishmael or Edom (Christendom) was a question which medieval Jews debated. Outside of Spain, Christian notions varied. The first Christians to have contact with the Muslims labelled them Hagarenes, accepting, through this matronymic, a notion of shared Abrahamic ancestry. However, medieval Christian Bible commentary allegorically denied the Semitic identity of post-Crucifixion Jews, linking them instead to another son of Noah, the mocking Ham.[2]

Morever, by the mid-fourteenth century, rising Christian hostility toward Judaism, at least in the West, expressed itself in greater sympathy for Islam and an implicit denial of common human ancestry with the Jews. Thus, the earliest versions of the mid-fourteenth century *Mandeville's Travels* praise Islam for its affinities with Christianity, acknowledge a shared Noahide ancestry with the Saracens, but deny such links to Judaism and Jews. Rather, the Jewish image is fixed in a bloodcurdling parody of Jewish messianism, according to which the Ten Lost Tribes of Israel, led by the Antichrist, sally forth from the Caspian hills to join their fellow Jews throughout the world in order to wreak havoc on Christians and place them under a Jewish yoke.[3]

Despite the fact that *Mandeville* was the most widely read work of secular literature in Europe during the Renaissance, it has been neglected by students of Christian attitudes toward other religions, who have tended to focus on other works which had comparatively narrow influence. *Mandeville* has been regularly revised throughout the nearly 650 years of its existence, but the expressions of hostility, greater against Judaism than Islam, and the assumption of non-affinity between the two religions, seem to have been maintained in most versions. However, there are at least two exceptions.

The early Italian printed versions link the Jews with the Saracens as descendants of Shem—a genealogy taken for granted by Bible-quoting Christians after the Reformation, but one not assumed by earlier readers and listeners who probably knew the story better from Mandeville than from Scripture.[4] Later, this awareness had spread to northwestern Europe as well. It is evidenced by at least two English versions (London, 1677 and 1684) which confirm the ties between Islam and Judaism by asserting that Muhammad had a Jewish mother.[5] Why should the Italian versions have been the first to introduce this change? Possibly they, more than northern Europeans, were already aware of the migration of Sephardi Jewry from Christendom to the lands of Islam commencing with the persecutions of 1391 in Iberia. By the seventeenth century, this new attitude had spread beyond the Mediterranean.

Between the fifteenth and the seventeenth centuries, a significant change took place in Christian attitudes toward Judaism and Islam, which helped to shape what nineteenth-century observers took for granted. This shift can be seen in a version of the Antichrist-Jewish alliance which had been popularized by Mandeville, but which now appeared with a significant variation in the early sixteenth century. It surfaced in a sermon printed and repeatedly reprinted by an important colleague of Martin Luther, Johannes Brenz (1499–1570). This broadsheet, one of the most widely read of its time, reads much like a summary of far longer tracts written by Luther and his friend, Justus Jonas (1493–1555), on the same subject. In Brenz's version, the Jews are indeed to sally forth with Antichrist. But there is more. Brenz preached in the aftermath of the first Ottoman siege of Vienna in 1529, when Germans lived in fear of a Turkish invasion. His text was entitled *How Preachers and Laymen Should Conduct Themselves if the Turk Were to Invade Germany.*[6] It is therefore not surprising that Turks should not only intrude into Vienna, but elsewhere as well. Indeed, Brenz identifies the Jews with the Turks—a linkage which Luther also made common in his own tracts. Brenz explains that the so-called ancient prophecies of a military alliance of ferocious Jews led by Antichrist should be interpreted to refer not just to Jews but also to Muhammad and the Turk.

This assimilation of the old Jewish adversary to the resurgent Muslim enemy became a commonplace from the sixteenth century, reflecting Jewish settlement in the East following the expulsion from Iberia. The role of the Jews in Ottoman lands, exaggerated into an image of conspiratorial helpmate to the new Antichrist, helped revalidate, reconfirm, and modify old myths about the Jews as conspiratorial Christ-killing enemies of mankind.

Palgrave in Brief

By the nineteenth century, the apocalyptic character of such visions had faded along with the Turkish threat, but the notion of Jewish-Muslim religious affinity and Jewish-Arab racial fraternity remained strong. It was to express itself in the life and letters of William Gifford Palgrave and, through his posthumous influence, in the ideas of British statesmen. Palgrave does not figure prominently in today's readings of Middle Eastern history. But in the mid-nineteenth century he was the instigator of a plot which, a half-century later, served as the model for the British-organized Arab Revolt of 1916. He involved the French government, the Society of Jesus, and the Holy See in a political-religious conspiracy to forge an alliance of bedouin tribes. This alliance would overthrow the Ottoman Empire, establish an Arab kingdom under French influence, and convert Muslims to Christianity. His highly misleading account of this adventure was one of the most popular works about the Arabs in the nineteenth century.

He was christened William Gifford Palgrave, but later called himself "Michael Suhail," "Selim Abu Mahmud el-Ays," "Hajji Mahmud Ibn Isa" as well as "Michael" or "Michel-Xavier Cohen."[7] Significantly it was as Père Cohen, S.J., that Palgrave obtained the personal backing of Louis Napoleon, the emperor of France (r. 1852–70), who funded the mission and instructed the Quai d'Orsay to place its consular posts in Syria and the eminent orientalist Charles Schefer (1820–1902) in its service.[8] It was as Père Cohen, S.J., that Palgrave sought the permission of Pieter Beckx (1795–1887), the father-general of the Society of Jesus, who, in turn, obtained the approval of the Sacred Congregation for the Propagation of the Faith.[9] And it was as Père Cohen, S.J., that Palgrave received the blessing of Pope Pius IX who was comforted by the possibility "however remote of seeing Christianity established anew amongst the unbelievers."[10]

How did Father Cohen come by his name? And by what form of reasoning is he to be considered a Jew?[11] Palgrave was born in London in 1826. His mother came from old East Anglian stock, but his father had been born a Jew, Francis Ephraim Cohen (1788–1861). Francis Cohen had converted from Judaism, married into a well-connected Anglican family, and in the process abandoned his own name for the maiden name of his new mother-in-law, Palgrave. Like Disraeli, he paid what Heinrich Heine once called the "entry ticket" to European society, and once he did so, his career, like Disraeli's, took off. By the time he died in 1861, he had gained membership in the Royal Society, an honorable career at the bar, a knighthood, and a record of distinction as historian and archivist. His four sons (William Gifford was the second) matched their father's example, but in the different fields of literature, banking, journalism, and the civil and foreign service.

William Gifford initially gave every sign of continuing his father's pattern. Well-educated at Charterhouse and Oxford, he seemed poised for a conventional career. But in 1847, he unexpectedly set off to join the East India Company's army. In India he abandoned Anglicanism for Catholicism; even more dramatically, he left the army for the Society of Jesus. His studies brought him first to Rome and then, in 1855, to Lebanon, the center of the Jesuit mission in the East. He spent the next years teaching, traveling, and preaching. He also mastered Arabic to the point that he became the leading Catholic preacher in Beirut. In 1860, a peasant revolt in a district of Mount Lebanon burst into a civil war between the Maronites and Druze. During the conflagration he was forced to flee to France. It was during this exile from the East that he conceived his grandiose scheme for Arabia.

In formulating his proposals, he was very much influenced by a number of sources. These included the radical program of his Jesuit teacher for the conversion of China; Lamartine's *Voyage en Orient* which publicized the idea of a Napoleonic-Arab alliance against the Ottomans and the British; and Ottoman propaganda against the Wahhabis, which portrayed them as enemies of Islam and therefore possible allies of Europe. This is evident from his correspondence with fellow Jesuits as well as the extensive and detailed memoranda which he prepared for his superiors, and which are to be found in the archives of the Society in Rome. At this point, before his actual contact with Arabia proper, he was convinced that the Wahhabi Muslims were ripe for conversion to Christianity and ready for leading an alliance with the French.

He embarked on the mission in 1861, returning to Beirut in 1863. He discovered that the Saudis were neither likely conspirators nor likely converts. He did contact other elements in the peninsula, notably the Āl Rashīd dynasty, who seemed more willing to cooperate. But before he could return to organize them, his cover was blown and the Ottoman authorities demanded that he be bundled out of the country as quickly as possible. He was never to return to the Middle East as a Jesuit. Profoundly discouraged, he abandoned Catholicism for Protestantism.

After he left the Jesuits, he wrote an account of his adventures, *Narrative of a Year's Journey through Central and Eastern Arabia,* which was a best-seller in English and appeared quickly in French and German translations. This was probably the most popular European book about the Arabs before Lawrence's *Seven Pillars of Wisdom.* It was arguably the first, and undoubtedly the most widely read and influential articulation of the case for Arab self-determination published in Europe. It was also very much the deceptive and vindictive work of a spurned lover. Having pinned his hopes on the Wahhabis, he was deeply disappointed that they did not respond to his missionary overtures. Accordingly, he described them in the blackest of terms. They were the dourest of the dour, the most fanatic of the fanatic. He accepted their definition of Islam as the true and most accurate reflection of the message of Muhammad, for which he felt little sympathy. (He thought rather better of other elements within Islam, notably of Sufism, so alien to the Wahhabiyya.) Eventually he married and joined the British Foreign Office, which posted him to obscure consulates as far from the Arab world as possible. In 1888 he died in Montevideo, Uruguay.

This short biography only hints at the complexities in Palgrave's life—a hint conveyed by his brief use of the name Cohen. In what sense can we even speak of Palgrave as a Jew? And to what degree did his Jewishness—if it can be established—contribute to his appreciation for and articulation of Arab identity? Finally, how did he influence David George Hogarth, a principle architect of British policy in the Middle East?

Jewish Names

On the surface, neither generation of the Palgrave family had much of a Jewish character. Yet in the life of Sir Francis, a significant residue of Jewish identity remained beneath his conversion. The father maintained a large library which contained many rare and important works of Judaica, including—and this is significant—the latest works in contemporary Jewish scholarship, written by the leading lights of the vital German Jewish movement of intellectual revival founded in the midst of Jewish emancipation and known as the *Wissenschaft des Judentums*. At the behest of the most famous Jew of the nineteenth century, Sir Moses Montefiore (1784–1885), he also contributed to Jewish learning in Palestine.

His son's Jewish identity was much more flamboyant, although less grounded. For many of his Jesuit years, he resurrected his Jewish origins by calling himself Cohen. His Jesuit colleagues were astounded that he would eat no meat at their table. His knowledge of Hebrew surprised them. But they were even more shocked when, while effortlessly reading aloud a Hebrew manuscript brought for his perusal, he stopped in mid-course to explain his refusal to pronounce the name of God, the tetragrammaton that pious Jews treat as ineffable.

In correspondence with his father, he would hearken back to the wanderings of his Hebraic forebears, journeys which his own travels as a Jesuit reenacted. In a least one letter home, he interspersed words spelled out in Hebrew block letters: the name Mordechai, the words *hatunah* (wedding), *'egel* (calf), *'olat tamid* (burnt offering). His brothers remarked upon how frequently Gifford's mind turned to their "Judaic extraction."

The adoption of Cohen as his last name was the most public and flamboyant aspect of his judaizing behavior. Since name change is an obvious indicator of identity, this is worth some attention. Until he reached Lebanon in 1855, he had been content with Palgrave. He then started calling himself Michael Suhail. *Suhayl* is the Arabic for the constellation Canopus, the inconstant one, inconsistently rising either at the end of the summer or the beginning of the fall. The earliest usage of his Hebrew name seems to date from 1857, the year of his ordination as a Catholic priest. The desire to present himself as a priest by vocation and a *cohen* by descent might have prompted the change. Calling himself Cohen was one peculiar way of publicly asserting the appropriateness of his new status.

Yet he was inconsistent about this name. In 1857, when he revived his father's original name, he did not immediately abandon Suhail, which he continued to use in correspondence with his family and with his Jesuit superiors. Not until his pilgrimage to Palestine in 1859 did he consistently call himself Cohen. The first letter so signed was written from Nazareth. Thus, it was only after establishing a tie with his ancestral land that he publicly proclaimed his ancestral name—a curious parallel to the apparent influence of a voyage to Palestine upon the young Disraeli, a few decades earlier. Subsequently, he used his Jewish name in all his dealings with the Jesuits, the French government, and papal authorities.

With his family he was less consistent, using either Cohen or Palgrave or both. During the undercover voyage, he adopted Muslims names. Significantly, it was as Cohen that he conceived and pursued his grandiose political and religious scheme for Arabia. Only after the abject failure of his mission, and his breach with the Catholic Church and the Society of Jesus, did he abandon his priesthood—and his "Cohenate."

Politics of Identity

Palgrave's Jewish identity and the role it played in shaping his view of the Arabs were regularly noted by his contemporaries. Richard Francis Burton (1821–90), in the notes to his edition of *The Arabian Nights* and in the preface to the third edition (1879) of his *Personal Narrative of a Pilgrimage to Al-Madinah and Meccah* (a book less successful than Palgrave's *Central and Eastern Arabia*), drew upon confidential official documents to denounce Father Michael Cohen for his frequent changes of religion. By contrast, Reginald Stuart Poole (1832–95), nephew and disciple of the famous lexicographer, Edward William Lane (1801-76), praised him, and repeatedly quoted him as an authority alongside his uncle's *Arabic-English Lexicon.* Significantly, Poole noted that one of the qualities that made Palgrave's work so excellent was his "innate sympathy with the Semitic race."[12]

Clearly, a case can be made for a peculiar but nonetheless real form of Jewish identity in William Gifford Palgrave. But what about his role in Arab nationalism, and more importantly what about the nature of the relationship between the Jewish and Arab elements present in his life?

First, Palgrave played a crucial if unacknowledged role in shaping the Western image of the Arab. Since the Western image was to assist in the creation of Arab political identity itself, this is no mean influence. Palgrave wrote with unique authority, for he was the first (and for many decades the only) European to travel widely through central and eastern Arabia. Eloquence and romantic mystery made his narrative the most widely read book in Europe about the Arabs. In the nineteenth century, it sold more editions than Burckhardt, Burton, Doughty, the Blunts, and all the other Victorian travellers in Arab lands combined. It established Palgrave as the authority on matters Arabian for the rest of his life. On the whole, Palgrave created a largely positive image, which was supportive of European recognition of the Arabs as a distinct national group worthy of self-determination.

By Arabs, Palgrave meant the inhabitants of the Arabian peninsula, especially those of the towns and villages. Far from being the driftwood of the desert, they were a noble people who, because of the misfortunes of Turkish misrule and the excesses of their religion—particularly the version promoted by the Saudis—had fallen on hard times. He turned the normal usage of "Arab" as bedouin on its head. Excluding the desert nomads (whom he, like most town-dwellers, heartily despised), the Arabs were an able and civilized people. Denying the role of Islam, he created for the Arabs a secular Arab identity. And he paid the Arabs what was, for his audience, the very highest of tributes by calling them "the Englishmen of the East." Palgrave wrote that if only they could be rid of the Ottoman yoke, they could re-emerge proud and independent. As for the adjoining peoples of Egypt and Syria, he proposed that they be allied with the Arabs of the peninsula, although he recognized that there were differences between them.[13]

At the same time, he detested the Saudis, whom he painted black with the brush of intolerance and fanaticism. He felt that only Arabian rivals of the Saudis could furnish the leadership which could revive the past glory of the Arabs. In retrospect, his assessment was a remarkably accurate prediction of the eclipse of the Saudis by their rivals, the Āl Rashīd, during the decades after Palgrave's visit in 1862–63.

Palgrave published and popularized this secular vision of the noble Arab, restive under Turkish misrule, more than a decade before the call by a Melkite Catholic from Lebanon, Ibrāhīm al-Yāzijī (1840–1906), for the Arabs to arise and awake—a call which formed the basis for George Antonius's claim that Arab Christians of Lebanon originated Arab nationalism. Yāzijī's famous proto-nationalist, anti-Turkish ode serves as the epigraph of Antonius's book, *The Arab Awakening.*[14] And perhaps here, too, one can trace the influence of Palgrave. Palgrave had very close ties with the Melkite (or Greek) Catholics, that is the Arabic-speaking communicants of the Greek Orthodox Church who had accepted the leadership of, and had become united (hence Uniates) with the pope in Rome. His travel companion on the journey across Arabia later became their patriarch. As an educator in the Jesuit schools of Beirut, Ghazir, and Zahle during the 1850s and 1860s, he taught the contemporaries of Ibrāhīm al-Yāzijī, along with other Melkite Catholics. Perhaps he even taught Ibrāhīm himself. He was concerned to make his pupils, whatever their religious background, aware of all that they had in common, particularly as Arabs. In particular, he desired to foster what he called an awareness of the common "patriarchal way of thinking," by which he meant those religious and non-religious traditions of the Abrahamic heritage shared by Arabic-speaking Jews, Christians, and Muslims

This is manifest in a letter he wrote his father in 1858, which illustrates the way in which he combined a pro-Arab sensiblity, an outspokenly anti-British and anti-imperial political attitude, and a highly idiosyncratic sense of Jewish identity. In the letter, Palgrave writes:

> I am becoming a great friend with the Arabs in general and a perfect Paria for the Europeans, especially for my old acquaintances the English so much so that the British Consul thought himself obliged to write to his government complaining of the harm I do them by word and deed. Poor fellow, please God, I will do them yet much more. Meanwhile as I have put myself long before under French protection I laughed at the complaining consul, and with a note to the French Government silenced the English plaints. If it ever happened that you had official dealings with me it is to the French Consul and not to the English with whom I have nothing to do, not even a bow of civility that you should write, for I am the מרדכי ["Mordechai" written in block Hebrew letters] of this latter.[15]

This letter warrants careful attention. It contains a veiled reference to a British complaint that he had harmed "them by word and deed." Indeed, several months earlier, in the fall of 1857, Palgrave made repeated "vituperating" comments about the English in general and British Indian policy during the Great Mutiny in particular. He said the British deserved to lose since they oppressed the native population, and he welcomed what he hoped would be the impending victory of the mutineers. Speaking as a veteran of the East India Company's military, he warned his Arab audience to beware the beguilements of the British. These comments were reported back to the British consul in Beirut, who lodged a series of formal protests with the French government, the papal nuncio, and the Society of Jesus, in an unsuccessful effort to expel or silence this unwelcome agitator. What particularly worried the consul was that Palgrave was "a most popular preacher in this place, in fact, the only preacher of any note amongst the Native Roman Catholic Community."

Then there is the odd way in which Palgrave tied his struggle with the consul to his own Jewishness, playing Father Mordechai to Consul Haman. Palgrave's assertion of his Jewish identity as part of his alienation from the British was not simply a private notion expressed in a letter home, but rather a consistent attitude maintained in public. This emerges clearly in the report the British consul sent to London: "Father Michael has made it known in this country that he is of Jewish origin from India; he has studiously repudiated his British nationality. Upon asking him the name of his family he said it was that of the 'Cohen'."[16]

Palgrave's linkage of the three elements—Jewish, pro-Arab, and anti-European—might seem too bizarre to merit further attention, except for the fact that it echoes a commonplace of European thought in the nineteenth century: the Jew as Oriental. To paraphrase Disraeli, the Jews were simply Arabs off horseback. The theme is deployed by other English, French, and German writers as well. For the famed French scholar of religion and Semitic languages, Ernest Renan (1823–92), the mind of the East was to be plumbed through the literature of the Jews. The well-known historian Heinrich von Treitschke (1834–96) wrote in 1879 that despite their assimilation, "there will always be Jews who are nothing but German-speaking Orientals."[17]

In that very same year, most perniciously of all, Wilhelm Marr (1818–1904) popularized and perhaps coined the term "anti-Semitism," thereby suggesting that hatred of Jews was not some superstitious medieval religious prejudice, but was a scientifically-sanctioned opposition to the entire Eastern race, of which the Jews were the quintessential example. Marr, anticipating his contemporary, Theodor Herzl, thought that Palestine was a natural destination for the Jews, since they were racially close to the Muslims.[18] In Palgrave's support for the Arab cause, he may well have internalized then-current European assumptions about the Jews' affinity to other so-called Oriental peoples.

His peculiar and idiosyncratic Jewishness was not only Arab; it was also Christian. In a sense, he created his own syncretistic religion. In 1840 John Henry Newman (1801–90) published *The Church of the Fathers,* which lay the groundwork for his own and others' conversion from Anglicanism to Catholicism. Newman had been Palgrave's spiritual idol; he devoured the book. By becoming Father Cohen, a priest by descent and vocation, Palgrave united "the church of his fathers" with the "church", i.e. synagogue, of his own fathers. The next task was to bring his Muslim brethren into his union as well. The journey through the desert to convert and unite the Arabs grew out of his conviction that as one son of Abraham, he was uniquely qualified to bring the truth of the New Israel to the other offspring of Abraham, the children of Hagar.

Clearly this strange life must be seen against the background of European Jewish emancipation, the movement that brought Jews out of the self-contained, legally autonomous community of the ghetto into the modern world as individuals, citizens of the newly invented nation-state, free and equal, tremulous and insecure. All who came through this process faced the challenge, in the words of Sir Isaiah Berlin, of how "to replant themselves in some new and no less secure and nourishing soil." They, too, needed firm moorings and "since they were not born with them, [they] invented them. They did this only at a price of ignoring a good deal of reality seen by less agonised, more ordinary, but saner men."[19] Gifford Palgrave found these moorings in his scheme for religious syncretism and national independence for the Arabs. They were, after all, "Jews on horseback," to quote (and not paraphrase) Disraeli, and his plot indeed reads as though it came from the pages of a Disraeli novel.

During Palgrave's years of missionary service in the Middle East, he maintained a peculiar dual identity: Semitic-Jewish-Arab in ethnic-national terms, and Christian in terms of religion. It was this bifurcated vision which enabled him to envisage a comparable bifurcation for the Arabs, with whom he identified as fellow Semites. Palgrave sought to redefine and create a new identity for them, just as he had for himself. Since their religious and ethnic identities as Muslims and Arabs were so intertwined as to be inseparably one, he had to separate these two elements in order for his mission to succeed. Once their Arabness was no longer linked to their being Muslim, he could convert them while they yet maintained their authentic heritage. And once this link of peoplehood and religion was broken, the Arabs could be organized in revolt against the Muslim Ottoman Empire. Palgrave's personal and national vision evokes a phenomenon described by Erik Erikson, a pioneer in the study of identity and history: "Such a man makes his individual 'patienthood' representative of a universal one, and promises to solve for all what he could not solve for himself alone."

The failure of his solution for the Arabs of the peninsula meant the failure of his solution for himself, hence his profound hatred of the Wahhabis, who were an instrument of his fall. However, the combining of what might anachronistically be called Jewish and Arab ethnicity, as well as his vision of national self-determination distinct from religious identity, made an important contribution to political discourse about the Middle East. Palgrave made a plea for the Arabs decades before Wilfrid Scawen Blunt (1840–1922) issued a similar appeal for an Arab awakening and Arab independence. Through his book and his secret mission through Arabia, Palgrave created a powerful political agenda, and a practical program for gaining it, which were to be largely realized half a century later during the First World War.

Prophet of Arab Revolt

In 1918, Harry St. John Philby (1885–1960), then serving the British cause on the Arabian front, inserted a seemingly irrelevant attack on Palgrave into an official report.[20] Philby, who was to became famous as an explorer, later argued that the Jesuit was an impostor who had never entered Arabia. Palgrave's dogged defender in the public controversy which then ensued was David George Hogarth (1862–1927), an authority on travellers in the Middle East whose own writing and thinking were much influenced by Palgrave. Hogarth was also T.E. Lawrence's mentor, and the *éminence grise* of British Arab policy during the war. What brought Hogarth, a man of tact who avoided personal controversy, into conflict with Philby?[21]

Each stood for more than himself. Hogarth led the Cairo-based Arab Bureau, which was at loggerheads with Philby's employer, the India Office. Hogarth realized that Philby's attack was really directed against the policies of his bureau, specifically, those policies which it fostered and the India Office opposed: the Arab Revolt of 1916 (which Lawrence of Arabia made famous in the West), the very concept of Arab nationhood represented by the Hashemites, and British support for Zionist claims in Palestine—support for which Hogarth expressed sympathy. All these found their inspiration and justification in Palgrave's distinction between national and religious identities, and his combination of Jewish and Arab identities.

Palgrave was the unacknowledged influence in much of Hogarth's writing and thinking about the Arabs. In Hogarth's two major works on the subject, *The Penetration of Arabia* (1905) and *Arabia* (1922), there are scores of instances where the Palgravian presence is apparent. In the first book, the longer of the two, which is annotated and carefully indexed, the degree of influence is immediately apparent: Palgrave is one of the most frequently cited authorities. Hogarth carefully and thoroughly read Palgrave's work, so much so that he unconsciously integrated its ideas into his own thinking. This is also apparent in the second book, which is much shorter, more an essay than a work of detailed scholarship. Here, too, a careful reading reveals the presence of Palgravian themes and thinking about the Arabs.

Thus, Hogarth's response to Philby's attack on Palgrave was hardly surprising, since Philby had attacked one of the fundamental sources for Hogarth's own views on the Arabs. On the face of it, the attack seemed confined to pedantic issues of geographical arcana. But both participants realized that matters of high state policy were also at stake. This is because, just as Philby and Hogarth were jousting over Palgrave in public, they were jousting over policy towards the Arabs in the secret councils of Whitehall.

An insight into this intertwining of geography and politics is afforded by a record in the archives of the Royal Geographical Society in London.[22] The occasion was the annual awards dinner of 1920, when Hogarth was to bestow the society's Gold Medal upon Philby, in honor of Philby's explorations in Arabia. The Royal Geographical Society was then, before the founding of the Royal Institute of International Affairs, the leading and effectively sole forum for the public discussion of matters of international concern. Attending this dinner were the leading political and military figures of the British Empire, notably Lord Curzon (1859–1925), who was himself not only an explorer in his own right, and past president and benefactor of the society, but also the chief British official in charge of coordinating policy toward the Arab world.

Thus Hogarth and Philby had as influential and important an audience as they were ever likely to gain. The remarks prepared by each have been preserved. Their arch and purposeful multiplicity of meaning reveals how much more was going on than met the eye. Hogarth, the presenter, spoke first. Before praising Philby's geographical achievements, he hinted at politics:

> I could tell you a good many things about Mr. Philby if I liked—things about his political activities; things about his great friend, that black-bearded Assyrian King, who manages to bring Nejd so frequently into ~~my mind~~ the lime-light.

The "Assyrian King" was of course Philby's friend and patron, 'Abd al-'Azīz ibn 'Abd al-Raḥmān, known in the West as Ibn Saud (1880–1953)—descendant of the dynasty which Palgrave had tried to convert to Catholicism and whose fanaticism he then denigrated in his book.

Hogarth consistently cited that same fanaticism as a reason to avoid British entanglement with the Saudis. When Philby's turn came, he could not resist replying in turn.

> I do not propose to enter now into any controversy with Dr. Hogarth. I have my controversies with him in other places, and I do not yet know whether he has admitted he is in the wrong. Until I know that I do not feel safe to tread on the subject any more.

The use of the plural, "controversies" and "other places," alerts us to the number and complexity of Philby and Hogarth's disagreements. Everyone in the know at this meeting realized that both Hogarth and Philby were locked in many debates, and that each debate could stand in for the other. The allegedly geographical forum of the society's dinner provided an opportunity for Hogarth to comment on Philby's political leanings. Philby's award for geographical exploration—discoveries which supposedly discredited Palgrave—gave Philby the excuse to remind the audience of all his interrelated disagreements with Hogarth. Both, without saying so, were acknowledging that Palgrave was present at the roots of their contest.

And so for more than seventy years, Palgrave, the quasi-Jew, was present and influential in the formulation, dissemination, and implementation of ideas which have made the modern Middle East. His was a pervasive contribution, which deserves to be recognized. He was one of those Europeans who fostered the policies which created and shaped the world of the Arabs, linked them with the Jews, and thereby promoted the assumption of Semitic fraternity which allowed the British to believe that support for Zionism could be consistent with support for Arab nationalism.

Notes

1. Allan Harris Cutler and Helen Elmquist Cutler, *The Jew as Ally of the Muslim: Medieval Roots of Anti-Semitism* (Notre Dame: University of Notre Dame Press, 1986). The larger claims of this work, i.e. that anti-Islamic sentiment is at the root of anti-Semitism, are not persuasive.
2. *Biblia Latina cum Glossa Ordinaria: Facsimile Reprint of the Editio Princeps, Adolph Rusch of Strassburg, 1480/81,* intro. by Karlfried Froehlich

and Margaret T. Gibson (Turnhout: Brepols, 1992), 41.

3. See Benjamin Braude, "The Sons of Noah and the Construction of Ethnic and Geographical Identities in the Medieval and Early Modern Periods," *William and Mary Quarterly* (3d series) 54 (1997): 103–42; idem, "*Mandeville's* Jews among Others," in *Pilgrims and Travellers to the Holy Land, Proceedings of the Seventh Annual Symposium of the Philip M. and Ethel Klutznick Chair in Jewish Civilization,* eds. Bryan F. LeBeau and Menahem Mor (Omaha, Neb.: Creighton University Press, 1996), 141–68.
4. See Italian versions of *Mandeville's Travels:* (Milan, 1480), quire K vii recto; (Milan, 1496), quire M iii verso; (Milan, 1497), quire I iv recto; (Bologna, 1488), quire H i recto; (Bologna, 1492), quire F iv recto ; (Bologna, 1497), quire G iv recto; (Florence, 1492), quire H i recto; and (Venice, 1496), quire L iv recto.
5. *The Voyages and Trauailes of Sir John Maundeuile Knight. Wherein is set downe the Way to the Holy Land, and to Hierusalem: As also to the Lands of the great Caane and of Prester John, Inde, and diuers other Countries: Together with the many and strange Meruailes therein* (London, 1677), chapter 46, sign. F 3 v and (London, 1684), chapter 46, pp. 68–70.
6. Johannes Brenz, *Wie sich Prediger und Leien halten sollen, so der Türck das Deudsche Land vberfallen würde* (Wittenberg, 1537), leaf C2, quoted in John W. Bohnstedt, *The Infidel Scourge of God, the Turkish Menace as Seen by German Pamphleteers of the Reformation Era* (Philadelphia: Transactions of the American Philosophical Society, New Series, vol. 58, part 9, 1968), 50.
7. See Benjamin Braude, "The Heine-Disraeli Syndrome among the Palgraves of Victorian England," in *Jewish Apostasy in the Modern World: Missionaries and Converts in Historical Perspective,* ed. Todd Endelman (New York: Holmes and Meier, 1987), 126; William Gifford Palgrave, *Narrative of a Year's Journey through Central and Eastern Arabia (1862–63),* 2 vols. (London: Macmillan, 1866), 1:152; "Translated purport of a statement made by Aboo-Eesau on the 22nd of April 1866," Layard Papers, British Library, Additional Manuscripts, 39, 119, f. 529.
8. See letters of Michel Cohen S.J. and Charles Schefer to Napoleon III, Hamah, 31 August 1861, Memoirs et documents, Turquie, CXXIII, nos. 13 and 14, 33–34, 35–38, Archives du Ministère des Affaires Étrangères, Paris.
9. Father-General Pieter Beckx, S.J. to Cardinal Barnabo, Rome, 9 June 1861, in "Udienze di nostro signore del 1861," vol. 137, no. 19, p. 652, in the Archives of the Sacred Congregation for the Propagation of the Faith, Rome.
10. Letter of Father Cohen, Beirut, 28 July 1861, in "Lettres de Laval," a collection of missionary reports privately distributed within the Society of Jesus.
11. Braude, "Heine-Disraeli Syndrome."
12. Richard Francis Burton, *A Plain and Literal Translation of the Arabian Nights*

Entertainment, now intituled The Book of the Thousand Nights and a Night, (n.p., n.d. [1886?]), 10:189n.; idem, *Personal Narrative of a Pilgrimage to al-Madinah and Meccah,* 3d ed. (London, 1879), 1:vii–viii; Reginald Stuart Poole, "Pagan and Muslim Arabs," *Fortnightly Review,* 15 October 1865, 555.

13. Palgrave, *Narrative,* 1:70, 143.
14. George Antonius, *The Arab Awakening* (London: H. Hamilton, 1938).
15. W.G. Palgrave to Sir Francis Palgrave, Beirut, 24 February 1858, Palgrave Family Archive.
16. Moore to Clarendon, Beirut, 11 November 1857, Political no. 44 with enclosures, 13 November, Political no. 45 and Hammond to Moore, 1 December 1857, Public Record Office, FO78/1300, and Ministère des Affaires Étrangères to de Lesseps, 29 December 1857, Correspondance politique, Turquie, Beyrouth, XI, 164 ff.
17. Paul Mendes-Flohr, "Fin de Siècle Orientalism, the Ostjuden, and the Aesthetics of Jewish Self-Affirmation," in his *Divided Passions: Jewish Intellectuals and the Experience of Modernity* (Detroit: Wayne State University Press, 1990), 77–132, esp. 81.
18. Moshe Zimmerman, *Wilhelm Marr, the Patriarch of Anti-Semitism,* (New York: Oxford University Press, 1986), 87, quoting Wilhelm Marr, *Vom jüdischen Kriegsschauplatz* (Bern, 1879), 42–43.
19. Isaiah Berlin, *Against the Current: Essays on the History of Ideas,* ed. Henry Hardy (London: Hogarth Press, 1979), 284.
20. The report was twice printed: *Report of a Trip to Southern Najd and Dawasir by H. St. J. Philby, C.I.E, I.C.S. on special duty in Central Arabia, July, 1918* (Simla: Goverment Monotype Press, 1918), 14–15 deals with Palgrave, catalogued as India Office Records, L/PS/20/C 169; and *Southern Nejd, Journey to Kharj, Aflaj, Sulaiyyil and Wadi Dawasir in 1918 by H. St. J. B. Philby, I.C.S., Printed and issued by the Arab Bureau* (Cairo: Government Press, 1919), 20–22. It can also be found in the Public Record Office, FO 371/3859, ff. 98–139. This report was Philby's first essay in travel literature.
21. C.R.L. Fletcher, "David George Hogarth, President R.G.S. 1925–27," *The Geographical Journal* 71 (April 1928): 321–44, esp. 328.
22. Minutes of the 1920 Annual Dinner, Royal Geographical Society Archives, London.

3

Arminius Vámbéry: Identities in Conflict

Jacob M. Landau

In the summer of 1987, while I was a visiting professor at the University of Bamberg, I was invited to attend the dedication of a hall to the memory of Arminius Vámbéry (1831/2–1913), whose family is said to have originated in the town. What struck me most about this ceremony was that not a word in the many speeches remarked upon the fact that Vámbéry was a Jew.

Born Hermann Wamberger in 1831 or 1832, he magyarized his family name to Vámbéry, using Hermann and Arminius interchangeably.[1] His birthplace was a town near Bratislava in today's Slovakia; his mother-tongue was Hungarian, while much of the general culture of his early environment was German. Since practically all of his early education, until the age of twelve, was in the *heder*, it is quite likely that a conflict in determining his identity ensued early in his life, probably prompted by the many languages and cultures he encountered (and in many of which he became proficient). Identity conflicts, of course, were not unusual among many ethnic and religious groups in the area, but perhaps were even more in evidence amongst Jews, who were different both ethnically and religiously, and frequently had to contend with widespread anti-Semitism. This may have been an additional factor in attracting some of the Jewish intellectuals of that region to the study of other civilizations—a strategy for postponing a final definition of their own personal identity.

In Vámbéry's instance, his childhood in poverty, and the tauntings and beatings he endured because of his lameness, may have increased his sensitivity to the suffering of others. Time and again, in his autobiography and other works,[2] he shows compassion towards the physical and emotional suffering of other groups, such as slaves, and certain Muslim and other tribes which he encountered in his wanderings in the Ottoman Empire, Iran, and Central Asia. The Turkmens[3] and Tatars[4] are cases in point; so, too, are the Babis, in his travel account of Persia.[5] A scholar and traveller, essentially a self-made man, Vámbéry characteristically inclined to defend such groups, while condemning bigotry and what he called *Sektenhass*, or hatred of [religious] sects.[6]

However, Vámbéry's sympathies were more evident at the beginning of his career than later. In this, he differed strikingly from Ignaz Goldziher (1850–1921), his student. Goldziher's starting point in his Islamic studies was his own strong sense of commitment to Orthodox Judaism. It is not unlikely that his subsequent break with Vámbéry was at least partly motivated by Vámbéry's growing distance from Judaism and his enthusiasm for the modernization of the Islamic East in his writings. In his *Oriental Diary*,[7] Goldziher identified himself repeatedly with traditional Muslim anti-Westernism.[8]

This alienation between the two was hastened by Vámbéry's effort to integrate himself into the non-Jewish society of his time. During his travels in Central Asia, he more than once would have risked being put to death, had he identified himself as a Jew. Indeed, his assumed disguise of a dervish became almost second nature. But after his return to Budapest in 1864, he could not pass for someone other than he was, for Hungarians were well aware of his origins. True to form, he later boasted of how he had achieved fame and position despite having been born in a poor, lower-class Jewish family. He correctly perceived his Jewishness and humble origins as serious obstacles to advancement.

The Hungary of his time was not only permeated by anti-Semitism, but was also extremely class conscious. The aristocracy and upper middle class moved in closed circles, within their own social clubs that perpetuated ingrained prejudices. Vámbéry's entry into some of these circles in his later years was due almost entirely to external factors: his having been invited to stay with British political leaders, even to visit Windsor Castle; and his connections with royal oriental personages, such as the ruler of Iran, Nāṣir al-Dīn Shah (r. 1848–96), who visited Budapest in 1889. His introduction to Budapest's upper strata, however, remained merely formal, and he maintained very limited social contacts. Even his funeral, in 1913, was attended by very few representatives of the upper class. Vámbéry's status, an outsider who had penetrated (even "crashed") the scholarly establishment in Budapest by being appointed in 1865 as the first holder of the chair of oriental languages at the University of Pest, did not increase his popularity in a society very partial to formal schooling and official diplomas. Likewise, his frugal way of life was hardly conducive to social intercourse with the wealthy of Budapest.

Lastly, the strongly Catholic society of Hungary was disinclined to forget that Vámbéry had been born a Jew, while Jewish community leaders suspected him of having converted to Islam, or Christianity, or both. While there is no definite proof of any conversion, the fact that he often defined himself as a freethinker and adopted markedly non-religious attitudes in his behavior seemed sufficient proof of apostasy to the Hungarian Jewish establishment. Moreover, his appointment to a university chair and his marriage to the daughter of a Christian professor of pathological anatomy, Lajos Arányi, settled the matter for them.

On the other hand, the prevalent rumor that he had become a Protestant did little to endear him to Catholic society. The question of his conversion is far from settled, however. In his autobiographical writings, Vámbéry stated repeatedly that during his sojourn in the East, he had firmly rejected all suggestions that he become a Muslim. Later, when he applied to the Foreign Office in London for a pension, he could not produce a certificate of baptism which would have documented his date of birth. When questioned later on this point by the noted Zionist leader Nahum Sokolow (1859–1936), Vámbéry replied that "it is not water that is important, but race."[9] Lory Alder and Richard Dalby, Vámbéry's biographers, offer no conclusive proof of his conversion. Nor is this mentioned in a smaller, more recent book in Russian by M. Sominskii,[10] or in the available obituaries.[11]

There are numerous indications that whatever feelings of Jewish identity Vámbéry may have had, these, as Sokolow noted, were based on ethnic rather than religious ties. Again, on Sokolow's evidence, Vámbéry was proud of his Jewish origins. More than once, Vámbéry's writings expressed sympathy with persecuted Jews, such as those in Mashhad. His *Sittenbilder aus dem Morgenlande* contains a revealing sub-chapter on the Jews,[12] which starts as follows: "Nothing is more shocking—and let us immediately add, more distressing—than the sad lot of the Jews in the various lands of Muslim Asia."[13] Vámbéry sympathized with their poverty and insecurity, inveighing against the Muslims' hatred and oppression of the Jews.[14] Later, Vámbéry's stubborn efforts to persuade Sultan Abdülhamid II (r. 1876–1909) to grant an audience to Theodor Herzl, in 1901, may have been another indication of his readiness to help the Jewish national cause, even at the risk of injuring his own relations with the Ottoman court.[15]

Advocate for the Oppressed

Yet Vámbéry's brief involvement with Zionism was merely one aspect of his persistent campaigns on behalf of the oppressed. This found expression in the three broad categories of his writings, which perfectly complement one another.[16]

First, Vámbéry's scholarly research branched into linguistics and literature. His most memorable contributions remain his investigation of Chagatay and other East Turkic languages, mainly Özbek, and the critical editing of several Turkic literary manuscripts. The linguistic studies began in 1867 with *Çagataische Sprachstudien*,[17] followed by other works. Among his literary studies, *Die Scheibaniade, ein özbegisches Heldengedicht* is particularly noteworthy.[18] While somewhat outdated, these and other works are still used and referred to by Turcologists.

An extension of these literary studies was his examination of manners and customs in the Ottoman Empire, Iran and Turkestan. Vámbéry offers a perceptive, expert evaluation of the changes there in his *Sittenbilder aus dem Morgenlande*;[19] *La Turquie d'aujourd'hui et d'avant quarante ans*;[20] *Der Islam im neunzehnten Jahrhundert*;[21] and his *Über die Reformfähigkeit der Türkei*.[22] In these works, Vámbéry demonstrates his self-perception as an advocate of the East in Europe, and as an interpreter of the West in the Ottoman Empire, Iran and Central Asia.

A second category of his writings contains his romantic travel accounts, beginning with *Travels in Central Asia*,[23] amplified in *Life and Adventures*,[24] continuing in various volumes which supplemented it in French, German, Hungarian and Italian,[25] and culminating with *The Story of My Struggles*.[26] These books were directed at a wider readership and established Vámbéry's popularity with a European public increasingly interested in the Muslim East and its supposed mysteries, in an era of relative affluence when tourism was becoming increasingly common.

A final category was comprised of Vámbéry's political works. Although these were written in a scholarly style, they were published with specific goals in mind. His books *Hungary in Ancient, Mediaeval, and Modern Times,*[27] and *The Story of Hungary,*[28] are especially characterized by their pronounced nationalist tone. Patriotism has often been a convenient meeting-ground for majority and minorities, and Jews have more than once distinguished themselves by wholehearted patriotism in eastern and central Europe—a posture Vámbéry may have been eager to emphasize, in order to dispel criticism of his close relations with British political circles.

Hungary was ardently nationalist in the second half of the nineteenth century, and preoccupied with the "villainy" of Czarist Russia, which had helped to impose the Dual Monarchy and left Hungary to play second fiddle to Austria. Thus, the thrust of Vámbéry's political writing was invariably against Russia, and many of his books, articles and letters to the British and German press warned against what he perceived as aggressive Russian imperialism. Some of these papers were later collected in his *Central Asia and the Anglo-Russian Frontier Question.*[29] The first two papers, which are also the volume's largest, are suggestively entitled "The Rivalry of Russia with England in Central Asia,"[30] and "Fresh Advances of Russia in Central Asia."[31] A subsequent book, *Westlicher Kultureinfluss im Osten,*[32] consists of two lengthy articles discussing the cultural influence of Russia and Great Britain, respectively.[33] A third long paper examines the "Future of Islam,"[34] concluding that the impact of Western penetration into Muslim areas is unstoppable. In these two books, and in his own personal contacts in Great Britain, he issued frequent warnings against Russia's designs in Turkestan and Afghanistan as part of its master plan to invade India.

The scholarly studies, the travel accounts, and the political writings combine to convey Vámbéry's perceptions of race and nationalism. A good example can be found in his "Freiheitliche Bestrebungen in moslimischen Asien."[35] His linguistic and ethnographic studies repeatedly attempted to prove that the similarities of the language structures of the Hungarian and the Turkic peoples show a common origin and that the ancestors of the Hungarians had emigrated from Central Asia. Indeed, in his introduction to *Travels in Central Asia,*[36] he allowed that one of the main goals of his travels was to examine the relations between Hungarian, Finnish and Tatar. Vámbéry's *Das Türkenvolk in seinen ethnologischen und ethnographischen Beziehungen geschildert* was an endeavor to prove ethnic affinities among Hungarians, Turks, Tatars and others.[37] His travel records presented additional evidence for common origins, while his political writings argued that Russia was the common arch-enemy of Hungarians, Ottomans, Persians and the Turkic groups in Central Asia.

In subscribing to Hungarian anti-Russian patriotism, Vámbéry simultaneously searched for signs of nationalism amongst Turkic groups, such as the Tatars. As early as 1868, Vámbéry devoted an entire chapter of his book *Sketches of Central Asia*[38]—also published in German in the same year as *Skizzen aus Mittelasien*[39]—to the Turanian idea, contending that all Turkic groups belong to one race, subdivided by physical characteristics and customs. This was an attempt, subsequently adopted by other Turanists in Hungary, to end the profound sense of Hungarian isolation in a hostile environment. One of the main arguments of Vámbéry's book on Hungary was that Hungarians and Turco-Tatars have the same ethnic origins and characteristics. Later, he was one of the first, if not the very first European to "discover" the nationalist awakening of the Tatars, in a series of articles published in English and German between 1905 and 1907. There he also praised the efforts of Tatar leaders towards cultural revival—efforts Vámbéry regarded as a striking success.[40]

At about the same time, Vámbéry's affection for peoples of the East found a somewhat unexpected expression in his pamphlet *Le Péril jaune*, published in 1904.[41] The date, of course, is not fortuitous. It was the Russo-Japanese War that stirred Vámbéry's interest in and sympathy for the peoples of East Asia. His concern for Japan, which had hardly interested him earlier, was strengthened by his persistent anti-Russian suspicions. His main argument in this pamphlet was that Japan did not represent "a yellow peril," but rather "a rosy future" for Europe and Asia, since it would contain Russian expansionist ambitions.[42]

To sum up, Vámbéry's political writing (as well as his activities) suited the general thrust of Habsburg foreign policy. While careful not to antagonize Russia unduly, many Austrian and Hungarian officials considered Russia as their main rival and implacable enemy. Throughout the late nineteenth century, they suspected Russia of fomenting ethnic nationalism in the Habsburgs' Balkan possessions. By encouraging Russophobia in Great Britain and promoting Turanism in Hungary and among such Turkic groups as the Tatars, Vámbéry was in tune not only with Hungarian political sentiments, but also with the strategic interests of Habsburg policies.

To the last, Vámbéry himself remained keenly interested in politics and actively involved in them. His own Jewishness had little evident relationship to this, but it may have made Vámbéry's advocacy of the oppressed more passionate still.

Notes

1. The best biography of Vámbéry remains Lory Alder and Richard Dalby, *The Dervish of Windsor Castle: The Life of Arminius Vambery* (London: Bachman and Turner, 1979).
2. *Arminius Vambery: His Life and Adventures Written by Himself* (London: T. Fisher Unwin, 1884). The book has been reprinted repeatedly.
3. See Vámbéry's "Die Turkomanen und ihre Stellung gegenüber Russland," *Russische Revue* 3 (1873): 438–53.
4. See below, n. 40.
5. Arminius Vámbéry, *Meine Wanderungen und Erlebnisse in Persien* (Pest: Gustav Heckenast, 1867), introduction and *passim.*
6. E.g., ibid., 288–89. This book was published in the same year in Hungarian, too, entitled *Vándorlásaim és élményeim Perzsiában* (Pest: Gustav Heckenast, 1867).
7. Raphael Patai, *Ignaz Goldziher and his Oriental Diary* (Detroit, Michigan: Wayne State University Press, 1987).
8. See also Lawrence I. Conrad, "The Dervish's Disciple: On the Personality and Intellectual Milieu of the Young Ignaz Goldziher," *Journal of the Royal Asiatic Society*, 1990: 225–66.
9. Nahum Sokolow, *Ishim* (Jerusalem: Ha-Sifriyah Ha-Zionit, 1958), 406.
10. M. Sominskii, *Armin Vambery* (Jerusalem: Leksikon, 1987).
11. Such as Rudolf Tschudi's in *Der Islam* 5 (1914): 107–8; Vilmos Prohle's in *Keleti Szemle* 14 (1913–14): 1–3 and Bernát Munkácsi's in *Ungarische Rundschau* 3 (1914): 513–32; 4 (1915): 88–113; 386–408.
12. *Sittenbilder aus dem Morgenlande* (Berlin: A. Hofmann, 1876), 249–55.
13. Ibid., 249.
14. Ibid., 250.
15. A decline in favor with certain Turkish circles has continued to this day, as exemplified in the hostile biography by Mim Kemal Öke, *İngiliz casusu prof. Arminius Vambery'nin gizli raporlarında II. Abdülhamid ve dönemi* (Istanbul: Ucdal, 1983).
16. The most detailed bibliography of Vámbéry's works is Gy. Hazai, *Ármin Vámbéry 1832–1913* (Budapest: Hungarian Academy of Sciences, 1964). See also Alder and Dalby, *The Dervish of Windsor Castle*, 498–505.

17. Leipzig: Brockhaus, 1867.
18. Vienna, 1885.
19. See above, n. 12.
20. Paris, 1898.
21. Leipzig: Brockhaus, 1875.
22. Budapest: F. Kilian, 1877.
23. London: John Murray, 1864.
24. See above, n. 2.
25. The French translation reads *Voyages d'un faux derviche dans l'Asie Centrale* (Paris: Hachette, 1865); the German, *Reise in Mittelasien* (Leipzig: Brockhaus, 1865); the Hungarian, *Közáp-Ázsiai utazás* (Pest, 1865); the Italian, *Viaggi di un falso dervish nell'Asia Centrale* (Milan: E. Treves, 1873). It appeared in Turkish translation in Istanbul in 1879.
26. 2 vols., London: T. Fisher Unwin, 1904.
27. London: T. Fisher Unwin, 1887.
28. New York: Putnam, 1886.
29. London: Smith, Elder, 1874.
30. Ibid., 1–66.
31. Ibid., 67–166.
32. Berlin: D. Reimer, 1906.
33. Ibid., pp. 1–138, 139–284.
34. Ibid., 285–436.
35. *Deutsche Rundschau* 20 (Oct. 1893): 63–75.
36. See above, n. 23.
37. Leipzig: Brockhaus, 1885. Despite its provocative thesis, the book sold only 300 copies in its first ten years.
38. London: W.H. Allen, 1868.
39. Leipzig: Brockhaus, 1868.
40. A. Vámbéry, "The Awakening of the Tatars," *The Nineteenth Century* 52 (February 1905): 217–27; idem, "Die Kulturbestrebung der Tataren," *Deutsche Rundschau* 33, no. 10 (July 1907): 72–91. See also Jacob M. Landau, *Pan-Turkism: From Irredentism to Cooperation* (Bloomington: Indiana University Press, 1995), 2.
41. Budapest: Gustave Ranschburg, 1904.
42. Ibid., 38.

4

Abraham Geiger: A Nineteenth-Century Jewish Reformer on the Origins of Islam

Jacob Lassner

In 1832, the German Arabist Georg Wilhelm Freytag (1788–1861) encouraged his student, Abraham Geiger (1810–74), to enter an academic competition. The contest, sponsored by the Philosophical Faculty of the University of Bonn, called for an enquiry into those themes of the Qur'an which were derived from Judaism ("Inquiratur in fontes Alcorani seu legis Mohammedicae eas qui ex Judaismo derivandi sunt"). In retrospect, the query as defined by the professors at Bonn seems insensitive to Muslim claims that the Qur'an is God's word and thus unique. But that lack of sensitivity to a fundamental tenet of Islam caused no concern, let alone reaction, among learned Europeans of the time.

Young Geiger took up his mentor's challenge and produced a work that merited the prize and then a doctorate at the University of Marburg. The Latin dissertation was revised, enlarged, and subsequently published in German as *Was hat Mohammed aus dem Judenthume aufgenommen?*, "What did Muhammad borrow from Judaism?"[1]—a title that implies, even more strongly than the Latin assignment, that Muhammad's prophetic utterances were entirely his own, the product of a fertile human mind exposed to Jewish influence, rather than a tongue moved by divine revelation.

The expanded dissertation, which the author published at his own expense, received significant acclaim and remained, with all the limitations of an 1830s doctoral project, an interesting, indeed important study.[2] Throughout the nineteenth century and even beyond, Geiger's book remained a point of departure for reflective scholars who continued to be interested in the origins of Islam. Theodor Nöldeke (1836–1930), perhaps the greatest Semiticist of the century, opined in 1860 that Geiger's epoch-making work, although in need of revision, remained in every sense a classic.[3] The reprinting of Geiger's essay in 1902 occasioned a less favorable assessment by leading Arabists. Both Hubert Grimme (1864–1942) and Josef Horovitz (1874–1931) found it wanting in retrospect, and concluded that the quest for the Jewish influence on the Qur'an required a more sophisticated conceptual focus and a wider range of primary sources than those examined by Geiger, as many new sources had come to light in the seventy years since publication of Geiger's work.[4]

These led to new studies of Jewish themes in Islam. But even the most thorough of the later authors, Heinrich Speyer (1897–1935), was obliged to concede Geiger his enduring place in the scholarship on the subject. Writing almost a century after Geiger, Speyer was still able to appreciate the extent to which his predecessor combined great learning in Jewish and Muslim sources to elucidate the Prophet's views of the biblical past and its *dramatis personae.*[5] Even now, Geiger can be read, with all his limitations, as more than simply a mirror of early modern scholarship on Muhammad's mission and faith.

In many if not all respects, Freytag's student was ideally suited to broach the subject of the competition. Geiger was a child prodigy of a rigorously traditional Jewish background, who began to read the Bible in the original Hebrew at three, the Mishna at four, and the Talmud at six. Geiger's ability to absorb sacred texts soon rendered formal religious schooling inadequate. As a result, he abandoned his studies at the traditional *heder* and continued his education at home, first under the tutelage of his father and then an elder half-brother, Solomon, himself a gifted talmudic scholar. Although the family was primarily interested that their gifted child study classical Jewish sources—his father and brother were both rabbis of the old school—young Geiger developed broader interests in the relatively liberal atmosphere of Frankfurt.[6]

In Frankfurt, young Jews intoxicated by the spirit of the Enlightenment tended to enroll at the Philanthropin School, a Jewish institution offering a wide range of secular subjects in preparation for university studies. Because Geiger's family feared secular education might prove corrupting, they did not consider the Philanthropin School appropriate. But they could not suppress his intellectual interests nor his desire for a university education. As a result, he acquired a knowledge of Greek and Latin in a somewhat desultory fashion, as well as a firm command of literary German, all of which set the stage for the great leap into the secular world of the *Kollegia.*

Geiger enrolled at Heidelberg in 1829 and then transferred to Bonn. Given his thorough grounding in Hebrew and Aramaic sources and his particular interest in (Jewish) speculative theology, Geiger gravitated to oriental languages and general philosophy. But he also saw a need to partake of cultural history and classical philology, subjects in which he was not so well grounded, owing to his lack of formal training in the humanities. At Bonn, Geiger became acquainted with other young Jewish men who, like himself, were attracted to the fruits of the Enlightenment, and who were to play, as he did, a major role in the religious and intellectual life of nineteenth-century Jewry. After completing his university studies, Geiger secured a pulpit in Breslau and later emerged as one of the leading proponents of modern Reform Judaism and a central figure for university-educated Jews, engaged in *Wissenschaft des Judentums,* the historically-oriented study of the Jewish religion and people.[7]

For Geiger, the dissertation submitted at Marburg and the doctorate it earned for him was the beginning of a lifelong quest to march in step with the scholarly and aesthetic sensibilities of the times and to make the study and practice of Judaism less parochial. He saw the Jews not through the narrow lens of received Jewish experience, but as a people rooted in the larger story of civilization, in this case the story of Judaism and Islam. His dissertation also revealed the inherent value of an orientalist scholarship struggling to become free of the overt Christian bias that still resonated strongly in the nineteenth century. In that sense, Geiger's study of the relationship between Jewish sources and the Qur'an may be seen as an early attempt at modern comparative religion, a subject which Geiger and others like him helped to liberate from religious apologetics and transform into a respected discipline.

Islam Esteemed

Generally speaking, Geiger had great respect for the pure monotheism of Islam and the free spirit of enquiry he associated with the Muslim faith. In a series of essays on Judaism and history published in 1865, he contrasts Islam, which "always left itself favorable to the cultivation of science and philosophy, with a [pre-modern] Christian church that increasingly nourished a repugnance of science and reason. In that mental state [produced by the church], Judaism could not prosper as it did in the realms of Islam."[8] Geiger then invokes memories of Muslim Spain, for him a culturally rich environment which produced Jews at the cutting edge of intellectual trends. It would seem that in Geiger's imagination, the intellectual milieu of Muslim Spain bore resemblance to nineteenth-century Germany, a breeding ground of university-trained Jews at the forefront of current knowledge. It is certainly possible, if not probable, that this parallel already informed the outlook of Geiger's younger years, including the period in which he wrote his prizewinning essay.

No less than Antoine-Isaac Silvestre de Sacy (1758–1838), the founder of modern Arabic studies and Freytag's teacher, gave the essay an extensive review.[9] The great Arabist, who was much interested in Jews and Judaism, congratulated the author on his vast erudition and commended him for disengaging the study of Islam from religious polemics: "He [Geiger] renders almost superfluous all the preceding discussion which I would call prejudicial." Nevertheless, even Silvestre de Sacy could not help but observe that the author seemed a bit generous in his evaluation of Muhammad.[10]

Geiger refers to Muhammad as a *schwärmer*, that is an "enthusiast," a term which in ecclesiastical parlance can become the less neutral "zealot" or the more highly charged "fanatic." Yet the context of Geiger's remarks clearly reveals that, in opposition to a long established Christian tradition, he did not regard Islam's prophet as a self-serving adventurer. Muhammad's highly critical attitude and hostile behavior towards the Jews and Judaism is well attested in the Qur'an and other Islamic sources. Yet Geiger, the Jew (and by then on his way to becoming a pulpit rabbi), considered Muhammad to have been motivated by sincere religious beliefs: "We should not at all imagine that we are to regard [Muhammad] as a deceiver who deceived intentionally... [Muhammad] seems to have been a genuine enthusiast who was himself convinced of his divine mission."[11] According to Geiger, Muhammad was absolutely obsessed with the idea of uniting the religions of the world for their mutual well-being under the banner of Islam. Muhammad sincerely viewed each of his decisions as the product of divine inspiration. No doubt, that included, for Geiger, Muhammad's expulsion of the Jewish tribes from Medina, the attack on the Jewish oasis of Khaybar, and the extermination of the adult Jewish males of the Banū Qurayẓah. There were admittedly times when the Muslim prophet's "ambition and love of power were the incentives to his action, but even so the harsh judgment generally passed upon him [by Europeans] is unjustifiable."[12]

Silvestre de Sacy, who would have considered himself the representative of an enlightened outlook, goes on in his review to describe Muhammad in far less charitable terms. The Muslim prophet was a "skilled imposter, premeditated in all his actions and cold-bloodedly evaluating all that which favored and assured the success of his ambitious projects."[13] (Silvestre de Sacy seems to have demanded of Muhammad a higher plane of moral behavior than that which he expected from the religious and political establishment of his native France. After all, in his own lifetime, he experienced the ancien régime, the Revolution, the Reign of Terror, the Napoleonic wars, and the politics that restored the monarchy.) And his was not the only review chiding Geiger for being overly sympathetic to Muhammad and, by implication, to Islam.[14]

While in today's climate of doing third world history, Geiger would hardly be regarded as sympathetic to the "natives" and their culture,[15] his scholarly rather than strictly polemical objective was considered of particular value in a most unexpected quarter. Some sixty years after the appearance of the prizewinning essay, the Rev. G.A. LeFroy, not a university professor but the head of the Cambridge Mission in Delhi, India, contracted a certain Miss F.M. Young of Bangalore, a member of the Ladies League in aid of the Delhi mission, to translate Geiger's work into English, so that missionaries could make use of it in proselytizing the local Muslims. By showing the Jewish underpinnings of the text held most sacred by all Muslims, the missionaries of the Delhi League hoped to inspire in the natives a greater appreciation of Christianity—not quite what Geiger had in mind for his prizewinning work, but a tribute in any case to his extensive learning and the important connections between Jewish and Muslim tradition. The translation appeared in 1898, bearing a title more sensitive to Muslim claims for the divine authorship of the Qur'an. The English reincarnation of *Was hat Mohammed aus dem*

Judenthume aufgenommen? was published simply as *Judaism and Islam.*[16]

As fate had it, Geiger did not devote himself to the study of Islam, and never again published a work that dealt specifically with Islam or the Muslims. Rather, he concentrated his energies and enormous analytical talent on the Jewish sources and the reform of Judaism.[17] Nevertheless, following the path begun by him, various scholars, mostly Jewish and, as was Geiger, mostly trained during their young years in classical Jewish sources, grappled intermittently with the Islamization of Jewish themes and, more generally, with the origins of the Islamic community and faith.[18]

Given what we now know of the transmission of culture and of the tendentiousness of early Arabic historiography, there is much in Geiger and his nineteenth- and twentieth-century successors that will strike us as naïve and judgmental. The vaguest similarities in Jewish and Muslim traditions were considered proof of direct cultural borrowing; differences were too often ascribed to textual distortion or even perversion. Learned orientalists, however sympathetic to Islam, charged medieval Muslims, directly or indirectly, with failing to quote accurately or footnote adequately those Jewish traditions that were said to inform Muslim texts, including the Qur'an, the book revered by the Muslim faithful as God's eternal and immutable word. This broad charge, whether stated or implied, rested upon two questionable assumptions: that the transmission of literary artifacts was consciously initiated and carefully programmed by the Muslims; and that the artifacts themselves were always discernible to the borrowers. Neither assumption reflected the complex interaction of closely linked cultures, especially in the early and fluid stages of contact. That the history of the ancient Israelites became a site contested by Jews and Muslims is beyond question, but the manner in which the religious tradition of the borrower was made different from the tradition borrowed was ever so subtle, certainly more subtle than the early orientalists realized.[19]

The Muslim-Jewish Symbiosis

A rather different view of Jewish-Muslim contacts obtained when orientalists wrote of intellectual links in later times, that is, after the victorious Muslim armies brought the faithful into direct contact with civilizations that had inherited the philosophical and scientific legacy of the ancient world. At that later time, intellectual contact between Jews and Muslims, at least as regards philosophy and science, was marked by an open sharing of knowledge and a common vocabulary of ideas. Rather than serve as a site contested by Jews and Muslims, the venerated Greek past, when studied by them, shaped intellectual and religious concerns that were common to both monotheist communities, a fact duly noted and with much approval by modern scholars.

Given Geiger's interest in formulating a Judaism that could reach beyond the narrow and parochial, it might seem odd, at first glance, that the intellectual synergy of medieval Jewish and Muslim philosophers never became one of the more compelling subjects for his own keen intellect. One can only speculate how Geiger would have represented that intellectual milieu had he made it the major objective of his own scholarly work, and how, viewing it in his usual meticulous fashion and with his striking analytical skills, he might have considered the interaction of medieval Jewish and Muslim thinkers appropriate to modern Jews trying to adapt their ancient faith to the best intellectual and moral impulses of their own age.[20]

As did many of his contemporaries, Geiger gives the intellectual milieu of the Judeo-Islamic world high marks. He thus acknowledges that a truly vibrant culture flourished among Spanish Jewry when they lived under Islamic as opposed to Christian rule.[21] In an aside relevant to his reformist agenda, and more generally to *Wissenschaft des Judentums,* he asserts that the Jews of Islam had a deeper point of entry into the meaning of scripture and the principles of Judaism, and more refined methods of scholarly enquiry.[22] In sum, the Jews of Muslim Spain would seem to have had the kinds of tools that Geiger valued for his project of adapting the best of Judaism's past to the contingencies of a nineteenth-century present.

Indeed, the mystique of Spanish Jewry, with its refined aesthetic and intellectual tastes and its sense of public decorum, had taken root among German Jews who embraced the Enlightenment. Pronounced sentiment preferring Sepharad (Spain) to Ashkenaz (western Europe) appear already at the end of the eighteenth century. Some twenty years prior to his brief assessment of Spain, Geiger, taking part in a dispute on synagogue liturgy, strongly favored Spanish religious poetry because of its grammatical, literary, and philosophical superiority to the Ashkenazi *piyyutim* heard regularly in German houses of worship. Where Hebrew was to be read aloud, he preferred, as did other reformers, the Sephardic pronunciation. There was, no doubt, a perceived need that the holy tongue not sound like Yiddish, the Judeo-German dialect for which Jews were ridiculed by Christians.[23]

That is not to say Geiger could not be critical of his learned Spanish forebears. Having acknowledged the intellectual vibrance of Spanish Jewry, he becomes coy, particularly as regards the orientation of Spanish Jewry's most profound thinkers, the philosophers. He appears to view medieval philosophy as a discipline devoid of practical import and therefore of limited relevance for someone who wished to be identified as a quintessential modern Jew and not simply a vestige of the Middle Ages or ancient Judaism. With the exception of Maimonides, he sees the medieval philosophers as abstract thinkers, unconcerned with the quotidian world, and lacking interest or learning in the Talmud. They appear as the kind of individuals who lack the impulse and training to pursue what is truly important to Geiger: recovering the legal-historical context in which Judaism developed over its lengthy history.

For Geiger, a proper understanding of Jewish beliefs and practices requires taking measure of the environment in which they unfolded. That holds true not only for later Jewish experience, but for the biblical period as well. Geiger, who was familiar with and sympathetic to the broad outlines of higher biblical criticism, saw the history of the Hebrew scripture as interwoven with the history of its people. And so he regarded the biblical text as a response to historical exigencies, rather than the product of a single sublime revelation. Accepting that, he thought it possible for learned scholars to reconstruct the inner history of Israel's faith from the external history of the biblical text. But the Bible is not Geiger's main concern. It is the literary output of the rabbis and the environment in which rabbinic texts unfolded that holds his utmost attention. For it is the world of the rabbis that continued to dominate the outlook and behavior of contemporaneous Jewry entering the modern age.

The contextualization of rabbinic sources is no mere intellectual exercise. For Geiger, the proper understanding of Jewish beliefs and practices enables the truly modern Jew to restructure Jewish life by retaining, in reshaped form, useful ideas and practices of the past. At the same time, Geiger enjoins us to abandon what may have been the useful creation of a former time and place, but which in his age would have been regarded by himself and other German reformers as anachronisms. The reform platform called for Jews to become an accepted religious group within an all-embracing German society, as opposed to an alien nation subject to degradation because of its vestigial markers of difference. Judaism was to be regarded as a religion bearing universal values, applicable in any given place or time, rather than the ideological and ritual relic of earlier Jewish particularism. And so Geiger is uncomfortable with the Middle Ages, even the relatively tolerant milieu that has come to be described as the Jewish-Muslim symbiosis. Judaism's past can provide much food for thought and useful modes of behavior. But for Geiger, not even the best of times past are templates with which to create the present, the positive experiences of Muslim Spain notwithstanding.[24]

Because of his abiding passion for reforming contemporary Jewish life, Geiger's intellectual pursuits were confined primarily to the history of Jewish law and institutions.[25] As regards Islam, his literary production never extended much beyond his initial foray into Islamic origins. That is a pity. With his wide Jewish learning and enormous intellectual gifts, he would have had an even more substantial impact in tracing the path of Islamic origins and, more generally, the Jewish influence on Islam, especially as numerous and rich sources, Muslim and Jewish, were brought to light in the decades following his early work on Muhammad and the Qur'an. Had he devoted himself to more strictly defined Islamic themes, there is every likelihood that his contributions would have been equally pathbreaking. However, our concern here is not with that which might have been, but that which was.[26]

Positivism and Philology

I referred earlier to the naïvety of the early orientalists and the judgmental tone with which they discussed Muhammad and the origins of Islam. One should not be misled by this seemingly harsh assessment of Geiger and the nineteenth-century scholars who followed in his path. The search for the Jewish origins of Muslim tradition never was a frivolous enterprise, nor was it fueled by a compulsion to denigrate the achievement of Islam, let alone offend Muslim sensibilities. In attempting to recover the Islamic past, including the life and times of Muhammad, Jewish scholars enthusiastically embraced the general outlook of the modern university and molded it to their own particular concerns. In sum, the orientalists, Jewish and non-Jewish, were consumers of contemporaneous intellectual fashion, much like their critics today. Guided by a positivist outlook, armed with well-honed philological skills, and supremely confident of their research methods, earlier generations of scholars went about the task of stripping sources bare in order to reveal their textual and ideological strata. The purpose of this reductive enterprise was to recover earlier sources and kernels of ideas that had imbedded themselves in new literary environments—in the case of Geiger and his successors, Jewish themes in Muslim texts.

Concurrent with this kind of literary archeology, at which it might be said Geiger was well ahead of his time, there was the perceived need to recreate the past for scholarly rather than narrowly defined parochial needs. The objective, whether realized, or even realizable, was to discover a different culture rather than inscribe contemporary values on it. Some now view this as a vain enterprise. No one is unburdened by cultural baggage, and there is always the danger of recreating the "other" in our own image—or worse yet, in a negative image that suits particular concerns of the moment. That process of self-delusion is often subtle; at times it may even be subconscious. But it is hardly part of a cultural conspiracy, as some critics of the orientalists have claimed.[27]

On the whole, Jewish orientalists studying Islamic civilization were sympathetic to the Muslims and their faith, much more so than Christian scholars of the time. Geiger took the lead in being more gracious to Muhammad than his Christian colleagues, although he made many barbed criticisms of the Muslim prophet and Islam. He considered Muhammad ignorant and incapable of finding easy acceptance among the intelligent and learned. Success came to Muhammad not because of any clarity of vision or extraordinary powers of persuasion, but because contemporaneous Muslims were already predisposed to accept a message which essentially was Judaism recast.[28]

But leaving such views of the Prophet and his faith aside, Geiger's essay stands up, on the whole, surprisingly well, in particular its conceptual framework. That is all the more remarkable, considering that he was a product of the first or second generation of scholars specifically trained to explore the civilization of Islam without the declared intention of disputing Muslim religious claims. Geiger and like-minded Islamicists were in tune with a general drift away from dogmatic theology and its residual effects on historical interpretation and writing. There is also a quality to Geiger's analysis that is well ahead of its time. Even current scholars interested in cultural transmission are likely to find him an interesting read. The general questions that serve as his point of departure for tracing Jewish influence on the Qur'an could have been the foundation of a dissertation prospectus in an *orientalistik seminar* or a Near Eastern studies program well into the 1960s, before the post-modernist assault on the epistemological foundations of literary and historical research made it impolitic to offer confident answers to questions of influence.

Above all, there is Geiger's broad learning in both Jewish and Muslim matters. His erudition at the age of twenty-two is impressive, indeed remarkable for the time in which he wrote. When he entered the prize competition, Geiger had access to and consulted almost all the sources then available in printed editions, as well as important manuscripts. It boggles the imagination to think of what Geiger might have accomplished had he possessed the numerous Muslim and Jewish texts that came to light later in the century, works that are directly relevant to the subject of his enquiry. In any case, his accomplishment represents a milestone in oriental studies, a methodological breakthrough that continues to warrant the attention of modern scholars.

Geiger's Questions

Geiger begins his work on Judaism and Islam with a general observation about the sociology of knowledge. He notes that scholars often grasp intuitively what they later discover to be true as a result of carefully constructed "scientific" projects. Geiger would find strange the contemporary view that intuition itself is culturally constructed, and may thus subvert scientific enquiry, or at least shape research to obtain anticipated or even desired results. In keeping with the emerging mood of the nineteenth century, Geiger has supreme faith in his capacity to move from "correct" intuition to "scientific" understanding. He points out that the thesis of his dissertation, namely that "Mohammed in his Qur'an borrowed much from Judaism as it was presented to him," had long been recognized as probable. As such, Geiger would no doubt have conceded that the thrust of his doctoral thesis, although intuitively correct, was not original. It was left for him to prove, however, that the generally-held supposition of Jewish origins—the view of the Bonn faculty and presumably others as well—was indeed true.

According to Geiger, that could not be done by producing a catalogue of isolated data or by presenting an inventory of apparent adaptations from Judaism (as might have been a scholar's agenda at an earlier time). Rather, he sought to combine the literary facts with a larger picture of the life and times of Muhammad, an approach which could establish probable cause for the borrowing of Jewish themes by furnishing both the need for that borrowing and the means by which it could be accomplished.[29] That is, he applied to the problem of Islamic origins the same conceptual framework that he would later use in his Jewish researches. There can be little doubt that the broad outlines of Geiger's approach to texts and history were already well established even before he completed his doctoral dissertation.

Geiger begins with a series of interrelated questions. Did Muhammad wish to borrow from Judaism? Did the Muslim prophet have a general objective in mind that led him to Judaism as a source of potential religious inspiration? For some modern scholars, an opening gambit that invokes authorial intention is a non-starter. But Geiger, like his nineteenth-century confrères, is made of bolder stuff when it comes to reading texts and cultures. His query would seem to imply that Muhammad consciously looked to the Jews and the Jewish past when establishing his own faith and in formulating a Muslim world view. That he regarded Muhammad and not the Almighty as the author of the Qur'an is self-evident. Indeed Geiger explicitly states it: he refers to Muslim scripture as "his [Muhammad's] book," the product of a seventh-century Arab's literary imagination and oracular skill.[30]

Geiger then asks whether Muhammad could have borrowed from Judaism. Assuming that the Muslim prophet saw some clear advantage in borrowing from the older monotheist faith, did he actually have the means to acquire Jewish tradition, oral or written? And if he did, was he limited in his ability to interrogate Jewish sources? In stating this question as he has, Geiger obviously is laying the groundwork to explain the disparities between the Qur'anic and Jewish exposition of biblical themes, based on Muhammad's learning (or his lack of it, as Geiger is wont to put it). In his later historical essays, Geiger describes the Muslim prophet as an ignoramus lacking a finely tuned mind, a view already established, but in less sharply worded language, in his prizewinning essay. Accordingly, Muhammad had no direct familiarity with Jewish sources and had to rely largely on traditions acquired by way of learned Jewish converts to Islam, figures such as 'Abdallāh ibn Salām, a "legendary" rabbi mentioned in Arabic sources and thus known, however vaguely, to orientalists of the time.[31]

But Geiger recognizes that not all deviations from Jewish tradition stem directly from ignorance or from a smattering of learning acquired from his Jewish informants. A lack of direct familiarity with Jewish sources need not be the only explanation for Muhammad's distorting familiar biblical and rabbinic accounts. Ever reflective, Geiger asks if there could have been reasons for Muhammad to deliberately alter authentic Jewish traditions that he might have acquired, albeit haphazardly, from his learned rabbi-teachers.[32] Even if Muhammad had both the means and broad incentive to make free use of certain Jewish themes, were there not circumstances that could have militated against particular borrowings, or, in any event, limited the extent of what could be borrowed and then safely repeated to a Muslim audience? Put somewhat differently, Geiger assumes that the author of the Qur'an was conscious of the need to Islamize specifically Jewish themes, so as to authenticate his own religious message and establish a new monotheist identity at the expense of his Jewish adversaries. With this last assumption, Geiger raises the larger problem of contextualizing the work held sacred by the Muslims. Or, as he put it: "Was borrowing [from the Jews] compatible with the rest of [Muhammad's] agenda?"[33] The question that has lost none of its force in the ensuing 160 years since it was first formulated.

From the outset, Geiger is aware of the problematic nature of determining religious influence and its measurement. The existence of parallel themes in the Qur'an and Jewish religious texts may be important to any study of Judaism and Islam. But for Geiger it is not, in and of itself, conclusive proof of borrowing, or, in any case, direct borrowing. He recognizes that many religious ideas of a general nature found common expression in the religious environment that gave rise to Islam.[34] Geiger thus allows for a wide variety of possible influences on Muslim scripture. That would have been self-evident to him even after a cursory reading of the Qur'an, which contains many moral aphorisms common to monotheism in general. That being so, it is not that broad monotheist sentiment that excites Geiger's scholarly imagination, but the transfer of specific material from identifiable written sources of Jewish provenance, or from oral traditions supposedly originating in written Jewish texts.

Geiger, aware of the temptation to range far afield in search of sources that will support a presumptive case of borrowing, urges caution to a degree that is unusual for a scholar of his time. He would not have trusted taxonomies of folklore, nor would he have regarded that way of classifying knowledge as particularly useful to his own work. In so many words,

Geiger instructs us to be wary of back projections. Just because literary artifacts of a later period inform our reading of the Qur'an does not mean that the Qur'anic text was inspired by these later sources. In an age that had invested much effort in linking fairy tales and myths of highly disparate cultures, Geiger was not one to have concluded that all of history, myth, and literature is a variation of Cinderella and the story of the Flood, told and retold again and again.[35]

For Geiger, texts and the ideas that emerge from texts are the products of a particular location and age, and are governed by specific historical circumstances, as for example is the prodigious intellectual output of the Jews in Muslim Spain, to which he referred in his later essays.[36] Muhammad's Qur'an therefore should be regarded as a response to the historical contingencies of the moment. Charting responses to historical contingency was the larger agenda of *Wissenschaft des Judentums,* which emerged a decade of so before young Geiger earned his doctorate.[37] And so, in thinking about Geiger and his work on Islamic origins, we are forced to reflect about Geiger the Jew as well as Geiger the Islamicist. Arabists who retain interest in Geiger do so because of his essay, his only Islamicist project. But can we really understand that project without the larger Jewish context that informs it? I refer not only to Geiger's intimate acquaintance with traditional Jewish sources, which is evident everywhere in his essay and which has always been appreciated by scholars, Jewish and non-Jewish alike. I refer also to the substantive changes taking place among enlightened Jews influenced by the liberating impulse of the "Science of Judaism"—Jews who, like Geiger, were captivated by the possibility of adapting their ancient faith to the contingencies of the modern. From that perspective, Geiger's study of the origins of Islam and his lifelong project to Reform Judaism are intertwined in a single intellectual construct.

Here too we are obliged to entertain a question of cultural influence, although it seems to have escaped the attention of scholars who write of modern Jewish history and thought. What, if any, is the relationship between Geiger's dissertation on Islamic origins, and the conceptual underpinnings of his reformist enterprise, a project which demands at every step a scientific explanation of Jewish origins?

Both projects are comparative and begin with the *sitz im leben* of texts. Geiger is well aware that it is often difficult to establish a context for a particular verse or series of verses in the Qur'an, let alone track possible Jewish influences. To narrow the odds against interpretive error, he was reluctant, at the outset, to rely on later sources, be they Jewish or Muslim. Rather, he chose to base his analysis of Muslim scripture on traditions that would have been known to Muhammad's Jewish informants and, therefore, available to Muhammad himself, most likely in fragmentary form.[38] The initial search for Jewish influences was thus confined to material in the Bible and Talmud, canonical and widely studied sources before the advent of Islam, as well as various *midrashim*. The midrashic sources were presumably the likes of the *Tanhuma*, a text that may be concurrent with Muhammad's mission, and the *Targum Sheni* to the Book of Esther, a well-known work which informs Geiger's analysis of the Qur'anic story of Solomon and the Queen of Sheba.[39] He does not mention the great Bible commentaries of the Middle Ages; even the earliest of these works was composed long after the Qur'an. It is of course true that the medieval commentaries contain older material, but much of that material would have been known to Geiger through his talmudic studies. He is also hesitant as regards some interesting passages in later *midrashim*, such as the *Pirke de Rabbi Eliezer* and the *Sefer ha-Yashar*, as he cannot date those passages with absolute certainty.[40] Geiger did not have access to the vast body of midrashic literature that came to light only later in the century.

Geiger also worked with a limited number of Arabic sources, partly because the corpus of materials then available was scant and partly because he applied the same rules of evidence to Muslim as well as Jewish writings. That is to say, he was reluctant to use later Islamic sources to recover the original meaning of the Qur'an, a task made all the more difficult because no known Arabic prose texts predate or are contemporaneous with Muslim scripture. Not about to shape his research to fit the contours of later Muslim writings, Geiger began his project "with the bare Arabic text of the Qur'an... and an intimate acquaintance with Judaism and its writings." The only non-Qur'anic Muslim material that he used at this stage was a hand copy of some passages from Bayḍāwī's commentary, a gift from his mentor Freytag. The passages from the manuscript explicate verses in Surahs 2 and 3, segments of Muslim scripture that presumably drew Geiger's attention because they encompass so many Jewish themes.

One should not conclude from Geiger's reluctance to use post-Qur'anic sources that he dismisses out of hand the insights of later generations of scholars. He would be the last to claim that understanding the past is possible only for those who actually experienced it. If that were so, he would have been forced to question his own views about the Qur'an, to say nothing of the manner in which he privileged his reading of Jewish sources. The recovery of contemporaneous meaning from ancient texts and institutions was the foundation of the reformist agenda, the driving force of Geiger's life, even as a young man. It is hardly disrespect for later Muslim writers and their views that occasions Geiger to reject them at the outset of his research. Rather, he wanted first to test the waters of his investigation by relying on original sources and the keenness of his own scholarly intuition. As with Jewish accounts, he preferred not to be influenced by commentary that postdated the primary sources, which in this study meant Muhammad and his informants. Explaining his initial decision to exclude later Muslim sources from consideration, Geiger declares: "I thus had the advantage of an unbiased mind; on the one hand of not seeing the passages [of the Qur'an] through the lenses of Arab commentators [save the fragments from Bayḍāwī], nor, on the other of finding in the Qur'an the views of the Arab dogmatists"—that is, the later religious establishment of theologians and jurists, Muslim analogs to the rabbis whose influence Geiger sought to counter by way of reform.[41] Only after the dissertation was completed did he turn to later Arabic sources, which confirmed for him many of his insights.

The Limits of a Method

But insight can be a very dicey business, particularly for a person of Geiger's manifest confidence. He may have been a model of circumspection when compared to many of his contemporaries, but most of today's scholars would be cautious where Geiger is bold. When he does cite later Arabic sources, his arguments resemble the commentaries themselves: forced attempts at supporting problematic assertions. For example, Geiger is doubtless correct in assuming that Muhammad's knowledge of Judaism was acquired by way of oral traditions, rather than any direct familiarity with written sources. But the path of that acquisition is anything but clear. Perhaps there really was an 'Abdallāh ibn Salām and a coterie of other rabbis who bore responsibility for instructing Muhammad in Jewish lore.[42] A supposition of Jewish informants hardly taxes credulity. Indeed, Muslim exegetes also assume that the Prophet had access to Jewish tradition, although from their perspective this alleged link could not be the source of his divinely revealed message. Nevertheless, the

Qur'anic evidence cited by Geiger for the historicity of 'Abdallāh ibn Salām and, beyond that, his alleged role in instructing the Prophet, is anything but convincing.[43]

Muslim scripture seeks to combat polytheist assertions that Muhammad's message is not God's revelation but information obtained from a human teacher relying on non-Arab sources. At one point it proclaims: "We know that they [the polytheists] say, 'It is a man [not God] who teaches him [i.e. Muhammad to compose the Qur'an].' The tongue [of the man] to which they hint is foreign; but this [Qur'an] is Arabic pure and clear [hence proof of its Arab origins and by extension its divine source]."[44] Clearly, the verse begs for explication. Who, if anyone, is the alleged teacher and what is the foreign tongue referred to by the polytheists in their vain attempt to discredit Allah's chosen messenger and his divinely inspired preaching? Geiger, who in this matter sides with the polytheists in denying that Muslim scripture is God's revealed word, understood the verse as showing "plainly that this man was a Jew."[45] The foreign tongue was presumably Hebrew and/or Jewish Aramaic. Turning then to later Qur'an commentary, he asserts that his (own intuitive) understanding of the text is in fact supported by the Muslim commentators, who "take this view [of the polytheists] and indeed think that it was [a reference] to 'Abdallāh ibn Salām."[46]

But it hardly follows that the Qur'anic verse refers explicitly to such a rabbi or indeed to any other teacher of Jewish descent. Nor is there a compelling reason to believe that the traditions, which Muhammad was accused of having learned, were understood by Muslims as having originally been in Hebrew or Aramaic. Nor, for that matter, do Muslim exegetes unequivocally link the mysterious informant of Qur'an 16:105 with Geiger's favored candidate, 'Abdallāh ibn Salām. Snippets of commentary to this enigmatic verse were well known among European scholars long before Geiger. The Qur'an translation by George Sale (ca. 1697–1736), which appeared a century prior to Geiger's essay, draws heavily on fragments from that Muslim interpretive tradition.[47] In a footnote to this verse, Sale refers to various individuals thought by Muslim scholars to have been the informant cited by the polytheists in their false accusation. Some of the figures proposed by the Muslim scholars are clearly Christians, their "foreign tongue" presumably neither Hebrew nor Jewish Aramaic. Indeed, there is no claim among the commentators known to Sale that the unnamed informant of this verse is in fact 'Abdallāh ibn Salām. When Sale introduces him, he does so not on the basis of Muslim commentary, but Christian sources attempting to implicate the Jews in the fabrication of a debased Muslim scripture. Geiger was surely well aware of Sale, and while he may not have actually used Sale's translation in writing his essay, he should have been, and no doubt was, familiar with the Arabic sources that Sale cited a century earlier. It would appear that Geiger's confidence in his own intuition was so strong as to shade his later analysis of the sources.

There are, to be sure, references in Muslim Qur'an commentary which do link 'Abdallāh ibn Salām and various learned rabbis to Muhammad and the rise of Islam. Geiger draws attention to them in order to support his view of Jewish influence on Muslim scripture. The Qur'an states: "Indeed, it [word of Muhammad's futurc revelation] is [mentioned] in the scriptures *(zubūr)* of ancient peoples. Was [reference to] it not [given as] a sign to them, so that the learned among the Israelites might know [of] it?"[48] The Qur'an thus argues that proof of Muhammad's prophethood was accessible to Jews who had expert knowledge of their own tradition. Those Jews are identified in the Qur'an commentary cited by Geiger as being five in number: Ibn Yāsīn; Tha'labah; Asad; Usayd; and the ubiquitous 'Abdallāh ibn Salām.[49]

It does not necessarily follow, however, that the Muslim commentary is itself free of tendentious shaping. At face value, the Qur'anic verse castigates the Jews (and also Christians) for not accepting Muhammad, even though their own scriptural tradition contains hints of his future coming. Muslim commentators moved the argument a step further. By giving identities to various Jewish rabbis who supported the Prophet, based on evidence implanted by God in Jewish tradition, they indicted all the other learned Jews who could and should have done the same, but refused to do so. The failure of these other Jews to follow suit and declare the authenticity of Muhammad's mission therefore arose not of ignorance but of a knowing disregard for their own sacred writings.[50] Faced with a need to identify Jews faithful to their tradition who converted to Islam, the Muslim exegetes merely rounded up the usual suspects, with the fabled 'Abdallāh ibn Salām in the lead. It is, if nothing else, quite a stretch for Geiger to accept Muslim commentary as definitive in this instance. But, having committed himself to the thesis that 'Abdallāh ibn Salām and some other rabbis were in fact Muhammad's informants, references to unnamed persons in enigmatic verses take on a clarity which is unwarranted. Again, there is no reason for current scholars to deny outright the existence of an 'Abdallāh ibn Salām or of other rabbis who might have served as conduits of Jewish learning for the Muslim prophet. But the evidence cited by Geiger—with characteristic forcefulness—is not likely to convince a skeptical audience of contemporary scholars.

Medieval Muslim authorities were very much concerned that Jewish materials had percolated into Islamic tradition, and they engaged one another in a lively debate as to the consequences of such borrowing.[51] There is no indication in Geiger's essay that he heard echoes of that debate, which was uncovered by a later generation of Jewish orientalists with access to more Muslim sources. But no Muslim writer, regardless of place or time, would have entertained the notion that the Qur'an itself was composed by Muhammad, let alone that he did so relying on Jewish informants. When Geiger speaks of having his insights confirmed by studying the later Muslim authorities, he refers to philological and literary observations gleaned from their works, and not to any Muslim discussion of Jewish influence on the development of the Qur'an.

The German version of the Latin dissertation relies on a number of sources that postdate Muslim scripture.[52] These include fragments of unedited Qur'an commentary; the chronicle of Abū al-Fidā'; and various Arabic texts that had been published in collections such as Bartholomé d'Herbelot's *Bibliothèque orientale*. Geiger was, of course, unable to benefit from literally thousands of Islamic manuscripts that have since come to light. He had none of the biographical literature on Muhammad and his times *(sīrah* and *ṭabaqāt),* nor the great chronicle of Ṭabarī which draws heavily upon that literature. Nor did he have access to the large body of *isrā'īlīyyāt,* Islamic tales of the ancient Israelites that are scattered throughout Arabic religious literature and belles-lettres. We can only speculate as to what Geiger might done had he had access to these materials which later came to light.

Geiger was very much a product of his own place and time: intellectually critical if not wary, but quite certain of his own judgement and therefore more than willing to take on heroic projects demanding broad conclusions—the kind of scholarship that today inspires extreme caution among Islamicists. As did many orientalists of the nineteenth century, he underestimated the elusiveness of his evidence and the complexities of recovering a remote past, that history which for Geiger was essential to understanding any civilization and its cultural artifacts. All his caveats aside, Geiger does not appear to have fully appreciated the dilemma forced upon him by his ambitious scholarly agenda. For Geiger, texts and religious institutions became truly understandable only when exposed to the full light of history, but our knowledge of worlds far removed from us in place and time is more often than not dependent on the written word itself. Even today, the origins of Islam remain shrouded in obscurity because the sole source of contemporaneous documentation is the Qur'an. And while later Muslim sources may well contain genuine echoes of Muhammad's activities and views, the historiography of early Islam is so tendentious as to render many if not all modern judgements shaky at best.

Bold Speculations

Still, it is the Qur'an that is the fulcrum of Geiger's investigation, and the book revered by Muslims is sufficiently rich in allusions to Jewish cultural artifacts to allow Geiger informed speculations about Muhammad's acquired Jewish learning, Muslim scripture, and borrowings from Judaism—or, as current scholars might put it, statements in the Qur'an that suggest links to Jews and the Jewish tradition.

For Geiger, the proof of Jewish influence on Muhammad must be grounded in two sets of facts. The first, quite obviously, is that which allows us to demonstrate that the artifact allegedly borrowed is of Jewish rather than Christian or ancient Arabian origin. For that, Geiger relied on his prodigious knowledge of Jewish sources (and a confidence in his scholarly intuition).

The second set of facts establishes a presumptive case for the alleged borrowing—a probable cause for integrating elements of other religions into an emergent Islam. He assumes that certain ideas are absorbed by a religious culture because of a proclivity or openness to the concepts of another culture. For the borrowers, these concepts may be radically new ideas, or ideas loosely linked to existing concepts of their own, which however are not yet concrete and therefore lack formal expression. These older concepts, already found in the host culture, then take definitive shape under the influence of foreign intervention. In such fashion, vague Arabian tendencies towards monotheism may have been be recast as complex religious doctrine. Or, put somewhat differently, the formulation of doctrine and legal rules in the Qur'an was dependent in a marked way on cultural borrowing from intellectually more mature religious traditions (of which Jewish tradition was, in Geiger's eyes, clearly the most sublime, and a likely avenue of influence). There were also specific reasons to borrow from monotheist traditions of the past. Geiger suggests a perceived need to legitimize the Prophet and his mission and, related to that, to appeal to the constituents of the larger monotheist community whose support he coveted.[53]

Geiger's hunt for links to older Jewish forms begins with tracking the vocabulary of Muslim scripture.[54] In Geiger's view, such new ideas are expressed through technical terms traceable to the primary culture, the source of the borrowing. So he reads the Qur'an with the aim of isolating words freighted with religious significance, terms which are not derived from Arabic but are rather Hebrew and Aramaic loan words originating in Jewish tradition. His list includes: *tābūt* (ark; Hebrew *tayva*): *tawrāt* (Torah), *jannah* (Paradise; Hebrew *gan* [*'eden*]); *jahannam* (Hell; Hebrew *gehennom*); *sabt* (Sabbath); *sakīnah* (divine presence or guidance; Hebrew *shekhinah*), and so on. Such words are pregnant with all sorts of religious connotations, certainly Jewish, but Christian as well, as Geiger concedes. But there are also Qur'anic words derived from Hebrew and Aramaic that are without a clearly defined religious connotation. There also words of Christian (Syriac) provenance. What then does Geiger's discussion of loan words tell us of a particular Jewish influence on Muslim scripture? The technical vocabulary cited by him and others may indeed allude to some acquired knowledge of Judaism (and also Christianity) but is that always a reflection of conscious borrowing? If so, to what purpose?

Geiger would have us believe Muhammad deliberately borrowed from the Jews to legitimize his monotheist enterprise.[55] That is, he went back to the mother of all monotheist faiths. But he could have turned elsewhere. Many religious ideas were common currency in the Arabian peninsula, there having been a powerful Christian as well as a Jewish presence in the region. Yet despite their obvious importance, neither the Christian nor the ancient Arab civilizations command Geiger's attention. He is aware that in order to make the certain claim for Jewish influence, he has to deny the probability or even possibility of Christian or indigenous Arab influences: "For [a] complete discussion... it would be necessary to write [additional] treatises to the one in which I am now engaged...the respective subjects would be (1) the points of contact between Islam and the ancient tradition of the Arabs, and (2) the points of contact between Islam and Christianity; only in this way could certainty on [Jewish influence] be attained."[56] But that is not how Geiger defines his mandate. Indeed, he goes on to say that such projects would lead him too far afield and, in any case, his methods allow him to demonstrate with scholarly accuracy the Jewish influence on the formation of the Qur'an, meaning religious concepts of Muslim scripture that are linked to the Jewish faith and those historical narratives of the Qur'an that are linked to the Jewish past.

But in drawing links between the Qur'an and Judaism, how useful is it to cite, as does Geiger, evidence from normative rabbinic sources? Arabian Judaism might have been quite eclectic and less informed by formal learning than the faith practiced in the Land of Israel and Babylonia, the major centers of Jewish settlement. Geiger himself describes Arabian Jewry, albeit in a later essay, as being situated far off in a corner (of the Jewish world), without a highly developed intellectual culture and without substantive knowledge of the Law. He then goes on to state that Arabian Jews had receded into the background of Jewish existence and so lived out their entire lives in obscurity.[57] It comes as no surprise that current scholars are somewhat less certain than the learned Geiger as to what Muhammad might have borrowed, and in what form, from Jews living in the Arabian environment of the time.[58]

Still, Geiger is no doubt right when he assumes that the Muslim prophet was aware of rabbinic sources (presumably filtered through the oral traditions of local Jewry). Does it necessarily follow, however, that Muhammad borrowed from the Jews specifically to address Jewish audiences, the proposed rationale for adopting Jewish artifacts? When Geiger writes, "It is evident that Muhammad sought to win the Jews to his side, and this could best be done by approximating their religious views," he clearly suggests that, at the outset of his dealings with the Jews, the Prophet regarded them as natural allies.[59] That is, from Muhammad's perspective, the Jewish tribes of the Hijaz had been prepped to accept his mission by teachings that emanated from their own prophets, who like himself were God's messengers.

Many Qur'anic passages connect Muhammad and the Muslims with the ancient Israelites and their spiritual leaders. Time and again, Muhammad is declared the last and strongest link in a chain of monotheist prophets that includes Moses and other biblical figures. Muhammad's prophetic vocation and its links to the Israelite past, so clearly enunciated in the Qur'an, are the fulcrum of Muslim belief and permeate later Muslim writing as well. The legitimation of Muhammad's prophethood is a ubiquitous theme of Qur'an commentary and of the extensive Islamic literature on biblical events and *dramatis personae*—

a body of texts subsumed under the rubric *isrā'īlīyyāt,* "Israelitica." With such declared linkages to the Israelite past, the Prophet could make claims on the allegiance of his Jewish neighbors. From the Muslim point of view, only ignorant Jews or those deliberately recalcitrant would have rejected Muhammad's call, rooted as it was in a tradition and past revered by the Jews themselves.[60]

But is there a necessary link between the expected conversion of the Jews and the Hebrew and Aramaic loan words that form part of the religious vocabulary of the Qur'an? Or does the use of such terms in Muslim scripture merely reflect the assimilation of Jewish artifacts that were part of a loosely defined monotheist milieu, a milieu which spread in time to western Arabia where there was a certain receptivity to monotheist ideas? For Geiger the question is not moot.

Having considered a concept as borrowed from Judaism if the technical terms expressing that concept are of Jewish origins,[61] Geiger turns to establishing the Jewish underpinnings of Muhammad's broader religious outlook, specifically, the Qur'anic positions on creed and doctrine, moral and legal rules, and, more generally, the Prophet's views on life.[62] He admits that determining the Jewish influence on Muhammad's view of the world, and the rules that govern Muslim behavior, is more complicated than analyzing vocabulary. Geiger is aware that certain general points of belief and behavior are common in different religious societies. Therefore, the expression of such beliefs in both Judaism and Islam is, in and of itself, no certain proof of borrowing. One must not only prove, through detailed references to Jewish sources, that an idea found in the Qur'an is rooted in Judaism. One must also show that this idea, as expressed in Islamic garb, is "in harmony with the spirit of Judaism" and is utterly inexplicable without its Jewish referent.[63] As previously noted, Geiger is very well aware that cardinal points of faith passed from Judaism to Christianity, so that one must be cautious as to whether these points as adopted in the Qur'an are, in fact, directly borrowed from the oldest of the monotheist faiths or from the daughter religion. As he puts it: "To decide whether these (cardinal) points... in the Qur'an have come from the Jews or from the Christians, we must direct our special attention to a comparison between the forms in which the beliefs are held in both religions, and the form in which they are presented to us by Muhammad."[64]

Current scholars will applaud Geiger's epistemological concerns and his stated caution. On the other hand, the evidence he chooses to illuminate the origins of Muslim doctrine seems to force the issue. What Geiger declares a direct borrowing from Jewish doctrinal property may belong, in fact, to a wider monotheist domain. For example, his contention that the unity of God was at that time found only in Judaism and Islam may receive oblique support from Muslim scripture, which chides Christians for their trinitarian views. But that hardly means Muhammad's pronouncements on Allah's unity were taken over directly and deliberately from the Jews and Judaism. The notion of a single, indivisible, and all-powerful deity was not necessarily foreign to the Arabian peninsula, a region far less remote and culturally isolated than popularly believed in Geiger's time. Along with residual beliefs in paganism, monotheist notions were very much in the air.

Regarding other doctrinal themes, Geiger similarly strains his evidence of Jewish influence. Among the alleged talmudic parallels to Qur'anic doctrine cited by him, there is not a single text that necessarily suggests direct cultural borrowing. Juxtaposing Geiger's talmudic references with citations from Muslim scripture, cautious scholars will be hard-pressed to conclude that Muhammad had a direct familiarity, even by way of oral tradition, with particular rabbinic passages. The operative words here are direct and particular. In each case cited by Geiger, there may have been an indirect Jewish influence, although the course of that alleged influence is anything but certain. And it is not always clear that Geiger is speaking of a direct and conscious borrowing from Judaism, or that he merely wishes to suggest a Jewish substratum to Muslim scripture—that is, a kind of subtext which can be recovered when the Qur'an is properly interrogated by a scholar of critical intelligence and broad learning in Jewish and oriental studies—such as Geiger himself.

Parallels in Practice

A more persuasive case can be made for linking the legal discussion of the Qur'an to actual Jewish customs and practices and, by implication, to the anticipated winning of Jewish support. Given the proximity of the Jews, especially after the emigration to Medina, the Prophet undoubtedly observed them practicing their religion firsthand. The endorsement of the fast of Yom Kippur, the setting of the orientation of prayer to Jerusalem, and fixing the initial daily cycle of prayer to reflect morning, afternoon, and evening worship, as in Judaism, most likely reflect a direct borrowing from the older monotheist faith, if not a deliberate attempt to influence Jews to accept the authenticity of the Prophet's mission. That is the view of most orientalists and subsequent historians.

Yet the Jews continued to resist Muhammad and his message, and so the concessions were withdrawn. The orientation of prayer was changed in the direction of Mecca, and the daily prayers were increased to five in number. The fast of Yom Kippur was superseded by the monthly celebration of Ramadan, and became for Muslims a commendable rather than obligatory act. Oddly enough, these proposed borrowings from Judaism are not mentioned at all by Geiger, even though they fulfill all his concerns for establishing a case of cultural transference. They are manifest during the Prophet's lifetime, they are most assuredly Jewish in origin, they are only comprehensible through their Jewish referent, and they are explicable as incentive for conversion of the Jews.[65]

Perhaps these borrowings seemed too mundane to merit Geiger's attention. With his great command of Jewish law, he focuses on less obvious connections.[66] Jews and Muslims alike pray while standing, but allow also for other positions. He notes that in both faiths, prayer while intoxicated was explicitly prohibited (Muslims, as opposed to Jews, later forbade intoxicants in all places and at all times). In both faiths, ritual ablutions are required before praying, but when water is unavailable, sand may be used for purification, an obvious concession to Jewish and Muslim travellers in desolate areas. Moreover, for Jews and Muslims, proper decorum requires that the worshippers follow a middle course between loud declarations and completely silent prayer. Geiger also observes the strong links between Jewish and Muslim family law, suggesting that Qur'anic legislation may be connected to Jewish practice. Among Jews and Muslims, divorced women must wait three months before remarrying; Jewish and Muslim mothers alike are obliged to nurse their children for fixed periods of time. For Jewish women, the prescribed time is two years; for Muslims it is the same if one factors in the period of a short-term pregnancy given at half a year.

Some of Geiger's proposed links seem less secure. He refers, for example, to Muslim and Jewish regulations for establishing the break between night and day for ritual purposes. Be it for fasting (Islam) or offering prayers (Judaism), the break is determined by whether or not there is sufficient light by which to distinguish a dark-colored thread (blue in Judaism, black in Islam) from one which is white.[67] There is also the regulation obliging men who have touched women to wash with water before saying their prayers, and the preference for congregational worship as against individual devotions.[68] But such practices may reflect customs widely practiced among many peoples of the region.

The most interesting links between Jewish and Muslim legal regulations are those Jewish customs and practices that were consciously rejected by Muhammad in an effort to create sacred space for the nascent Muslim community. Geiger cites a number of Qur'anic passages which offer Muslims a lighter obligation than that prescribed by Jewish custom and law.[69] Muslims fast from sunrise to sunset; Jews from sunset to sunset. Thus, it is legal for Muslims to have intercourse with their wives on the night preceding the fast, which for Jews marks the actual beginning of the fast day. Similarly, Muslims were allowed greater license than Jews to take pleasure from their women. As the Qur'an put it: "Your wives are your lands for plowing; so plow them as you wish."[70] According to biblical law, a woman who has been divorced, remarried, and then divorced again, cannot be united in marriage once more with her former husband. On the other hand, a Muslim man who has twice divorced his wife may remarry her if she has been married to another man and subsequently divorced by him.[71]

For Geiger, the clearest examples that Muhammad had firsthand knowledge of Jewish legal practice are his pronouncements on dietary restrictions.[72] He notes that the Qur'an refers explicitly to biblical laws in listing foods that are prohibited to the Jews: "For those who followed the Jewish law we forbade every animal without cloven hoof; and we forbade them the fat of the ox and the sheep, except that which comes from their backs or their entrails or is connected with a bone."[73] Elsewhere, the Qur'an, in keeping with Jewish practice, forbids carrion, swine, blood, and that which has been sacrificed to a false god.[74] As among Jews, meat must be properly slaughtered. It is thus forbidden to eat animals killed by strangulation or the blow of an ax, or dead animals killed by a fall from a mountain, or gored by another animal, or torn by wild beasts.[75] On the whole, Muslim dietary regulations were far less stringent than those of the Hebrew Bible, let alone talmudic law.[76] The Jews no doubt regarded Muhammad's dietary practices as lax in comparison with God's ordinances. The disparity between Jewish and Muslim dietary practices had to be a source of friction between the two communities, as Jews could not easily break bread with their Muslim neighbors. The Qur'an's response was to claim that the more prohibitive Jewish dietary laws were God's punishment for the iniquities of those who observed them.[77] In sum, as regards legal customs and practices, there is no question of a profound Jewish influence on the formation of Islam, as Geiger demonstrates.

The Biblical Narratives

Geiger's greatest contribution in this study is, without question, his analysis of the "Old Testament" narratives of the Qur'an: those stories in Muslim scripture that are loosely based on the Hebrew Bible.[78] Given his great command of rabbinic sources, Geiger is able to link the Qur'anic narratives not only to the biblical text but to the various permutations of biblical themes in Jewish legendary literature. He has no doubt that the "biblical" narratives of Muslim scripture are, in fact, derived from Jewish sources, even though Christians privilege the Old Testament.[79]

Geiger's analysis of the Qur'anic narratives is a subject that deserves separate and detailed treatment. Suffice it to say, Geiger regarded Muhammad as incapable of interrogating Jewish sources at first hand. It was through a folkloric oral tradition that the Muslim prophet and his followers grasped the sublime history of God's chosen people. He grants that the Qur'anic versions of the biblical past have an undeniable charm. The stories appealed to the Muslim prophet's poetic fancy, and their fairy-tale quality suited the intellectual level of his contemporaries. There is, to be sure, a dismissive tone to Geiger's comments.[80] A century and a half of subsequent scholarship have made scholars interested in the Jewish foundations of Islam a good deal more cautious than was Geiger about claims for borrowed cultural artifacts and, more generally, the complex processes of cultural transmission.

When Nöldeke mentioned Geiger in his monumental *Geschichte des Qôrans*, he wondered why the rabbis of the generation that followed Geiger did not take up the challenge of pursuing the line of research that Geiger had so ably opened.[81] Implicit in Nöldeke's query is an awareness that a more profound understanding of Islamic origins must rest, however schematically, on a deep familiarity with Judaism and the sources of its tradition.

Notes

1. *Was hat Mohammed aus dem judenthume aufgenommen? Eine von der Königl. Preussischen Rheinuniversität gekrönte Preisschrift* (Bonn: F. Baaden, 1833); English trans., *Judaism and Islam,* trans. F.M. Young (Madras: Printed at the M.D.C.S.P.C.K. Press, 1898) and reprinted (New York: Ktav Publishing House, 1970) with an introduction by Moshe Pearlman (Perlmann). The translation is cited throughout as *Judaism and Islam.*

2. Reviews of this work are listed in Victor Chauvin, *Bibliographie des ouvrages arabes ou relatifs aux Arabes publiés dans l'Europe chrétienne de 1810 à 1885*, 12 vols. (Liege and Leipzig: H. Vaillant-Carmanne, 1892–1922), 10:4–5. See also Gustav Pfänmuller, *Handbuch der Islam.-Literatur* (Berlin: W. de Gruyter, 1923), 98ff.
3. *Geschichte des Qôrans*, ed. Friedrich Schwally (2d. ed.; Leipzig: T. Dieter, 1909–38), 208 ff. Retains Nöldeke's remarks originally published in the Göttingen edition of 1860.
4. Hubert Grimme in *Orientalistische Literaturzeitung* 7 (1904): 226ff.; J.H. in *Zeitschrift für die hebräische Bibliographie* 6 (1903): 10.
5. Heinrich Speyer, *Die biblischen Erzählungen im Qoran* (Berlin, 1931; repr. Hildesheim: G. Olms, 1961), vii–viii.
6. An appreciation of Geiger that appeared after his death was that of his close friend, the Semiticist Joseph Derenbourg (Dernburg), *Abraham Geiger* (Paris, 1875). The most detailed evaluation of Geiger's life and works remains the volume assembled by his son Ludwig with the collaboration of various leading figures from the world of German-Jewish scholarship on the centennial anniversary of Geiger's birth. See Ludwig Geiger et al., *Abraham Geiger: Leben und Lebenswerk* (Berlin: G. Reimer, 1910). The early years of his life are discussed in the biographical section written by his son. See 5–19 for his early years at Frankfurt, Heidelberg and Bonn. Note also the later work of Max Wiener which was translated into English as *Abraham Geiger and Liberal Judaism* (Philadelphia: Jewish Publication Society of America, 1962). Wiener's book consists of a short biography followed by excerpts from Geiger's correspondence, works, sermons and lead articles. Quite a bit of Geiger's work was published after his death by his son Ludwig as *Abraham Geigers Nachgelassene Schriften*, 8 vols. (Berlin: Louis Gerschel, 1875–78). Commemorating the centennial of Geiger's death, the Hebrew Union College–Jewish Institute of Religion held a colloquium. The papers were subsequently edited by Jakob J. Petuchowski as *New Perspectives on Abraham Geiger* (New York: Hebrew Union College, 1975).
7. The rabbinical years prior to his permanent position in Breslau are discussed in *Leben und Werke*, 19–49; the years when he was firmly established at Breslau, 50–174. For a broad background of the times, see Ismar Schorsch, *From Text to Context* (Hanover, N.H.: University Press of New England, 1994).
8. *Das Judenthum und seine Geschichte*. 2 vols. in 1 (2d ed.; Breslau: Schletter, 1865, 1871). A less than adequate English translation by Charles Newburgh was reprinted as *Judaism and its History in Two Parts* (Hanover, N.H.: University Press of America, 1985). Citations are to the English translation; at times I emend the translation so as to render it more idiomatic. As regards the aforementioned quote, see *Judaism and its History*, 354 ff. The general

tone of Geiger's comments about Islam throughout this work is nevertheless quite harsh and at times all too dismissive, however much he seeks to distance himself from contemporaneous criticism of Islam and the Muslims among Europeans. See, for example, chapter 4 entitled "Islam," 247–59.

9. *Journal des Savants* (1835): 162–74.
10. Ibid., 163.
11. *Judaism and Islam*, 24.
12. Ibid. 25.
13. *Journal des Savants* (1835): 164. Silvestre de Sacy also had some substantive criticisms regarding Geiger's use of Jewish technical vocabulary to identify loan words in the Qur'an, a process which Geiger believed demonstrated a direct borrowing from the Jews. See 165ff.
14. See, for example, the review of H.E. (Ehwald) in *Göttingische gelehrte Anzeigen* 1 (1834): 438–40. Contrast that assessment with H.L. Fleischer's more balanced and scholarly review: "Über das Arabische in Dr. Geigers Preisschrift: *Was hat Mohammed aus dem Judentume aufgenommen?*" originally published in 1841 and repr. in his *Kleinere Schriften,* 3 vols. (Leipzig: Hirzl, 1885–88), 2:107–38.
15. Note that Geiger continued to be highly critical of Islam's spiritual component and of the intellectual background of its earliest community even at the time of his later work on Judaism and its history. See n. 8 above.
16. See n. 1 above.
17. A full list of Geiger's publications was compiled by M. Stern in Ludwig Geiger's biography, *Leben und Werke*, 414–70.
18. Among these many works one may cite Max Grünbaum, *Neue Beiträge zur semitischen Sagenkunde* (Leiden: Brill, 1893); Hartwig Hirschfeld, *Jüdische Elemente im Qoran* (Berlin: author, 1878); Israel Schapiro, *Die haggadischen Elemente im erzählenden Teil des Korans* (Berlin: G. Fock, 1907); D. Sidersky, *Les origines des légendes musulmanes dans le Coran* (Paris: Geuthner, 1933); the aforementioned work of Heinrich Speyer (see n. 5 above) ; and more recently Abraham I. Katsh, *Judaism in Islam* (New York: Sepher-Hermon Press, 1980). A contemporary of Geiger, the Islamicist Gustav Weil, wrote *Biblische Legenden der Muselmänner* (Frankfurt a.M.: Literarische Anstalt, 1845); tr. into English as *The Bible, the Koran and the Talmud* (London: Longman, 1846). Unlike Geiger's highly analytical essay, Weil's work is entirely descriptive.
19. I take up these issues in *Demonizing the Queen of Sheba* (Chicago: University of Chicago Press, 1993), esp. chapters 5, 6.
20. Geiger was, to be sure, interested in Jewish philosophers and indeed devoted some attention to them. They were, however, very much secondary to his real interests—the development of Jewish law and ritual practices—as can easily be gleaned from the complete list of his scholarly work. See *Leben*

und Werke, 414–70. The lengthy appreciation of Geiger's research also found in that work (235–400) includes six pieces by eminent scholars. They fall under the rubrics: Introduction; Systemic Theology; Practical Theology; Bible; History (including Jewish history and literature, the history of sects and the development of law [*halacha*], and the exegetical schools of northern France); and Philology (*sprachwissenschaft*). There is no separate listing for philosophy.

21. An extended essay on Judaism in Spain is found in chaps. (lectures) 8–10 of his *Judaism and its History*.
22. Ibid., 352
23. The myth of Sephardic supremacy is dealt with by Schorsch, *From Text to Context*, 71–92.
24. *Judaism and its History*, 340ff.
25. As regards Geiger's historical outlook and his talmudic studies, see the concise and reflective papers of Michael A. Meyer, "Abraham Geiger's Historical Judaism," and David Weiss Halivni, "Abraham Geiger and Talmud Criticism," in *New Perpectives on Abraham Geiger*, 3-16, 31–41. One should note that as regards "Historical Judaism," Geiger and the other children of the Enlightenment were much influenced by similar trends among Christians anxious to discover the historic roots of their faith. Geiger was quite familiar with Christian biblical scholarship and apparently much influenced by it, as can be seen from his later *magnum opus* on the biblical tradition, *Urschrift und Übersetzungen der Bibel in ihrer Abhängigkeit von der inneren Entwicklung des Judentums* (Breslau: J. Hainauer, 1857). For Geiger's interest in biblical scholarship, see Nahum M. Sarna, "Abraham Geiger and Biblical Scholarship," *New Perspectives*, 17–30.
26. Two confidantes from his early years, Joseph Derenbourg (1811–95) and Solomon Munk (1805–67), both pursued academic careers in France. Derenbourg specialized generally in Arabic and Islamics; Munk became the premier scholar of the time in Judeo-Islamic philosophy.
27. See the influential work of Edward Said, *Orientalism* (New York: Pantheon, 1978). The text of the new edition of Said's work is essentially the same. Said apparently is not interested in the Jewish dimension to nineteenth-century scholarship.
28. *Judaism in History*, 252–53 picking up the general thrust of his prizewinning essay.
29. *Judaism and Islam*, 1–2.
30. Ibid., 3–4.
31. Ibid., 17ff.; reiterated in *Judaism and History*, 252ff.
32. *Judaism and Islam,* 21ff.
33. Ibid., 21.
34. Ibid., xxx–xxxi (1970 pagination is followed throughout when referring to the intro.)

35. Ibid., xxxi–xxxii.
36. See n. 21 above.
37. See n. 25 above and Schorsch, *From Text to Context*, 149–205.
38. Refer to nn. 34, 35 above.
39. *Encyclopaedia Judaica*, s.v. "Tanhuma," "Targum Sheni." The dating of both texts is highly problematic. Geiger's use of the *Targum* to explicate the Qur'anic story of Solomon and the Queen of Sheba is found in *Judaism and Islam*, 147ff. For a discussion of Jewish sources and the Qur'anic and later Muslim versions of the Solomonic tale, see Lassner, *Demonizing the Queen of Sheba*. The dating of the *Targum* is discussed on 131–32.
40. The problem of comparing the Qur'an with Jewish midrashic texts is that the dates of the *midrashim* are so uncertain. Moreover, a later midrashic text may preserve material which antedates its composition. Earlier texts may, in turn, feature interpolations composed long after the text was originally formulated. The *Pirke de Rabbi Eliezer* as we presently have it is clearly a composition of Islamic times. It does not necessarily follow, however, that all the material contained therein is of later provenance. Clearly, the safest course to follow as regards paths of Jewish influence is to confine oneself to the Bible and Talmud as Geiger sought initially to do.
41. *Judaism and Islam*, xxxi.
42. See n. 31 above. Regarding Muhammad's Jewish teachers, the standard treatment remains S.D. Goitein's "Mi hayyu rabbotav hamuvhakim shel Muhammad," *Tarbiẓ* 23 (1953): 146–59. See also his "Isra'iliyat," *Tarbiẓ* 6 (1936): 89–101. Note also the work of Moshe Perlmann on early Jewish converts to Islam: "A Legendary Story of Ka'b al-Aḥbār's Conversion to Islam," in *Joshua Starr Memorial Volume* (New York: Conference on Jewish Relations, 1953), 85-99: and his "Another Ka'b al-Aḥbār Story," *Jewish Quarterly Review* (Philadelphia) 45 (1954): 48–51.
43. *Judaism and Islam*, 26ff.
44. Qur'an 16:105.
45. *Judaism and Islam*, 27.
46. Ibid., 27–28.
47. Sale's translation was first published in 1734. The edition I utilized was that introduced by D. Ross and published by Frederick Warne and Co. (London and New York, 1921). The text cited here is p. 267 n. 2. Sale relied heavily on Edward Pococke's *Speciae Historiae Arabum* and Lodovico Marracci's *Alcorani Textus Universus*, both works well known and used by Geiger. For Geiger's Western sources, see *Judaism and Islam*, xxxi–xxxii.
48. Qur'an 26:196, 197.
49. *Judaism and Islam*, 28.
50. This is a common feature of Muslim polemical tradition. A discussion of Muslim polemics can be found in S.D. Goitein, "B'ne Yisrael u-mahloktam," *Tarbiẓ* 6 (1936): 410–22; Jacob Lassner, "The Covenant of the Prophets:

Muslim Texts, Jewish Subtexts," *Association for Jewish Studies Review* 15 (1990): 207–38; idem, "The Origins of Muslim Attitudes Towards the Jews and Judaism," *Judaism* 39 (1990): 498–507; and Moshe Perlmann, "The Medieval Polemics Between Islam and Judaism," in *Religion in a Religious Age*, ed. S.D. Goitein (Cambridge, Mass.: Association for Jewish Studies, 1974).

51. That debate is dicussed in M.J. Kister, "Ḥadditū 'an Banī Isrā'īla walā-ḥaraja: A Study of an Early Tradition," *Israel Oriental Studies* 2 (1972): 215–39.
52. Geiger discusses these sources *en passant* in his preface, xxxi–xxxii.
53. *Judaism and Islam*, 29ff.
54. Ibid., 30–64.
55. Ibid., 21ff.
56. Ibid., 29–30.
57. *Judaism and its History*, 254. These sentiments are also expressed, although somewhat less strongly, in *Judaism and Islam*, 6.
58. On that question, see the introduction to Reuven Firestone, *Journeys in Holy Lands: The Evolution of the Abraham-Ishmael Legends in Islamic Exegesis* (Albany: State University of New York Press, 1990), and Lassner, *Demonizing the Queen*, ch. 6.
59. For Geiger's assessment of Muhammad's relations with the Jews, see *Judaism and Islam*, 4–21.
60. See n. 50 above, esp. Lassner, "The Covenant of the Prophets."
61. *Judaism and Islam*, 30–45.
62. Ibid., 45–73.
63. Ibid., 45–46.
64. Ibid., 46.
65. Geiger refers to these borrowings in his later essays on Jewish history. See *Judaism and its History*, 258–59.
66. *Judaism and Islam*, 64–70.
67. Ibid., 68–69.
68. Ibid., 67–68.
69. Ibid., 157–61.
70. Qur'an 2:223. Muslims stand accused of licentiousness in the polemical literature of both Jews and Christians.
71. Qur'an 2:230, as opposed to Deut. 24:1–4.
72. *Judaism and Islam*, 159.
73. Qur'an 6:147.
74. Qur'an 2:168, 6:146.
75. Qur'an 5:4
76. *Encyclopaedia Judaica*, s.v. "Kashruth."
77. Qur'an 4:158. Although it does not refer specifically to Jewish dietary laws, it is so understood by Muslims.

78. *Judaism and Islam,* 75–156.
79. Ibid., 73–75.
80. See n. 8 above.
81. See n. 3 above.

5

Ignaz Goldziher on Ernest Renan: From Orientalist Philology to the Study of Islam

Lawrence I. Conrad

In 1889, the Eighth International Congress of Orientalists convened in Stockholm, and as the climax of a full and fruitful program King Oscar II of Sweden presented the Congress' Gold Medal to Dr. Ignaz Goldziher (1850–1921). For Goldziher, this was a time of great professional triumph: the first volume of his *Muhammedanische Studien* had just been published and was already being hailed as a masterpiece; the second, the final draft of which he took with him to Stockholm, was eagerly awaited on all sides.[1] Now his peers had collectively recognized his central role in his field. It was also a time for personal stocktaking; only a few months later, on 1 June 1890 (his fortieth birthday), he set down in writing a résumé of his life and career to that point, and then for the next twenty-nine years kept the record up to date with accounts of events of importance or concern to him.[2] Neither he nor his colleagues say so in so many words, but with the benefit of more than a century's hindsight, we are perhaps justified in wondering if already in 1889 he was being recognized as the founder of a new field of scholarship—Arabic and Islamic studies.[3]

Since his death in 1921, this distinction has routinely been conceded as a matter of manifest fact;[4] but while the choice certainly seems to be the obvious one, it is worth asking why Goldziher in particular has been singled out for this honor and what, in specific terms, his contribution was to the creation of this field. It was not, for example, just a matter of an impressive curriculum vitae. Had this been the decisive factor, one might ask why we should not attach similar importance to his older colleague Theodor Nöldeke (1836–1930), who was likewise honored at the Stockholm congress and who had already published his monumental *Geschichte des Qorâns* when Goldziher was only ten years old.[5] In the following remarks, then, I should like to consider the sense in which Goldziher played a founding role in his field and the relation of his Jewish background to his intellectual development and career, with particular reference to his critique of the French historian and philosopher Ernest Renan (1823–92).[6]

It must be stated from the outset that such an enquiry takes one into vexed and complicated territory. On the one hand, this is a topic that falls within the purview of nineteenth-century European intellectual history rather than Arab-Islamic studies. It thus raises such issues as the factors that influence the formation of new fields of scholarly endeavor and why they should assume formal academic form in the first place, the professionalization of scholarship, nationalism and its impact on communal relations in Hungary, and the influence of the Enlightenment on the Jewish communities of central and eastern Europe.[7]

My remarks must also call into question some of the formulations of Edward Said in his influential *Orientalism.* As one of Said's more important conclusions decisively contradicts my own basic argument, it is there that I will begin; and indeed, it is to issues arising from his book that many of my remarks will be directed.[8]

Said on Renan and the Orientalist Enterprise

Said has argued that orientalist scholarship in Europe began with and was essentially founded by the work of Antoine-Isaac Silvestre de Sacy (1758–1838) and was dominated by scholars in France and England from the late eighteenth to the mid-twentieth century: "to speak of Orientalism therefore is to speak mainly, although not exclusively, of a British and French cultural enterprise."[9] In this enterprise the key role was played by Ernest Renan,[10] and in particular by his Aryan/Semitic theory of intellectual and moral dichotomy. In his *Histoire générale et système comparé des langues sémitiques* (1855),[11] which won him the Académie des Inscriptions et Belles-Lettres' coveted Prix Volney already in 1847, he argued that determining factors of language shaped the ways in which so-called "Aryan" and "Semitic" peoples did and could think. According to this scheme of things, the "Aryan genius" is specifically gifted in and inclined toward perception of multiplicity, the observation and assessment of which expresses itself in polytheistic religion, mythology, philosophy, and science, and hence, with practically unlimited scope for further progress and development. The "Semitic genius," on the other hand, is specifically gifted in and inclined toward the perception of unity, the apprehension and contemplation of which expresses itself in monotheistic religion and theology. As Semites do not seek to assess the disparate phenomena of the world in any critical fashion, they have neither mythology, nor science, nor philosophy, nor plastic arts, nor even civil life, all of which presume an interest in the endless varieties that the world displays and an effort to make sense of them. Semitic culture is thus invariably "arrested" by its own limitations and is inherently incapable of the heights to which Aryan culture can ascend.

In pursuing and refining the work of Silvestre de Sacy, it was Renan's task, as Said sees it, "to solidify the official discourse of Orientalism, to systematize its insights, and to establish its intellectual and worldly institutions." Once this had been achieved, orientalism remained "unchanged as teachable wisdom (in academies, books, congresses, universities, foreign-service institutes) from the period of Ernest Renan in the late 1840s until the present in the United States." That is, orientalism became a static system of ideas that, after Renan, generated no new ways of conceptualizing the subject of its study and analysis. All subsequent work—specifically, that of the German orientalists and their disciples—simply "refined and elaborated techniques whose application was to texts, myths, ideas, and languages almost literally gathered from the Orient by imperial Britain and France."[12]

This demotion of the role of central European scholarship to a purely secondary function of assimilation was already recognized by Said himself as a potential focus for criticism,[13] but while several commentators have queried his view,[14] he has not retreated from it—so far as I know—up to the present day. For our purposes here, this would mean that Goldziher was not the founder of anything, much less the field of Arab-Islamic studies; his intellectual pedigree can be traced back through H.L. Fleischer (1801–88), one of his teachers in Leipzig, to Silvestre de Sacy, who taught Fleischer, and thus into the Anglo-French mainstream of orientalism that for Said dead-ends with Renan. That the career of Goldziher is to be viewed in this way is in fact specifically stated by Said.[15] Elsewhere he argues that "... if you look at the Austro-German School of Orientalism, there is nothing there that fundamentally contradicts the general view of the Orient.... It's not something which they in any way dispute. It's simply taken for granted."[16]

One must first observe that Said presents an oversimplified picture of the background to Renan. On the one hand, in the eighteenth century there was a prominent tendency, motivated by religious considerations, to promote the "Semitic" tradition over the "Aryan." Serious works were written to argue, for example, that the *Iliad* and the *Odyssey* were of Hebrew origin, and that the myth of Hercules came from the book of Joshua.[17] On the other hand, and more importantly, it is difficult to credit the curious linearity that Said postulates for the development of orientalism from Silvestre de Sacy to Renan. As is amply attested by the vast oriental collections of such centers of orientalist learning as Leiden and Berlin, where there were no imperial considerations to stimulate interest in the Orient, or at least (in the case of the Netherlands) not in the Middle East, it is a gross error to characterize European orientalist scholarship as dependent upon "imperial Britain and France" for access to texts.[18] The orientalist tradition in the Netherlands and Germany was already well-established by the eighteenth century. In Leiden the decisive impetus (if one is to think in terms of contributions of individuals) had been provided by Jacob Golius (1596–1667), and the treasures of the Warnerian Library provided materials for study by an expanding circle of scholars; in Germany a founding figure may be identified at Leipzig in Johann Jacob Reiske (1716–74), who had been trained at Leiden.[19]

Within France itself it is hard to see how any decisive role can be assigned to Silvestre de Sacy as the personal inaugurator of an intellectual paradigm to which Renan was heir. Silvestre de Sacy certainly attracted a large throng of students, and his literary contributions were numerous and important; Goldziher considered that in Silvestre de Sacy's time he "represented the embodiment and sum of all knowledge about the Muslim East in Europe."[20] But it was probably Napoleon's invasion of Egypt in 1798, more than any initiative by Silvestre de Sacy himself, that focused European attention on the Near East as an important area of study and on Paris as the place to undertake such work. For years he had been an obscure civil servant, and he did not assume his professorial chair at the École spéciale des langues orientales vivantes until 1795;[21] all of the works to which he owed his renown were published after the invasion of Egypt. But even this was insufficient to make him an exclusive focus of academic attention as a teacher, and certainly it is precarious to trace to his influence the ideas and conclusions of all of his students and students' students who were eventually to do—like him—important and influential work on the history of Arabic culture and Islam. Through much of the nineteenth century, aspiring orientalists routinely studied with specialists in many subjects and languages and often derived crucial methodological inspiration and insights from teachers far removed from the fields in which the student later did his most important work.

Renan was a typical example of this. It was at the seminary of St. Sulpice that he studied with the biblical scholar Arthur-Marie Le Hir (1811–68), who turned his academic zeal from mathematics to philology and the Old Testament.[22] And though almost all of his orientalist scholarship was devoted to Semitica, most particularly biblical and Arabic studies, Renan's most important teacher was the renowned Indologist Eugène Burnouf (1801–52), who treated Renan almost like a son, supported him both before and after his success in the Volney competition, and encouraged him with advice. Renan's correspondence reveals that he practically worshipped Burnouf; as he wrote to his sister Henriette: "In sum, dear friend, I have found in him the man for whom I was searching, the true philosopher-scholar, who represents the kind of man I would like to be and whom, in so far as my abilities allow, I want to do all I can to imitate."[23] His overarching concern with the fusion of orientalist philology with history and philosophy was inspired by Burnouf, as was his approach to the relation between language and race. Burnouf also introduced him to his collaborator Christian Lassen (1800–76), from whose monumental study of ancient India Renan sought authoritative sanction for his views on Semitic character.[24] And beyond the figure of Burnouf stood not Silvestre de Sacy, but the pioneering linguist Franz Bopp (1791-1867) and the philosopher Wilhelm von Humboldt (1767–1835), who in the wake of the discovery of the connections between Sanskrit and European languages promoted the notion of a language as an organic manifestation of the particular character of those who speak it.[25] To the objection that Bopp was also a student of Silvestre de Sacy, the response is that the main influence on Bopp was from another teacher, the Sanskritist Alexander Hamilton (1762–1824), and that in Bopp's case the presence of Silvestre de Sacy was of little consequence.

The same is ultimately true for Renan as well. He dedicated *Langues sémitiques* to Bopp and regarded his own work as a continuation of Bopp's;[26] but in all of his long career, and through the many thousands of pages he produced, he makes only a few passing references to Silvestre de Sacy and assigns him no particular importance for his own intellectual or professional development. Silvestre de Sacy was primarily a compiler, editor, and translator, and Renan had little esteem for such scholars, whom he compared to masons who perform useful services but have no understanding of the structure they are helping to erect.[27] All this speaks decisively against Said's claim that orientalists after Silvestre de Sacy simply copied and rewrote him.[28]

It must also be said that Said's characterization of the central and unassailed position of Renan himself cannot possibly be true; Renan was acutely aware that his *Langues sémitiques* was flawed in various ways,[29] and any degree of reading in nineteenth-century literature on the subject will reveal that Renan's theories were attacked, revised, and reinterpreted all across the Western world almost as soon as he published them in 1855. That Semitic peoples also possessed vigorous mythic traditions had in fact already been argued at length before Goldziher: the examples of Abraham Geiger (1810–74)[30] and Heymann Steinthal (1823–99)[31] in Berlin, François Lenormant (1837–83) in Paris,[32] and George Smith (1840–76) in London[33] are but four prominent cases of many that could be cited. Even where Renan's views were accepted, they did not generate a monolithic view of the Orient, as Said suggests they did; rather, their deployment by different scholars often resulted in "proof" of exactly opposite conclusions on one and the same issue.[34]

When we find Goldziher questioning Renan's theories, it is thus important to bear in mind that he was not the first or the only scholar of his time to do so. His views are important because they illustrate the thinking of a scholar who not only opposed Renan, as others did, but also argued for an alternative way forward that provided the decisive impetus for a new field of study that still thrives today.

Goldziher and His Early Critique

As is well known, the young Goldziher was sent by the Habsburg ministry of education to Germany in 1868 to pursue his doctoral studies. After spending some months in Berlin, he proceeded to Leipzig and took his

Ph.D. with Fleischer late in 1869; the following year and a half allowed him further opportunity for study and research in Leipzig, Leiden, and Vienna, and in the fall of 1872 he returned to Pest, received his lecturer's diploma, and began to teach in the university.[35] There one of his very first priorities was to refute Renan.

Goldziher's motivations had much to do with his own intellectual development and his experiences in Germany. Much impressed by the works of Alfred von Kremer (1828–89) on the cultural history of Islam,[36] Goldziher conceived a plan to write at an even more ambitious level, and in sum, to integrate the history of Eastern cultures into a grand synthesis that would incorporate the insights of historical studies (both ancient and medieval), ethnography, comparative religion, theology, and what would now be called social history.[37] Not surprisingly, then, he used his tour of Europe in 1868–72 to pursue topics ranging far beyond the field of Arabic and Islam: Judaica, Egyptology, Syriac and Sanskrit (both of which he later taught), classical Greek and Latin philology, philosophy, ethnography, psychology, and theology.

The paradigm according to which this vast material was to be interpreted was provided by the Haskala, or Jewish Enlightenment,[38] and in particular by the thought of Abraham Geiger, with whose works Goldziher had already become familiar as a student in 1865.[39] Geiger was an influential and powerful rabbi in Frankfurt and Berlin, an outspoken liberal, and a scholar much influenced, on the one hand, by the work of David Friedrich Strauss (1808–74) and the Tübingen school led by Ferdinand Christian Bauer (1792–1860) where religious texts were concerned, and on the other, by Moses Mendelssohn (1729–86) and ultimately Immanuel Kant (1724–1804) in more general philosophical terms.[40] One of Geiger's most important theses, and one that was to influence Goldziher for all of his life, began with the proposition that all texts—including religious scriptures—are human creations. They are not truths in and of themselves, since all texts record the past within a complex matrix of motivating presuppositions, ideas, and arguments that in many cases may completely defeat the Rankean quest for "what actually happened." The strictly rational and critical study of such texts promised to reveal not merely factoids to be strung together into descriptive narratives but, more importantly, the various stages of development through which any society passes in coming to terms with fundamental issues. As these layers of particularist interpretation and development in a text are stripped away, one comes closer to discovering the quintessential core of concerns with which the whole discussion had begun.[41] As earlier stages tend invariably to be the more basic and fundamental ones, it is at these levels that one can discern a more universal dimension revealing enduring values shared with other communities and religions.

As I have sought to show elsewhere,[42] Goldziher was decisively influenced by Geiger's thinking not only from his studies in Berlin and Leipzig, two of the foremost centers of the Haskala in Germany, but also from his exposure to the writings of Strauss and Bauer, which, as he describes in his *Tagebuch*, enabled him to understand Geiger more clearly.[43] Already in Leipzig, and then back in Pest, his early Hungarian writings seek to apply Geiger's ideas to the comparative history of Islam and Judaism.[44] But a formidablc obstacle was posed by the eminent Renan, whose widely circulated theories bore three fatal implications for the sort of Haskala-inspired scholarship that Goldziher planned to pursue.

First, if Semitic peoples were *a priori* incapable of the great soarings of imagination and reflection that comprised the pristine core that Geiger ultimately sought to reveal, then the systematic study of Judaism and Islam held little promise. Second, if the cognitive processes of Aryans and Semites are distinct and separate from the start, and then proceed in entirely different directions thereafter, there can be no universal dimension to whatever one finds at the heart of any issue or problem under investigation. Third, if the culture and intellectual life of Semites inevitably grinds to a halt in theology, then the challenges of the modern world, in so far as these require solutions transcending those of traditional theology, cannot be met by either Jewish or Muslim intellectuals whose thought has any relevance at all to their faith or religious heritage. That is, in Judaism and Islam there is no meeting ground between modernity and religious reform; or conversely, for a Jew or Muslim to embrace the modern world is to forsake one's heritage and religious identity, and indeed, to despise and reject it.

Though Geiger and Nöldeke were on generally good terms, they often crossed swords on precisely such matters;[45] Goldziher was now to do so with Renan. Upon his return to Pest from his European study tour in 1872, his writing and lecturing immediately begin to reflect a sharp antagonism to Renan's work, and on his study tour of the Near East in 1873–74 he spent many evenings in Cairo with Jamāl al-Dīn al-Afghānī (1839–97) discussing religious reform. Although the specific subject of their conversations is not recorded by Goldziher, it is likely that Renan, whom al-Afghānī was later to attack in a spirited critique of his own, was an item high on the agenda.[46] This is especially probable in light of the fact that Goldziher was by then well advanced in his writing of a detailed refutation of Renan. Exactly when he began the book is impossible to say, but in his introduction he states that, inspired by the research of Steinthal, he originally wrote a series of lectures in Hungarian for teaching purposes and at first had no plans for combining these into a major work.[47] Publication of a preliminary statement[48] confirmed his earlier suspicions that there would be little interest in his work among either publishers or readers in Hungary,[49] and he had already decided to translate his lectures into German and publish them in a revised form abroad.[50] Much of the work was done before he left for the Near East, and he continued the project in various places during his travels.[51] He speaks, for example, of how chapter 4, on how societies formulate visions of their past in terms of their current means of livelihood and production, was written in the Hotel Damas in Jerusalem.[52] Back in Europe in 1876, this work was published in Leipzig under the title of *Der Mythos bei den Hebräern*.[53]

This book has often been overlooked or dismissed because of Goldziher's adherence to currently circulating theories about the relation of the Old Testament to solar mythology, ideas that were eventually shown to be mistaken. Far more important, however, is the way in which this tome of over 400 pages, his first extended work, considered the question of how ancient peoples conceptualized and related images of their past in terms relevant to their present situation, and both explicitly and implicitly refuted Renan's theories in their entirety. Further material was adduced in an 1881 collection of studies on Islamic topics,[54] and after Renan's death in 1892 Goldziher again returned to this subject in his "Renan as an Orientalist," a 100-page memorial study.[55]

In these studies, as well in some shorter pieces published from time to time, mostly in Hungarian, his line of argument is consistent. In *Mythology among the Hebrews* Goldziher first points out that mythology is reflective of the most basic stage in the development of intellectual life and the formation of communal identity. It is not possible to speak of an identifiable people possessed of any culture at all as devoid of myth, and indeed, the ubiquity of mythology and the existence of very similar myths in societies that cannot have been in contact with one another indicates that myth-making is a universal phenomenon common to all peoples. There is thus no good reason to suppose that the creation of myth, which with language ranks as one of the most primordial psychological acts of the human mind, is limited by ethnic or linguistic considerations. Renan's contrary theories, while formulated with supreme elegance, simply serve as proof that mere dogma can sometimes come to dominate even serious scholarship and gain authority among non-specialists.[56] Though Renan seeks to explain historical phenomena on a grand scale, Goldziher says, his theses are themselves anti-historical; his proposition of polytheism and monotheism as given *a priori* and separately in two different parts of mankind, for example, allows no place for the development of monotheism from polytheism, or for the emergence of polytheism from some system of belief that is mythic, but not specifically religious. For Goldziher, Renan's theory amounts to an assertion that Judaism and Islam had not developed into or from anything—they were just "there," like a person who had no childhood or adolescence, but simply sprang into being as an adult.[57] As Goldziher saw it, then, the task was not to replace Renan's simplistic schema with another:

> We see clearly how worthless such clever fancies are, that enable one to embrace with a stroke of the pen a domain which geographically fills more than half of the inhabited world, and chronologically stretches from remotest antiquity down to the most recent times.[58]

He also observes that Renan's famous maxim: "The Semites have never had any mythology,"[59] can only be saved from mockery as self-evident absurdity by engaging in the most arbitrary sleight-of-hand, much like the claim that such-and-such a race cannot digest food or bear children would require fairly acrobatic redefinition of such notions as "digestion," "food," "procreation," and "child."[60] Similarly dismissive is his reaction to Renan's thesis that myths apparently common to Semites and Aryans are to be attributed to "common prehistoric traditions" formed by the two peoples in their "original common dwelling place." This obviously anti-historical argument Goldziher ranks among ploys that "have cut away the ground from any scientific investigation of the question."[61]

On the question of the categories of "Semitic" and "Aryan," Goldziher had further criticisms to air. First, the affinities of languages within a language family do not necessarily translate into social realities. Buṭrus al-Bustānī (1819–83), for example, whom he had met in Beirut,[62] had found it much easier to learn English than Syriac; through the long history of Ottoman rule in Hungary, Turkish had contributed nothing more than a few loan words to Hungarian, though the two tongues belong to the same family.[63] Goldziher also rejected Renan's paradigm of "genius" expressed in terms of such categories, not because Goldziher denied the validity of ethnic categories (he did not), but rather because he did not see these as the determining factors in the progress of thought or culture: "There is no such thing as a psychology particular to a given race." To the extent that myths do not reflect basic human psychology, they represent reactions to changing political, economic, and social circumstances through which a people has passed; this in turn makes the task of studying them an essentially historical one.[64]

At this point one sees that Goldziher's position was not motivated by a particularist interest in redeeming the religious credentials of Judaism or the venerable dignity of the Jewish people, but rather by an effort to secure for the Jews and Judaism what he considered to be their proper place in the broader course of civilization. Following the lead of Geiger, here as elsewhere, he wished to stress their contributions to universal questions relevant to all peoples, and as with Geiger's research into the Old Testament this involved the concession of large-scale borrowing and development and the rejection of all modern research that did not take this into account:

> It is a mistaken, and anything but the right sort of reverence, when we would rather leave unknown or misunderstood a region of literature which we all love and venerate, and to which we owe most of our moral and religious ideals, than trace its elements and analyse their psychological and literary history, so as to understand the object of our love.[65]

It is impossible, he argued, that a primitive nomadic people like the ancient Israelites should have developed on their own the political institutions, the sophisticated legal and doctrinal system, the concern for ethics, and the mature world view that one sees in the early books of the Old Testament. This can only have been the result of borrowing from a settled and more advanced people, and in the case of the Israelites these sources are easy to identify. Upon entry into Palestine they adopted from the Canaanites and Phoenicians such sedentary notions as judgeship, kingship, priesthood, and the temple;[66] much later, during the Babylonian exile, they assimilated from their masters such themes as Creation, the Fall, the Flood, and the Tower of Babel.[67]

In light of these arguments it becomes distinctly unsurprising to find that the ire of the irascible Goldziher was invariably provoked by ideas and individuals that promoted or perpetuated attachment to religious literalism, since such thinking seriously obstructed the promotion and understanding of the broad patterns of historical change that he deemed central to his task as a scholar. A case that he found especially irritating was Jerusalem, which he visited in November–December 1873 and regarded as "torn to pieces by denominational swindle."[68] Utterly dismissive of pilgrims as obsessed with their superstitions, he observes that "one cannot take two steps without running into a so-called holy place to which legend ties its swindle."[69] Christian-Jewish disputes attract a similar response; on arguments over whether Jeremiah slept in the pit for 70 or 200 years, he comments: "I, of course, cannot be the arbiter in this learned difference of opinion."[70] His brief diary comments in fact reflected an ongoing concern in this area, and his views were eventually expressed in systematic form in an essay arguing, among other things, how futile it was for archeologists to swarm over the terra firma of Palestine in an effort to dig up the topography of the Bible.[71] One must therefore set aside as uninformed Said's interpretation of Goldziher's "dislike of Mohammed's anthropomorphisms" (known to Said only from Waardenburg in any case) as indicative of his participation in an orientalist consensus on the "latent inferiority" of Islam.[72] As can now be seen quite clearly, Goldziher's views on such matters in Islam spring directly and consistently from his attitude toward religion in general, and are inspired not by Renan, Silvestre de Sacy, and French orientalism, but rather by Geiger, the Tübingen school, and Enlightenment thought in central and eastern Europe.

In some quarters, especially England, Goldziher's book was well-received. Elsewhere, where it was criticized, he considered that opposition was due to Christian evangelical considerations and the rabbis' fear that the triumph of his views would reduce literalist piety and hence their opportunities for extra income.[73] In Hungary there was at first no reaction at all: the book was studiously ignored and the *Pester Lloyd*, a prestigious Budapest paper, did not even mention that it had been published. When the Jewish community did discover it, however, hundreds signed a petition protesting that such an enemy of religion should be secretary of the Neolog community and demanded his removal.[74] The reaction of Renan himself to the copy of the book sent to him by Brockhaus at Goldziher's request was quite conciliatory. In his letter of response he thanked his young Hungarian colleague and assured him that "on this subject, as on all others, I am quite devoid of prejudice."[75] His findings had been that compared to other peoples the Hebrews were but little inclined to mythology, "though certainly, like all peoples, they had myths." In his view, the key issue was this relative distinction between myth and mythology and the extent to which they were to be found among the ancient Israelites. "In forming my own opinion on this point, I will take your learned publication into most serious account."[76]

If Renan was impressed by Goldziher's challenges to his theories, this did not move him from his central thesis that Semitic peoples were morally and intellectually inferior and had no contribution to make to philosophy and the exact sciences, i.e. the fields most closely identified with modernity in Europe. At the Sorbonne on 29 March 1883 he delivered his famous lecture "L'islamisme et la science," in which he argued this position in detail, and the publication of this paper the following day in the *Journal des débats* immediately provoked a critique from Goldziher's old friend Jamāl al-Dīn al-Afghānī, who was in Paris at the time, and a reply from Renan.[77] This renowned exchange has frequently been discussed by others,[78] and here it will suffice to note that while Goldziher was eventually to express his approval of al-Afghānī's criticisms of Renan,[79] earlier he does not seem to have been moved by the debate.[80] He certainly agreed with al-Afghānī's arguments that Islam is superior to Christianity and that British colonialism in India was to be deplored, but he probably would have argued that these were not the central points to be made in reply to Renan.

In the following year Goldziher and his wife planned a two-month tour through Württemberg, the Black Forest, and Strassburg to Paris, and when Renan received a letter advising him of these arrangements he replied that he would be "pleased and honored" to receive Goldziher. The two met twice in May 1884 at the Collège de France, where Renan had assumed the directorship the previous year, and as the discussion included Goldziher's study tour in the Near East and his relations with al-Afghānī, his 1876 critique and Renan's 1883 exchange with al-Afghānī must have ranked high on their agenda.[81] Even after Renan's death Goldziher still recalls the awe he felt upon meeting him in Paris: "How many great men have I seen face to face, and how many have I heard speak? I now think of the—for me—unforgettable meeting with Renan, May 1884."[82] On the other hand, while Goldziher exchanged hundreds of letters with colleagues with whom he had much to share, he appears to have been in contact with Renan only twice: once in 1876 when *Mythology among the Hebrews* was published, and again in 1884 when his travel plans took him to Paris. One therefore suspects that while the two seem to have respected one another at the time, they never had much to exchange by way of scholarly views.

It is interesting to see how frequently Goldziher's interest in the Arab world and the Islamic heritage surfaces in his first major book. Considering the subject, it is significant that he does in fact choose to bring in Arab and Islamic materials. In addition to the references to al-Bustānī and the Ottomans, he cites numerous passages that sustain his case for the universality of mythology and support his broader arguments on cultural change. This ancient Arab lore includes stories about various stars and constellations seeking the hand of another star in marriage, avenging slain relatives, and grieving for the departed lover. What is this material, he asks, if not genuine ancient nomadic mythology?[83] One finds equally fascinating mythic material in such areas as related tales of nomadic life, an Arabic parallel to the story of Oedipus, and an account of Hāshim, his birth, and the meaning of his name.[84]

Ethnic Genius and the Issue of Originality

Overall, Goldziher remained satisfied with his results of 1876 and planned to move on to his broader agenda for research into the history of Eastern cultures.[85] Unfortunately, this ambition was quickly complicated by factors beyond his control, in the first instance by the failure of his promised professorship to materialize. This issue has been discussed elsewhere by myself and others; here it will suffice to say that in 1874 a combination of anti-Semitism and local politics made it impossible to appoint Goldziher over Péter Hatala (1832–1918), an errant clergyman who had come into conflict with the Vatican over the doctrine of papal infallibility and had to be stored in some place less visible to Rome than the Faculty of Theology.[86] For Goldziher, the result was that the need for employment obliged him in 1876 to accept the position of secretary of the Neolog community of Budapest, a job for which he had neither the talent nor personality. Though assured that a university position would soon be found for him, he was to spend the next twenty-nine years in this post, until his colossal international reputation finally obliged the university to appoint him to a professorial chair when Hatala retired in 1905. In the interim, Goldziher had little time for research; as he describes in his *Tagebuch*, the works for which he was famous were all researched during his brief moments of leisure and spare time through the year, and then written up in their final form during his summer holidays in the mountains or by the sea.[87] It may also be doubted whether even a full academic position in Budapest would have provided him with the time and resources necessary to conduct research on the scale he originally envisaged; certainly his post as a petty bureaucrat did not do so.

In 1880 one of his respites from his administrative duties took him on a four-week holiday to the Carpathian resort of Lucsivna, where he organized six already-prepared Hungarian papers into a book entitled *Islam: Studies on the History of the Muhammedan Religion*.[88] The first of these essays, entitled "The Religion of the Desert and Islam," renews his critique of Renan and the latter's notion of "le génie arabe," specifically, in order to show that Islam was not and could not have been the product of any such "Arab genius." After reviewing the contradictory theories of several leading orientalists of the day, including Renan,[89] he proceeds to describe pre-Islamic ways of life in detail and demonstrate how antithetical they were to Islam. The values of the Arabs of ancient Arabia were encapsulated in the idea of *muruwwa*, or "tribal virtue," a complex of ideals treasured for the glory and fame they brought to the individual and the tribe, but conceding little to religious or moral sensibilities.[90] Just as one can see among the bedouin tribes of modern times (i.e. those known to Goldziher from the accounts of such explorers as C.F. Volney, E.H. Palmer, Richard Burton, Lady Anne Blunt, H.B. Tristram, and Eduard Rüppell),[91] the Arabs of ancient Arabia had no use for prayer or self-denial, rejoiced in physical pleasures of all kinds, and adhered to various barbarous and immoral customs. Their fetishes were of only meager religious content, and they took seriously hardly anything that was sacred to Islam.[92] Not surprisingly, the notables of Mecca opposed or resisted Islam and the first Muslim dynasty of the Umayyads also showed little religious sentiment.[93] Anything to which the label of "the Arab genius" could be attached must thus be rejected as contributing to the rise of Islam in any positive sense, since these aspects of Arab life all stood in opposition to Islam. Indeed, Islamic institutions and traditions ought more rightly to be attributed to the "génie" of the *'ajam*, the non-Arabs.[94]

The critique of Renan's proposition of ethnic genius or spirit was also pursued in several other works bracketing the publication of *Islam*; this was clearly a major interest of Goldziher's after the publication of *Mythology among the Hebrews*, where the subject had not received full attention. In these essays he insisted that neither Arabic grammar, nor

Islamic law or dogma, nor Arabic historical writing were the products of "le génie arabe," as Renan had proposed: in all cases, the formative processes were more complicated and involved the interplay of various competing and complementary currents of development. A scholar of Syriac as well as Arabic, Goldziher was able to argue that just as Islamic dogma was stimulated by discussions within the Eastern church, so Arabic grammar can be shown to have made use of Syriac models.[95] The same applies to Islamic law, which developed mainly in the conquered territories outside of Arabia in the eighth century and adopted many of the legal conventions and even terminology of the law schools of the church.[96] In historiography one again must reject the role of "le génie arabe," for the Arabs, who traditionally had possessed no systematic sense of history, did not give rise to Arabic historiography. It was, in fact, Muslims of Persian origin who contributed most to the rise of Arab historical writing, and in the sciences and philosophy translations from the Greek were the work of Persians and Syriac-speaking Christians.[97]

The aim in these essays was not to deny the achievement of the Arabs, any more than the aim of *Mythology among the Hebrews* had been to diminish the accomplishments of the ancient Israelites. But for Goldziher, Renan's arguments for the identification of various fields of cultural and social endeavor as specific to distinct categories of ethnic predisposition, to the exclusion of participation by other peoples, was essentially anti-historical. No people lived in isolation, and collaboration and synthesis were the rule rather than the exception.

He was therefore impatient with the discussions—common in his time—of originality: picking apart a theme or idea to determine what was original and what was not, so as to arrive at a "score" enabling one to judge relative contributions to the history of civilization. His response to this sort of work is already to be found in the conclusion to *Mythology among the Hebrews*:

> Has Homer lost his attractiveness since we have subjected him to critical analysis, or the divine Plato forfeited any of his divinity since we have discovered some of the sources of his ideas? For the fact of Originality is not the only criterion of the admirable. Not only that which is cast in one piece from top to toe, is one whole: an alien substance which becomes a civilising agent to that in which it rests, and a patchwork which has turned out a harmonious whole, are not less admirable or perfect. Julius Braun says very justly: "There is another and indeed the highest kind of originality, which is not the beginning but the result of histori-

cal growth—the originality of mature age. We have this, when an individual or a nation has gathered up all existing means of culture, and then still possesses power to pass on beyond them and deal freely with all elements received from the past."[98]

Much the same attitude is evident in Goldziher's later *Muhammedanische Studien*:

From the point of view of cultural history it is of little account that Muhammed's teaching was not the original creation of his genius which made him the prophet of his people, but that all his doctrines are taken from Judaism and Christianity. Their originality lies in the fact that these teachings were for the first time placed in contrast to the Arabic ways of life by Muhammed's persistent energy.[99]

And still near the end of his life, on the eve of the First World War, one finds a similar argument:

When the historian of civilization appraises the effect of an historical phenomenon, the question of originality does not claim his principal attention. In an historical evaluation of Muhammad's work the issue is not whether the contents of his revelation were a completely original, absolutely trail-blazing creation of his soul. The Arab Prophet's message was an eclectic composite of religious ideas and regulations. The ideas were suggested to him by contacts, which had stirred him deeply, with Jewish, Christian, and other elements, and they seemed to him suited to awaken an earnest religious mood among his fellow Arabs. The regulations too were derived from foreign sources; he recognized them as needed to institute life according to the will of God.[100]

All this is, of course, closely tied to influence from Geiger and the Haskala, which had stressed that the critical assessment of communal history—that of the Jews in Geiger's case, but in fact any community's past—would lead back through successive stages of borrowing and development and end in a core of ideas and beliefs that were not necessarily "original" to the people under consideration, but rather typical of peoples living in similar circumstances.[101]

Late in this series of essays on ethnic genius, the research agenda underlying Goldziher's ongoing critique was seriously undermined by his continuing professional difficulties in Budapest. Though his scholarship was respected and his burgeoning international reputation admired, his impassioned advocacy of Jewish reform and campaigning for the agenda of the Haskala were generally not well received. A decisive moment arose in the winter of 1887–88, when he prepared a series of six lectures on the subject of "The Essence and Evolution of Judaism," in which he argued forcefully for the views of Geiger on the modernization of the faith.[102] Accusing the prevailing rabbinic structures of betraying the Prophetic ideal, he advocated a comprehensive reform aimed at the fusion of a pristine Judaism with strictly rational and scientific thinking. These lectures were a colossal failure. The Haskala had by this time lost whatever momentum it had once had in Hungary, and Goldziher himself, already regarded with suspicion as "a menace to Judaism," was now vilified as "a bad speaker" as well. Attendance at his lectures dwindled, and the sixth he cancelled "for the sake of my honor."[103]

The fact that his inability to reach his co-religionists on a topic of immediate interest should lead him to abandon his plans for his broad-ranging research agenda illustrates how committed he had been to a Geigerian perspective and the idea that comparative historical research was a path to the discovery of truths of universal and contemporary relevance. As Goldziher was in any case an insecure man constantly in need of recognition and approval,[104] it may also be that the embarrassment he suffered at this time convinced him that it was futile to try to pursue such ambitious plans under the exceedingly negative conditions of his current employment, which contrasted drastically to the warm and engaging reception his ideas on religious reform had received among Muslim intellectuals in Damascus and Cairo.[105] The year 1889 also witnessed the death of his inspiration for his project, Alfred von Kremer himself, and in a letter to Baron Victor Rosen (1849–1908) in St. Petersburg he admitted that this too discouraged him.[106] In any case, a few years later he identified this troubled period as the time when he decided to abandon his other studies and concentrate on Arabic philology and history and the study of Islam.[107]

The Memorial Essay on Renan

Ernest Renan died in Paris on 2 October 1892, and two weeks later the Hungarian Academy of Sciences, of which he had been a foreign member, asked Goldziher to deliver a memorial lecture on him at the Academy. His remarks that day in his diary indicate that his attitude toward the Frenchman had soured considerably since his visit to Paris in 1884:

> I will begin to assemble the ideas for the lecture. It was very sensible of me to declare from the outset that I could undertake the task only on condition that I limit myself to "Renan as an Orientalist." It would be wicked for me to offer myself up as a sacrifice to the singing of Renan's praises as a New Testament critic and historian of the rise of Christianity. It will be as useful to attach R. to Le Hir, Quatremère, and Burnouf as to celebrate him as a student of Strauss and Bauer. Yes, he was such a student, and because of this he disliked the Tübingen [colleagues].[108]

Six months later, in May 1893, he again records his progress in his diary:

> I have begun to write my essay on "Renan as an Orientalist." The theme is tremendously attractive for me. In two days I have drafted two chapters: a) Renan as a professor, b) R. as a Bible critic. Much remains for me to put pen to paper. The man has the soundest views on *contemporary* Israel. He is the most dangerous anti-Semite, because he is right. The only dangerous one is the one who is right. One cannot match him. The pompous phrase is for the moment and for the rabble. Honorable people use no such phrases, and with them one can never refute truths.[109]

There is nothing here to indicate what it was that had provoked Goldziher, but rather than one of Renan's older studies it was probably his *Histoire du peuple d'Israël*, the first three volumes of which were published before Renan's death, the fourth in 1893, as Goldziher prepared his critique, and the fifth in the following year.[110] In this massive work of 1,600 pages, Goldziher is not once cited or mentioned, and as is rendered obvious in an early chapter entitled: "Monotheism, Lack of Mythology,"[111] no concession had been made to his 1876 critique. Indeed, in the course of his extensive reading of Renan's works for his essay, Goldziher would have discovered—much to his chagrin—that while Renan had made frequent use of research by other scholars of biblical and Arab-Islamic studies, he nowhere cites Goldziher's work on any subject in any of his published writings.[112]

In these two passages in his *Tagebuch*, Goldziher reveals views that he was apparently unwilling to state in print. A bitter critic of Christianity for what he saw as its absurd doctrines, intolerance, and aggressive evangelism,[113] he had no wish to be associated with a celebration of Renan as a historian of the faith. Renan's *Vie de Jésus*[114] bears some affinities with the methods of Strauss, but these are more apparent than real, and Goldziher's comment on Renan's dislike for the Tübingen circle refers to Renan's critical comments on them in his memoirs[115] and to his political differences with Strauss in the wake of the Franco-Prussian War of 1870.[116] In any case, as a critic of what he regarded as Renan's erroneous and racist theories, he was disinclined to associate him with Strauss, Bauer, and the Tübingen school, by which he had himself been profoundly influenced. As he had hinted already in 1876, he was also annoyed by the way Renan's elegant but pompous style lent undeserved authority to his theories in the eyes of non-specialists.[117] Indeed, he seems to suspect that Renan's style is part of a deliberate attempt to mislead.

On the other hand, his own extremely negative views of the rabbinical establishment of modern Judaism, not to mention his disastrous experiences in Budapest as an advocate of reform, led him to concede that while Renan was a dangerous anti-Semite, the peril of his views derived from the fact that they accurately described the state of contemporary Judaism. It was difficult to argue against the theory that Semites were incapable of imaginative, rational, and scientific inquiry when this, for Goldziher, was precisely the conclusion suggested by the rabbis' attitude toward reform. He would have felt obliged to agree, for example, with this deliverance from Renan's introductory study for his translation of the Book of Ecclesiastes:

> A strange people, in truth, and made to present all kinds of contrasts! They have given God to the world, and hardly believe in Him themselves. They have created religion, and are the least religious of peoples; they have founded the hope of humanity in a kingdom of Heaven, yet all their sages keep telling us that one ought not to occupy oneself with anything but worldly affairs. The most enlightened races take seriously what they have preached, while the latter laugh at them. Their ancient literature has excited the fanaticism of all the nations, but they see its weak points better than anyone.[118]

Goldziher's impassioned views on the need for a return to the pristine Judaism of the Prophets would probably have also led him to agree with Renan's view that the Talmud was a "wicked book" and the source of the "perverse genius of Judaism."[119]

Pointing to such factors as Renan's explicit denunciation of anti-Semitism, his protest against the Tisza-Eszlar blood libel in 1882, his efforts with Victor Hugo (1802-85) to organize relief committees for the Jews of Russia, and the fact that he was himself the victim of anti-Semitic attacks and was accused of being in the pay of the Rothschilds,

Shmuel Almog has sought to exonerate Renan of the charge of anti-Semitism, arguing that he was "not consciously anti-Semitic."[120] One may accept this, assuming that Almog means that Renan simply could not bring himself to admit that his pet theories were in fact not only racist but anti-Semitic as well. A visit to Athens and the Acropolis, for example, convinced him that perfection is to be found only among the ancient Greeks. This discovery moved him to compose his famous "Prière sur l'Acropole" (1876), which among other things speaks about how "an unseemly little Jew" got his way and turned the world into a desert in which no flower grew for a thousand years.[121] Elsewhere he argues that the Jews have been so universally detested through the ages that there must be some legitimate cause for the phenomenon. This justification he finds in their haughty sense of superiority, badtemperedness, quarrelsome nature, and their withdrawal from society to live among themselves—all of which made them disagreeable neighbors.[122] He also comes down forcefully on the side of the traditional Christian anti-Semitic line holding the Jews collectively responsible for the crucifixion of Jesus. In his version of this charge he states that while Jews in modern Europe might rightly complain if they are persecuted for this, the fact of the matter remains that Jesus was killed according to the Mosaic law: "Nations bear responsibilities just as individuals do, and if ever a crime was the crime of a people, it is the death of Jesus."[123] Renan's works are full of such condescending and finger-wagging flourishes; conscious or not, they make it difficult to defend him from the charge of anti-Semitism without—as Goldziher would say—a questionable redefinition of the term at issue.

The summer of 1893 witnessed further work on Goldziher's memorial essay, and the first two weeks of another respite from his official duties were almost entirely devoted to finalizing his text.[124] On 28 November he reports on the culmination of his efforts:

> At the Academy yesterday evening, in front of a numerous audience that included very prominent figures, I read a part of my study on "Ernest Renan as an Orientalist" in place of a memorial lecture on the foreign member of the Ac. I reaped—as the newspapers say—"stormy applause." The study actually ranks among my best works in the general fields, and during its preparation it was nurtured with great passion and inner interest.[125]

It would be most valuable to know which part of his study Goldziher chose to present, especially in light of the interest and favorable reception his lecture received. No information on this is available, but again, it seems likely that he would have selected some of his material on Renan's *Histoire du peuple d'Israël*, the posthumous volumes of which were appearing in print as he spoke. In any case, it is clear from his *Tagebuch* entries that the lecture marked the climax of a project to which he attached great importance.

Goldziher begins his study by reiterating his intention to limit his study to Renan's career as an orientalist and to exclude works on philosophy and the rise of Christianity. Based on a comprehensive collection of the autobiographical details in Renan's oeuvre he then sketches out his intellectual development and early career; contrary to Said, who links Renan primarily with Silvestre de Sacy, Goldziher more correctly sees his primary influences as having come from Le Hir[126] and especially Burnouf.[127] Through this part of his text Goldziher's tone is generally appreciative, and he makes a point, for example, of stressing the value to young aspiring orientalists of the *Rapport annuel* of the Société asiatique.[128]

Where specific works of Renan's are concerned, however, Goldziher's verdict is decidedly negative. Returning to the *Histoire générale et système comparé des langues sémitiques*,[129] and indeed, to the theme of style we have already seen in his 1876 critique and in the *Tagebuch*, he characterizes the work as an encyclopedia intended "to charm at the same time the ear and spirit of the reader," and its author as the self-proclaimed Bopp of Semitic studies.[130] A critical reading of his book will reveal that its argument is sustained not by genuine evidence but rather by a host of *a priori* assumptions about race and the "monotheistic instinct," baseless generalization from one people to the whole race to which they belong across vast expanses of time, and dramatic pronouncements such as: "The desert itself is monotheist." This last dictum Goldziher counters with a comparative argument already familiar to us from earlier works. The seventh-century Arabs were at heart pagan polytheists and only submitted by force of arms; when the monotheistic faith of Islam did spread among them, their life as a people was not transformed in any way different from the ways in which conversion to Christianity had transformed the Aryans. Renan's arguments are thus, in the first instance, ahistorical, and further, cannot be redeemed by renewed investigation since the relevant evidence either does not exist or, where it does exist, decisively contradicts him.[131]

In the next section of his study, Goldziher comments on the more Islamically-oriented works of Renan, most particularly in the field of philosophy.[132] He is distinctly unimpressed with Renan's alleged sympathies for Islam, and instead points to the polemical agenda of his notorious 1883 Sorbonne lecture on "L'islamisme et la science" and the ensuing exchange with Jamāl al-Dīn al-Afghānī.[133] Renan's theories would of course lead one to expect no philosophy in the Semitic Middle East, yet it is possible to trace out important contributions by Syriac-speaking Christians between the sixth and eighth centuries AD, and a vigorous tradition of philosophy culminating in the *Tahāfut al-falāsifa* by al-Ghazālī (d. 505/1111) and the countering *Tahāfut al-tahāfut* by Ibn Rushd (d. 595/1198). Renan writes all this off as possible only among those who have engaged in a kind of intellectual insurrection against their own heritage and (in the case of Muslims) faith, but again one sees how his arguments are based on his own dogma rather than evidence. In any case, the first part of his book on Ibn Rushd and his philosophy[134] must be dismissed as a failure, since it was written without recourse to either al-Ghazālī's or Ibn Rushd's most important contributions to the subject.[135]

The most extensive discussion in Goldziher's study considers Renan's *Histoire du peuple d'Israël*;[136] the four sections (5–8) devoted to this work display a greater sense of unity than that encountered elsewhere in the essay, and as suggested above, it may well be that Goldziher's Academy lecture was drawn from these sections. Numerous biblical scholars—including Heinrich Ewald (1803–75), Johann Vatke (1806–82), Abraham Kuenen (1828–91), and Julius Wellhausen (1844–1918), to name only the most eminent—are cited throughout the discussion, and by comparison Renan is found sorely wanting. In his book he faulted colleagues who were so accustomed to "discoveries through the microscope" that they could not perceive the "broad vistas" that he saw,[137] but Goldziher viewed things differently. Renan's last major work was based on the same premises and methodologies as his *Langues sémitiques*, and thus was subject to the same criticisms and reservations. An astonishingly dogmatic work, it deploys a broad range of elegant but specious analogies to argue propositions for which no real evidence exists. Some of these are already familiar from the usual Renanian répertoire. The motif of the broad expanse of the desert as the source of monotheism crops up again, for example, and for Goldziher illustrates how Renan's arguments can amount to nothing more than speculation based on mere observation of topography.[138] Elsewhere one finds that numerous biblical figures have their counterparts in modern Europe: Solomon is somehow comparable to Louis XIV, Hosea to a preacher or puritan pamphleteer in the age of Oliver Cromwell, Zorobabel to an Ottoman pasha, Isaiah to Armand Carrel (1800–36) or Émile de Gerardin (1802–81), Ezekiel to Charles Fourier (1772–1837), etc.[139] In yet other cases the effort is synchronize ancient Israelites with supposedly comparable Greeks: Josiah with Solon, Ezra and Nehemiah with Pericles, and so forth.[140]

A final section of the essay deals with Renan's research in Semitic paleography, Phoenician antiquities, his travels in the Near East, and his work on the *Corpus inscriptionum semiticarum.*[141] Here Goldziher is less critical of him, but it is interesting to observe that he in no way identifies with him or sees any parallels to his own career. Yet parallels there were. Just as Goldziher's youthful abilities had led to promises of a chair in Pest for which he was clearly the most qualified candidate, Renan had been a bright student and promising scholar apparently destined for the chair of Hebrew, Chaldaic, and Syriac languages at the Collège de France upon the death of Étienne Quatremère in 1857. Both were disappointed by factors involving religious intrigue and prejudice: Goldziher by unwillingness to appoint a Jew, Renan by the Catholic Church's unwillingness to have a renegade seminary student and notorious heretic appointed to a chair involving biblical exegesis. Both were sent on trips to the Near East to allow the storm to pass: Goldziher on a study tour ostensibly to learn Arabic dialects and the official Arabic of international diplomacy, Renan to Lebanon to collect ancient inscriptions. Both returned in unexpected triumph with major works in hand: Goldziher's *Mythology among the Hebrews* and Renan's collection of inscriptions that was to comprise the basis for the *Corpus inscriptionum semiticarum.* Yet in neither case did success redeem the situation at home: Goldziher's position was sacrificed to the need to conceal Péter Hatala from the ire of Rome, and Renan, though appointed to his chair, was soon transferred to the Bibliothèque Nationale for lecturing along lines offensive to Catholic sensibilities, refused the new position, lost his chair, and henceforth had to live from his literary efforts until his restoration to the chair in 1870.[142] Both men displayed an irresistible urge to rail against the powerful authorities of traditional religion, and yet seemed to be genuinely shocked and surprised at the inevitable backlash.

Goldziher would have known all this from his extensive reading on Renan's youth and early career,[143] and especially from the latter's *Souvenirs d'enfance et de jeunesse* and his *Questions contemporaines*, which he frequently cites. But his antipathy for Renan was apparently such that it never occurred to him, even in his diary, and much as he had esteemed the great man in his youth, to draw the obvious comparisons between their professional lives.

This antipathy finds its clearest expression not in Goldziher's extensive criticisms of Renan's flawed methods or arguments, nor even in his judgments on him as an anti-Semite, but rather, I think, in a brief passage in "Renan as an Orientalist" in which he cites yet another pithy dictum of Renan's, this time one in which the French scholar declares: "Criticism is an exercise in anatomy that ought to allow the object of its study to live."[144] But this is precisely where, for Goldziher, Renan's work was most to be faulted. Sharp and unrelenting historical criticism was one thing, and Goldziher himself was one of its most successful and influential proponents; however unsettling and destructive it might seem in some quarters, it cleared the way for more accurate assessment and cogent understanding. But Renan's research on matters "Semitic" was quite another matter. It systematically demeaned and deprecated the object of its study, robbed it of historical worth, defined it almost wholly in terms of negative attributes,[145] denied its relevance as anything more than an artifact, and even then insisted that it be judged against the standard of values and norms of another people and another time *a priori* privileged and protected from the same harsh scrutiny directed at other peoples. Renaniana was a slippery sphere: one could hold it or drop it, but not work with it. Having demonstrated, along with other scholars, how flawed it was in both conception and execution, Goldziher wisely decided to drop it and urged others to do the same.

The Legacy of Arab-Islamic Studies

"Renan as an Orientalist" marked the final major contribution by Goldziher to the critique of Renan, and in important ways it was a tangent from which he subsequently withdrew.[146] As discussed above, the 1880s marked the time when he decided henceforth to limit his work to a more restricted agenda of Arabic and Islamic topics. The immediate results of the shift were quite dramatic, though the influence of his earlier sources of inspiration continued undiminished. Turning to the rather disjointed collection of Hungarian essays he had published in 1881,[147] he pruned out the first three chapters, translated them into German, revised them heavily with copious annotations (the Hungarian originals bear almost no documentation or references to sources) and many additions of new material, and published the work thus produced in Halle in two volumes in 1888–89. This was his monumental *Muhammedanische Studien.* Other classics were of course to follow: a series of ground-breaking studies on Arabic literary themes in 1896–99[148] and a volume of six lectures on Islamic religious subjects in 1910,[149] to name only two. Though some of his essays were quite lengthy, he never produced a long continuous monograph on a single subject.[150] The format of collected studies or lectures remained his favored mode of presentation throughout his career, and perhaps reflects the limitations imposed by a work schedule that allowed him little continuous time for his scholarly research.

In all these works Goldziher applied the same methodology that he had learned ultimately from Strauss, Bauer, and the Tübingen school, appreciated as relevant to his own liberal way of thinking as a result of his exposure to Geiger, and first advocated and applied himself in his critique of Renan. The method he espoused, and which he was the first to apply systematically to the study of Islam on such a broad-ranging scale, viewed texts not as depositories of mere facts that research should ferret out and line up one after another, but as sources in which one could discern the stages of transformation through which a community based on a common religious vision had passed as it struggled to come to terms with a host of new situations and problems. By careful and critical analysis of these sources, one could extrapolate important new insights on such processes of development not only in religious thought, but in literature, social perceptions, and politics as well.

It is important to bear in mind that if all this sounds perfectly conventional now, more than a hundred years after the publication of *Muhammedanische Studien*, it was a completely novel departure in the late nineteenth century. The way forward suggested by Geiger's work had already been explored, it is true, by two of his most enthusiastic orientalist followers prior to Goldziher: Wellhausen had applied his formulations to the pre-exilic books of the Old Testament,[151] material that even the powerful Geiger had not dared to touch, and Nöldeke's *Geschichte des Qorâns* likewise involved a fairly straightforward transplant of Geiger's methods to the study of the Qur'an.[152] But *Muhammedanische Studien*, on the other hand, encompassed the entire vast range of Arab-Islamic literary culture—historical texts, poetry, *adab*, proverb collections, Qur'anic exegesis, doctrinal works, *fiqh, ḥadīth,* biographical dictionaries, and so forth—and from them laid out an incredibly rich vista of historical experience that not only had not been known before, but even had not been sought. It would be no exaggeration to say that Goldziher's colleagues were stunned by his work; Nöldeke, for example, conceded that he would never have dared to review *Muhammedanische Studien* had he not felt that others were no less unprepared for the appearance of such a book and equally unqualified to assess it.[153]

Muhammedanische Studien and the works that followed from Goldziher's pen not only imparted new discoveries, ideas, and methodologies, they also set a standard. Arab-Islamic history as a string of facts extracted from a few key texts continued to be written, of course, as indeed history was pursued in other fields.[154] But it was the model of Goldziher that, even in his own lifetime, came to be recognized as marking the way genuinely serious scholarship on the subject should proceed. Though too little is as yet known to comment in detail, I would at least suggest that this had a major impact on the professionalization of the study of Arabic and Islamic culture and history. Work of the sort undertaken by Goldziher required a full mastery of the Arabic language, detailed reading in and command of a vast array of sources, and a well thought-out critical methodology to bring to bear on the evidence. His example could only be followed by those with a systematic university training and continuous access to specialized library resources on a large scale; this may well have been a factor in the decline of the role played by such types as gentleman scholars, colonial administrators, adventurers, and missionaries, who by the time of Goldziher's death in 1921 had to a considerable extent been displaced by a new generation of professional academics legitimated by quite different structures of learning and authority.

This is not to argue that Goldziher was a flawless paragon of virtue, either personally or in intellectual terms. He seems never to have realized that his own fiery convictions did not entitle him to treat with contempt those whose own views—perhaps equally heartfelt—differed from his. He was clearly obsessed with the wrong that the world had done him by diverting him from his anticipated professorship to what he regarded as a menial position as secretary of the Neolog community, and his *Tagebuch* leaves no doubt that in this role he could become quite difficult and unpleasant. So far as one can tell, his joy in life was his academic work; as will have been noticed from the examples cited above, trips abroad were undertaken for purposes of attending orientalist congresses or conducting research in foreign libraries, and holidays within Hungary always seem to have been engulfed by efforts to finalize papers and books for publication.[155]

Intellectually he also had his faults and shortcomings. Throughout his life he was keen to serve as an objective and sympathetic observer of the Islamic world and its history, but his works are not entirely free from ethnic slurs, usually aimed—as in his comments on Jewish topics—at figures or groups opposed to his universal paradigm for true religious and communal progress. Being a member of a religious minority and a citizen of a country in which many patterns of communal identity were active may have enriched his professional point of view on medieval Arab-Islamic history, but he seems never to have realized that these inputs could distort as well as clarify. His early dismissal of the Arab role in the rise of Islam,[156] for example, clearly reflects an overly slavish adherence to a methodological paradigm at the expense of the personal element that, paradoxically enough, was otherwise so extremely important to him.

Many of these excesses disappeared when Hungarian works were rewritten in German for exposure to his professional peers in Europe, but this too involved certain problems. Goldziher was possessed of a colossal ego; he exulted in his skills as a scholar, prided himself in his academic accomplishments, and considered that the honors that streamed his way were simply his just deserts. All the same, however, he had limited self-confidence and constantly feared for his reputation among his fellow orientalists. He was never sure whether his work was that of inspired brilliance, as he hoped, or deluded fancy, as he feared. His *Muhammedanische Studien*, for example, languished in his desk for years, and was published only at the persistent insistence of his close friends.[157] As he corrected the proofs of the first volume he continued to be ill at ease:

> I saw nought but the most hideous disgrace. In my imagination I heard the disdainful laughter of Nöldeke, saw De Goeje shrugging his shoulders and D.H. [Müller] turning up his nose; the friends, the "coercers," I saw disappointed in their expectations, withdrawing their support.[158]

The same self-doubt arose in the case of his *Abhandlungen zur arabischen Philologie*, and then again with the *Vorlesungen über den Islam*. Although in the latter case Goldziher was at least pleased with his work and confident of its reception,[159] the final text still went to press only after considerable pestering by friends and colleagues.[160] His habit of writing first in Hungarian was thus a deliberate tactic designed to afford him time to view his work in print and decide how to proceed.[161]

The transition to German usually resulted in the appearance of a far more mature piece of work, and it was always much better documented. But one thing that fell by the wayside in such shifts was his willingness to state explicitly what his methodology really was. One rarely sees references to Geiger, for example, in his German publications, and explanations of his approach to texts, though present, are not all that recognizable as such unless one knows what to expect in the first place. This silence on method—what one might more generally describe as a failure of nerve—was such that in his obituary for Goldziher, C.H. Becker (1876–1933) characterized his scholarship as displaying a "reverential fear of hypotheses."[162] This is of course untrue, but it was to a large extent Goldziher's own fault that while his works were immediately mined and quoted for specific points, his broader vision for the study of the history of the Middle East, Judaism, and Islam was not appreciated and pursued until attention was drawn to it long after his death by Joseph Schacht (1902–69).[163] It is therefore necessary to draw a clear distinction between the influence of Goldziher in terms of the specific knowledge and conclusions imparted in his German works, which have been appreciated and built upon since his own lifetime, and the broader methodological insights implicit in these works, but mainly spelled out in his Hungarian contributions and therefore of far more recent impact on scholarship.

In the present context two final questions need to be addressed. First, did Goldziher's critique of Renan form any part of some overall conception of what he thought orientalism was all about? And second, did the fact that Goldziher was Jewish make any difference to him or to his work as a scholar?

Though he rarely speaks of such matters in his German publications, Goldziher frequently expresses his views on orientalist scholarship and orientalism as a professional calling in his Hungarian works and personal letters. Significantly, the clearest statement on the subject comes in his memorial essay on Renan, where in the prelude to his discussion of *Langues sémitiques* he asks the question directly: "What does the word 'orientalist' really mean?" His answer is at one level the obvious one: an orientalist is "a scholar who has decided to take up the study of the spiritual traditions of Eastern man." But further, he says, the value of the scholarship of any one researcher as compared to another depends upon the perspectives he adopts, the aims for which he strives, and the extent to which these are relevant to "the great questions in the history of human thought." The great syntheses are thus the contributions that are celebrated and remembered: hence the reputation of Renan, the subject of Goldziher's paper.[164] But in a formulation that exactly contradicts Renan's use of the very same metaphor,[165] he argues that such synthetic work stands on the foundations prepared by other scholars, those "who with laudable industry produce the little building blocks that neither indicate anything of the dimensions of the structure ultimately to be built from them, nor the purpose that the building will serve, but that are nevertheless of great importance in the generation of scholarship's material results and ancillary aids."[166] Among the scholars he had in mind here was probably von Kremer, whose works he had earlier praised in terms very similar to those in the letter to Baron Victor Rosen already cited above.[167]

What then did Goldziher consider the common task of orientalists and orientalism to be? Here again he leaves us in no doubt. In his 1868 interview with Baron Jószef Eötvös (1801–71), minister of religion and public education for Hungary, to justify his plans for doctoral studies in Germany, he had "explained the importance of the study of mankind's institutions in terms of their historical development in religious and political life."[168] The same viewpoint appears again in his memorial essay on Renan, where he identifies the task of orientalism as the study of the Eastern world and its various literatures for the purpose of discovering their contribution to human thought. This history cannot be written from a Western viewpoint alone; it is up to orientalist scholarship to provide the missing dimension of Eastern history and culture essential for a truly universal perspective.[169]

This highly idealistic perspective, if distinctly unsurprising from Goldziher in light of the powerful influence on him from Geiger and the Haskala, was of course one that many scholars of the day did not share. Still, Goldziher appreciated and acknowledged their contributions even when their own perspectives clashed sharply with his on matters of great importance to him. A bitter critic of Westernization and Western influence in the Near East, he nevertheless held in very high regard such scholars as Christiaan Snouck Hurgronje (1857–1936), who held a post in the colonial administration of the Dutch East Indies and regarded Islam as a political opponent to be disposed of on the way to the assimilation of Asia to Western civilization,[170] and von Kremer, who served in the Habsburg diplomatic corps and sat on the international commission for the supervision of the Egyptian national debt.[171] He deplored the anti-Islamic prejudice that was so often passed off in academic dress in his day,[172] yet one of his closest personal friends and professional colleagues was Nöldeke, whose publications and private correspondence flaunt bigotry and prejudice of a level that Goldziher must have found highly offensive.[173] His ire was quickly inflamed by frauds, opportunists, and general incompetents whose work made little or no contribution to knowledge,[174] and he had little patience for the "Talk Machines," the "Professores Linguarum Orientalium" who mastered languages but put them to no further use.[175] But, apart from such types, he seems to have regarded his field as a fraternity of colleagues[176] working in different ways toward goals to which he attached great importance. He clearly sensed a spirit of solidarity among orientalists. One of his last students recalls Goldziher advising him of two things he must do "if you want to prosper in life:" give lectures at the orientalists' congresses, and "answer every letter or card you receive, even if your answer be negative."[177] And when this solidarity was broken by the First World War, which witnessed the cashiering of colleagues from the academies of opposing nations and the turning of scholarship to propaganda purposes, he rightly saw the damage as serious and potentially irreversible.[178]

Finally, what role did Goldziher's Jewish background play in all this? The answer may seem obvious in light of what has been said above, but the question does need to be asked in light of the fact that Goldziher was a Hungarian nationalist who, like so many other assimilated Jews in Habsburg domains at the time, had seen in the Compromise of 1867—wrongly, as it was to prove—the dawning of a new age in which the emancipated Jews were being invited to play a full participatory role in society at large. He looked to Jewish religious reform as a means to achieve the assimilation of Jews as citizens in their own countries, and (like Geiger) he had no sympathy for ideologies that conflicted with this aim, including Zionism.[179]

As is well known, he declined numerous offers of prestigious positions and professorships outside of Hungary throughout his career. Once it became clear that the promised professorship in Budapest was to be denied him at the eleventh hour, his supporters abroad made efforts to situate him elsewhere. Contacts in Austria and Germany sought to gain him a place in the Habsburg ministry of education, and the Egyptologist Georg Ebers (1837–98), one of his former teachers, campaigned on his behalf for directorship of the Khedivial Library in Cairo. In 1885 he was offered a professorship at Prague that Nöldeke urged him to accept. After the publication of *Muhammedanische Studien*, further opportunities arose: a professorship at Heidelberg in 1893 (with virtual guarantee of succession to Nöldeke within a few years), the chair at Cambridge in succession to William Robertson Smith (1846–94) the next year, and similarly prestigious offers from Strassburg, Paris, Cairo, Jerusalem, and various universities in the United States.[180] All these he declined, despite his profound unhappiness with his situation as a frustrated academic. His place, he considered, was in Hungary: as he told two of his last students, "Scholarship has no country, but the scholar does have his country."[181] In this maxim one can see, first, the enduring influence of the Compromise of 1867 and the connections between Reform Judaism and Magyar nationalism,[182] and second (and related to this), some of the zeal of the Goldziher of the 1870s, when statements in his *Keleti naplóm* reflect a conviction that however relevant a reformer's views might be to other peoples, it is to his own people and on his own ground that he should express himself.[183] The fact that Goldziher continued to publish his work on Judaism and modern issues largely in Hungarian is surely to be seen in this light.

For Goldziher, religion was a matter of personal spiritual identity and a basis for common action toward universal goals shared with those of other faiths. The sanctity of religious identity—whether among Jews or Muslims—was an extremely important issue to him, and threats to such identity at the personal or communal level he opposed with great hostility. He despised Christian missionaries and those who, like Vámbéry, converted for the sake of material gain,[184] and he was dismayed at the effects of Westernization in the Near East. As indicated above, his critique of Renan in large part sprang from his conviction that Renan's work was destructive and demeaning, and, because it was so far off the mark, revealed no way forward. Though surprisingly tolerant of bigotry among his scholarly colleagues, Goldziher was a man of high religious ideals himself. He saw the study of Islam as a means to gain further insights into and confirmation of ideals relevant to Jews and Muslims alike. In the end, he considered that the conclusions he was reaching had a specifically universal dimension to them, and found them crucial to his own personal sense of spiritual and professional fulfillment, especially during his long years of frustrated and only intermittent participation in academic life.

His starting point was the challenge posed by the modern world to the situation of Jewry in central and eastern Europe. Had this been of no concern or relevance to him personally, one would wonder why he ever should have taken up the study of Islam, an exceedingly obscure subject in the Pest of his youth,[185] and thus, whether *Muhammedanische Studien* or any of his other classic works would ever have seen the light of day.

Notes

1. *Muhammedanische Studien* (Halle: Max Niemeyer, 1889–90); ed. and trans. S.M. Stern and C.R. Barber, *Muslim Studies* (London: George Allen and Unwin, 1967–71).
2. *Tagebuch*, ed. Alexander Scheiber (Leiden: E.J. Brill, 1978); cf. 117–21 for the Stockholm congress.
3. Even his most eminent colleagues recognized that his methodologies and analyses far surpassed the work being done by others. See, for example, 162–63 below.
4. See, for example, Róbert Simon, *Ignác Goldziher: His Life and Scholarship as Reflected in His Works and Correspondence* (Leiden: E.J. Brill, Budapest: Magyar Tudományos Académia, 1986), 13–76; Johann Fück, *Die arabischen Studien in Europa bis in den Anfang des 20. Jahrhunderts* (Leipzig: Otto Harrassowitz, 1955), 226–31; Jean-Jacques Waardenburg, *L'Islam dans le miroir de l'occident*, 3d rev. ed. (Paris and the Hague: Mouton, 1962), index; Lawrence I. Conrad, "The Dervish's Disciple: On the Personality and Intellectual Milieu of the Young Ignaz Goldziher," *Journal of the Royal Asiatic Society*, 1990: 225–66; idem, "The Pilgrim from Pest: Goldziher's Study Tour to the Near East (1873–1874)," in *Golden Roads: Migration, Pilgrimage and Travel in Mediaeval and Modern Islam,* ed. Ian Richard Netton (London: Curzon Press, 1993), 110–59.
5. Theodor Nöldeke, *Geschichte des Qorâns* (Göttingen: Verlag der Dieterichschen Buchhandlung, 1860). On the importance of this work, written as Nöldeke's entry in a prize competition, see Fück, *Arabischen Studien in Europa*, 217–18. An extensively revised version was published under the editorship of Friedrich Schwally and later Gotthelf Bergsträsser and Otto Pretzl (Leipzig: T. Weicher, 1909–38).
6. On Renan, see Harold W. Wardman, *Ernest Renan: A Critical Biography* (London: Athlone Press, 1964). For an assessment of Goldziher's critique from the perspective of the history of racism, see also Maurice Olender,

Les langues du paradis: aryens et sémites, un couple providential (Paris: Gallimard, 1989), 153–75.

7. For some preliminary observations, see Conrad, "The Pilgrim from Pest," 118–38.
8. Cf. the brief treatment of the subject in my "The Pilgrim from Pest," 142–45.
9. Edward W. Said, *Orientalism* (London: Routledge and Kegan Paul, 1978), 1, 3–4, 98, 123–30.
10. This was not the first time that Said had turned his attention to Renan. See his *Beginnings: Intention and Method* (Baltimore: Johns Hopkins University Press, 1975), 215–22, where Renan's *Vie de Jésus* (1863) is discussed. Cf. also Tim Brennan, "Places of Mind, Occupied Lands: Edward Said on Philology," in *Edward Said: A Critical Reader*, ed. Michael Sprinker (Oxford: Blackwell, 1992), 74–95.
11. Critical edition in Renan's *Oeuvres complètes*, ed. Henriette Psichari (Paris: Calmann-Lévy, 1947–61), 8:127–589.
12. Said, *Orientalism*, 6, 17–18, 19, 105, 130–48, 197.
13. Ibid., 18.
14. E.g. Edward Mortimer during the discussion of Said's speech at the 1979 International Press Seminar, *The Arab Image in Western Mass Media* (London: Outline Books, 1980), 110–11.
15. Said, *Orientalism*, 18–19, 105.
16. *The Arab Image in Western Mass Media*, 110–11. There is nothing in these passages or elsewhere to indicate that Said had ever actually read anything by Goldziher.
17. E.g. Gerard Croese (1642–1710), a historian of the Quakers and author of a work entitled *Homeros Hebraios, sive Historia Hebraeorum ab Homero Hebraicis nominibus ac sententiis conscripta in Odyssea et Iliade* (Dordrecht: Theodore Gorie, 1704).
18. The Islamic holdings at the Leiden University Library roughly equal those of the British Library (ca. 23,000), and those of the Deutsche Staatsbibliothek in Berlin and the Bibliothèque Nationale in Paris are again about the same (ca. 12,000). See Geoffrey Roper, ed., *World Survey of Islamic Manuscripts* (London: Al-Furqān Islamic Heritage Foundation, 1992–94), 1:275–90 (Paris), 320–29 (Berlin); 2:365–76 (Leiden); 3:471–90 (London).
19. See Johann Fück, "Die arabischen Studien in Europa vom 12. bis in den Anfang des 19. Jahrhunderts," in *Beiträge zur Arabistik, Semitistik und Islamwissenschaft,* eds. Richard Hartmann and Helmuth Scheel (Leipzig: Otto Harrassowitz, 1944), 128–37, 143–57, 163–68, 174–78, 189–208; Peter Bachmann, *Yūḥannā Ya'qūb Rāyska: mu'assis al-dirāsāt al-'arabīya fī Almāniya* (Beirut: Orient-Institut der Deutschen Morgenländischen Gesellschaft, 1974).

20. Ignaz Goldziher, *Die Ẓâhiriten. Ihr Lehrsystem und ihre Geschichte* (Leipzig: O. Schulze, 1884), 1; trans. and ed. Wolfgang Behn, *The Ẓāhirīs: Their Doctrine and their History* (Leiden: E.J. Brill, 1971), 1.
21. See Fück, "Die arabischen Studien in Europa," 226–27.
22. The relevant materials are assembled and discussed in G. Pondaven and Louis Le Guennec, *Un maître de Renan à Saint-Sulpice: M. l'abbé Le Hir de Morlaix* (Brest: Imprimerie de la Presse Libérale, 1923).
23. Ernest Renan to Henriette Renan, Paris, 19 May 1847, in Renan's *Lettres de famille (1838–71)*, ed. Psichari in *Oeuvres complètes*, 9:996. For similarly effusive praise of Burnouf, see ibid., 937, 967–68, 971, 973–74, 975, 979, 1010, 1111, 1148, 1167, 1174–75; also Ernest Renan to Charles Daremberg, Rome, 4 March 1850, in Renan's *Correspondence*, ed. Psichari in *Oeuvres complètes*, 10:78; Renan, *Langues sémitiques*, 544; idem, *Questions contemporaines* (1868), ed. Psichari in *Oeuvres complètes*, 1:121–26 (originally written as an obituary for Burnouf in the *Moniteur universal*, 13 June 1852, on the day after his death). Renan also dedicated his *L'avenir de la science* (1848) to Burnouf; ed. Psichari in *Oeuvres complètes*, 3:729–32.
24. Christian Lassen, *Indische Alterthumskunde* (Bonn: H.B. Koenig, and Leipzig: L.A. Kittler, 1847–62), 1:414–17. Cf. Renan, *Langues sémitiques*, 146 n. 1.
25. Cf. Salomon Lefmann, *Franz Bopp. Sein Leben und seine Wissenschaft* (Berlin: Georg Reimer, 1891–97); Richard Albert Wilson, *The Miraculous Birth of Language* (London: J.M. Dent, 1942), 34–36.
26. *Langues sémitiques*, 134.
27. Renan, *Questions contemporaines*, 129 (originally published in the *Journal des débats*, 20 October 1857), with the interesting caveat that his comment, made with reference to Étienne Quatremère (1782–1857), should not be taken as criticism.
28. *Orientalism*, 177.
29. See Ernest Renan, *Souvenirs d'enfance et de jeunesse* (1883), ed. Psichari in his *Oeuvres complètes*, 2:905, referring to the book as "a very imperfect essay that I presented to the Volney competition in 1847."
30. *Urschrift und Übersetzungen der Bibel in ihrer Abhängigkeit von der innern Entwicklung des Judentums* (1857), 2nd ed. by Paul Kahle (Frankfurt am Main: Verlag Madda, 1928), 20–100. More will be said about Geiger below; cf. also the contribution of Jacob Lassner to this volume.
31. Two of his studies are reprinted as appendices to Goldziher's *Mythology among the Hebrews* (n. 53 below), 363–446. Cf. also the discussion of Steinthal's influence on Goldziher in ibid., xxviii–xxix; *Tagebuch*, 87, 138.
32. Primarily in his *Les premières civilisations: études d'histoire et d'archéologie* (Paris: Maisonneuve, 1874), 2:81–99, 113–46.

33. *The Chaldaean Account of Genesis* (London: S. Low, Marston, Searle, and Rivington, 1876). This work on cuneiform parallels to legends in the book of Genesis was a landmark in its time and went through four editions in its first year of publication. Goldziher's view of Smith and his work was again extremely positive; see his "George Smith," *Egyetemes philologiai közlöny* 1 (1877): 22–35, 102–10, 160–67.
34. Cf. the summary in *Mythology among the Hebrews*, 5–9.
35. Conrad, "The Pilgrim from Pest," 121–26.
36. Alfred von Kremer, *Geschichte der herrschenden Ideen des Islam. Der Gottesbegriff, die Prophetie und Staatsidee* (Leipzig: F.A. Brockhaus, 1868); idem, *Culturgeschichte des Orients unter den Chalifen* (Vienna: Wilhelm Braumüller, 1875–77). Both books were frequently cited by Goldziher in his own publications.
37. *Tagebuch*, 113, 115. Goldziher's appreciation of von Kremer is discussed in Simon, *Ignác Goldziher*, 31–34.
38. See David Philipson, *The Reform Movement in Judaism* (London: Macmillan, 1907), 3–379; Max Wiener, *Jüdische Religion im Zeitalter der Emanzipation* (Berlin: Philo Verlag, 1933); Michael A. Meyer, *Response to Modernity: A History of the Reform Movement in Judaism* (Oxford: Oxford University Press, 1988), 3–212.
39. *Tagebuch*, 28–29, 33.
40. See Horton Harris, *David Friedrich Strauss and His Theology* (Cambridge: Cambridge University Press, 1973); idem, *The Tübingen School* (Oxford: Clarendon Press, 1975).
41. The classic formulation of Geiger's thinking along these lines was his *Urschrift und Übersetzungen der Bibel.* On this work see Felix Perles, "Lebenswerk. Der Gelehrte," in *Abraham Geiger. Leben und Lebenswerk,* ed. Ludwig Geiger (Berlin: Georg Reimer, 1910), 316–27; Wiener, *Jüdische Religion*, 251–53.
42. Conrad, "The Pilgrim from Pest," 124–25.
43. *Tagebuch*, 39; cf. also 153.
44. Ignaz Goldziher, "Mit nyerhetünk a beduin élet ismerete által az Ó-Testamentom megértésére nézve?," *Protestáns tudományos szemle* 1 (1869): 73–76; idem, "A nemzetiségi kérdés az araboknál," *Értekezések a nyelv és széptudományok köréből* 3, no. 8 (1873): 1–64; idem, "Mahommed és az arab nemzeti hiúság," *Athenaeum* (Budapest) 1 (1873): 148–57.
45. E.g. Abraham Geiger, *Nachgelassene Schriften*, ed. Ludwig Geiger (Berlin: Louis Gerschel Verlagsbuchhandlung, 1875–78), 5:342.
46. *Tagebuch*, 68 (where he calls him "the Afghan Abd-al-Dschakâl" and characterizes him as "an anti-English agitator, exile, journalist, and polemicist against Renan"), 108 ("my Afghan friend Dschelâl al-Dîn and his exiled companions"). On the Renan–Afghānī debate, see below, 149.

47. *Mythology among the Hebrews*, xv, xxix (cf. n. 53 below).
48. See his "A sémi faj őshazájáról és vándorlásáról," *Nyelvtudományi Közlemények* 12 (1875): 285–340.
49. Simon, *Ignác Goldziher*, 74, 89, citing a review of the work in a Budapest periodical.
50. *Mythology among the Hebrews*, xv.
51. Cf. *Tagebuch*, 74; also *Keleti naplóm*, trans. Raphael Patai as *Ignaz Goldziher and His Oriental Diary: a Translation and Psychological Portrait* (Detroit: Wayne State University Press, 1987), 101, 121, where he alludes to work on the book with evident relish.
52. *Tagebuch*, 74.
53. *Der Mythos bei den Hebräern und seine geschichtliche Entwicklung. Untersuchungen zur Mythologie und Religionswissenschaft* (Leipzig: F.A. Brockhaus, 1876). I have used the translation by Russell Martineau, *Mythology among the Hebrews and Its Historical Development* (London: Longman's, Green, and Co., 1877), which contains further additions and corrections by the author.
54. *Az Iszlám. Tanulmányok a muhammedán vallás története köréből* (Budapest: Magyar Tudományos Académia Könyvtára, 1881), 1–100.
55. "Renan mint orientalista," *Emlékbeszédek a M.T. Akadémia elhúnyt tagjai fölött* 8.2 (1894): esp. 20–33. Here I will follow the separate pagination given for Goldziher's text in the *Emlékbeszédek*.
56. *Mythology among the Hebrews*, xxi–xxiii, 1–5.
57. Ibid., 5–7.
58. Ibid., 6.
59. Renan, *Langues sémitiques*, 148.
60. *Mythology among the Hebrews*, 7–8.
61. Ibid., 327–28.
62. Cf. *Oriental Diary*, 109.
63. *Mythology among the Hebrews*, 237–42.
64. Ibid., 35–48.
65. Ibid., 327–28.
66. Ibid., 231–58.
67. Ibid., 316–36; "George Smith," 22–35, 100–10, 160–67.
68. *Oriental Diary*, 132.
69. Ibid., 135, 136.
70. Ibid., 135. Cf. Jeremiah 38:1–13.
71. "Palesztina ismeretének haladása az utolsó három évtizedben," *Értekezések a nyelv és széptudományok köréből* 13, no. 3 (1886): 43–49.
72. Said, *Orientalism*, 209, citing Waardenburg's *L'Islam dans le miroir de l'occident* in general.
73. Goldziher had extremely negative opinions of both Christian evangelism

and the Jewish rabbinical establishment. On the former, see below, n. 113. On the latter, see Conrad, "The Dervish's Disciple," 236–37; idem, "The Pilgrim from Pest," 127–29.

74. *Tagebuch*, 86–89. Years later the matter had still not been forgotten or forgiven. In 1912 a rabbi in Vágujhely raised a protest that such an enemy of religion as the author of *Mythology among the Hebrews* should be on the faculty of the rabbinical seminary (*Tagebuch*, 272).
75. On this startling denial of racism and the question of Renan's anti-Semitism, see below, actual pages.
76. Renan to Goldziher, als, Paris, 14 September 1876 (Library of the Hungarian Academy of Sciences, Oriental Collection). This was exactly the sort of quibble that, as we have already seen, Goldziher dismissed as unhelpful to discussion of the subject.
77. German translations of Renan's lecture, al-Afghānī's critique, and Renan's reply are usefully collected in Renan's *Der Islam und die Wissenschaft* (Basel: M. Bernheim, 1883).
78. See Nikkie Keddie, *Sayyid Jamāl ad-Dīn "al-Afghānī": A Political Biography* (Berkeley and Los Angeles: University of California Press, 1972), 81–92, 189–99.
79. "Renan mint orientalista," 34–36.
80. Cf. *Tagebuch*, 63, where he hardly does more than acknowledge his awareness that the exchange had occurred.
81. Renan to Goldziher, als, Paris, 20 May 1884 (Hungarian Academy of Sciences, Oriental Collection); *Tagebuch*, 108.
82. *Tagebuch*, 153.
83. *Mythology among the Hebrews*, xxxiv–xxxv.
84. Ibid., 79–87, 188–89, 334–35.
85. There has long been a tendency, set in motion by well-intended younger colleagues of Goldziher, to dismiss *Mythology among the Hebrews* as an anomalous and misconceived product of his youth and a work that he later disowned. See, for example, C.H. Becker, "Ignaz Goldziher," in his *Islamstudien* (Leipzig: Verlag Quelle und Meyer, 1924–32), 2:505, describing the work as " a book on which I pass no judgment, but which played no role in the later life of Goldziher and about which he himself later wished to know nothing further." But Simon (*Ignác Goldziher*, 74–75) has demonstrated that this view is completely false, and the continuing influence of the book's main themes will be seen in the remainder of this study.
86. *Tagebuch*, 75–76. On the context see Simon, *Ignác Goldziher*, 49–52; also Miklós Maróth, "The Reception of Arabic Philosophy at the University of Budapest," in *The Introduction of Arabic Philosophy into Europe*, eds. Charles E. Butterworth and Blake Andrée Kessel (Leiden: E.J. Brill, 1994), 105–6, on the subsequent rivalry between the two scholars.

87. *Tagebuch*, 92–93. Cf. also *Keleti naplóm*, Jewish Theological Seminary (New York), Ms. Small Collections Box 1, 108–9, an appendix on Goldziher's travels between 1876 and 1900, not included in Patai's *Oriental Diary* translation.
88. *Tagebuch*, 93; *Keleti naplóm*, 108. On the book, see above, n. 54, and the further discussion below.
89. *Az Iszlám*, chap. 1: "A sivatag vallása es az iszlám," 4, for Renan.
90. Ibid., 15–22.
91. Ibid., 37–45.
92. Ibid., 6–14, 46–86.
93. Ibid., 92–99.
94. Ibid., 100.
95. "A nyelvtudomány történetéről az araboknál," *Nyelvtudományi közlemények* 14 (1878): 309–75.
96. "A muhammedán jogtudomány eredetéröl," *Értekezések a nyelv és széptudományok köréből* 11, no. 9 (1884): 1–23.
97. *A történetirás az arab irodalomban* (Budapest: Magyar Tudományos Acadêmia, 1895).
98. *Mythology among the Hebrews*, 328. The quotation is from Julius Braun, *Naturgeschichte der Sage: Rückführung aller religiösen Ideen, Sagen, Systeme auf ihren gemeinsamen Stammbaum* (Munich: F. Bruckmann, 1864–65), 1:8.
99. *Muhammedanische Studien*, 1:12; = *Muslim Studies*, 1:21.
100. *Vorlesungen über den Islam*, 2nd ed., 3–4; = *Introduction to Islamic Theology and Law*, 5 (cf. n. 149 below).
101. Cf. Geiger, *Urschrift und Übersetzungen der Bibel*, 20–100.
102. Ignaz Goldziher, *A zsidóság lényege és fejlődése*, ed. József Bánóczi and Ignác Gábor (Budapest: Népszerü Zsidó Könyvtár, 1923–24), the first five lectures from which are reprinted from *Magyar-Zsidó Szemle* 5 (1888): 1–14, 65–80, 138–55, 261–79, 389–406.
103. *Tagebuch*, 111–12.
104. Conrad, "The Dervish's Disciple," 225–66.
105. Ibid., 240–42; idem, "The Pilgrim from Pest," 115, 134–37.
106. Quoted in Fück, *Arabischen Studien in Europa*, 226 n. 577.
107. *Tagebuch*, 110.
108. Ibid., 153.
109. Ibid., 159.
110. Ed. Psichari in Renan's *Oeuvres complètes*, vol. 6.
111. Ibid., 57–67.
112. Not even in his chapter on comparative mythology in his *Nouvelles études d'histoire religieuse* (1884), ed. Psichari in *Oeuvres complètes*, 7:740–45, where he considers some of the same themes that Goldziher had discussed;

nor even, for that matter, in his correspondence, though in 1892–93 Goldziher would not have had access to much of this. It is also interesting to note that while his personal library of more than 6,000 volumes contained numerous books on Islamic and Arabic themes written by the leading authorities of his time, Renan possessed none of the many seminal contributions to these subjects authored by Goldziher; see *Catalogue de la bibliothèque de M. Ernest Renan* (Paris: Calmann Lévy, 1895), 160–80.

113. Conrad, "The Dervish's Disciple," 236; idem, "The Pilgrim from Pest," 129–32.
114. Ed. Psichari in Renan's *Oeuvres complètes*, 4:10–427.
115. *Souvenirs d'enfance*, 893, referring to "an exaggerated school, that of the Protestants of Tübingen, minds without literary tact and without a sense of proportion, to which, thanks to the Catholics, the study of Jesus and the age of the Apostles has found itself almost entirely abandoned."
116. Ernest Renan, *La réforme intellectuelle et morale* (1871), ed. Psichari in *Oeuvres complètes*, 1:409–75. Cf. Henriette Psichari, *Renan et la guerre de 70* (Paris: A. Michel, 1947).
117. *Mythology among the Hebrews*, 4, referring to "a scheme of race-psychology invented by Renan himself, which at the first glance seems so natural and sounds so plausible when described with all the elegance of style of which he is master, that it has become an incontestable scientific dogma to a large proportion of the professional world—for even the territory of science is sometimes dominated by mere dogmas—and is treated by learned and cultivated people not specifically engaged in this study as an actual axiom in the consideration of race-peculiarities." Cf. also Olender, *Les langues du paradis*, 169–71.
118. Ernest Renan, *L'Ecclésiaste* (1882), ed. Psichari in *Oeuvres complètes*, 7:554.
119. Renan, *Histoire du peuple d'Israël*, 1038.
120. Shmuel Almog, "The Racial Motif in Renan's Attitude to Jews and Judaism," in *Antisemitism Through the Ages*, ed. Shmuel Almog (Oxford: Pergamon, 1988), 255–78.
121. *Souvenirs d'enfance*, 756.
122. *Histoire du peuple d'Israël*, 1198–205.
123. *Vie de Jésus*, 341.
124. *Tagebuch*, 162; *Keleti naplóm*, 108.
125. *Tagebuch*, 165–66.
126. "Renan mint orientalista," 8–10.
127. Ibid., 15–20.
128. Ibid., 32–33, referring to a regular feature section in the *Journal asiatique*.
129. Ibid., 23–30.
130. Ibid., 25–27. On Franz Bopp, the renowned Sanskrit philologist, see above, 141–42.

131. Ibid., 23–30.
132. Ibid., 33–47.
133. Ibid., 34–35.
134. *Averroès et l'averroïsme: essai historique* (1852), ed. Psichari in Renan's *Oeuvres complètes*, 3:21–142. The part in question comprises Renan's account of the life, works, and doctrines of Ibn Rushd, while later sections deal with the reception of his philosophy in Europe.
135. "Renan mint orientalista," 41–43. Cf. *Catalogue de la bibliothèque de M. Ernest Renan*, 173–74, showing that to the end of his life Renan owned very few of the texts by or studies on al-Ghazālī or Ibn Rushd that were becoming available through the course of the nineteenth century. It is of course true that in Paris he would have had easy access to such books without purchasing them himself, but this could also be said of any of the many other topics represented in his large personal library.
136. "Renan mint orientalista," 49–88.
137. Ibid., 61–62.
138. Ibid., 78.
139. Ibid., 69–70.
140. Ibid., 74–75.
141. Ibid., 88–100.
142. Discussed by Renan in detail in his *Questions contemporaines*, 143–80. Cf. Wardman, *Ernest Renan*, 77–78.
143. "Renan mint orientalista," 1–20, 88–94.
144. Ibid., 72. The quotation is from Renan's *Nouvelles études*, 807, in a chapter on Buddhism with reference to the historical settings that give rise to myths.
145. Renan specifically insists on this point; see his *Langues sémitiques*, 155.
146. Apart from his later study on historiography (n. 97 above), Goldziher also subsequently reviewed the published correspondence between Renan and his lifelong friend Marcelin Berthelot (1827–1907); "Renan és Berthelot leverezése," *Budapesi Szemle* 96 (1898): 261–90. This work was unavailable to me as this paper was being written.
147. *Az Iszlám*, n. 54 above.
148. *Abhandlungen zur arabischen Philologie* (Leiden: E.J. Brill, 1896–99). See Simon, *Ignác Goldziher*, 105–25; Conrad, "The Pilgrim from Pest," 139–40.
149. *Vorlesungen über den Islam* (Heidelberg: Carl Winter, 1910); trans. Andras and Ruth Hamori, *Introduction to Islamic Theology and Law* (Princeton: Princeton University Press, 1981). A second German edition was published by Franz Babinger (Heidelberg: Carl Winter, 1925) on the basis of Goldziher's own interleaved copy of the book bearing many additions.
150. His *Ẓâhiriten* (1884) was an essay originally intended for inclusion in *Muhammedanische Studien*; see *Ẓâhiriten*, v; = *Ẓāhirīs*, xiii. His last ma-

jor work, *Die Richtungen der islamischen Koranauslegung* (Leiden: E.J. Brill, 1920), consists of his Olaus Petri Lectures, delivered at the University of Uppsala in September 1913.

151. Julius Wellhausen, *Geschichte Israels* (Berlin: Georg Reimer, 1878), better known in its second ed., *Prolegomena zur Geschichte Israels* (Berlin: Walter de Gruyter, 1883); trans. J.S. Black and Allan Menzies, *Prolegomena to the History of Israel* (Edinburgh: A. and C. Black, 1885). Cf. Lothar Perlitt, *Vatke und Wellhausen* (Berlin: Alfred Töpelmann, 1965), 153–243. On his career in Arab-Islamic studies, see Fück, *Arabischen Studien in Europa*, 223–26; Kurt Rudolph, *Wellhausen als Arabist* (Berlin: Akademie Verlag, 1983).
152. Ludwig Geiger, *Abraham Geiger*, 153, 154, 228, 324, 325, 410–11; also Nöldeke in *Zeitschrift der Deutschen Morgenländischen Gesellschaft* 20 (1866): 457.
153. *Wiener Zeitschrift für die Kunde des Morgenlandes* 5 (1891): 43.
154. On the traditional attitude toward the task of the historian in nineteenth-century European intellectual life and the quest for the past "wie es eigentlich gewesen," see Edward Hallett Carr, *What Is History?* (New York: Random House, 1961), 5–7; Karl-Georg Faber, *Theorie der Geschichtswissenschaft*, 5th ed. (Munich: C.H. Beck, 1982), 10–13.
155. See above, nn. 81, 87–88, 124.
156. See above, 151–53.
157. This is mentioned in *Muhammedanische Studien*, 1:ix = *Muslim Studies*, 1:9.
158. *Tagebuch*, 115.
159. Ibid., 257, 262–63, 268.
160. See S.D. Goitein, "Goldziher as Seen Through His Letters," in *Ignace Goldziher Memorial Volume*, eds. Samuel Löwinger and Joseph de Somogyi (Budapest: Globus, 1948), 1:9–12 (Hebrew section, with letters in the original German).
161. Cf. Conrad, "The Pilgrim from Pest," 110–11.
162. Becker, "Ignaz Goldziher," 508.
163. Joseph Schacht, *Origins of Muhammadan Jurisprudence* (Oxford: Clarendon Press, 1950).
164. "Renan mint orientalista," 20.
165. See above, n. 27.
166. "Renan mint orientalista," 20.
167. Above, n. 106.
168. *Tagebuch*, 34.
169. "Renan mint orientalista," 22.
170. Christiaan Snouck Hurgronje, *Politique musulmane de la Hollande* (Paris: Ernest Leroux, 1911); Harry J. Benda, "Christiaan Snouck Hurgronje and

the Foundations of Dutch Islamic Policy in Indonesia," *Journal of Modern History* 30 (1958): 338–47; Conrad, "The Dervish's Disciple," 248–49.

171. Simon, *Ignác Goldziher*, 31.
172. *Az Iszlám*, 341–82; "L'avenir de l'Islam," *Questions diplomatiques et coloniales* 11 (January–June 1901): 600–2.
173. See the Goldziher-Nöldeke correspondence edited in Simon, *Ignác Goldziher*, 157–419. Cf. also Hartmut Fähndrich, "Invariable Factors Underlying the Historical Perspective in Theodor Nöldeke's *Orientalische Skizzen*," in *Akten des VII. Kongresses für Arabistik und Islamwissenschaft*, ed. Albert Dietrich (Göttingen: Van der Hoeck und Ruprecht, 1976), 146–54; Conrad, "The Dervish's Disciple," 248–49. Said (*Orientalism*, 209) presents one of Nöldeke's most outrageous deliverances as typical of orientalism's view of its topic of inquiry, but again he errs for lack of adequate information. Nöldeke's fiery Prussian nationalism and openly bigoted attitude toward non-European peoples were a source of constant embarrassment to his colleagues, and the "Nöldeke problem" comes up repeatedly in correspondence among them.
174. Especially his former teacher Arminius Vámbéry (ca.1831/2–1913); see Conrad, "The Dervish's Disciple," 243–64; idem, "The Pilgrim from Pest," 124–25.
175. *Tagebuch*, 56 (again with reference to Vámbéry); "Renan mint orientalista," 22.
176. In Goldziher's day there were as yet very few scholars working on the Middle East who were women.
177. Joseph de Somogyi, "My Reminiscences of Ignace Goldziher," *Muslim World* 51 (1961): 9.
178. *Tagebuch*, 282–311; "A háború és a tudósok szolidaritása," *Magyar Figyelő* 4 (1914): 250–54; also the correspondence with Nöldeke in Simon, *Ignác Goldziher*, 371–89.
179. Conrad, "The Dervish's Disciple," 236–38, 262–64; idem, "The Pilgrim from Pest," 128–29.
180. Cf. the summary in Simon, *Ignác Goldziher*, 57–60.
181. Bernát Heller, "Ignác Goldziher," *Magyar-Zsidó Szemle* 44 (1927): 273; de Somogyi, "Reminiscences," 15–16.
182. Conrad, "The Pilgrim from Pest," 120, 128.
183. *Oriental Diary*, 99, 100–1, 105, 132.
184. Conrad, "The Dervish's Disciple," 236, 247–48, 256–57; idem, "The Pilgrim from Pest," 130.
185. Outside of Vienna, where von Kremer was based when not serving in a political capacity in the Near East, there was no position in Habsburg domains for the study of Arabic, Arab history, Islam, or the Islamic world more generally until 1865, when Vámbéry, returning from his dervish trip

to Central Asia and resounding acclaim in England after a successful lecture tour, was appointed to a post in the University of Pest at the behest of emperor Franz Josef I (r. 1848–1916) and over the objections of many of the faculty. In 1865–66 he had two students, one of them Goldziher, and in the following year he had none. See *Tagebuch*, 25–26. Cf. also Lory Alder and Richard Dalby, *The Dervish of Windsor Castle: The Life of Arminius Vambery* (London: Bachman and Turner, 1979), 235–45; Conrad, "The Dervish's Disciple," 253–56.

6

The Death of an Orientalist: Paul Kraus from Prague to Cairo

Joel L. Kraemer

> Though we have raised quite a few excellent scholars in the study of Arab-Islamic culture, one may say that after Goldziher, who was one of the founders of the modern study of Islam, there has not been a scholar like Kraus in this field who combined so many signs of scholarly genius.
>
> —D.H. Baneth

The orientalist Paul Kraus died in Cairo, by his own hand, on Thursday, 12 October 1944, just two months before his fortieth birthday. Kraus shared his apartment in Zamalek (7 Ahmad Hishmat Pasha Street) with the brothers Albert and Cecil Hourani, serving then with the British in Egypt. It was they who discovered the body. Returning at lunchtime to the flat, they found the bathroom door locked from the inside. Peeking through the keyhole, they saw Kraus' body hanging from a conduit pipe by the cord of his bathrobe. They called the doorman *(bawwāb),* then the police, and informed university authorities. The Czech consulate was notified, as Kraus was a Czech national. The deceased's closest friends—Ṭāhā Ḥusayn, Max Meyerhof and Ḥasan Ibrāhīm Ḥasan—rushed to the scene. Kraus was brought to the hospital of Qaṣr al-ʻAynī, and was buried the next day (Friday) in the Jewish cemetery in Cairo. These and other graphic details were reported by the press.[1] Among the mourners present were the Hourani brothers and Aubrey (Abba) Eban. Cecil Hourani and

Eban bore the coffin. Eban, then a major in the British army, informed Kraus' wife Dorothee of the tragedy.[2]

Why would Paul Kraus have killed himself? He was a young and eminent scholar, with splendid achievements behind him and vast scholarly projects ahead. In a way, the fate of Paul Kraus epitomizes the tragedy of European Jewish scholars caught in the maelstrom of the Second World War, uprooted, displaced, living in exile. As a lecturer at Fuad I University in Cairo and Farouq I University in Alexandria, Kraus was immersed in the intellectual life of Egypt. He published major works there, contributed to local journals, and had close ties with Egyptian scholars and intellectuals. His Arabic was impeccable. Yet as a European and a Jew, Kraus had come to feel abandoned in Cairo in this last autumn of the war—and of his life.

Prague and Reise nach Osten

It was Paul Kraus' destiny to have been born in Prague at the beginning of this century, and so to be afflicted by the tragedy that befell European Jewry in its fourth decade. He was born on 11 December 1904. His father was Sigmund Kraus, a businessman ("Geschäftsmann aus Prag"). His mother was Henriette née Katz.[3] In his curriculum vitae, he gave most of these details, noting (as was customary) that he was of the Jewish religion and a Czechoslovakian citizen.[4] Kraus graduated with distinction from the Deutsches Humanistisches Gymnasium in Prag-Smichov, and then studied oriental languages at the Deutsche Universität in Prague.[5] Kraus' teachers were the Arabist Max Grünert (1849–1929), the Indologist Moritz Winternitz (1863–1937), the historian of philosophy Isidor Pollak (1874–1922), and the papyrologist Adolf Grohmann (1887–1977).

The Deutsche Universität was a modern division of the medieval Charles University, which had been split into separate Czech and German universities, often using the same buildings. Conflict between Czech and German students occasionally erupted into open violence. Although German-speaking Jewish students joined German students in the *Halle* (the reading and lecture hall for German students), they were excluded from German nationalist associations and student societies. A few formed their own Zionist students' organization, Bar Kochba, in which Hugo Bergmann (1883–1975) was the leading figure.

The atmosphere of Prague in the early twentieth century is familiar from the life and works of Franz Kafka (1883–1924).[6] Prague retained vestiges of its medieval origins and was filled with monuments evocative of the past: the Castle, Charles University, St. Vitus' Cathedral, the Old-New Synagogue, and the Jewish cemetery. Prague was charming and mysterious, part of its charm being its "multiculturalism" as a city of three peoples *(Dreivölkerstadt)*—Czechs, Germans and Jews—though this diversity also caused social tensions.[7] Prague was a linguistic melée, an ethnic potpourri of the Habsburg Empire, heart and crossroads of Europe. Early in this century, Prague nurtured linguistic genius and literary creativity: Jaroslav Seifert (1901–86), Rainer Maria Rilke (1875–1926), and Gustav Meyrink (1868–1932); the "Prague Circle" of Kafka, Franz Werfel (1890–1945), Max Brod (1884–1968), and Oscar Baum (1883–1941); and the Prague linguistic school.[8]

Kraus was a product of this intensely intellectual climate. But early in the twentieth century, Zionism also struck roots in Prague, and became a significant focus of group identity.[9] Many of Prague's German-speaking Jews felt an uneasy *Inseldasein,* an isolation and constriction, a need to escape, and Zionism provided one answer. Jews were mainly proponents of German culture, a minority submerged within a large Czech majority.[10] The Czechs regarded German-speaking Jews as Germans and foreigners. Yet the Prague Jews did not feel solidarity with Germans, and some felt more of a kinship with the Czechs. The Prague Jew has been characterized as driven by a craving for acceptance, for relief from a sense of being alien even at home. The literature of Prague Jews reflects insecurity and a vague sense of guilt. So one becomes a wanderer. The pilgrim, the wayfarer, the wanderer appear often in Czech literature and are emblematic of Prague's German-speaking Jews.[11]

Kraus left Prague in 1925 for Palestine as a member of a group of pioneers of the Czech branch of the Blau-Weiss Bewegung, and joined a kibbutz. But he became disillusioned with kibbutz life, and in 1926 he left to study at the Hebrew University in Jerusalem.[12] His friend Hans Lewy (1904–45) perceived in this early vacillation a tendency to detachment and displacement. His multiple displacements, wrote Lewy, belonged to his "nomadic nature." In his youth, he detached himself from life in Prague and embraced Zionism, only to abandon Zionism soon thereafter. He was, says Lewy, "un passant qui ne s'enracina nulle part." Yet his being *un passant,* as shall be seen, was often by constraint, *malgré soi,* and at several junctures of his life he might have liked nothing better than to settle down permanently. While in Palestine he even made a move in that direction, marrying Hadassa Mednitzky (d. 1993).

But in one respect Kraus never wavered, and his life trajectory never departed from the course he set as a young man. He was ultimately committed from start to finish to a passionate labor of love: to philology, meaning the study of ancient texts—editing, translation, interpretation—as a way of discovering new knowledge about human civilizations.

Before returning to Europe, Kraus spent time in Egypt, Syria and Palestine. In Jerusalem, in addition to his studies at the Hebrew University, he studied at the American School of Oriental Research with William Foxwell Albright (1891–1971), who was to become the doyen of American archeologists, and with Romain François Butin (1871–1937).[13] He also studied at the École Française Orientale in Damascus with Edouard Dhorme (1881–1966), Raphael Savignac (1874–1951), Albert Leopold Vincent (1879–1968), and Antonin Jaussen (1871–1962). Kraus' scholarly interests centered upon Bible, Semitics and archeology.

Berlin before the Storm

In 1927, Kraus ended his first *Reise nach Osten,* and enrolled at the University of Berlin, to study under its renowned faculty of orientalists. Kraus completed his doctorate in Semitics in 1929. His thesis dealt with Babylonian epistolography, and was characteristically thorough, meticulous and mature.[14] His principle advisor was the Assyriologist Bruno Meissner (1868–1947).[15] Kraus also drew close to Eugen Mittwoch (1876–1942),[16] and studied under Carl Heinrich Becker (1876–1933)[17] and Hans Heinrich Schaeder (1896–1957),[18] thus laying the foundations for his subsequent study of Islamic civilization.

Kraus' doctorate propelled him to a leading place among scholars in cuneiform studies and Semitic languages, and his career was launched. But while Kraus never lost interest in the ancient Near East, Semitics, and the Hebrew Bible, a turning-point occurred when he met Julius Ruska (1867–1949). A secondary school teacher, Ruska had become fascinated by the Islamic natural sciences.[19] In particular, he became intrigued by the transmission of Greek science to the world of Islam, and wrote on the "Lapidary of Aristotle."[20] After coming across Abū Bakr al-Rāzī's *Kitāb sirr al-asrār,* Ruska began to study the history of chemistry and alchemy in Islam. He corresponded with Max Meyerhof (1874–1945), a specialist in Islamic sciences and medicine, and a close collaboration ensued. Meyerhof sent copies and photostats of Arabic manuscripts to Ruska, including Jābir b. Ḥayyān's *Book of Seventy* and *Book of Poisons.*

Kraus also met Meyerhof during this period, and they remained close friends and companions in science until the end. Meyerhof was one of the most remarkable Jewish orientalists of the twentieth century. Born in Hildesheim, Germany, Meyerhof studied medicine, specializing in ophthalmology. He visited Egypt in 1900–1, then returned in 1903 as chief of the Khedivial Ophthalmic Clinic, and stayed until 1914, studying and treating eye diseases, which were rampant in the country due to poverty and ignorance. In 1914, Meyerhof went back to Europe, serving in the German army in the war. He returned to Cairo in 1923, and remained there until his death in 1945. Meyerhof wrote widely on the history of medicine and on the transmission of science, medicine and philosophy from Greek into Arabic. He treated eye diseases by day and studied his books and manuscripts and prepared his articles by night, still having time to partake of Cairene life. His combination of medical practice and scholarship evokes Maimonides, on whom he wrote extensively.[21]

Ruska established the new Research Institute for the History of the Natural Sciences (Forschungsinstitut für Geschichte der Naturwissenschaften) in Berlin with the support of Becker, who had been named Prussian minister for culture and education in 1925. Kraus became Ruska's assistant in 1929 following Martin Plessner (1900–73), who had assisted Ruska from 1927 to 1929.[22] Later, in 1931, the research institute was joined with the new Institute for the History of Medicine and the Natural Sciences (Institut für Geschichte der Medizin und der Naturwissenschaften) as part of the University of Berlin.

Kraus' view of Ruska reflected some of his own scholarly aims and methods. Ruska's energies were devoted, Kraus wrote, to one main purpose: "To recognize the role of Arabic science in the transmission of Greek thought to medieval Europe and to trace its historical evolution." Ruska studied works that earned Islamic civilization glory in the Christian West, primarily Arabic mathematics, astronomy, chemistry and medicine. Ruska, who urged study of primary sources and suspected conventional views, went by this maxim: "Do not adhere to the traditional opinions, go back to the sources." Although Ruska was engrossed in esoteric subjects like alchemy, he abjured a mystical or spiritual approach. He was attracted to alchemy as nascent chemistry, not as allegory and mystical-gnostic speculation. In particular, he wanted to show that al-Rāzī's alchemy was experimental chemistry, and that it influenced the development of European chemistry.[23]

Under Ruska's influence, Kraus became fascinated by the alchemist Jābir b. Ḥayyān (Geber of the Latins). Jābir was a mysterious figure, traditionally portrayed as the disciple of the sixth Shi'ite Imam Ja'far al-Ṣādiq (d. 765), a dating that had been accepted by historians of chemistry. However, discoveries of new Jābir material by Meyerhof and by Hellmut Ritter (1892–1971) made Ruska doubt the conventional dating. In addition, Kraus found evidence placing the Jābir writings at the end of the ninth century and beginning of the tenth, and linked the Jābir b. Ḥayyān corpus with radical Shi'ism, showing that it had gnostic and Ismā'īlī tendencies. Kraus' central idea was that the Jābir corpus belonged to Qarmatian-Ismā'īlī propaganda, and paved the way for a great religious revolution.[24] Kraus' dating and his Ismā'īlī hypothesis radically revised conventional notions about the Jābir corpus. More recent scholars, it should be noted, primarily Fuat Sezgin, have criticized Kraus' theories, favoring the more conventional and traditional opinions.[25] Pierre Lory, an expert on Arab alchemy, has also modified some of Kraus' theses. Lory regards Jābir b. Ḥayyān as a mythical figure representing an old esoteric tradition, and he sees the corpus as laying the ground for a fundamental cultural and religious revolution—not merely a Qarmatian or Ismā'īlī-Fatimid revolution, but a transformation of human society by a cosmic descent of the spirit to the sublunary world.[26]

Hans Lewy, a friend from Berlin days, described Kraus' monastic dedication to research during this period of work in the institute, his sequestering of himself for days and nights. Lewy recalled Kraus telling with sparkling eyes how he persuaded an Ismā'īlī Muslim from India, Husayn F. Hamdani, to lend him for one night the precious manuscript linking the Jābir corpus with Ismā'īlī literature. After a long vigil, Kraus returned triumphant at dawn to the institute, his work done.[27]

Lewy marveled at Kraus' reclusive dedication to scholarship: "la vie recluse en science, la liberté de l'esprit." According to Lewy, Kraus never talked about current events and never made a frivolous remark. His personality exercised a strong attraction, and his devotion to the spirit of research won hearts. He was obsessed with the subjects he explored. Ancient languages were not dead for him. He actually used them, and wrote letters in Akkadian and Syriac. He declaimed poetry in Arabic. Kraus, wrote Lewy, was a philologist in the precise sense of the term: "a lover of logos as word, signification, power and act."[28]

In March 1932, Kraus became a *privatdozent* at the University of Berlin in Semitic languages and Islamic studies. My teacher Franz Rosenthal (b. 1914), the Yale orientalist, informed me on the basis of his "Studienbuch" from the university, that Kraus taught him second-level Arabic in the summer of 1932, and third-level Arabic and a course on Greek science in Islam in the winter of that year. (Kraus did not teach him elementary Arabic; this the student was expected to do on his own, and Kraus told Rosenthal to study Brockelmann's grammar.)

Throughout their later correspondence,[29] Kraus expressed great solicitude for Rosenthal's development and personal welfare. Rosenthal remained in Berlin after the Nazis came to power, while Kraus by then was safely in Paris (and subsequently in Cairo). Most of the correspondence relates to academic matters, particularly Graeco-Arabic studies. But there are personal references. In an early letter, Kraus asked Rosenthal not to address him as "Dr.", and signed his own signature as "Kraus."[30] He also encouraged Rosenthal to submit a monograph for the prestigious Lidzbarski Prize, and Rosenthal did so successfully—but as a Jew was precluded from receiving the award.[31]

La belle epoque

The conducive atmosphere for research in Berlin was devastated by the Nazi rise to power in January 1933.[32] At the beginning of 1933, when Kraus heard that Jews working in the institute in Berlin had been dismissed, he decided to leave.[33] Kraus' colleagues Hans Lewy and Martin Plessner emigrated to Palestine (and when Kraus and his wife later divorced, she returned to Palestine with her daughter). For Kraus, however, Palestine was not an option after his disillusionment with Zionism in the 1920s. Instead he went to Paris in April 1933, a move made with the assistance of his teacher, Becker. There Louis Massignon (1883–1962), who was to become a lifetime friend, assisted the young refugee. Massignon later wrote about Kraus' arrival in these words: "In 1933, a young Czech orientalist, a refugee, Paul Kraus, was sent to me by our friend C. H. Becker, who had told me about his precocious abilities."[34]

The three years Kraus spent in Paris, from April 1933 until 1936, were joyous, fruitful, and fondly remembered.[35] He had fellowships in 1933–34 and 1934–35 from the Caisse Nationale des Sciences, then under the Ministry of National Education. By 1935, his fellowship application listed seven major publications and three more in preparation, and had the formal sponsorship of the leading lights of French Arab and Islamic scholarship: Massignon, William Marçais (1872–1956), Abel Rey (1873–1940), and Maurice Gaudefroy-Demombynes (1862–1957).[36]

From November 1933, Kraus taught courses at the École Pratique des Hautes Études, V^e section–Sciences Religieuses. In 1933–34, he lectured on "Études sur l'école des Mu'tazilites." In 1934–35, he taught "La théologie de Naẓẓām" (explications of texts of Naẓẓām preserved in the *Kitāb al-Ḥayawān* of Jābir). In 1935–36 he taught "Plotin chez les Arabes." Beginning in 1933–34, he also gave courses at the Institut d'Histoire des Sciences et des Techniques of the University of Paris, directed by Abel Rey, where he also taught a course with his friend Shlomo Pines (1908–90).[37]

Kraus knew Pines from his Berlin days,[38] and they corresponded after Kraus reached Paris. In a letter to Pines, written in late 1933 or early 1934, Kraus described his initiation at the École: he has begun teaching and has six students, most of them Arabs, for whom it is the same whether he speaks French with flaws or not.[39] In another letter from this period, Kraus announced to Pines his discovery of a crucial passage concerning the nature of the Jābir corpus.[40]

The École was a place of incredible intellectual ferment when Kraus taught there. During his first year in Paris, Alexandre Koyré (1892–1964) was conducting his famous seminar on Hegel's religious philosophy.[41] Koyré's nomadic career bore some resemblance to that of Kraus. Born in Taganrog in Russia, Koyré, who was Jewish, was educated in Germany, moved to Paris in 1919, and received his doctorate there in 1929. In 1931 he became director of the École Pratique des Hautes Études.

Kraus and Koyré also were similar in outlook. Koyré believed in the unity of human thought at its highest level;[42] so, too, Kraus considered science a unity, and joined this idea with a belief in an international confraternity of scholars, linking Prague, Jerusalem, Berlin, Paris, Cairo.[43] And while Kraus did not participate in Koyré's seminars, he remained friendly with Koyré in later years, when both were in Cairo.

When Koyré left for Cairo in January 1934, the seminar was taken over by Alexandre Kojève (Kojevnikoff) (1902–68), another distinguished Hegel scholar and a Jew, who led it until 1939. Kojève was born in Russia, moved to Heidelberg, then to Berlin, and finally to Paris in 1932. The seminar under his direction was attended by a remarkable constellation of people, who studded the intellectual firmament of Paris for many years.[44] The young Russian émigré succeeded in enthralling Paris by his teaching of Hegel, and he became a lifelong friend of Kraus' brother-in-law Leo Strauss (1899–1973), whom he knew from Berlin.[45]

The École des Hautes Études was then located in the main building of the Sorbonne. It was more receptive to foreign students than the main part of the university, and became a haven for the Russian and German émigrés of the 1930s, many of them Jews. Jewish émigrés from eastern and central Europe, like Kraus, Koyré, Kojève, and Strauss, found in Paris—in the ancient classrooms of the university, in the libraries, and in the cafés and book shops along the Boulevard Saint Michel, the Rue des Écoles, Rue Saint Jacques, the Latin Quarter, and the Luxembourg Garden— a stimulating environment for their creativity and genius.

Paul Kraus thrived in this atmosphere, and (as was his custom) collaborated with other scholars. One was Henry Corbin (1903–78), a participant in the Hegel seminars, who worked with Kraus in editing a philosophical-mystical work by the twelfth-century mystic Shihāb al-Dīn al-Suhrawardī.[46] Corbin, French translator and disciple of Heidegger, became a prodigious scholar, whose interests embraced Sufism, Shi'ism, and also alchemy. Corbin leaned toward the more occult aspects of alchemy, more in harmony with Carl G. Jung's psychological approach to this field of study.[47]

The Paris years were crowned by Kraus' collaboration and friendship with Louis Massignon.[48] What was it that united the aristocratic French orientalist, Louis Fernand Jules Massignon, with this Jewish émigré from Prague? Massignon was born in 1883 into a distinguished family. His father, Fernand Massignon (1855–1922), a sculptor and painter ("Pierre Roche"), moved in the most select Parisian literary and artistic circles, and saw to it that his son travelled widely and studied at the finest institutions. Massignon's *itinéraire et courbe de vie* catapulted him in 1926 to the pinnacle of academic achievement, a chair in the Collège de France. From 1932, Massignon also had a chair in Islam at the École des Hautes Études. Kraus, a prodigy, was verging on his thirties without a proper university appointment.

We know something of Kraus' first impression of Massignon from a letter to Shlomo Pines, written at this time. Kraus related that he had read proofs of Massignon's "Salmân Pâk,"[49] a Persian contemporary of Muhammad and a semi-legendary figure, who is said to have converted from Christianity to Islam. Kraus finds Massignon's study a "très audacieuse construction comme ensemble mais pleine de détails fort intéressants." Kraus then speaks highly of Massignon and his lectures, expressing regret that Pines cannot attend them.[50]

With all the differences in background, life circumstances and age, the friendship between Massignon and Kraus became close and devoted. Friendship and confraternity were dominant themes in Massignon's life and thought, and Kraus was among Massignon's most intimate friends. Over the years, these had included his childhood companion and famous Sinologist Henri Maspéro (1883–1945); the ascetic hermit Charles de Foucauld (1858–1916); and a renegade Spanish grandee, converted to Islam, named Luis de Cuadra (1877–1921).[51] Massignon and Kraus were magnetic personalities drawn to one another by a kind of elective affinity. Massignon saw in Kraus a linguistic genius and superb philologist, who could assist him with his work; Kraus looked to Massignon as mentor, patron and *maître.*

That said, Kraus and Massignon differed fundamentally in their approach to scholarship. Kraus, a secular, uncommitted Jew, studied the history of Islamic sciences and the transmission of Greek science and philosophy to Islamic civilization as a classicist would study Plato, Aristotle or Plotinus. Kraus immersed himself in Arabic and Islamic sciences without identifying spiritually with his subject. Massignon's approach to Islam was committed, *engagé.* He was a Catholic of a mystical type, and his spirituality commingled with his study of Islam. Massignon had undergone a conversion experience, a "visitation de l'étranger," which inspired a "retour à l'Église" in 1908.[52] He belonged to a group of intellectuals identified with the renaissance of French Catholicism early in the century.[53] Ultimately, in 1950, Massignon would be ordained a Greek Catholic (Melkite) priest in Cairo.[54]

In his *itinéraire spirituel* and understanding of Islam, Massignon was deeply influenced by the Belgian writer Joris-Karl Huysmans (1848–1907), a friend of his father, who had experienced a rebirth in Catholicism. Massignon met Huysmans in 1900 and was captivated by his "conversion" and spiritual teaching.[55] Huysmans' idea of life as a spiritual journey and his notion of substitute suffering transformed Massignon. Massignon came to see Hagar and Ishmael as prefigurations of disinherited Muslims and of all who are disinherited. Huysmans' notion of surrogate suffering coincided with the concept of *badal* (surrogacy) close to Massignon's heart. Massignon founded a Badaliyya society along with some Christians living in the Middle East as a bridge between Christianity and Islam.[56]

Massignon saw Christianity and Islam through the lens of the tragic figure of the mystic al-Ḥallāj (857–922).[57] Al-Ḥallāj, who was "martyred" in Baghdad for heresy, represented for Massignon a direct parallel to the suffering of Jesus on the cross. As Christianity had suffering and compassion at its foundation, so too (according to Massignon) did Islam. Indeed, he regarded suffering as fundamental to Semitic and Jewish psychology: "This brings us to a fundamental problem of Semitic, and particularly Jewish, psychology, in its most 'Kierkegaardian' aspect: There is a hidden but divine good in suffering, and this is the mystery of anguish, the foundation of human nature."[58] Massignon's mystical Catholicism belonged to the core and essence of his being, and it informed his entire understanding of Islam. This makes the companionship with Kraus so beguiling and intriguing.

Whereas Kraus examined Islamic civilization historically by way of origins and sources *(Quellenforschung),* Massignon explored the internal development of Islam and was unconcerned with foreign influences. He regarded the Qur'an as a revealed book, and believed that Sufism evolved autonomously around the central theme of mystical union. Instead of looking for external influence—Christian, Jewish, Jewish-Christian, Iranian or Neoplatonic—Massignon sought an internal reconstruction (a "décapement mental") of Sufism. He wanted to reach the heart of the phenomenon by introspection and sympathy, and by penetrating into the feelings and intentions of the believers themselves.[59]

I believe that to understand another culture, we must hope for a combination of intimate understanding and reflective detachment, for an equilibrium of presence and absence, proximity and distance. Massignon was all presence and proximity. Kraus balanced proximity and distance. Scholarly detachment demands attention to context and history; its premise is that no phenomenon emerges by parthenogenesis or springs full-grown like Athena from the brow of Zeus. Kraus never relinquished the philological-historical discipline he acquired in Prague and Berlin, which provided the bedrock for all his research.

It must not be forgotten, however, that Massignon was also an authority on texts, a master of Arabic philology, who was fascinated by religious and mystical terminology.[60] Kraus' own teacher, the meticulous Hans Heinrich Schaeder, appreciated Massignon's *Passion of al-Hallaj,* and Massignon's concentration on religious terminology and linguistic form influenced Schaeder's own study of religion.[61] Thus, we should not overdraw the routine contrast between German *Genauigkeit* and French *esprit.* Moreover, Massignon's early study of Islam came under the powerful influence of the man he properly regarded as the founder of modern Islamic studies, the Hungarian Jewish orientalist, Ignaz Goldziher (1850–1921), whom he first met in 1905 at the Fourteenth International Congress of Orientalists in Algiers.[62] Massignon made his way in his early career through links to Goldziher and other established orientalists.

Even though Massignon's study of Islam was *engagé* and *mystique,* he respected the philological skills of Jewish scholars like Goldziher and Kraus. Goldziher had helped him with his *Kitâb al-ṭawâsîn,* and Kraus contributed to his *Akhbâr al-Ḥallâj.* Massignon was impressed by the appreciation that Goldziher, Kraus and other Jews showed for al-Ḥallāj, and tried to explain their attraction to Sufi texts. He writes:

> "Ḥallājians," in the broad sense, are to be found even in [the people of] Israel. They exist among those who yield "priority" to Arabic vis-à-vis the other Semitic languages as explaining grammar and reasoning, sifting their art, condensing their wise maxims. This is the same intellectual attraction for the essentially Semitic rhythm of the Ḥallājian sentence that prompted mediaeval Caraïtes to transcribe Ḥallājian poems and prose into Hebrew letters; that led Ignaz Goldziher in 1912 to bend over the proofs of *Ṭawāsīn,* revising my efforts at translation; and that determined Paul Kraus, before his death ["avant de disparaître dans le désespoir"] to reprint in Aleppo in 1943, as a farewell addressed to our friendship, the sections of our *Akhbâr al-Ḥallâj* in which the Essential Desire burns.[63]

According to Massignon, then, it was the Semitic rhythm of the language that captivated Goldziher and Kraus. Massignon seems to have implied that these Jewish orientalists were attracted by the rhythm of the "the letter," rather than by "the spirit."

Massignon tells about his collaboration with Kraus in the preface to the third edition of *Akhbâr al-Ḥallâj.*[64] He relates how Paul Kraus, having begun his admirable studies on the history of medieval Arab scientific thought, from the Hellenizing philosophers to the Ismāʻīlīs, was attracted by the Ḥallājian texts, and how he offered to help resolve the captivating enigma of the *Akhbār al-Ḥallāj.* Massignon sees the attraction to al-Ḥallāj as a change of direction for Kraus, and in a profound sense it was. For while Kraus continued his work on Jābir b. Ḥayyān and Islamic science, begun under Ruska in Berlin, in Paris he came under the spell of the mystical texts of al-Ḥallāj. Massignon writes: "For two years of his life, he devoted himself to his host as well as to the task of a critical reconstruction of a grand intellectual adventure, a passion for the truth." Massignon cites Kraus' fundamental contribution to establishment of the text, his definitive classification of pericopes, and his encouraging the reexamination of the chain of transmission *(isnād),* which Massignon did after Kraus' death. Kraus helped Massignon revise his French translations of the pericopes of the *Akhbār:*

> Furthermore, within three years Paul Kraus had assimilated our language, nearly achieving mastery; he asked me to retouch my translations of the pericopes of the Akhbâr into French, striving, as [the Arabist] Émile Dermenghem has described it at the time, "towards technical precision, through some kind of heroic asceticism, even if that meant relinquishing the purely literary and dynamic beauty."

Massignon writes that Kraus imparted to him his intellectual scruples in the problem of translation—"l'horreur sémitique répudiant toute idolâtrie des formes belles." Kraus' translations are "abstraites, algébrisants, presque logisticiennes."[65]

Like Kraus' description of Massignon's "Salmân Pâk" as "very audacious," Massignon's emphasis on Kraus' "technical precision" and "abstract, algebraic, nearly logical translations" is not unequivocally laudatory. Nevertheless, perhaps aware of his own exuberance and impatience with certain technical aspects of scholarship, Massignon astutely appreciated what Kraus had to offer him.

Massignon wrote his preface to *Akhbâr al-Ḥallâj* thirteen years after Kraus' death. He had by then become familiar with Kraus' theory of Semitic metrics developed in the last years of Kraus' life. But he had discovered this theory independently. Writing about the rhythm of the Qur'an, "la merveille secrète d'un rythme infra-métrique," he notes Kraus' attraction to the same ideas. Separated from him after 1940 by the war, Kraus gradually arrived at the same conclusions regarding "Semitic" texts like the Hebrew Bible. Massignon says that Kraus' studies on biblical metrics demonstrated a primitive rhythm which the Hebrew possessed within an Arabic "vocalisation basale." Thus, Kraus' ideas on Semitic metrics (which put off Jewish scholars in Jerusalem in 1943, as we shall see presently) were shared by Massignon, who had also embraced these ideas.[66]

Massignon adds a personal note to his preface. Before going to his death, Kraus remembered "what he promised me before our separation," to make the *Akhbār al-Ḥallāj* known in the Orient to the great Muslim public. Kraus had sent a selection of pericopes from the *Akhbār* to "our friend Sami Kayali in Aleppo," for publication in the review *al-Ḥadīth.*[67] Massignon cites "the last words of Paul Kraus" from this article: "the voice of Ḥallāj is the cry threatening the one who is about to drown himself: 'stop, stop, don't get wet in the water;' it is also the invitation of seduction to the martyr, and the coquetry of beauty that carries away its Elected Ones."[68]

Kraus' three years in Paris were intense and glorious.[69] He received a *licence ès-lettres* on 3 March 1935, and was planning to complete a *doctorat ès-lettres.*[70] The theses he proposed to submit were "Jābir ibn Ḥayyān, essai sur l'histoire des idées scientifiques dans l'Islam,"[71] and a *thèse complémentaire* entitled "La critique religieuse de Razi." The first was presented, but the *thèse complémentaire* was never submitted. For Kraus stood on the verge of yet another displacement. As a foreigner in France, he could not obtain a university post, which was a government appointment. "If you only were a Frenchman," said Massignon to Kraus ruefully, the sense being that Massignon would have kept Kraus in Paris if he had not been a foreigner.[72]

There was a candidacy for a position in Aligarh, India. In a letter of 2 May 1936, Ziauddin Ahmed, vice chancellor of the Aligarh Muslim University, wrote to the finance minister of Hyderabad State, Sir Akbar Hydari, informing him that Otto Spies (1901–81), professor of Arabic, had resigned, and requesting that Kraus be asked to detail his qualifications. "The fact of his being a Jew is not a disqualification for service in the Aligarh University," wrote the vice chancellor. "We would like to appoint the best man on minimum salary." Sir Akbar Hydari forwarded the letter to Kraus requesting his résumé.[73] However, nothing came of the initiative.

Hans Lewy later wrote that Kraus could have gotten a teaching appointment at the Hebrew University, "which the authorities offered him in 1936 and 1937." He declined. This decision, wrote Lewy, had a fateful influence on his life, and he lived to regret it. Later, in the autumn of 1939, Lewy related, Kraus visited Palestine for the first time since his youth. The people were more open-minded than he had expected, and he found friends and interest in his research. This brief visit, Lewy continued, transformed his ideas about Palestine and the Hebrew University, and he realized that he could remain a true European in Jerusalem. Lewy wrote that "his old love for his people was reawakened. This was a secret and subdued love."[74] But in 1936, Kraus made a different choice, preferring Cairo to Jerusalem.

Into Egypt

Through Massignon, Kraus was offered and accepted a teaching post at the Egyptian University in Cairo. Massignon had taught there in 1912, on the recommendation of Goldziher. Now Massignon recommended Kraus to his old friend Ṭāhā Ḥusayn (1889–1973), dean of the faculty of arts and the outstanding Egyptian intellectual of his day, who would become Kraus' next mentor.[75] Blind from the age of two, Ṭāhā Ḥusayn had written his doctoral thesis at the Egyptian University, on the blind poet Abū al-'Alā' al-Ma'arrī.[76] He subsequently studied in Paris, where he wrote a second doctoral thesis, on Ibn Khaldūn's social philosophy.[77] He later issued a flood of writings: short stories, novels, criticism, philosophy, translation. His choice of subjects revealed his intellectual independence as a free-thinking poet and a philosopher-historian.

Ṭāhā Ḥusayn had every reason to feel an affinity with Kraus. He saw Egypt as part of wider Mediterranean civilization, and linked its destiny to ancient Graeco-Aegean civilization—that is, with the West.[78] He viewed Arabic culture at its best as continuing the culture and political thought of ancient Greece. Schooled in Paris and married to a French woman, he also had a strong predilection for French culture and philosophy, and through his prolific translations introduced the Egyptian reading public to the French classics. Ṭāhā Ḥusayn was also controversial, and his doubts concerning the authenticity of pre-Islamic Arabic poetry had raised a storm in literary, political and religious circles. In 1932, he was driven from the university and the deanship of the faculty of arts in a political controversy. But in 1934 he was restored to his professorship, and in 1936, with the election victory of allies in the Wafd party, he was reinstated as dean.[79]

Ṭāhā Ḥusayn was partial to the critical method of orientalists. He had been nurtured in the relatively open atmosphere of the Egyptian University in the early twentieth century, when its faculty included such renowned foreign scholars as Massignon, Enno Littmann (1875–1958), C.A. Nallino (1872–1938), and David Santillana (1855–1931). For Ṭāhā Ḥusayn, it was perfectly natural that Kraus should continue their tradition, and one of his first acts as dean was to authorize Kraus' employment.

Not long after arriving in Cairo, Kraus described his feelings to Rosenthal in a letter:

> After a rather difficult time getting organized, etc., I feel really happy in the new milieu and my new activity in the university. The enthusiasm may naturally be premature, since the setbacks (intrigues, anti-Semitism, etc.) will certainly recur soon. However, in the meantime, I have never dreamed that there would be so much and so rich a harvest here. Perhaps it will suffice if I tell you that the Dār al-Kutub [National Library] has no less than 40,000 uncataloged manuscripts, which no one has looked into, and Azhar and the University Library have 7,000. I have not the slightest need to go to Istanbul.[80]

Kraus wrote that at the university he teaches textual criticism and Semitic languages. His being on good terms with Ṭāhā Ḥusayn gives him much joy ("Besonders viel Freude macht mir das gute Verhältnis zu Taha"). He also has had the chance of meeting other orientalists rather often, and mentions Massignon, Littmann, Nallino, Hamilton A.R. Gibb (1895–1971), August Fischer (1865–1949), and especially the Tunisian, Sayyid Ḥasan 'Abd al-Wahhāb. They had all come to Cairo for the meetings of the Arabic Language Academy.[81]

At the end of 1937, Kraus met a young and promising scholar visiting Cairo. Bernard Lewis (b. 1916) had left London for Paris when he was twenty to study with Massignon, at the suggestion of Lewis' teacher, Hamilton Gibb. As Lewis later recalled, Gibb had written on Lewis' behalf "to an extraordinarily brilliant man called Paul Kraus. But unfortunately Kraus had left Paris and went to Cairo. Gibb had a very high regard for Kraus, and I do believe he was at least as anxious for me to see and consult Kraus as for me to see Massignon. But Massignon found Kraus a job in Cairo, so I didn't see him in Paris."[82] Kraus' impressions from meeting Lewis are recorded in a letter to Franz Rosenthal (2 May 1939), then in London: "You must certainly get to know Bernard Lewis, who teaches Islamic history at [the] S[chool of] O[riental] S[tudies]. Write to him in my name....He is very young, very competent, and ready to undertake whatever needs to be done."

Kraus spent the summer of 1938 (until early October) in Paris. He writes a postcard (13 September 1938) to Rosenthal about scholarly matters and sends regards to Mittwoch. In further correspondence Kraus congratulates Rosenthal on winning the Lidzbarski Prize and urges him to leave Berlin for Paris. Kraus believed that it would not be difficult to get a residence permit through Massignon or Marçais. Later that month (28 September), he asks Rosenthal to understand that "in these days of great tension and general nervousness" he has not been able to do much.

> I have spoken with Massignon who is ready to take the necessary steps which the situation allows....In general I am, if only the situation were better, rather optimistic. You must only have a little patience. Since I must leave soon, I have agreed with M[assignon] that I would give him a written memorandum concerning the situation.

The attempt to bring Rosenthal to Paris did not come to fruition.

While in Cairo, in 1938, Kraus worked feverishly on editing texts. In a postcard sent to Rosenthal from Cairo (9 April 1938), Kraus wrote that "in general I have very much work to do here and am terribly tired," noting that his edition of al-Rāzī's philosophical writings are in press and will appear in the summer, and that he is preparing a critical edition of *Kitāb al-Ḥayawān* of al-Jāḥiẓ.[83] Kraus was eager for contact and cooperation with other scholars. In a postscript to a postcard to Rosenthal (14 May 1938), he writes that Murād Kāmil (1907–75), an Egyptian colleague, had been in Cairo for a few days. He had spoken with him briefly, came away favorably impressed, and hopes that their cooperation will go well when Kāmil returns.[84]

While in Egypt, Kraus attempted to become a French citizen, perhaps to secure a regular affiliation to the Institut Français d'Archéologie Orientale du Caire (IFAO). Pierre Jouguet (1869–1949), director of the IFAO, in a letter written in Paris, "le 26 Juillet 193-,"[85] certifies that Paul Kraus desires to be naturalized as a Frenchman, and has been "attached" to the institute as of October 1936.[86] It is not known whether this request succeeded. But Kraus' desire dissipated after the Munich Pact of September 1938 and the German annexation of Sudentenland (an agreement to which France was a signatory). Constance Padwick (1886–1968), a missionary who befriended Kraus in Cairo, wrote this in a letter to Massignon about Kraus and his wife Bettina: "They were, ever since Münich, passionate Czech patriots and Paul said that in spite of it all the trouble you took to get him French naturalisation, he was glad that at the last he decided to remain Czech, dearly as he loved France. Otherwise he would have felt that he had betrayed Czecho-slovakia when her hour of sorrow came."[87]

Kraus thus remained completely dependent on his temporary university appointments in Egypt, and viewed growing student unrest with consternation. The atmosphere on the campus fueled suspicions, and mail addressed to Kraus at the university did not always reach its destination. "Your offprint which you sent to the university has apparently gotten lost," he wrote to Rosenthal from Cairo (14 May 1938). "It is not the first time that this happened." Again to Rosenthal, he reports bad news (24 March 1939): "The dance goes on and the end is not in sight. The events of the last weeks have also made me unwell, as we once wrote. Great confusion prevails here." He refers to university strikes and brawls that are more serious than ever, and adds: "Taha has resigned and the whole faculty is totally ruined *(kaputtgeschlagen).*"

Despite this, Kraus went on with his research. He informs Rosenthal that he has finished his work on Jābir b. Ḥayyān; his al-Rāzī volume will appear in eight to ten weeks; and a series of small articles is underway. Rosenthal had suggested that they coedit Alfarabi's *Philosophy of Plato,* and Kraus was "naturally very much in agreement," but wrote that it would be difficult to solve problems by correspondence. In the end, the difficulties in coediting the Alfarabi text from a distance were insurmountable. In a letter to Rosenthal (2 May 1939), Kraus writes that he is happy to hear that Rosenthal is doing Alfarabi's *Philosophy of Plato* with Richard Walzer (1900–75).[88] Kraus reports that publication of the first volume of al-Rāzī is very advanced and that Jābir b. Ḥayyān will go into print; at least publication is assured. But wartime conditions in Cairo and shortages of paper made publishing difficult. Kraus wrote (27 January 1941) that publication of his *Plotin chez les Arabes* and the second volume of al-Rāzī had been cancelled.

Along with academic hardships caused by the war, Kraus' life was beset by personal tragedy. Kraus had met his wife, Bettina Strauss, during his Berlin period; she was the sister of Leo Strauss. Julius Ruska and Kraus directed her doctoral dissertation, entitled "Das Giftbuch des Śānāq."[89] The study was inspired by a suggestion by Max Meyerhof, who put a copy of a Cairo manuscript at her disposal. Paul and Bettina were married on 20 December 1936 in Cairo. On 23 January 1942, Bettina died after childbirth. The baby, named Jenny, was brought to Kibbutz Ma'aleh ha-Hamishah on the outskirts of Jerusalem.[90] She was later sent to New York to her uncle, Leo Strauss,[91] who adopted and raised her.[92]

The death of Bettina Strauss was a traumatic shock for Kraus. Hans Lewy described the impact: "the pallor, the dull and fatigued glance, and psychological balance barely maintained. He had lost the taste for life ('Il avait perdu le goût de vivre')."[93] Constance Padwick, in her letter to

Massignon, wrote: "One could hardly imagine Paul's existence there without her. She shouldered most of the practical worries of life, and she was his work companion as well, typing all his mss, looking up references, and so on." Yet Charles Kuentz, who knew Kraus during those hard years, wrote:

> All the obstacles would have paralyzed the efforts of many others, but for a man with sacred fire nothing counts but the result attained. And the more somber life became for him, the more he launched into professional occupations and studies. Although he found a diversion and a certain consolation, he also drew on an exaltation and a fever which could only be dangerous....He vibrated to all that is beautiful because it is true, in the world of the senses and the intelligible world. He had an alert curiosity, and investigated historical truth in all its forms. He went on reading, writing, speaking, and thinking, without apparent fatigue; to search, to discover, to understand.[94]

The appreciation of his work won him public distinction on 9 March 1942, when he was elected to the prestigious Institut d'Égypte by a unanimous vote.[95]

A Theory and its Critics

As he brought the two Jābir volumes to completion, Kraus thought to return to Semitica. He was competent in all the Semitic languages: Hebrew, Arabic, Akkadian, Aramaic, South Arabian and Ethiopic (in addition to Greek, Latin and Persian). Kraus began to articulate a theory on Semitic and biblical metrics—a complex argument that can only be adumbrated here. Kraus claimed that many Semitic epics, hymns and prose texts were originally in poetry, and had a carefully marked metric system. He extended this theory to the Hebrew Bible.[96]

Kraus' theory involved a revolutionary critique of modern biblical scholarship. Biblical science, he contended, was an outgrowth of the seventeenth- and eighteenth-century rationalism of Astruc, Spinoza, Hobbes. It also inherited Arab rationalism (Ibn Rāwandī, Abū Bakr al-Rāzī, Abū al-Barakāt al-Baghdādī, Maimonides, Ibn Ezra), which was directly linked to the biblical criticism of Celsus and Porphyry and the religious criticism of Epicurus. In the nineteenth century, biblical criticism was made scientific by Julius Wellhausen (1844–1918) and others, and became universally accepted. Its basis was a historical and evolutionist pragmatism, expressed in the so-called documentary hypothesis. Wellhausen and his precursors assigned documents J and E to the eighth and seventh centuries BC, and dated P (for Priestly Code) after the Exile, long after the Prophets. The Law thus comes after the Prophets according to Wellhausen's school, whose conclusions became universally accepted. The entire conception of the history of ideas of Israel was based on this chronology.

Against this approach, Kraus adduced what he called "a delicate and marvelous instrument," namely, "la phonétique historique et la linguistique générale." Kraus rejected the documentary hypothesis. Using the principles of historical phonetics and general linguistics, he claimed that the epic recitals of the Hebrew Bible were actually composed in a meter resembling that of classical Arabic poetry. Against the nineteenth century "German criticism" of Wellhausen, Kraus contended that biblical texts were authentic documents belonging to the epochs which sacred tradition assigned to them and not late compilations.[97]

Buoyed with optimism, Kraus set out to lecture on his theory. In late February 1943, he was in Beirut, delivering a series of talks. He spoke on 24 February at the Lycée Français; his theme was "Du nouveau dans les études relatives à l'Ancien Testament."[98] And on 26 February he lectured there on "Les Relations diplomatiques et littéraires entre la Syrie et l'Egypte au 14ème siècle avant Jésus Christ."[99] In this talk he showed that his linguistic method also applied to other ancient languages, notably Assyro-Babylonian, the diplomatic and literary language used in Syria and the Near East during the second millennium BC. Kraus also lectured on Arabic literature. He spoke on al-Jāḥiẓ to the Cénacle de la Culture on 28 February at the home of its president, Jamīl Bayhum.

The Lebanese Arabic newspaper *al-Jumhūr* at the time showed Paul Kraus, "a great guest of Lebanon," along with various dignitaries and the soon-to-be-famous Syrian professor of history at the American University of Beirut, Constantine Zurayk (b. 1909). Kraus appears as a slight seated figure with sparkling eyes, engulfed by robust Lebanese notables.[100] He also gave a lecture on Radio-Levant on "Rythme poétique arabe et son rapport avec la poésie sémitique."[101] After returning to Egypt, Kraus lectured on "Du nouveau dans l'Ancien Testament" at the Collège de Faggalah.[102]

Kraus attached great importance to reaching Arab audiences, and at the time of the Levant trip, he commenced a series of fifteen articles in the journal *al-Thaqāfa* under the title "Min Minbar al-Sharq," "From the Eastern Pulpit."[103] He used this forum to acquaint Arab readers with the Arab cultural heritage, by sharing his own scholarly projects. Kraus wrote on Graeco-Arabic subjects, but he also presented his new theory on the metrics of Arabic and Semitic poetry. According to Kraus, Arabic chancellery style *(inshā')* retained Assyrian and Aramaic forms, "so that the ancient and modern East are remarkably one." The meters of Assyrian poetry were identical to Arabic poetic meters, which are thus proven to be ancient Semitic. He also wrote on Arabic literature, including Ḥamza al-Iṣfahānī, the Shu'ūbiyya, the *Kitāb al-Bukhalā'* of al-Jāḥiẓ, Abū Isḥāq al-Naẓẓām, Mu'tazilism, and Saladin's physician Ibn Jumay'.[104] Kraus also had praise for the work of his Arab and Egyptian colleagues, and especially the research of his friend, 'Abd al-Raḥmān Badawī (b. 1905) on the history of Greek thought and Greek philosophy. He lauded Badawī's attempt to give cultivated *(mustathqif)* youth of the East the results of Western scholarship on Greek philosophy. (As it happened, he inadverently offended Badawī by mentioning his "slips" *[hafawāt]*, which Kraus was quite willing to pardon because a certain manuscript had not been available to him.) Kraus' mastery of Arabic and Arabic literature was a source of awe to his Egyptian colleagues and students.[105]

But in September 1943, Kraus unfolded his theory before a more skeptical audience in Jerusalem, at a moment when an appointment at the Hebrew University hung in the balance. Prior to his visit, Kraus had written to Gershom Scholem (1897–1982) of the Hebrew University about his theory, and inquired about obtaining a visiting professorship there. He had every reason for wanting to be in Jerusalem: his daughter was nearby and he had friends at the university. Kraus sent Scholem a précis of his article on Tel-Amarna, which was part of his projected "Études sur les mètres sémitiques." He described, somewhat apologetically, the difficulties he was having with his theory. After a "long interruption, filled with disquiet, failure, despair," he had arrived at positive results that would challenge Old Testament scholarship. The letter clearly reflected Kraus' mercurial mood swings from despair to confidence (see appendix 1 below).

In Jerusalem, he lectured at the Hebrew University (in French), and at the Hebrew Teachers' Seminary in Beit ha-Kerem (in Hebrew). The invitations to the all-important university lecture simply said: "Paul Kraus will give a talk on his biblical research." Hans Lewy, who was present, described the "unforgettable soirée in Jerusalem"—unforgettable for all the wrong reasons. The talk, wrote Lewy, was totally bizarre, unlike anything the audience had ever heard from a scholar. It was "without head or tail, without any train of thought, without an attempt to define or prove, in a medley of all languages and with histrionic effects." The audience had the impression that this excited person was a man of genius, the event unprecedented. However, writes Lewy, when the glitter faded and critical intelligence took over, the hour of the skeptics arrived. Lewy noted that Kraus himself realized the weaknesses of his theories and went through a period of crisis marked by ups and downs.[106] The professors who had befriended and encouraged him now distanced themselves from him.[107] Scholem in particular was not persuaded by Kraus' theories. In a letter from Kraus to his friend D.H. Baneth (1893–1973), written in early 1944 after his visit to Jerusalem, he wrote: "Please tell Scholem that the letter he announced to me in Jerusalem has never arrived."[108]

In June 1944, Kraus remarried in Jerusalem. With his new wife, Dorothee Metlitzki, he traveled to Beirut, where he had business with the Catholic Press. Upon their return to Jerusalem, Dorothee Metlitzki relates, he realized that he had no prospects at the Hebrew University. During his stay in Palestine, Kraus told her of his own disappointment with his theory on Semitic and biblical metrics, his sense that his reputation as a scholar had been undermined. His Jerusalem friends—D.H. Baneth, Hans Lewy, Shlomo Pines—later noted his extreme mood swings, from buoyancy and exhilaration to dejection and despair.[109]

"A man who isn't wanted..."

Without prospects in Jerusalem, Kraus was even more dependent upon his teaching posts at King Fuad I University (the Egyptian University had been renamed after the king in 1940), and at the King Farouq I University in Alexandria. This in turn was contingent upon the position and status of Ṭāhā Ḥusayn, Kraus' Cairene mentor and patron, whose own prospects were bound up with the fortunes of the Wafd party. Since Ṭāhā Ḥusayn's restoration to the deanship in 1936, he had been on the rise. In the course of 1942, he was made adviser to the minister of education in the Wafd cabinet, and was named the first rector of the new King Farouq I University in Alexandria. Kraus could not have had a more influential patron.

But early in 1944, with the end of the war in sight, the political situation in Egypt grew unsettled. Anti-British (and anti-foreign) sentiment ran high, fomented by the Muslim Brotherhood and the Young Egypt Society. The Wafd government had grown unpopular among nationalists by its collusion with the British through the war. By the spring, the position of the Wafd was uncertain: the opposition had gained momentum, and the young King Farouq (r. 1936–52) was determined to remove the Wafd prime minister, Muṣṭafā al-Naḥḥās (1879–1965).[110] On 8 October 1944, the king finally found an adequate pretext to dismiss the Wafd cabinet, and summoned Aḥmad Māhir (ca. 1886–1945), leader of the Sa'dist party, to form a new government.

As a result of the change of government, Ṭāhā Ḥusayn was on his way out: on 16 October, he would resign all his administrative positions.[111] But before that, on 12 October, Ṭāhā Ḥusayn performed the sad duty of informing Kraus that he would be dismissed.[112] Kraus' colleague, Yaḥyā al-Khashshāb, met him around noon that day in the university. Kraus shook al-Khashshāb's hand, and told him that he had asked for him at the university and then at home. Al-Khashshāb had no indication from Kraus' demeanor that he would return home and immediately end his life.[113]

Kraus' mood had been gloomy even before 12 October. *The Palestine Post,* reporting from Cairo (14 October), said that he had appeared depressed ever since his recent return from Palestine, although he discussed his difficulties and plans in a normal way. He had not come back to Cairo with Metlitzki; she had a medical complication which required an immediate operation in Jerusalem. (She was still in hospital when Aubrey Eban came to Jerusalem with news of Kraus' suicide.) Cecil Hourani was also a witness to a change in Kraus. When Kraus had gone to Palestine in 1944 to remarry, he offered to lend Hourani and his brother Albert the use of his Zamalek apartment. Upon his return, Kraus asked the Houranis to stay on with him until his wife was able to join him. "I had felt that something had happened during his last visit to Palestine," wrote Cecil Hourani in retrospect. "He had lost much of the liveliness and humour which I had so much enjoyed when we first met."[114] Doubts about his scholarly worth, the lost prospect of an appointment at the Hebrew University, and concern about his wife already weighed heavily on Kraus even before the bad news struck him on 12 October.

In such a predicament, a person may inflate the gravity and severity of events, magnifying them out of proportion. Kraus had been sacked, but the war was drawing to a close, and his chances of finding employment in a major European or American university were excellent. Others in his position were making just that transition. Kraus' friend Koyré, for example, had left Egypt and reached the United States in 1941, where he became a professor at the New School for Social Research in New York. There he had established, with several colleagues, what was called l'École Libre des Hautes Études. This American École was a refuge for European victims of Nazism, mainly French and Belgian (Georges Gurvitch, Jean Wahl, Roman Jakobson, Claude Lévi-Strauss, George Sarton). Kraus' brother-in-law, Leo Strauss, was also initiated to American academic life at the New School (as was Hannah Arendt).[115]

But Kraus seemed to have lost his way. In the last four months of his life, he spent much time with Constance Padwick.[116] Her letter to Massignon described Kraus' mental state during these last months of his life. After Bettina died, she wrote, he could not cope with working on the third volume of Jābir b. Ḥayyān, with which she had been helping him. He turned to his interests in comparative grammar, and then developed his metric theory. He went through a period of ecstasy, elation and nervous excitement, and then darkness, despondency and illness. He was dogged by allegations that he had embezzled money designated for buying books for the libraries of the Cairo and Alexandria universities. And there was his own disappointment at the reception accorded to his theory, and the damage this had done to his own sense of integrity.[117]

We can never know what is in the soul of another human being.[118] But the concatenation of events, the accumulation of disappointments and tragedies, must have made the world seem so inimical and hostile that Kraus saw no point in going on.

There is an implausible account of the tragedy that nevertheless cannot be omitted. On 6 November 1944, Lord Moyne, British minister resident in the Middle East, was assassinated in Cairo by two Palestinian Jews, members of the terrorist group Lehi. The prospective assassins had stolen across the Egyptian border from Palestine. According to Cecil Hourani, someone informed him that among the papers of the assassins, the police found a list of Cairene safe houses, including Kraus' apartment. Hourani finds it difficult to believe that someone as gentle as Kraus could have been associated with the terrorists who killed Lord Moyne. Still, writes Hourani, "the thought remains in my mind that it may have been just that contrast between a natural gentleness and the desperate plight of the Jews in Europe, which drove some of them, with whom he may have had connections of friendship or collaboration at an earlier period of his life, to terrorism, and which brought him to suicide, that final escape from the necessity of making impossible choices."[119] Some Egyptians believed that Kraus was involved in the assassination. 'Abd al-Raḥmān Badawī thought that Kraus was caught up in the plans to murder Lord Moyne but changed his mind, and found there was no way out. Others held that the Zionists had murdered Kraus because he knew too much.[120] It may be that some Egyptians favored such an explanation out of remorse at the way he had been treated at the end. In counterpoint, S.D. Goitein records in his diary (13 October 1944) opinions of professors at the Hebrew University, reporting that Scholem thought the Egyptians had killed him.[121] There is no evidence to support any of these speculations, and it is implausible that Kraus would have offered his apartment as a "safe house" for the assassins, as the Hourani brothers were living there with him.[122]

Yaḥyā al-Khashshāb ended his moving elegy for Kraus by praying that Allah "have mercy on him but not on those who troubled his life."[123] That life, said Charles Kuentz in his eulogy, could be summarized by Proverbs 3:13–14: "Happy is the man who finds wisdom, the man who attains understanding. Her value in trade is better than silver; her yield, greater than gold." Kraus did attain precious understanding, but happiness eluded him; circumstances of time and place worked against him. Ultimately, his tragic end evokes the words of the landlady to the land surveyor in Kafka's *Castle:* "You are not from the Castle, you are not from the village, you aren't anything. Or, rather, unfortunately, you are something, a stranger, a man who isn't wanted and is in everybody's way."[124]

Appendix 1
Letter from Kraus to Gershom Scholem (in French, dated 30 December 1942)[125]

I sent you recently by an acquaintance of mine through D.H. [Baneth][126] a précis of my article on Tel-Amarna. Don't judge ill of it; it is a small résumé of my communication to the [French] Institute, destined at most to be a signpost: the finished study, set aside because of other urgent works, which will contain the entire phonetic, philological and "orthographo-logical" justification will appear one day in my "Études sur les mètres sémitiques." Please tell this to Polotsky,[127] who may be disappointed by the "meager" apparatus of my article.[128]

After a long interruption, filled with disquiet, failure, despair [*pleine d'amertume, d'insuccès, de désespoir*],—of which you, in Jerusalem, were the patient witness—I undertook two weeks ago my work on Semitic metrics and want to tell you that the results pass every expectation. All the "foolish" ideas which I shared with you in Jerusalem are nothing when measured against reality, the facts. The consequences for Hebrew, for the OT, are inestimable. Not only for grammar, phonetics, etc., but also and above all for literary criticism, for all this scaffolding of arbitrary ideas, of *petitiones principii,* of bad taste which one calls "the science" of the Old Testament. The whole collapses, not one stone remains on another. You recall how, at Jerusalem, I was troubled by the very numerous texts which refused any "metric analysis." Since then, I have found the key, and an astonishing key. Your wife may be disappointed. These are not only hendecasyllables or enneasyllables, but even, or above all, in the most ancient epic texts, heptasyllables, with variations of accent which are found exactly this way in classical Arabic metrics (thus! Finally there it is!). The surprises which await us are such that I cannot formulate them in a letter, written furthermore for a totally different reason.

You recall that at Jerusalem I talked to you about the possibility of giving courses at your university as a visiting professor, during the months of May–July, for example. Our semester here ends the first week of May and I might be able to get rid of the burden of examinations if I were invited to give lectures at your [university]. I do not yet have any idea about the theme, or the possible themes, to choose, but I am keen that they should relate to general Semitic philology, including Arabic and Islam, without my being assigned to one of the departments, castes in the hermetic division of the university organization. I am writing to you this early concerning this so that you may speak with your dean (G.S.)[129] and prepare the ground if you believe that the idea is "sound". I would rather give more "seminars" than ordinary (?) "lectures" which always have for me the air of something artificial. For all the rest, I give you free hand. N.B., speak about it also with Baneth and Guttman, and perhaps with Weil and Mayer.[130]

According to all expectations, I will come to Jerusalem for two weeks toward the 16 February (our semester vacation) to see my daughter (about whom I have, incidentally, some very good news). On this occasion, I would like to give my lecture in French, if possible, in the French Cultural Circle. Please speak about it with Duff.[131]

And if your Oriental Institute wishes to invite me to give a public lecture on the anniversary of the death of the lamented Billig,[132] I see no problem. In that case, I would naturally chose an Islamic theme.

That is all for the moment. I await your response, and ask you to transmit my best wishes to all my friends in Jerusalem. Remember me also to your wife, and trust, dear friend, in my sincerity.

Paul Kraus
7 Ahmad Hishmat Pasha
Zamalek

Appendix 2

The Kraus Papers and Library

Paul Kraus left behind a considerable amount of scholarly materials. Aside from his extensive library, including valuable manuscript materials, there were his own notes, papers and projected works. After his death, Dorothee Metlitzki came to Cairo to find out what happened and to put things in order. With the help and advice of Boris Grdseloff,[133] she bound the manuscript materials and copy-books into bundles and delivered them to Charles Kuentz at the Institut Français d'Archéologie Orientale (IFAO) "*for safekeeping* without any kind of authorization as to their use whatsoever" (her emphasis). The Czech consul (a Mr. Lienhardt) was informed.

A letter from Massignon to Leo Strauss (9 July 1945) shows that he took an active interest in the papers at an early stage. He writes from Cairo on stationery of the IFAO:

> Paul Kraus' death was such a sorrow. I paid a visit to the little Jany [sic] Kraus in Jerusalem. We hope you shall be for her a father. Paul's widow...has given, through the Czechoslovachian legation, to the French Archaeological Institute (here), the care of keeping Paul's manuscripts. They are already here, and I am classifying them with Dr. Ch. Kuentz, the Director, another friend of Paul (who was officially "Attaché" to the Institute). The Czechoslovachian legation is asking from the other heirs of Paul the confirmation of Paul's widow's decision,—and I hope you shall agree with her; so as to enable our Institute to see how to make the preparation of the unfinished works of Paul between specialists having been his friends (Walzer for Galien: printing finished in Beirut; Pines; you).[134]

The IFAO was, accordingly, interested in holding the papers so as to prepare Kraus' unfinished works for publication.

This objective was only partially achieved.[135] Kraus' tragic death interrupted his work at an advanced stage. After finishing *Jâbir ibn Ḥayyân–Contribution à l'histoire des idées scientifiques dans l'Islam,* Kraus planned to crown his monumental work with a comprehensive study of the religious and philosophical thought of Jābir and the relations between alchemy and radical Shi'ism.[136] The remaining drafts and notes were classified by Henry Corbin in 1946. But many scholars had access to these documents at the IFAO, and the papers were already in disarray at an early period. In February 1988 and March 1989, Pierre Lory visited the IFAO and found the material arranged along with boxes containing notes of works on Arab medicine, Aristotelianism, and the Hebrew Bible. Reading the dossiers, notably those concerning the Shi'ite doctrines of Jābir, he found that entire chapters from the projected book were missing, as were the Jābir manuscript materials which Kraus possessed. Lory describes three parts to this *Nachlass:* a typed text in German of a book on the religious thought of Jābir, written prior to 1936 (Corbin's dossier no. 91); dossiers of notes for lectures and personal reflections on general themes; and notes on Imāmism and connections with the Qarmatians.[137]

More evidence for the disarray of the collection may be found in correspondence between Leo Strauss and Charles Kuentz.[138] On 1 May 1946, Strauss wrote:

> M. Massignon informed me that your institute intends to distribute the unfinished works of Paul Kraus among specialists who had been his friends. I have worked together with Kraus on Farabi, and we studied together the Al-milla al-fadila, and the paraphrase of Plato's Laws in particular. When we were both still in Berlin, I ordered photographs of the mss. of these works, which Kraus later took to Cairo in order to prepare an edition and translation. There must be among his papers, a rough German translation of the paraphrase; the translation, dictated to me by Kraus, was entered by me into a blue exercise book, if I remember well. I should appreciate it very much if, in accordance with the plan of your institute, you would let me have these materials at your earliest convenience. I would like to start to work on these materials at once. May I avail myself of this opportunity and ask you whether you have heard anything about the last period of Kraus' life? We never received any information but the bare fact that he is no longer alive.

Strauss wrote this almost two years after the tragic event!

Kuentz replied (on 29 June 1946) that he has found the rough copy *(brouillon)* of the translation of the paraphrase of the *Laws,* but that he did not find photos of the manuscript of *al-Milla al-Fāḍila* or any other text of Alfarabi. He adds that "The papers of my deceased friend are in the greatest disorder, yet all hope is not lost." Strauss continued to work on Alfarabi's paraphrase of the *Laws* and other materials, and the study of Alfarabi was carried forward by his student Muhsin Mahdi.

A few years later, Dorothee Metlitzki received a request from Albert Hourani and H.A.R. Gibb to authorize a transfer of the papers to Oxford.

(They said that Gibb would have brought Kraus to Oxford had he not died so suddenly.) She gave her authorization, indicating that Jenny Kraus, or her uncle in her name, should be asked for their consent. Many years later, Dorothee Metlitzki met Prof. M. Manzalaoui and heard from him about his attempt to get the papers for Oxford University. According to him, Richard Walzer had gotten power of attorney from the family, which he transferred to Manzalaoui, to try to have the *Nachlass* sent to Oxford. This was in 1954. But the IFAO was unwilling to surrender the materials.[139]

As a postscript, it may be added that the IFAO agreed in the autumn of 1997 to release the papers to Paul Kraus' surviving heir, his daughter, Jenny Strauss Clay.

Dorothee Metlitzki had hoped that the Hebrew University would buy Kraus' library of books. S.D. Goitein served as intermediary, but nothing came of the plan. Eventually, Denyse Mosseri-Dreyfuss, of the prominent Cairene Mosseri family, and a friend of Kraus, purchased the library and gave it as a gift to Cairo University.[140]

Notes

Acknowledgments. I wish to express my gratitude to Jenny Strauss Clay for sending me valuable documents and material pertaining to her father, Paul Kraus; to Dorothee Metlitzki, Kraus' widow, for help answering questions and clarifying events; to Hélène Rosenberg, daughter of Hadassa Mednitzky and Shlomo Pines, for precious information and documents; to Franz Rosenthal for putting at my disposal his correspondence with Kraus and for other help; to Rémi Brague, Gad Freudenthal, Maurice Kriegel and Muhsin Mahdi for discussing Kraus with me in Paris; to Cecil Hourani in London; to Ouri Pines and Josef Stern for Kraus' letters to Shlomo Pines; to Shlomo Zucker and Tzvi Langermann of the Hebrew University and National Library; to Sharon Albert for help with the Strauss Archive at the University of Chicago, and to Joseph Cropsey for permission to consult it. My gratitude for information on the assassination of Lord Moyne goes to Prof. Joseph Heller; Shraga Peled of Haganah Archives; Hannah Armoni of the Lehi Museum; Amira Stern of Beit Jabotinsky; Yitzhak Shamir; Yafah Tevuah; and Benjamin Gefner. Thanks to Lucia Hochberg for information on Jenny at Kibbutz Ma'aleh ha-Hamisha; and to Ayala Gordon for material from diaries of her father, Prof. S.D. Goitein. For other assistance, I am grateful to Clark Gilpin, Ralph Lerner, Aviva Wilkov Kraemer, Eli Alshech, Judith Pfeiffer, and Ursula Wokoeck.

1. *La Bourse Égyptienne*, 13 October 1944; *Palestine Post*, 14 October, 1944; *al-Ahram*, 15 October 1944. The Egyptian press described Albert and Cecil Hourani as British officers; in fact, Albert was in government service.
2. Dorothee Metlitzki, personal communication and letter, 13 May 1997. Metlitzki was married to Kraus at the time (see below), and is today professor emerita of English at Yale, well known among Islamicists for her book *The Matter of Araby in Medieval England* (New Haven: Yale University Press, 1977). Cf. Cecil Hourani, *Lebanon and Beyond* (London: Weidenfeld & Nicolson, 1984), 45. Abba Eban, *An Autobiography* (New York: Random House, 1977), 38ff., describes this time of his life in Cairo, but does not mention Kraus.
3. This according to Kraus' birth certificate, courtesy of Jenny Clay Strauss.
4. See Kraus' published dissertation, *Altbabylonische Briefe aus der Vorderasiatischen Abteilung der Preussischen Staatsmuseen zu Berlin*, 2 vols. (Leipzig: J.C. Hinrichs, 1931–32), 78; Rémi Brague, "Paul Kraus: Person und Werk (1904–1944)," in Paul Kraus, *Alchemie, Ketzerei, Apokryphen im frühen Islam: gesammelte Aufsätze*, ed. R. Brague (Hildesheim: G. Olms, 1994), vii.
5. For background, see Gray Cowan Boyce, *The University of Prague: Modern Problems of the German University in Czechoslovakia* (London: R. Hale, 1937).
6. For Kafka in this context, see Hartmut Binder, *Kafka: ein Leben in Prag* (Munich: Mahnert-Lueg,1982). The standard biographies by Max Brod, Ronald Hayman and Ernst Pawel are very informative.
7. At the beginning of the century, the population of Prague numbered 414,899 Czechs (92.3%) and 33,776 Germans (7.5%), of whom 25,000 were of Jewish background; see Angelo Maria Ripellino, *Magic Prague*, trans. David Newton Marinelli (Berkeley: University of California Press, 1994), 19. Hans Tramer, "Prague—City of Three Peoples," *Publications of the Leo Baeck Institute, Year Book* 9 (New York, 1964), 305, says that the 1900 population consisted of 415,000 Czechs, 25,000 Jews and about 10,000 (non-Jewish) German-speaking subjects of the Habsburg Empire.
8. See Max Brod, *Der Prager Kreis* (Stuttgart: Kohlhammer, 1966); Jindrich Toman, *The Magic of a Common Language: Jakobson, Mathesius, Trubetzkoy, and the Prague Linguistic Circle* (Cambridge, Mass.: MIT Press, 1995). On the creativity of minority groups writing in the language of a majority culture, see Gilles Deleuze and Felix Guattari, *Kafka: Toward a Minor Literature*, trans. Dana Polan (Minneapolis: University of Minnesota Press, 1986).
9. Max Brod and Felix Weltsch, *Zionismus als Weltanschauung* (Mährische-Ostrau: R. Farber, 1925), esp. 77ff.
10. Tramer, "Prague—City of Three Peoples," 305.

11. Ripellino, *Magic Prague*, 21, 38, 48, 56. Consider Appollinaire's story, "Le passant de Prague," whose hero meets the figure of the Wandering Jew; discussed by Ripellino, *Magic Prague*, 254–57.
12. See Hans Lewy, "À la mémoire de Paul Kraus," given at a commemorative reunion on 17 January 1945 under the auspices of the School of Oriental Studies of the Hebrew University, first published in *Moznayim* 5 (1945); trans. into French by S. Pines, *La Revue du Caire, Revue de Littérature et d'Histoire* 15 (1945): 132–38, quote at 132. Lewy has him studying briefly at the Hebrew University and then returning directly to Berlin. Hans (Yohanan) Lewy (1904–45) was a classics scholar. He studied at the University of Berlin, emigrated to Palestine in 1933, and later taught classics at the Hebrew University. His field was late Jewish Hellenism.
13. Butin, an archeologist and biblical scholar, had written on the excavations and protosinaitic inscriptions at Serabit el Khadem and on the Massoretic text of the Pentateuch.
14. Kraus, *Altbabylonische Briefe* (see n. 4 above). The study is dedicated to Isidor Pollak, who had given Kraus his first stimulus to scholarship.
15. On Meissner, see Johann Fück, *Die arabischen Studien in Europa bis in den Anfang des 20. Jahrhunderts* (Leipzig: Otto Harrassowitz, 1955), 315.
16. Mittwoch, a Jewish orientalist, was close to Kraus and typifies the polymathy of the professors in Berlin. He worked in Arabic and Arabic literature, South Semitic philology, Hebrew and Hebrew inscriptions, and Turkish. He also participated in editing Moses Mendelssohn, *Gesammelte Schriften. Jubiläumsausgabe*, eds. I. Elbogen et al. (Berlin: Akademie Verlag, 1929–38). On Mittwoch, see Fück, *Die arabischen Studien in Europa,* 314.
17. On Becker, one of the founders of modern Islamic studies, see Josef van Ess, "From Wellhausen to Becker: The Emergence of *Kulturgeschichte* in Islamic Studies," in *Islamic Studies: A Tradition and its Problems*, ed. Malcolm H. Kerr (Malibu, Calif.: Undena Publications, 1980), 27–51; M. Batunsky, "Carl Heinrich Becker: From Old to Modern Islamology," *International Journal of Middle Eastern Studies* 13 (1981): 287–310; and C. Essner and G. Winkelhane, "Carl Heinrich Becker (1876–1933), Orientalist und Kulturpolitiker," *Die Welt des Islams*, n.s. 28 (1988): 154–77.
18. O. Pritsak, "Hans Heinrich Schaeder," *Zeitschrift der Deutschen Morgenländischen Gesellschaft (ZDMG)* 108 (1958): 24–25.
19. The information on Julius Ruska comes mainly from Paul Kraus, "Julius Ruska," *Osiris* 5 (1938) (= *Iulio Ruska Oblatum*): 5–20. See also Fück, *Die arabischen Studien in Europa,* 323; Rudolf Winderlich, *Julius Ruska und die Geschichte der Alchemie*, Abhandlungen zur Geschichte der Medizin und der Naturwissenschaften, 19 (Berlin: E. Ebering, 1937), 5–19 (appreciation), 20–40 (bibliography).
20. Julius Ruska, *Das Steinbuch des Aristoteles* (Heidelberg: C. Winter, 1912). The lapidary was known in medieval Latin and Hebrew translations; the

Arabic is from the mid-ninth century. Ruska found that it was from Syrian-Persian medical schools.

21. On Max Meyerhof, see Penelope Johnstone's preface to Meyerhof's *Studies in Medieval Arabic Medicine* (London: Variorum Reprints, 1984).
22. Martin Plessner was an expert on the classical heritage in Islam; he emigrated from Germany to Palestine in 1933 and became a professor at the Hebrew University in 1955. All three worked on the precious Ps.-Apollonius, *Kitāb Sirr al-Khalīqa.* H.S. Nyberg (1889–1969) possessed the most valuable manuscript materials for its study. Sigrid Kahle, in her biography of her father, *H.S. Nyberg: en vetenskapsmans biografi* (Stockholm: Norstedts, 1991), 240, reports that in 1936 Kraus wrote to Nyberg about *Sirr al-Khalīqa*, and Ruska also wrote to Nyberg about editing it. Kraus stressed that he had four Paris manuscripts copies. But Nyberg had not given up his own intention to edit the work. Kahle relates further (542), concerning the fate of *Sirr al-Khalīqa*, that Ruska, Kraus and Plessner all wished to work on it, but that her father finally turned over his materials to Ursula Weisser, a pupil of Fuat Sezgin, who edited it.
23. Julius Ruska, *Al-Rāzī's buch Geheimnis der geheimnisse,* Quellen und Studien zur Geschichte der Naturwissenschaften und der Medizin, vol. 6 (Berlin: J. Springer, 1937).
24. Paul Kraus, *Jâbir ibn Ḥayyân–Contribution à l'histoire des idées scientifiques dans l'Islam–Jâbir et la science grecque,* Mémoires présentés à l'Institut d'Égypte, 44–45 (Cairo: l'Institut français d'archéologie orientale, 1942–43; repr. Paris: Belles Lettres, 1986); idem, *Le Corpus des écrits jâbiriens,* Mémoire présenté à l'Institut d'Égypte (Cairo, 1943).
25. Fuat Sezgin, *Geschichte des arabischen Schrifttums* (Leiden: E.J. Brill, 1967–), 4:132–269, accepts E.J. Holmyard's view that Jābir was the son of a druggist Ḥayyān killed in Khurasan (107/725) with other Shi'ite agents, and that he was a pupil of Ja'far al-Ṣādiq. See also Sezgin's critique of Kraus in *Zeitschrift der Deutschen Morgenländischen Gesellschaft (ZDMG)* 114 (1964): 255–68, and Plessner's reply in Kraus' defense, *ZDMG* 115 (1965): 23–35. In a review of modern literature, Sezgin writes (*Geschichte des arabischen Schrifttums*, 4:175ff.) that Ruska first accepted an eighth-century date but abandoned it in 1930 after Kraus wrote about his early findings on Jābir and the Ismā'īliyya in "Dschābir ibn Ḥajjān und die Ismā'īlījja," in *Der Zusammenbruch der Dschābir-Legende* (*=Dritter Jahresbericht des Forschungsinstituts für Geschichte der Naturwissenschaften*) (Berlin, 1930), 23–42.
26. Pierre Lory, *Alchimie et mystique en terre d'Islam* (Lagrasse: Verdier, 1989), 15, refers to criticisms of Kraus in the works of Sezgin, Toufic Fahd, Seyyed Hossein Nasr and Henry Corbin. For the following, see Lory's own critique, 85f., 96f.
27. Lewy, "À la mémoire de Paul Kraus," 132–34.

28. Ibid.
29. Franz Rosenthal kindly put at my disposal copies of fourteen letters and postcards he received from Kraus between 1936 and 1941 (from Cairo).
30. Letter of 1 October 1936 from 139 Bd. St. Germain to Dr. Fr. Rosenthal in Berlin.
31. Letter of 15 August 1936, from 139 Bd. St. Germain VIe, Paris. The Lidzbarski Prize was announced at the International Congress of Orientalists in August 1938. The *Preisarbeit* was *Die aramäistische Forschung seit Th. Nöldeke's Veröffentlichungen* (Leiden: E.J. Brill, 1939). Kraus dwelt on the Lidzbarski Prize incident in his correspondence with Rosenthal; it caused him tension *(Spannung)*. The unfairness epitomized for him the academic and other injustices that he experienced so keenly in his own life.
32. As universities and research institutes were state bodies, professors, lecturers and researchers were state officials. The Restitution of the Civil Service decree of 7 April 1933 required that non-Aryan officials be dismissed, leading to the sacking of 1,200 scholars and scientists within two years. See Norman Bentwich, *The Rescue and Achievement of Refugee Scholars: The Story of Displaced Scholars and Scientists 1933–1952* (The Hague: M. Nijhoff, 1953), 1.
33. Lewy, "À la mémoire de Paul Kraus," 136.
34. Louis Massignon and Paul Kraus, trans., *Akhbâr al-Ḥallâj*, 3d ed. (Paris: Vrin, 1957), 5, after the dedication: "À la mémoire de Paul Kraus, mort à Zamalek, le 12 octobre 1944." Lewy, "À la mémoire de Paul Kraus," 136, says that Kraus sent a telegram to Louis Massignon and several days later received an answer. See also Ch. Kuentz, "Paul Kraus (1904–1944)," *Bulletin de l'Institut d'Égypte* 27 (1944–45): 432; and Yaḥyā al-Khashshāb, "Paul Kraus" [in Arabic], *al-Thaqāfa* 6 (24 October 1944), 17. Lory, *Alchimie et mystique*, 161–62, publishes a letter that Massignon wrote to Kraus from Paris concerning a Jābir fragment, and dated 14 December 1932—before they met in 1933.
35. For details of the Paris period, see also Brague, "Paul Kraus: Person und Werk," ix.
36. The application is in the possession of Jenny Strauss Clay.
37. Brague, "Paul Kraus: Person und Werk," x. Gad Freudenthal has informed me that Kraus taught together with Pines at the Institute. This must have been between 1937 and 1939, when Pines taught there. Shlomo Pines was born in Paris, studied at the University of Berlin, and emigrated to Palestine in 1940 (on the last boat from Marseilles). He became professor of general and Jewish philosophy at the Hebrew University in 1961. See Sarah Stroumsa, "Shlomo Pinès: le savant, le sage," *Journal Asiatique* 278, no. 3–4 (1990): 205–11; W.Z Harvey, "Professor Shlomo Pines and his Approach to Jewish Thought," *Shlomo Pines Jubilee Volume* (Jerusalem, 1988), 1:1–15. Abel Rey wrote widely on ancient and modern science.

38. Their relationship was close and complex. In Berlin in 1932, Pines fathered the daughter of Kraus' wife, Hadassa Mednitzky. Kraus and Pines nonetheless remained close friends. The daughter, Hélène Rosenberg (Ilana Kraus), who now lives in Paris, relates that Pines spoke of Kraus as a great influence upon him, and she had the impression that Kraus was the only scholar whom Pines genuinely admired.
39. The letter is addressed to "Cher Menia." It was found in Pines' Jerusalem apartment in 1997 by his son Ouri Pines and Josef Stern. The contents point to Pines as addressee: Ouri Pines informed me that "Menia" was a name of endearment used only by close members of the family.
40. Letter of 3 June 1933 from 7 Square Grangé (XIIIe Arr.), in the papers of Pines. Kraus had found a passage in Ibn Maṭrān's *Bustān al-Aṭibbā'* (from Abū Sulaymān al-Sijistānī's *Ta'ālīq*), showing that a person living toward the end of the tenth century was writing tracts and ascribing them to Jābir b. Ḥayyān.
41. Koyré's seminar in 1932–33 on Hegel's religious philosophy at the École Pratique des Hautes Études, Section des Sciences Religieuses, included Georges Bataille, Henry Corbin, Aron Gurvitsch, Raymond Queneau, Leo Strauss, and Eric Weil. See Michael Roth, *Knowing and History* (Ithaca: Cornell University Press, 1988), 95; Alexandre Koyré, *De la mystique à la science,* ed. Pietro Redondi (Paris: Ed. de l'École des Hautes Études en Sciences Sociales, 1986), 13.
42. G. Jorland, *La science dans la philosophie: les recherches épistémologiques d'Alexandre Koyré* (Paris: Gallimard, 1981), xx.
43. Lewy, "À la mémoire de Paul Kraus," 134.
44. These included Raymond Queneau, Henry Corbin, Georges Bataille, Jacques Lacan, Eric Weil, Maurice and Jacques Merleau-Ponty, Denyse Mosseri, André Breton, and Jean Hyppolite. See Dominique Auffret, *Alexandre Kojève* (Paris: B. Grasset, 1990), 238.
45. For Strauss and Kojève, and their correspondence, see Leo Strauss, *On Tyranny*, rev. ed., eds. Victor Gourevitch and Michael S. Roth (New York: Free Press, 1991); Roth, *Knowing and History*, 126–33; Shadia Drury, *Alexandre Kojève* (New York: St. Martin's Press, 1994), 143–60.
46. Massignon had encouraged Corbin to study Suhrawardī; see Pierre Rocalve, *Louis Massignon et l'Islam* (Damascus: Institut Français de Damas, 1993), 52; Henry Corbin and Paul Kraus, "Le Bruissement de l'Aile de Gabriel," *Journal Asiatique*, 227 (July–September 1935): 1–82.
47. Henry Corbin, *L'alchimie comme art hiératique*, Bibliotheque des mythes et des religions, vol. 3, ed. Pierre Lory (Paris: Herne, 1986).
48. On Massignon, see Christian Destremau and Jean Moncelon, *Louis Massignon* (Paris: Plon, 1994); and Mary Louise Gude, *Louis Massignon: The Crucible of Compassion* (Notre Dame: University of Notre Dame Press, 1996).

49. See Louis Massignon, "Salmân Pâk et les prémices spirituelles de l'Islam iranien," in his *Opera Minora,* 3 vols., ed. Youakim Moubarek (Beirut: Dar al-Maaref, 1963), 1:443–83 (first published in 1934); English trans., *Salman Pak and the Spiritual Beginnings of Iranian Islam,* trans. Jamshedje Maneckji Unvala (Bombay: J.M. Unvala, 1955); extracts in Massignon's *Parole donné,* 3d ed. (Paris: Seuil, 1983), 98–129; Herbert Mason, *Testimonies and Reflections: Essays of Louis Massignon* (Notre Dame: University of Notre Dame Press, 1989), 93–110. Massignon attributed to Salmān Pāk, like al-Ḥallāj, a role as intecessor in his "conversion." See Rocalve, *Louis Massignon,* 70.
50. In the undated "Dear Menia" letter; see n. 39 above.
51. Herbert Mason, *Memoir of a Friend: Louis Massignon* (Notre Dame: University of Notre Dame Press, 1988), 43–44; Rocalve, *Louis Massignon,* 14. Like Kraus, all three met tragic ends: Maspéro perished in Buchenwald, Foucauld was murdered by Saharan tribesmen, Cuadra took his own life.
52. On the "conversion," see Massignon, *Parole donnée,* 281–83; Daniel Massignon, "Le voyage en Mésopotamie et la conversion de Louis Massignon en 1908," *Islamochristiana* 14 (1988): 127–99; Destremau and Moncelon, *Louis Massignon,* 42–81; Gude, *Louis Massignon,* 27–56.
53. Massignon's Catholic friends included Jacques Maritain, Paul Claudel, Pierre Teilhard de Chardin, Gabriel Marcel, François Mauriac, Georges Bernanos, and Jean Daniélou; see Mason, *Memoir,* 36.
54. On Massignon's ordination, and the resulting controversy (the Vatican opposed the ordination), see Destremau and Moncelon, *Louis Massignon,* 311–18; Gude, *Louis Massignon,* 178–84.
55. Guy Harpigny, *Islam et Christianisme selon Louis Massignon* (Louvain-la-Neuve: Université Catholique de Louvain, 1981), 42–54. Huysmans worked as a clerk in the French ministry of the interior and had a brilliant literary career first as an author of decadence (in *A Rebours*) and then in a series of novels, *Là Bas* (1891), *En Route* (1895), and *La Cathédrale* (1898), a kind of autobiographical trilogy in which he describes his spiritual path to a Catholic mysticism and spirituality.
56. Mainly with Mary Kahil, a Greek Catholic living in Egypt, with whom he had a close relationship and a long correspondence, on which see Louis Massignon, *L'Hospitalité sacrée,* ed. Jacques Keryell (Paris: Nouvelle Cité, 1987).
57. During Massignon's first years of thesis writing, he thought that al-Ḥallāj had converted to Christianity (this according to Massignon's son, Daniel); see Rocalve, *Louis Massignon,* 124 n. 5.
58. See his "Nature in Islamic Thought," in Mason, *Testimonies,* 83. See Jacques Nantet, "L. Massignon et le judaïsme," in Jean-François Six, ed., *Louis Massignon,* Cahiers de l'Herne, no. 13 (Paris: Herne, 1970), 220–24, and at 223–24, where Massignon's idea (prompted by a conversation with

Magnes) is quoted: "les persécutions millénaires ont fait du peuple d'Israël le type exemplaire de la personne déplacée."

59. See Rocalve, *Louis Massignon*, 51ff., 99–100 on his "Revolution Copernicienne" and *metanoia*. See also Henry Corbin, "L. Massignon," in Jean-François Six, ed., *Louis Massignon*, Cahiers de l'Herne, no. 13 (Paris: Herne, 1970), 57.
60. Corbin, "L. Massignon," 57.
61. See Schaeder's review in *Der Islam* 15 (1925): 117–35.
62. See Massignon's appreciation, "Ignace Goldziher (1850–1921)," in his *Opera Minora*, 3:391–99.
63. See Louis Massignon's preface to *La Passion de Husayn Ibn Mansûr Hallâj: martyr mystique de l'Islam*, new ed., 4 vols. (Paris: Gallimard, 1975), 1:25; trans. Herbert Mason, *The Passion of al-Hallaj: Mystic and Martyr of Islam*, 4 vols. (Princeton: Princeton University Press, 1982), 1:lx. (Mason has a note on this page saying that Paul Kraus worked closely with Louis Massignon on *Akhbâr* until his death in 1946, instead of 1944. It appears that the phrasing in Massignon, *Akhbâr al-Ḥallâj*, 6, "ce que je ne pus faire qu'après sa mort, en 1946," has misled Mason and Fück into thinking that Kraus died in 1946.)
64. The third edition was published in 1957, twenty-one years after the 1936 edition.
65. Massignon, *Akhbâr al-Ḥallâj*, 6.
66. Ibid. See also Massignon, "Réflexions sur la structure primitive de l'analyse grammaticale en arabe," in *Parole donnée*, 327–42 (first published in 1954).
67. See Paul Kraus, "Akhbār al-Ḥallāj," *al-Ḥadīth* 18, no. 7 (July 1944): 289–300.
68. Massignon, *Akhbâr al-Ḥallâj*, 6.
69. According to Kuentz, "Paul Kraus," 432, "these were fruitful years for him which he always remembered with a bit of nostalgia," adding, "Mais l'Orient l'attirait." Kraus dedicated his *Jâbir ibn Ḥayyân* to his colleagues from the École.
70. Brague, "Paul Kraus: Person und Werk," x.
71. Paul Kraus, *Jâbir ibn Ḥayyân: essai sur l'histoire des idées scientifiques dans l'Islam* (Paris: G. P. Maisonneuve, 1936).
72. Personal communication from Dorothee Metlitzki, 13 May 1997.
73. The two documents are from the papers of Paul Kraus in the possession of Jenny Strauss Clay. Spies was professor of Arabic and Islamic studies at Aligarh from 1932 to 1936.
74. Lewy, "À la mémoire de Paul Kraus," 136: "Son vieil amour pour son peuple s'éveilla. Ce fut un amour secret et plein de pudeur." For the Jerusalem appointment, see *Encyclopaedia Judaica*, s.v. "Kraus, Paul Eliezer," where Martin Plessner writes that a post was offered to Kraus at the Hebrew University simultaneously with the Cairo offer in 1936. This offer is

also mentioned by D.H. Baneth in his necrology, "Paul Kraus," *Davar*, 19 October 1944; and by Shlomo Pines in a letter to Jenny Strauss Clay (undated). He was sought as a replacement for Levi Billig (1897–1936), born in London, who taught Arabic at the Hebrew University from 1926, and who was killed in the Arab uprising of 1936.

75. The literature on Ṭāhā Ḥusayn is vast. For broad lines, see Pierre Cachia, *Ṭāhā Ḥusayn* (London: Luzac, 1956); and Fedwa Malti-Douglas, *Blindness & Autobiography:* Al-Ayyām *of Ṭāhā Ḥusayn* (Princeton: Princeton University Press, 1988).
76. Ṭāhā Ḥusayn, *Dhikrā Abī al-'Alā' al-Ma'arrī*, 2nd ed. (Cairo: Maktabat al-Hilāl, 1922).
77. Taha Hussein, *Étude analytique et critique de la Philosophie Sociale d'Ibn Khaldoun* (Paris 1917) [Thèse de Lettres de l'Université de Paris].
78. See *Mustaqbal al-thaqāfa fī Miṣr* (Cairo: Maṭba'at al-Ma'ārif, 1938); trans. Sidney Glazer, *The Future of Culture in Egypt* (Washington: American Council of Learned Societies, 1954).
79. For the politics surrounding the deanship, see Donald M. Reid, *Cairo University and the Making of Modern Egypt* (Cambridge: Cambridge University Press, 1990), 120–25; Haggai Erlich, *Students and University in 20th Century Egyptian Politics* (London: Frank Cass, 1989), 77–86.
80. Letter of 16 Febuary 1937 from his address at 7 Ahmad Hishmat Pasha, Zamalek.
81. Ibid.
82. From an interview I conducted with Bernard Lewis and published under the title "Ba-Hipus ahar ha-Islam ha-Avud: Dialog 'im Bernard Lewis," *Zemanim* (Tel Aviv), no. 25 (Spring 1987): 18–31. Both Kraus and Lewis studied Ismā'īlism, as did another Jewish scholar, S.M. Stern (see the study on Stern by Shulamit Sela in this volume).
83. The ninth-century litterateur al-Jāḥiẓ interested Kraus over the years. He edited a volume of al-Jāḥiẓ treatises with his friend Muḥammad Ṭāhā al-Ḥājirī, *Majmū' rasā'il al-Jāḥiẓ* (Cairo: Lajnat al-Ta'līf wa'l-Tarjamah wa'l-Nashr, 1943).
84. Murād Kāmil worked in Ethiopic studies and wrote on the Copts of Egypt.
85. The year is unfortunately left blank; it was obviously 1938 or 1939.
86. Kraus was not a member of the Institute; in 1945, Massignon refers to him as having been "Attaché" (see appendix 2). Kraus is not listed among the members of the Institute in its centenary volume; see Jean Vercoutter, ed., *Institut Français d'Archéologie Orientale du Caire, Livre du Centenaire 1880–1980* (Cairo, 1980), xxv.
87. Constance E. Padwick was a missionary who befriended Paul and Bettina in Egypt, best known for her book *Muslim Devotions: A Study of Prayer-Manuals in Common Use* (London: SPCK, 1961). She wrote her letter to Massignon from Jerusalem on 16 October 1944, explaining the circum-

stances of Kraus' death. The letter was copied from the original in Massignon's possession by Jenny Strauss Clay, who kindly made it available to me. On Kraus' continuing affection for his place of birth, see al-Khashshāb, "Paul Kraus," 16–17: "How lovely in his eyes was the sight of the mountains and valleys of Prague. And the small house and small rose garden. How great was his yearning *(ḥanīn)* for his homeland."

88. *Alfarabius De Platonis philosophia*, Plato Arabus, vol. 2, eds. F. Rosenthal and R. Walzer (London: Warburg Institute, 1943).
89. Bettina Strauss, *Das Giftbuch des Śānāq: eine literaturgeschichtliche Untersuchung*, Quellen und Studien zur Geschichte der Naturwissenschaften und der Medizin, vol. 4, no. 2 (Berlin: J. Springer, 1935). Kraus reviews it in *Revue des Études Islamiques* 2 (1934), *Abstracta Islamica* 5: 196.
90. Jenny was placed in the kibbutz nursery. Jacob and Judith Princental (now Peri-Tal) were her adoptive family. Old-timers on the kibbutz, Shlomo Ben Haim and Mordechai Sandak, whom I met in the summer of 1996, remembered Paul Kraus and had been impressed by his Hebrew pronunciation of the letters ח and ע.
91. Leo Strauss was teaching then at the New School for Social Research; later he joined the political science department at the University of Chicago. When I visited Strauss in 1965, he mentioned his brother-in-law Paul Kraus and a theory he held concerning the book of Ecclesiastes. Strauss had high regard for Kraus and cites him in his writings; Kraus, in turn, wrote penetrating reviews of Strauss' early works. See the review of Strauss' *Philosophie und Gesetz* in *Revue des Études Islamiques* 4 (1935) = *Abstracta Islamica* 5:220–23; and on Strauss' "Eine vermisste Schrift Fārābīs," see *Abstracta Islamica* 5:227–28.
92. Jenny Strauss Clay is a professor of classics at the University of Virginia, and the author most notably of *The Wrath of Athena: Gods and Men in the Odyssey* (Princeton: Princeton University Press, 1983), and *The Politics of Olympus: Form and Meaning in the Major Homeric Hymns* (Princeton: Princeton University Press, 1989).
93. Lewy, "À la mémoire de Paul Kraus," 134–35. S.D. Goitein records in his diary (28 August 1942) that at a family dinner, Kraus' "depression did not leave him for a moment." He was upset because, he said, "I was sure that the Germans would enter Cairo two days after I left." (Field Marshal Rommel had taken Tobruk in June; he was not turned back until the British victory at El Alamein in November.) The war also took its toll on Kraus' susceptible nature. For the mood in Cairo during these years, see Artemis Cooper, *Cairo in the War: 1939–1945* (London: Hamish Hamilton, 1989).
94. Kuentz, "Paul Kraus," 433–34.
95. Ibid., 433.
96. Notebooks containing drafts for his lectures on Semitic metrics are preserved in the archives of the Hebrew University. Having been informed by

Dorothee Metlitzki that the Hebrew part of the *Nachlass* went to the Hebrew University on Mt. Scopus, I surmised that it might have come down to the Giv'at Ram campus after June 1967. Tzvi Langermann and Shlomo Zucker were kind enough to look into this and to locate the notebooks for me. I wish to thank the library for permission to publish from them. They are handwritten in French and contain Kraus' lectures delivered in 1943.

97. *La Syrie et l'Orient*, 26 February 1943, reporting one of his lectures.
98. *Le Soir*, 24 February 1943, announced the lecture. *La Syrie et l'Orient*, 26 February 1943, reported a positive reception to the lecture.
99. *La Syrie et l'Orient*, 23 February 1943, announced two lectures at the Lycée Français, on 24 and 26 February.
100. *Al-Jumhūr*, 26 February 1943.
101. *La Syrie et l'Orient*, 3 March 1943.
102. *La Bourse Égyptienne*, 27 March 1943, has an informed report on the lecture of Paul Kraus, distinguished Semitist and "maître de conférences" at the Egyptian University (signed by "J.L."), ending on a very positive note, describing "the original and fecund theory which opens a vast area of study and is supported by the results of archeology and history." Referring to "Le jeune savant de l'Université égyptienne," J.L. writes: "Il fait de l'excellent besogne."
103. The series began to appear in *al-Thaqāfa* 5 (1943) with instalments in no. 215 (9 February 1943), "Aflāṭūn 'inda al-'Arab," and no. 216 (16 February 1943), "Min ḥadīth Ḥunayn b. Isḥāq." He addresses the reader as "my dear friend" (*'azīzī*) and "the Arab reader." The series ended with *al-Thaqāfa* 6 (1944), no. 286 (20 June 1944).
104. Meyerhof had planned to work with Kraus on a book written by Ibn Jumay' and dedicated to Saladin. Meyerhof's aim, he later wrote, was "to publish the Arabic text with translation and commentary with the help of Dr. Paul Kraus, lecturer on Semitic languages at the Cairo University. The untimely death of that young and eminent scholar has prevented it for the time being." Meyerhof, "Sultan Saladin's Physician on the Transmission of Greek Medicine to the Arabs," *Bulletin of the History of Medicine* 18 (1945): 169–78, quote at 170.
105. Prof. A.I. Sabra, the historian of Islamic science at Harvard, writes (personal communication of 17 July 1997) of a tour de force lecture by Kraus on the poet al-Ma'arrī given in Alexandria. Kraus lectured on the most abstruse poetry, reciting by heart and commenting without notes. "Everybody watched this performance with awe."
106. Lewy, "À la mémoire de Paul Kraus," pp. 136–38.
107. However, Schalom Ben-Chorin wrote an enthusiastic review of Kraus' lecture; see his "Im Anfang War der Vers," *Jedioth uhadaschot*, 14 September 1943. It is also ironic that two elements of his revolutionary theory were also espoused by Hebrew University Bible professors. Yehezkel Kaufmann

(1889–1963) made a cornerstone of his approach a critique of Wellhausen's evolutionist hypothesis and his positing of an early date for the Priestly Code, in *The Religion of Israel*, trans. Moshe Greenberg (Chicago: University of Chicago Press, 1960). Umberto Cassuto (1883–1951) criticized the documentary hypothesis, in *The Documentary Hypothesis and the Composition of the Pentateuch*, trans. Israel Abrahams (Jerusalem: Magnes Press, 1961).

108. Letter from Cairo, 14 February 1944, preserved in the archives of the Hebrew University.
109. Baneth, "Dr. Paul Kraus," *Davar,* 19 October 1944; Pines, letter to Jenny Strauss Clay (undated).
110. P.J. Vatikiotis, *The History of Egypt from Muhammad Ali to Mubarak*, 3d ed. (Baltimore: Johns Hopkins University Press, 1986), 353; Jacques Berque, *Egypt: Imperialism and Revolution*, trans. Jean Stewart (New York: Praeger, 1972), 573ff.
111. Cachia, *Ṭāhā Ḥusayn,* 62, writes that a few days before the king dismissed the cabinet, Ḥusayn resigned from government service.
112. The source of this information is Shlomo Pines, and it is confirmed by Dorothee Metlitzki.
113. Al-Khashshāb, "Paul Kraus," 16. Al-Khashshāb felt very close to Kraus. He knew him from Paris days at the École des Hautes Études, and their ties were strengthened when they were faculty colleagues in Cairo.
114. Hourani, *Lebanon and Beyond*, 45. Hourani had met Kraus through 'Abd al-Raḥmān Badawī.
115. See Claus-Dieter Krohn, *Intellectuals in Exile: Refugee Scholars and the New School for Social Research* (Amherst: University of Massachusetts Press, 1993).
116. According to Goitein in his diaries, 12 October 1944.
117. Goitein reports in his diary entry of 13 October 1944 that on news of the tragedy, he heard from several sources that Kraus had said: "Only 60 per cent of my theory is correct, and I can live only with 100 per cent; I have to hang myself." Goitein mentons that after Kraus died, two letters arrived (to Prof. A. Frankel and Constance Padwick) in which he mentioned his concerns, especially his financial situation, but always ended on an optimistic note: "We have hope and good chances in the future."
118. Psalm 42:8.
119. Cecil Hourani, *Lebanon and Beyond* , 45–46. In an interview with Hourani in London, 23 May 1997, he said that the theory was "far-fetched" but still believed that it was possible under the terrible experiences of the war.
120. Badawī's theory was related to me by Muhsin Mahdi in April 1997. I spoke to Badawī in Paris in June 1997, but he had nothing more to say about Kraus.

121. The same rumor is mentioned by Shlomo Pines in an undated letter to Jenny Strauss Clay.
122. Depite the unlikelihood of Kraus' involvement in the assassination, I decided to speak with persons close to the event. Yitzhak Shamir, then one of the heads of Lehi and later prime minister of Israel, told me (interview, 4 September 1997) that he never heard of Paul Kraus, and that his apartment was not a "safe house." Yafah Tevuah, who was involved in the assassination, never heard of Kraus, nor had Bejamin Gefner, a Lehi operative active in Cairo. A survey of relevant archives—Haganah Archives, Lehi Museum, Beit Jabotinsky— also produced a negative result. Reports of the attack on Moyne and the investigation by the police are preserved in Public Records Office (London), FO 371/41515, J3969/J4016/33/66. Kraus is not mentioned anywhere in these records.
123. Bernard Lewis (in a letter of 10 July 1997) informed me that, when he asked Egyptian friends in 1945 what al-Khashshāb meant, they replied "that it meant first, those who had driven him into exile, and second, those who had made his life difficult at the university in Cairo." Lewis heard the Lehi story from Massignon. Lewis said he "dismissed the story as absurd and wildly out of characer, to which [Massignon] responded in the familiar manner with dark, conspiratorial hints."
124. Franz Kafka, *The Castle*, trans. Edwin and Willa Muir (New York: Knopf, 1930), 52; Franz Kafka, *Das Schloss* (Berlin: S. Fischer Verlag, 1935), 69. "Sie sind nicht aus dem Schloss, Sie sind nicht aus dem Dorfe, Sie sind nichts. Leider aber sind Sie doch etwas, ein Fremder, einer, der überzählig und überall im Weg ist."
125. The letter is from the archives of the Hebrew University and National Library at Giv'at Ram in Jerusalem. Dr. Maurice Kriegel kindly transcribed the French. The English translation is my own.
126. D.H. Baneth (1893–1973) was an Arabist and a close friend of Kraus; on Baneth, see the article by Hava Lazarus-Yafeh in this volume.
127. Hans Jacob Polotsky (1905–91) was a linguistic expert in Egyptology and Semitic languages. He taught at the Hebrew University from 1934.
128. The notes for this lecture are preserved in Kraus' notebooks at the Hebrew University. The published version appeared as "La forme littéraire des tablettes de Tel el-Amarna," *Bulletin de l'Institut d'Égypte* 24 (1942): 123–31.
129. He is referring humorously to Gershom Scholem himself.
130. Julius Guttman (1880–1950) emigrated from Berlin to Jerusalem in 1934 and became professor of Jewish philosophy at the Hebrew University. Gotthold Weil (1882–1960) was a Semiticist, Arabist and Turcologist, who emigrated from Germany and headed the National and University Library in Jerusalem from 1935 to 1946. Leo Ary Mayer (1895–1959) was a histo-

rian of Near Eastern art and archeology at the Hebrew University. He joined the university in 1925. On these and others, see the article by Hava Lazarus-Yafeh in this volume.

131. A.B. Duff (1899–1987) taught French at the Hebrew University and was an expert on de Gobineau. He had also written on Uriel Acosta.
132. See n. 74 above.
133. He was librarian of the Ludwig Borchardt Egyptological Institute in Cairo and a friend of Kraus, whom Dorothee Metlitzki later married.
134. The letter is from the Strauss archive at the University of Chicago. It was written in English.
135. The one instance was Galen, *Compendium Timaei Platonis*, Plato Arabus, vol. 2, eds. P. Kraus and R. Walzer (London: Warburg Institute, 1951).
136. Lory, *Alchimie et Mystique,* 41.
137. Ibid., 155ff.
138. Their correspondence is from the Strauss archive at the University of Chicago.
139. This account was given to me by Prof. Manzalaoui.
140. She was in Paris at the École with Kraus in the early 1930s, and participated in the Hegel seminar.

7

The Road from Mecca: Muhammad Asad (born Leopold Weiss)

Martin Kramer

In August 1954, there appeared in America a remarkable book, written by an author named Muhammad Asad and bearing the title *The Road to Mecca.* The book, a combination of memoir and travelogue, told the story of a convert to Islam who had crossed the spiritual deserts of Europe and the sand deserts of Arabia, on a trek that brought him ultimately to the oasis of Islamic belief. The book immediately won critical acclaim, most notably in the prestige press of New York, where it had been published by Simon and Schuster. One reviewer, writing in *The New York Herald Tribune Book Review,* called it an "intensely interesting and moving book."[1] Another reviewer, on the pages of *The New York Times,* placed the book in the pantheon of Arabian travel literature: "Not since Freya Stark," he wrote, "has anyone written so happily about Arabia as the Galician now known as Muhammad Asad."[2]

Muhammad Asad (1900–92) was a converted Jew, named Leopold Weiss at birth. He was no ordinary convert. Asad not only sought personal fulfillment in his adopted faith. He tried to affect the course of contemporary Islam, as an author, activist, diplomat, and translator of the Qur'an. Muhammad Asad died in February 1992 at the age of ninety-one, so that his career may be said to have paralleled the emergence of every trend in contemporary Islam.

As yet, however, there is no biography of Asad, and considerable obstacles await all who would attempt one. The most formidable of these is that the principal source for Asad's life remains Asad. No doubt this obstacle might be overcome, and this essay makes use of several additional sources for Asad's life. But the purpose here is more modest. It is to draw a very general sketch of Asad's life, and to place some emphasis upon the Jewish dimension of Muhammad Asad. For while Asad obviously distanced himself from Judaism, he adhered to a set of ideals that suffused the Jewish milieu from which he emerged. His failure to impart these ideals to contemporary Islam, and a repetitious pattern of rejection by his Muslim coreligionists, made of him a wandering Muslim, whose road from Mecca traversed an uncomprehending Islam before winding back to the refuge of the West.

The Drift from Judaism

Leopold Weiss was born on 12 July 1900, in the town of Lvov (Lemberg) in eastern Galicia, then a part of the Habsburg empire (Lvov is today in Ukraine). By the turn of the century, Jews formed a quarter to a third of the population of Lvov, a town inhabited mostly by Poles and Ukrainians. The Jewish community had grown and prospered over the previous century, expanding from commerce into industry and banking. Weiss's mother, Malka, was the daughter of a wealthy local banker, Menahem Mendel Feigenbaum. The family lived comfortably, and, wrote Weiss, lived for the children.[3]

From Weiss's own account, his roots in Judaism were deeper on his father's side. His paternal grandfather, Benjamin Weiss, had been one of a succession of Orthodox rabbis in Czernovitz in Bukovina. Weiss remembered his grandfather as a white-bearded man who loved chess, mathematics and astronomy, but who still held rabbinic learning in the highest regard, and so wished his son to enter the rabbinate. Weiss's father, Akiva, did study Talmud by day, but by night he secretly learned the curriculum of the humanistic *gymnasium.* Akiva Weiss eventually announced his open break from rabbinics, a rebellion that would presage his son's own very different break. But Akiva did not realize his dream of studying physics, because circumstances compelled him to take up the more practical profession of a barrister. He practiced first in Lvov, then in Vienna, where the Weiss family settled before the First World War.

Weiss testifies that his parents had little religious faith. For them, Judaism had become, in his words, "the wooden ritual of those who clung by habit—and only by habit—to their religious heritage." He later came to suspect that his father regarded all religion as outmoded superstition. But in deference to family tradition and to his grandfathers, young Leopold—"Poldi" to his family—was made to spend long hours with a tutor, studying the Hebrew Bible, Targum, Talmud, Mishna, and Gemarra. "By the age of thirteen," he attested, "I not only could read Hebrew with great fluency but also spoke it freely." He studied Targum "just as if I had been destined for a rabbinical career," and he could "discuss with a good deal of self-assurance the differences between the Babylonian and Jerusalem Talmuds."[4]

Nonetheless, Weiss developed what he called "a supercilious feeling" toward the premises of Judaism. While he did not disagree with its moral precepts, it seemed to him that the God of the Hebrew Bible and Talmud "was unduly concerned with the ritual by means of which His worshippers were supposed to worship Him." Moreover, this God seemed "strangely preoccupied with the destinies of one particular nation, the Hebrews." Far from being the creator and sustainer of mankind, the God of the Hebrews appeared to be a tribal deity, "adjusting all creation to the requirements of a 'chosen people.'" Weiss's studies thus led him away from Judaism, although he later allowed that "they helped me understand the fundamental purpose of religion as such, whatever its form."[5]

But this early disillusionment with Judaism did not lead to the pursuit of spiritual alternatives. In 1918, Weiss entered the University of Vienna. Days were given to the study of art history; evenings were spent in cafés, listening to the disputations of Vienna's psychoanalysts. ("The stimulus of Freud's ideas was as intoxicating to me as potent wine.")[6] Nights were given to passions. ("I rather gloried, like so many others of my generation, in what was considered a 'rebellion against the hollow conventions.'")[7] But as his studies progressed, the prospect of a life in academe lost appeal. In 1920, Weiss defied his father's wishes and left Vienna for Berlin to seek a career in journalism. There he joined the *littérateurs* at the Café des Westens, sold a few film scripts, and landed a job with a news agency.

Eastern Exposure

In the midst of this fairly unremarkable climb, Leopold Weiss took an unexpected detour. Early in 1922, a maternal uncle, Dorian Feigenbaum, invited Weiss to visit Jerusalem. Dorian, a psychoanalyst and pupil of Freud's, had initiated Weiss to psychoanalysis a few years earlier in Vienna. Now he headed a mental institution in Jerusalem. Weiss accepted the invitation, arriving in Egypt by ship and then in Palestine by train. In Jerusalem, he lived in Dorian's house, situated inside the old city a few steps from the Jaffa Gate. It was from this base that Leopold Weiss would first explore the realities of Islam. But his exploration would be prefaced by another discovery, of the immoralities of Zionism.

This stand was not a family inheritance. Although Dorian did not consider himself a Zionist, Weiss had another uncle in Jerusalem who was very much an ardent Zionist. Aryeh Feigenbaum (1885–1981), an opthalmologist, had immigrated to Palestine in 1913, and became a leading authority on trachoma whose Jerusalem clinics were frequented by thousands of Arabs and Jews. In 1920, he founded the first Hebrew medical journal; from 1922, he headed the opthamological department at Hadassah Hospital.[8] Weiss later omitted all mention of his Zionist uncle from *The Road to Mecca*—one of many suggestive omissions, hinting that the distancing from family and Zionism were linked.

But Weiss always presented his anti-Zionism as a simple moral imperative. "I conceived from the outset a strong objection to Zionism," Weiss would later affirm. "I considered it immoral that immigrants, assisted by a foreign Great Power, should come from abroad with the avowed intention of attaining to majority in the country and thus to dispossess the people whose country it had been since time immemorial."[9] This moral position was bolstered by a flash of insight Weiss experienced near the Jaffa Gate while observing a bedouin Arab, "silhouetted against the silver-grey sky like a figure from an old legend." Perhaps, he fantasized, this was "one of that handful of young warriors who had accompanied young David on his flight from the dark jealousy of Saul, his king?" Then, he says, "I knew, with that clarity which sometimes bursts within us like lightening and lights up the world for the length of a heartbeat, that David and David's time, like Abraham and Abraham's time, were closer to their Arabian roots—and so to the beduin of to-day—than to the Jew of today, who claims to be their descendant."[10]

In Jerusalem, Weiss began to confront Zionist leaders with the Arab question at every turn. He raised it both with Menahem Ussishkin (1863–1941) and Chaim Weizmann (1874–1952), and soon gained a reputation as a sympathizer of the Arab cause. Weiss also credited a new friend with assisting him greatly in Jerusalem: the Dutch poet and journalist Jacob Israël de Haan (1881–1924). By this time, De Haan's strange career had already taken its many turns: he had gone from socialist agitator to religious mystic, from ardent Zionist to fervent anti-Zionist. The Haganah would assassinate De Haan in 1924. De Haan fed Weiss's rejection of Zionism with grist, and also helped Weiss find journalistic work. And it was through De Haan that Weiss met the Emir 'Abdallāh (1882–1951) in the summer of 1923—his first in a lifetime of meetings with Arab heads of state.

In Palestine, Weiss became a stringer for the *Frankfurter Zeitung*, where he wrote against Zionism and for the cause of Muslim and Arab nationalism, with a strong anti-British bias. He published a small book on the subject in 1924,[11] and this so inspired the confidence of the *Frankfurter Zeitung* that it commissioned him to travel more widely still, to collect information for a full-scale book. Weiss made the trip, which lasted two years. At its outset, he found a new source of inspiration, during a stay in Cairo: Shaykh Muṣṭafā al-Marāghī (1881–1945), a brilliant reformist theologian who would later become rector of al-Azhar.[12] This was Weiss's first contact with Islamic reformism, and it left a profound impression upon him. Weiss concluded that the abysmal state of the Muslims could not be attributed to Islam, as its Western critics claimed, but to a misreading of Islam. When properly interpreted, in a modern light, Islam could lead Muslims forward, while offering spiritual sustenance that Judaism and Christianity had ceased to provide. Weiss spent the better part of the next two years travelling through Syria, Iraq, Kurdistan, Iran, Afghanistan, and Central Asia, growing ever more fascinated by Islam in its myriad forms.

The Conversion

Upon concluding his travels, Weiss returned to Frankfurt to write his book. There he also married Elsa, a widow, "probably the finest representative of the pure 'Nordic' type I have ever encountered," a woman fifteen years his senior, whom he had met before his last travels.[13] He was now settled into a comfortable routine. Yet he made no progress on his book: he was preoccupied and distracted, unable to put pen to paper in a summation of his travels. A quarrel with the editor of the *Frankfurter Zeitung* over his writer's block culminated in his resignation, and he moved to Berlin, where he took up Islamic studies and wrote as a stringer for lesser newspapers.

It was there, in September 1926, that Weiss experienced his second epiphany. He had had a flash of insight near the Jaffa Gate: the Arabs were the heirs of the biblical Hebrews, not the Jews. Now, on the Berlin subway, he had another flash. Watching the people on this train, in their finery and prosperity, he noticed that none smiled. Although positioned at the pinnacle of Western material achievement, they were unhappy. Returning to his flat, he cast a glance at a copy of the Qur'an he had been reading, and his eye settled upon the verse that reads: "You are obsessed by greed for more and more / Until you go down to your graves." And then later, in the same verse: "Nay, if you but knew it with the knowledge of certainty, / You would indeed see the hell you are in."[14] All doubt that the Qur'an was a God-inspired book vanished, wrote Weiss. He went to the leader of the Berlin Islamic Society, declared his adherence to Islam, and took the name Muhammad Asad.

Why the conversion? In 1934, Asad wrote that he had no satisfactory answer. He could not say which aspect of Islam appealed to him more than another, except that Islam seemed to him "harmoniously conceived... nothing is superfluous and nothing lacking, with the result of an absolute balance and solid composure." But he still found it difficult to analyze his motives. "After all, it was a matter of love; and love is composed of many things: of our desires and our loneliness, of our high aims and our shortcomings, of our strength and our weakness."[15] In the Feigenbaum family, it was more commonly thought that Asad's conversion stemmed from a hatred of his father, generalized to a contempt for the faith and people of his birth. Asad wrote to his father informing him of his conversion, but got no answer.

> Some months later my sister wrote, telling me that he considered me dead...Thereupon I sent him another letter, assuring him that my acceptance of Islam did not change anything in my attitude toward him or my love for him; that, on the contrary, Islam enjoined upon me to love and honour my parents above all other people... But this letter also remained unanswered.[16]

Asad's wife Elsa converted to Islam a few weeks later, and in January 1927 they left for Mecca, accompanied by Elsa's son from her previous marriage. On arrival, Weiss made his first pilgrimage; a moving passage at the end of *The Road to Mecca* describes his circumambulation of Ka'ba. Tragically, Elsa died nine days later, of a tropical disease, and her parents reclaimed her son a year later.

Asad of Arabia

So began Asad's Saudi period, which would form him as a Muslim. His six years in Saudi Arabia are recounted in *The Road to Mecca* in selective detail. Asad portrayed himself as a member of the inner circle of King Ibn Saud (1880–1953), dividing his time between religious study in Medina and palace politics in Riyadh. This intimacy with Ibn Saud can be confirmed in broad lines by an independent source. In late 1928, an Iraqi named 'Abdallāh Damlūjī, who had been an adviser to Ibn Saud, submitted a report to the British on "Bolshevik and Soviet penetration" of the Hijaz. It represents perhaps the most succinct confirmation of the role played by Asad in Saudi Arabia:

> Before concluding, I must bring attention to the person known as Asadullah von Weiss, formerly an Austrian Jew, now a Muslim, who resides presently near the holy shrine in Mecca. This Austrian Leopold von Weiss came to the Hijaz two years ago, claiming he had become a Muslim out of love for this religion and in pure belief in it. I do not know why, but his words were accepted without opposition, and he entered Mecca without impediment. He did so at a time when no one like him was allowed to do the same, the Hijaz government having recently passed a law providing that those like him must wait two years under surveillance, so that the government can be certain of their Islam before their entry into Mecca. Since that time, Leopold von Weiss has remained in Mecca, wandering the country and mixing with people of every class and with government persons. He then travelled to Medina, and stayed there and in its environs for several months. Then he was able—I have no idea how—to travel to Riyadh with King Ibn Saud last year, and he stayed in Riyadh for five months, seeing and hearing all that happened, mingling with the people and speaking with persons of the government. He does not seem to me to be a learned or professional man. His apparent purpose is to obtain news from the King, and especially from Shaykh

> Yūsuf Yāsīn, secretary to the King [and editor of the official newspaper *Umm al-Qurā*]. Asadullah uses this news to produce articles for some German and Austrian newspapers, in reply to the distasteful things written by some European newspapers on the Hijazi-Najdi court. This is the occupation of the Austrian Jew Leopold von Weiss, now Haj Asadullah the Muslim. What is the real mission which makes him endure the greatest discomforts and the worst conditions of life? On what basis rests the close intimacy between him and Shaykh Yūsuf Yāsīn? Is there some connection between von Weiss and the Bolshevik consulate in Jidda? These are mysteries about which it is difficult to know the truth.[17]

For British intelligence of the time, Bolshevism was an obsession, and Damlūjī's insinuation can be discounted. But from this account, it is clear that Asad did have exceptional access to the court of Ibn Saud. It is also clear that his status was not that of an adviser, but of a privileged observer, admitted to the court as part of the earliest Saudi efforts at public relations. Ibn Saud kept Asad close to him because this useful convert wrote flattering articles about him for various newspapers in continental Europe. (These newspapers, Asad wrote, "provide me with my livelihood.")[18]

According to Asad, he did finally become a secret agent of sorts: Ibn Saud employed him on a clandestine mission to Kuwait in 1929, to trace the funds and guns that were flowing to Fayṣal al-Dawīsh, a rebel against Ibn Saud's rule. Asad determined that Britain was behind the rebellion, and wrote so for the foreign papers, much to Ibn Saud's satisfaction.[19] Asad also began to settle down. He married twice in Saudi Arabia: first in 1928 to a woman from the Muṭayr tribe, and in 1930, following a divorce, to Munīra, from a branch of the Shammar. They established a household in Medina, and she bore him a son, Ṭalāl. Arabia was his home, so he worked to persuade himself: the Arabian sky was "my sky," the same sky that "vaulted over the long trek of my ancestors, those wandering herdsmen-warriors"—"that small beduin tribe of Hebrews."[20]

Arabia's sky enchanted Asad—but Arabia's ruler did not. Asad had shared the hope that Ibn Saud would "bring about a revival of the Islamic idea in its fullest sense." But as Ibn Saud consolidated his power, lamented Asad, "it became evident that Ibn Saud was no more than a king—a king aiming no higher than so many other autocratic Eastern rulers before him." Asad's indictment grew long, and he later made it public in *The Road to Mecca*. True, Ibn Saud had established order, but he did so "by harsh laws and punitive measures and not by inculcating in his people a sense of civic responsibility." He had "done nothing to build up an equitable, progressive society." "He indulges and allows those around him to indulge in the most extravagant and senseless luxuries." He had "neglected the education even of his own sons and thus left them poorly equipped for the tasks that lie before them." And he was incapable of self-examination, while the "innumerable hangers-on who live off his bounty certainly do nothing to counteract this unfortunate tendency." Asad's final verdict was that Ibn Saud's life constituted a "tragic waste":

> Belying the tremendous promise of his younger years, when he appeared to be a dreamer of stirring dreams, he has broken—perhaps without realizing it himself—the spirit of a high-strung nation that had been wont to look up to him as to a God-sent leader. They had expected too much of him to bear the disappointment of their expectations with equanimity; and some of the best among the people of Najd now speak in bitter terms of what they consider a betrayal of their trust.

Ibn Saud, in sum, was "an eagle who never really took to wing," a king who never rose beyond "a benevolent tribal chieftain on an immensely enlarged scale."[21]

Disappointed with Ibn Saud, Asad commenced a quest for the ruler, state, or society which would embody his ideal Islam. He briefly pinned his hopes on the Sanusi movement in Cyrenaica:

> Like so many other Muslims, I had for years pinned my hopes on Ibn Saud as the potential leader of an Islamic revival; and now that these hopes had proved futile, I could see in the entire Muslim world only one movement that genuinely strove for the fulfilment of the ideal of an Islamic society: the Sanusi movement, now fighting a last-ditch battle for survival.[22]

According to Asad, he went on a secret mission to Cyrenaica on behalf of the Grand Sanusi, Sayyid Aḥmad (1873–1932), then in exile in Saudi Arabia, to transmit plans for continuing the anti-Italian struggle to the remnant of the Sanusi forces. But the mission, in January 1931, was a futile one: Italian forces crushed the last of the Sanusi resistance later that year.[23]

By this time, Asad had fallen from favor. He gave no explanation in *The Road to Mecca* for his break with Ibn Saud, except his personal disappointment with the monarch. But other explanations also gained circulation. Some claimed that his last marriage proved his undoing: members of his wife's family were suspected of intrigues against Ibn Saud. Others pointed to his Jewish origins as a growing liability after 1929, when Arab-Jewish tensions in Palestine exploded in violence. What is certain is that he left Saudi Arabia in 1932, with the declared aim of travelling through India, Turkestan, China, and Indonesia.

Passage to India

Asad began with a "lecture tour" to India. According to British intelligence sources, Asad had linked up with an Amritsar activist, one Ismā'īl Ghaznavī, and intended to tour India "with a view to get into touch with all important workers." Asad arrived in Karachi by ship in June 1932, and left promptly for Amritsar.[24] There and in neighboring Lahore, he involved himself with the local community of Kashmiri Muslims, and in 1933 he made an appearance in Srinagar, where an intelligence report again had him spreading Bolshevik ideas.[25]

For Asad, the real attraction of Kashmir would have resided in its predicament as contested ground, where a British-backed maharaja ruled a discontented Muslim population. Beginning in 1931, Kashmiri Muslims in Punjab organized an extensive "agitation" in support of the Muslims in Kashmir. Hundreds of bands of Muslim volunteers crossed illegally from Punjab into Kashmir, and thousands were arrested. By early 1932, the disturbances had subsided, but the Kashmir government remained ever-wary.[26] Just what Asad did in Kashmir is uncertain. But on learning of his presence, the Kashmir government immediately wanted him "externed," although the police had no evidence to substantiate the intelligence report, and there appeared to be legal obstacles to "externing" a European national.[27]

With or without such prompting, Asad soon retreated from Kashmir to Lahore. There he met the poet-philosopher Muhammad Iqbal (1876–1938), himself of Kashmiri descent, who persuaded Asad to remain in India and work "to elucidate the intellectual premises of the future Islamic state."[28] From this point forward, Asad would be a Muslim intellectual, thinking, lecturing and writing on Islamic culture and law.

In March 1934 he published a pamphlet entitled *Islam at the Crossroads,* his first venture into Islamic thought. This work can only be described as a diatribe against the materialism of the West—as Asad put it, a case of "Islam *versus* Western civilization." Here Asad developed themes which would become widespread later in Islamic fundamentalist thought. Asad drew a straight line between the Crusades and modern imperialism, and held Western orientalists to blame for their distortions of Islam. This text went through repeated printings and editions in India and Pakistan. More importantly, however, it appeared in an Arabic translation in Beirut in 1946. Under the Arabic title *al-Islām 'alā mufṭariq al-ṭuruq,* it was published in numerous editions through the 1940s and 1950s. This translation had a crucial influence upon the early writings of the Islamist theoretician Sayyid Quṭb (1906–66), who drew extensively upon Asad in developing the idea of "Crusaderism."

In 1936, Asad found a new benefactor. The Nizam of Hyderabad had established a journal under his patronage entitled *Islamic Culture,* first edited by "Mohammed" Marmaduke Pickthall (1875–1936), a British convert to Islam.[29] Pickthall, best know for his English translation of the Qur'an, died in 1936, at which point Asad assumed the editorship of the journal. This placed Asad in touch with a wide range of orientalist and Indian Muslim scholarship, and he himself began to write scholarly pieces and translate texts.[30]

Intrusion of War

But another obligation began to assert itself—an obligation from the past. In *The Road to Mecca,* Asad wrote that his relationship with his father was resumed in 1935, after his father had come to "understand and appreciate the reasons for my conversion to Islam." Although they never met in person again, wrote Asad, they corresponded continuously until 1942.[31] However, Asad did return to Europe in the spring of 1939, with the intention of saving his endangered family. Nazi Germany annexed Austria in March 1938, enforcing the Nuremberg Laws in May. The life of Viennese Jewry became a succession of confiscations, persecutions, pogroms, and deportations. In October 1938, Asad resigned the editorship of *Islamic Culture,* and then left India. In April 1939, his Austrian passport was visaed in Vienna for entry to Britain and British India.[32] Afterwards he arrived in London, where he asked that this visa be extended: "I beg you to give me a prolongation of this visa till the end of this year as my parents will come in about 4 to 5 months. I have to settle many things for them."[33] ("Parents" was Asad's shorthand for his father and stepmother; his own mother had died in 1919.) This evidence hints that Asad made an eleventh-hour attempt at rescuing his Jewish family before returning to India in the summer of 1939.

But whatever the scope of these efforts, they ended abruptly with the German invasion of Poland and the British declaration of war against Germany in September 1939. Asad was detained immediately in India as an enemy national, and he spent the next six years in internment camps with Germans, Austrians, and Italians who had been collected from all over British-ruled Asia. Asad's camp, he wrote, was peopled by "both Nazis and anti-Nazis as well as Fascists and anti-Fascists."[34] During his internment, he established contact with his uncle in Jerusalem, Aryeh Feigenbaum, who sent him food, clothes, and money.[35] Asad was only released in August 1945. By then, the worst had befallen his family in Europe: his father, stepmother, and a sister were deported from Vienna in 1942, and they perished in the camps.

Asad would never write of his long years of detention. He was the only Muslim in his camp, and it seems he deliberately detached himself from his surroundings and the war, by thinking only of the "cultural chaos" into which Muslims had been plunged. "I can still see myself pacing day-in and day-out over the great length of our barrack room," asking himself why Muslims had failed to reach an "unambiguously agreed-upon concept of the Law."[36] He would not allow Europe's war to become his war, or the suffering of the Jews to become his suffering, as he moved ever more resolutely to a consolidation of his Muslim identity.

Upon Asad's release, he wholly identified with the cause of Pakistan, which he saw not simply as a refuge, but as the framework for an ideal Islamic polity. In 1947, Asad became director of the Department of Islamic Reconstruction in the new state, and he gave himself over to formulating proposals for its constitution. Asad's purpose in these proposals is clear: it is to establish an Islamic state as a liberal, multiparty parliamentary democracy. In the 1930s and 1940s, the idea of the Islamic state, in the hands of many ideologues, had been presented as antithetical to democracy, and similar to the totalitarian states of central Europe. Asad's work challenged that trend, finding evidence in the Islamic sources for elections, parliamentary legislation, and political parties.

But his own proposals, published in March 1948 as *Islamic Constitution-Making,* were never implemented. "Only very few, if any, of my suggestions have been utilized in the (now abolished) Constitution of the

Islamic Republic of Pakistan; perhaps only in the Preamble, adopted by the Constituent Assembly in 1949, can an echo of those suggestions be found."[37] Pakistan, he later said, did not work out as Iqbal and he had hoped it would. The new state had been "an historical necessity," and without it, "Muslims would have been submerged in the much more developed and intellectually and economically stronger Hindu society." But "unfortunately it did not quite develop in the way we wanted it to. Iqbal's vision of Pakistan was quite different to that of Mohammed Ali Jinnah [1876–1948, first governor-general of Pakistan], who did not in the beginning want a separation."[38] Pakistan became a state for Muslims, but its mission as an Islamic state was put aside by its secular founders. In 1949, Asad left domestic politics to join Pakistan's foreign service, eventually rising to the position of head of the Middle East Division of the foreign ministry. His transformation was now complete, down to his Pakistani *achkan* and black fur cap. In the beginning of 1952, after twenty years of continuous residence in the subcontinent, he came to New York, as Pakistan's minister plenipotentiary to the United Nations.

The West Again

So began Asad's road back to the West—a choice that would bring him fame and sever his links to living Islam. He came to New York alone, without his wife and son, and lived in a penthouse in Manhattan, attended by a servant-driver.[39] He soon found a new love, a striking contrast to his Arabian wife of over twenty years: Pola "Hamida," an American woman of Polish Catholic descent who had converted to Islam. Asad's marriage to Munīra now came undone, and he married Pola Hamida before a civil judge in New York in November 1952. He would remain with her for the next forty years, and this marriage to a Western convert presaged his evolving preference for an ideal Islam, distinct from the born Muslims who practiced it.

For some months in New York, Asad also reestablished a tie to his family in Israel. At the time, Aryeh Feigenbaum's daughter, Hemdah (1916–87), was living in New York with her husband, Harry (Zvi) Zinder (1909–91), press officer at Israel's information office (and later director of the Voice of Israel). Zinder later told an Israeli journalist the story of how Asad would dine with him in out-of-the-way restaurants, or visit the Zinders' home in Forest Hills. Asad even attended the bar mitvah of the

Zinders' son, and the Zinders attended his marriage to Pola Hamida. Zinder reported the contents of his table talk with Asad back to Jerusalem. Asad, he noted, remained an unequivocal enemy of Israel, but it might be possible to soften his animosity, and it would be worth the effort, given Asad's solid standing in the Pakistani foreign ministry. According to Zinder, the Mossad responded by proposing that he try to recruit Asad for pay, a proposal Zinder rejected "with both hands." "I knew he would refuse any payment," said Zinder years later, "that he would be enraged by the idea, and that he would sever all contact with me." In time, the contact weakened anyway; according to Zinder, Pola Hamida disapproved of Asad maintaining close ties with his family in particular, and Jews in general. Still, according to Zinder, Asad continued for some years to correspond with Hemdah on family matters.[40]

There could be no doubt from Asad's writing, and from Zinder's testimony, that Asad remained a fervent anti-Zionist. Yet for many years, Asad left the systematic indictment of the modern-day state of Israel to others. In 1947 he was fully preoccupied with the partition of India, and offered no published comment on the partition of Palestine and the creation of Israel. In the years that followed the 1967 war, he spoke out more frequently, especially on Jerusalem. "We cannot ever reconcile ourselves to the view, so complacently accepted in the West, that Jerusalem is to be the capital of the State of Israel," he wrote. "In a conceivably free Palestine—a state in which Jews, Christians and Muslims could live side by side in full political and cultural equality—the *Muslim* community should be specifically entrusted with the custody of Jerusalem as a city open to all three communities."[41] But given the fever of anti-Israel passion in the Arab world after 1967, Asad's criticism could only be described as restrained. As Pakistan was far removed from the conflict, more would not have been expected of him.

But Asad failed to meet other Pakistani expectations. One of Asad's colleagues on the Pakistani delegation made a scandal of his romance with Pola Hamida, and Pakistan's prime minister, Khwaja Nizamuddin, reportedly reacted strongly against the marriage. At the end of 1952, Asad offered his resignation, in the expectation his position would be confirmed. To his surprise, his resignation was accepted. It was not a clean break, and when Nizamuddin fell from power in the spring of 1953, the prospect of Asad's return to Pakistani service seemed real. But no offer materialized, and Asad was now pressed for funds. Acting upon the advice of an American friend, he proposed to write his story for the New

York publisher Simon and Schuster, which offered him a contract and an advance.[42]

Asad thus began work on the book that would make him famous. *The Road to Mecca,* written in New York, appeared in 1954, and won widespread praise for its combination of spiritual searching and desert adventure. As a testimony of conversion to Islam, *The Road to Mecca* is still unsurpassed, and its continued republication in Western languages attests to its power, for both general readers and sympathizers of Islam. An example of its influence may be found in the testimony of a twenty-one-year-old American Jewish woman named Margaret Marcus (b. 1934). Asad's book found a place on the shelves of the public library in Mamaroneck, New York, near her home. Her parents would not let her take out the book, so she read it in the library over and over: "What he could do, I thought I could also do, only how much harder for a single woman than for a man! But I vowed to Allah that at the first opportunity, I would follow his example."[43] The young woman later converted to Islam, took the name Maryam Jameelah, and moved to Pakistan, where she became one of the best-known ideologues of Islamic fundamentalism, famous for her methodical indictments of the West.[44]

One Western convert, however, took a dim view of Asad's book: H. St. John ("Abdullah") Philby (1885–1960). Philby, too, had converted to Islam in 1930, assuming Asad's place as the convert in the court of Ibn Saud. He, too, had dabbled in exploration and politics, and he had strong views on Asad's attempts at both. In his review of *The Road to Mecca,* Philby accused "Herr Weiss" of "vagueness and unusual naiveté." According to Philby, Asad was no more than a journalist in search of a story, a man without any flair for geographical work or political analysis.

> His bazar scenes, religious festivals, desert sunsets, *et hoc genus omne* of local color suggest a patchwork of newspaper articles or cuttings strung together for a new[s] story, in which the *leit-motiv* is provided by his own gropings toward an emotional dénouement.

In his most damaging insinuation, Philby wrote that there was "no independent contemporary evidence" that Asad had undertaken "secret missions" for Ibn Saud or the Grand Sanusi.[45]

If the book's value as a record of politics and exploration was doubtful, then at least it served as a faithful personal memoir. Or did it? On many points, noted Judd Teller (1912–72) in a review in *Commentary*, Asad had nothing to say on matters that demanded a say in the personal memoir of any European Jew. One of these was Asad's experience of Europe's anti-Semitism, nowhere mentioned by the author.

> Yet he was born in Galicia, where the Jews were caught up as scapegoats in the power struggles of the anti-Semitic Ukrainians and Poles and the dubiously tolerant Austrian government. He was brought up in Vienna, when it was the capital of European anti-Semitism. He left Berlin for his first visit to Palestine in the year when racist-nationalists assassinated Walter Rathenau. Did all this leave him untouched?[46]

Both Philby and Teller complained of the absence of another crucial point: Asad gave no reason for his decision to leave Arabia. (Teller speculated that it stemmed from heightened Jewish-Arab tensions in Palestine.) These criticisms suggested what is now obvious: *The Road to Mecca* cannot be read as a document of historical truth about Arabia, Ibn Saud, or even the author's life. It is an impressionistic self-portrait that suggests more than it tells. The face of its subject is in half-shadow.

But the omissions and elisions of the book did not detract from its commercial success. *The Road to Mecca* was translated from English into the major languages of Europe, and the royalties must have represented a windfall. The book also created demand for Asad's services as a lecturer, and his reputation in the West reached its pinnacle. But in Muslim lands, especially among Muslim activists, his choices raised troubling questions. The Pakistani ideologue Maulana Maududi (1903–79), in a letter written in 1961, expressed misgivings:

> I have great respect for [Asad's] exposition of Islamic ideas and especially his criticism of Western culture and its materialistic philosophies. I am sorry to say, however, that although in the early days of his conversion, he was a staunch, practicing Muslim, gradually he drifted close to the ways of the so-called "progressive" Muslim just like the "reformed" Jews. Recently his divorce from his Arab wife and marriage to a modern American girl hastened this process of deviation more definitely....Once a man begins to live the life of a true Muslim, all his capabilities lose their "market value." It is the same sad story with Muhammad Asad, who had always been accustomed to a high and modern standard of living and after embracing Islam, had to face the severest financial difficulties. As a result, he was forced to make one compromise after another.[47]

Asad, the critic of Western materialism, stood accused of succumbing to it; Asad, who first sought answers in Islam, now was suspected of questioning it. The disappointment Asad had come to feel for the actual practitioners of Islam had become mutual.

Translator of the Qur'an

Asad relocated to Geneva with Pola Hamida. There he began to contemplate a new project, ambitious in scope and significance: a new English translation of the Qur'an. Asad had not been satisfied with Marmaduke Pickthall's widely-used translation, since Pickthall's knowledge of Arabic had been "limited." As Asad later wrote:

> Familiarity with the bedouin speech of Central and Eastern Arabia—in addition, of course, to academic knowledge of classical Arabic—is the only way for a non-Arab of our time to achieve an intimate understanding of the diction of the Qur'an. And because none of the scholars who have previously translated the Qur'an into European languages has ever fulfilled this prerequisite, their translations have remained but distant, and faulty, echoes of its meaning and spirit.[48]

Asad began work on the translation in 1960. Such a large-scale project required the support of a patron, and he eventually appeared in the form of Saudi Arabia's King Fayṣal (r. 1964–75). Asad had known Fayṣal since 1927. He reestablished a link in 1951, when he paid his first visit to Saudi Arabia in eighteen years, and he nurtured the tie as Fayṣal began his ascent to the throne. Asad became one of Fayṣal's most fervent enthusiasts, seeing in him a vast improvement over Ibn Saud. "Whenever I reflect on the manner in which King Faysal rules over his realm," wrote Asad, "it appears to me as the fulfilment of every promise which the life of his father had held out and left open."[49] Still, Fayṣal was a dutiful son, and this praise could not cancel out Asad's stinging indictment of Ibn Saud, made in *The Road to Mecca.* As it happened, however, this obstacle was not insurmountable: in later editions of the book, Asad completely excised his enumeration of Ibn Saud's failings, replacing them with a few pages of banal ruminations on the desert.[50]

Fayṣal renewed Asad's Saudi patronage. In 1963, Fayṣal had the Muslim World League in Mecca subscribe in advance to Asad's planned translation, which he began to compile in Switzerland. Asad published a limited edition of the first nine surahs in 1964. At about that time, he moved to Tangier, settling in a comfortable villa surrounded by cypress trees and bougainvillaea, where he worked to complete the translation. In 1980, he published the full translation and commentary in Gibraltar, under the title *The Message of the Qur'ān.*

Asad's translation opened with this dedication: "For people who think." The spirit of the translation is resolutely modernist, and Asad expressed his profound debt to the reformist commentator Muhammad 'Abduh (1849–1905). As another convert later wrote: "In its intellectual engagement with the text and in the intimate, subtle and profound understanding of the pure classical Arabic of the Koran, Asad's interpretation is of a power and intelligence without rival in English."[51] There are many English-speaking Muslims who will attest to the appeal of this translation, and who rely upon it daily.

But the translation created a controversy among some Muslim clerics who disputed Asad's modernist and allegorical interpretations of some verses. Critics accused him of denying the existence of angels, the permissibility of concubinage, and the bodily ascent of Jesus to heaven.[52] In private, there were those who insinuated that the translation reintroduced *isrā'īliyyāt,* "Jewish distortions" akin to those allegedly introduced by the first Jewish converts to Islam. In 1974, even before the translation was published in full, it was banned in Saudi Arabia.[53] Asad was left to finish the work on his own, supported financially by his friends. Fortunately, Asad had many, including Shaykh Aḥmad Zakī al-Yamanī (b. 1930), the Saudi minister of oil and natural resources and "my brother-in-spirit," to whom Asad devoted a collection of his essays a few years later.[54]

The rejection of his translation was only one sign of the growing climate of intolerance that further disillusioned Asad. "Khomeini is worse than the Shah," he told journalists after the Iranian revolution. "He has nothing in common with Islam."[55] According another journalist, Asad took a dim view of fundamentalist chaos, the intolerance of extremists, and the patter about "Islamic science" and "Islamic education." The Muslims, he opined, had been "low down for so many centuries that now they think they have to assert themselves by saying we are different. They are human beings. They are not different." In particular, he championed the rights of women and opposed the fundamentalist campaign for the *ḥijāb.* "Many people think that if you put a veil over a woman's face and cover her, that is the way to Islam. It is not. In the time of the Prophet Muhammad, no *ḥijāb* existed except for the Prophet's wives and it is a wrong inference to say that this holds good for all Muslim women."[56]

His own early indictment of the West, *Islam at the Crossroads,* which found such an echo among fundamentalists, he himself came to regard as a "harsh book." Likewise, the once-powerful romance of the Arabs no longer held him in its grip. In 1981, he told a journalist that "it is possible that if I would come into contact with Arabs today for the first time, I would no longer be attracted by them."[57] Asad still remained enamored of Islam. Yet this ideal Islam was nowhere to be found in existing Islam, and could just as well be practised in Europe. It is said that Pakistan's president from 1978, General Zia ul-Haq (1924–88) tried to persuade Asad to return to Pakistan, but without result. In 1982, Asad left Tangier for Sintra, outside of Lisbon. He later moved to Mijas on the Costa del Sol in southern Spain. He remained articulate and lucid in interviews given as late as 1988.[58] In these last years, he reportedly began work on a sequel to *The Road to Mecca,* tentatively entitled *Homecoming of the Heart.* The title is said to have alluded to his contemplated return to Saudi Arabia at the invitation of Prince Salmān (b. 1936), governor of Riyadh and one of Ibn Saud's sons. It is not clear whether such a return was a realistic prospect, or whether the title hinted at a more spiritual homecoming. For Asad had neither completed this work nor returned to Arabia when he died in February 1992, at the age of 91. He was buried in the small Muslim cemetery in Granada.[59]

"Struck no root"

Few in the Muslim world took notice of Asad's passing. He had argued for a rational Islam; he had sought to reconcile Islamic teachings and democracy; he had tried to make the Qur'an speak to modern minds. His project, in fact, encapsulated ideals that drove the reform of Judaism, which by his parents' generation had largely served to ease Jews out of their faith altogether. Islam provided the last chance to achieve that ideal—the reform of a religion of law so that it could be made to live in a modern age, as a liberal force of continuing faith.

Unlike so many other Western converts to Islam, Asad chose also to live in Muslim societies, and worked to give Islam direction. But by advocating this reform, Asad remained a foreign body in contemporary

Islam, a transplant rejected time and again by his hosts. Saudi Arabia declined to keep him as a journalist; Pakistan, which he served as an official and diplomat, also broke with him; and the self-appointed guardians of Muslim orthodoxy shunned him as a Qur'an translator and commentator. Paradoxically, Asad won genuine acclaim in the West. There he found minds open to his ideas, and opportunities to publish and lecture. And there he ultimately found refuge from the late twentieth-century reality of Islam.

Asad's road to Mecca was the shorter journey, made headlong in the enthusiasm of youth. His road from Mecca was the longer journey, made painstakingly in an awareness of the contradiction between the promise of Islam and its contemporary practice—and his own equivocal position in it. For all Asad's fervor and belief, his Muslim answer never satisfied his Jewish question, put most poignantly by Asad to Asad: "Why is it that, even after finding my place among the people who believe in the things I myself have come to believe, I have struck no root?"[60]

Notes

1. S.C. Chew, review of *The Road to Mecca* in *New York Herald Tribune Book Review,* 15 August 1954.
2. Robert Payne, review of *The Road to Mecca* in *New York Times,* 15 August 1954.
3. Details on the family in Lodewijk Brunt, "Een Jood in Arabie; over het leven van Muhammad Asad," in *Neveh Ya'akov: Jubilee Volume Presented to Dr. Jaap Meijer on the Occasion of his Seventieth Birthday,* eds. Lea Dasberg and Jonathan N. Cohen (Assen: Van Gorcum, 1982), 182.
4. Muhammad Asad, *The Road to Mecca* (New York: Simon and Schuster, 1954), 55.
5. Ibid., 55–56.
6. Ibid., 58–59.
7. Ibid., 60.
8. *Encyclopaedia Judaica,* s.v. "Feigenbaum, Aryeh"; Haviv Kena'an, "Prof. A. Feigenbaum—Hasid ha-dugmah ha-ishit," *Ha'aretz,* 7 August 1964. The omission is all the more striking in that, at one point in *The Road to Mecca,* Asad writes that the eyes of Jerusalem's Arabs "seemed to remain clear and untouched by age—unless they happened to be affected by trachoma, that evil 'Egyptian' eye disease which is the curse of all countries east of the Mediterranean." *Road to Mecca,* 92.
9. Asad, *Road to Mecca,* 93.

10. Ibid, 91.
11. Leopold Weiss, *Unromantisches Morgenland; aus dem tagebuch einer reise* (Frankfurt: Frankfurter societäts-drukerei, 1924). The book is summarized by Wolf Kaiser, *Palästina—Erez Israel: Deutschsprachige Reisebeschreibungen jüdischer Autoren von der Jahrhundertwende bis zum Zweiten Weltkrieg* (Hildesheim: G. Olms, 1992), 267–83. Kaiser also discusses some of the contemporary criticism of reviewers. Asad wrote of his book that, "although its anti-Zionist attitude and unusual predilection for the Arabs caused something of a flutter in the German press, I am afraid it did not sell very well." Asad, *Road to Mecca,* 185.
12. Asad, *Road to Mecca,* 188.
13. Ibid., 142.
14. Qur'an, 102 (Sūrat al-Takāthur). The translation is Asad's.
15. Muhammad Asad, *Islam at the Crossroads* (1934; reprint, Lahore: Sh. Muhammad Ashaf, 1991), 4.
16. Asad, *Road to Mecca,* 311.
17. Arabic report (with translation) by Dr. Abdullah Damluji, no date, included in despatch from Political Secretary of High Commissioner for Iraq (Baghdad) to Consul (Jiddah), 18 December 1928, Public Records Office (London), FO967/22. Damlūjī had left Ibn Saud's service in September 1928 and returned to Iraq.
18. Asad, *Road to Mecca,* 48.
19. Ibid., chap. viii, "Jinns." On the Dawīsh affair, see Joseph Kostiner, *The Making of Saudi Arabia 1916–1936* (New York: Oxford University Press, 1993), 117–40.
20. Asad, *Road to Mecca,* 49.
21. Ibid., 177–81, for these assessments of Ibn Saud.
22. Ibid, 325.
23. Ibid., chap. xi, "Jihad."
24. "History sheet of Herr Leopold Weiss Alias Mohmmad Asad Ullah Vyce. An Austrian Convert to Mohammadanism," prepared by the Intelligence Bureau of the Government of India, included in letter from E.J.D. Colvin, Political Secretary, His Highness' Government Jammu and Kashmir (Jammu) to Lieut.-Col. L.E. Lang, Resident in Kashmir (Sialkot), 30 January 1934, India Office Records, R/1/1/4670. In *The Road to Mecca,* Asad dates his last Arabian journey to the late summer of 1932, which would place his final arrival in India at a date later than June.
25. C.I.D. report of 20 November 1933, India Office Records, R/1/1/4670.
26. On the Kashmir "agitation" of 1931–32, see David Gilmartin, *Empire and Islam: Punjab and the Making of Pakistan* (Berkeley: University of California Press, 1988), 96–99.
27. Lieut-Col. L.E. Lang, Resident in Kashmir (Sialkot) to B. J. Glancy, Political Secretary, Government of India, Foreign and Political Department (New

Delhi), 31 January 1934, India Office Records, R/1/1/4670.

28. Asad, *Road to Mecca,* 2.
29. On the journal, see Peter Clark, *Marmaduke Pickhtall: British Muslim* (London: Quartet Books, 1986), 61–62.
30. For a sample of his work, see his article "Towards a Resurrection of Thought," *Islamic Culture* (Hyderabad) 11 (1937): 7–16.
31. Asad, *Road to Mecca,* 311 n.
32. India Office Records, L/P&J/7/2678. This includes an extract, from Weiss's passport, of a visa for the United Kingdom and British India, granted at Vienna and issued on 24 April 1939. The authorization for the visa came directly from the Government of India in New Delhi, 9 February 1939.
33. Weiss, undated note to India Office in London, received at India Office on 8 June 1939; India Office Records, L/P&J/7/2678. Weiss gave his London address as 119, Old Church Street, Chelsea, S.W. 3.
34. Muhammad Asad, *This Law of Ours and Other Essays* (Gibraltar: Dar al-Andalus, 1987), 1.
35. Yossi Melman, "Goralo ha-Yehudi shel Muhammad Asad," *Ha'aretz,* 21 April 1989.
36. Asad, *This Law of Ours,* 1.
37. Muhammad Asad, *The Principles of State and Government in Islam* (new ed.; Gilbraltar: Dar al-Andalus, 1980), xi. This book built upon his *Islamic Constitution-Making.*
38. Mushtak Parker, "Death of a Muslim Mentor," *Middle East,* May 1992, 29.
39. Melman, "Goralo ha-Yehudi," quoting a despatch by Harry Zinder.
40. Ibid., quoting a despatch by Harry Zinder.
41. Asad, *This Law of Ours,* 169, 173.
42. Harry Zinder (New York) to Abba Eban, 30 April 1953, Israel State Archives, ISA/R693/Box 96, File 14.
43. Maryam Jameelah, *Memoirs of Childhood and Youth in America (1945–1962)* (Lahore: Muhammad Yusuf Khan, 1989), 109.
44. *Oxford Encyclopedia of the Modern Islamic World,* s.v. "Jameelah, Maryam."
45. H. St. John B. Philby, review of *The Road to Mecca,* in *Middle East Journal* 9 (winter 1955): 81–82.
46. Judd Teller, review of *The Road to Mecca,* in *Commentary* 18 (September 1954): 280.
47. Maududi (Lahore) to Margaret Marcus [Maryam Jameelah], 25 February 1961, in Maryam Jameelah, *Correspondence between Maulana Maudoodi and Maryam Jameelah* (Delhi: Crescent Publishing, 1969), 15.
48. *The Message of the Qur'ān, Translated and Explained by Muhammad Asad* (Gilbraltar: Dar al-Andalus, 1980), iv–v.

49. From the 1973 postscript to the 4th rev. ed. of *The Road to Mecca* (Gibraltar: Dar al-Andalus), 378.
50. Cf. 177–81 of the original 1954 ed. with 177–81 of the 4th rev. ed. of 1980.
51. Parker, "Death of a Muslim Mentor," 28–29.
52. Asad dealt with all these accusations in *Arabia, The Islamic World Review* (October 1981), 4.
53. Reinhard Schulze, *Islamischer Internationalismus im 20. Jahrhundert* (Leiden: Brill, 1990), 334 n. 59.
54. Asad, *This Law of Ours,* dedication page.
55. Quoted by Lisbeth Rocher and Fatima Cherqaoui, *D'une foi l'autre: Les conversions à l'Islam en Occident* (Paris: Seuil, 1986), 64.
56. Mushtak Parker, "Death of a Muslim Mentor."
57. Malise Ruthven, "Muhammad Asad, Ambassador of Islam," *Arabia: The Islamic World Review* (September 1981): 60, 62.
58. See the video "A Tribute to Muhammad Asad," filmed in 1988 and distributed by Islamic Publications International of Teaneck, New Jersey.
59. Details on these last years are provided by Mushtak Parker, "Death of a Muslim Mentor."
60. Asad, *The Road to Mecca,* 47.

8

The Transplantation of Islamic Studies from Europe to the Yishuv and Israel

Hava Lazarus-Yafeh

This is a short survey of the transplantation of Jewish European, mainly German, Islamic scholarship to the Yishuv—later, Israel—where it subsequently flourished to an amazing extent, first at the Hebrew University in Jerusalem, and then at other universities in Israel. This is not a comprehensive study by any means, and I shall not be able even to mention all those who were involved in the process. The transplantation was the result of teamwork which took decades to mature. It involved many scholars, as well as pivotal figures such as Jehuda Leib Magnes (1877–1948), the first chancellor of the Hebrew University. Here I shall focus upon only three of the many people who took part in the process: Josef Horovitz (1874–1931), the first director of the School of Oriental Studies at the Hebrew University; and Shlomo Dov Goitein (1900–85) and David Hartwig (Zvi) Baneth (1893–1973), two of its most outstanding teachers. I have relied upon my own memories, supplemented by material from the archives of the Hebrew University, in order to tell at least a part of the story.

When I came to the Hebrew University in Jerusalem in the early 1950s, I had no real understanding of how young the university was. Even had I known all the facts, I doubt I would have understood or cared. Several generations of students had already graduated from the university before me, including my teachers at the Reali School in Haifa. I and my friends took our studies at the Hebrew University for granted. I did not even realize how fortunate I was that most of my teachers were the same scholars who had initiated teaching at the university some twenty-five years earlier. (This was true only for oriental studies; in biblical studies, my other subject, great personnel changes had taken place in the same twenty-five years.) Among these veterans were the two most important of my teachers and the closest to my heart for many years: Shlomo Dov Goitein and David Zvi Baneth, who taught at the school from its inception through my years as a student in the 1950s and afterwards.

Both Goitein and Baneth, as well as Josef Horovitz, had excellent backgrounds in Jewish studies, by virtue of their upbringings. As was then customary, they had studied simultaneously in universities and in Jewish higher institutions (such as the Jüdische Hochschule in Berlin or in rabbinical seminaries). This developed their specific Jewish religious understanding of Islam, which is plainly evident in the work of all three, as well as in Goitein's unique personality. But in most other respects, they were very different from one another. Most notably, Goitein and Baneth were Zionists, Horovitz apparently was not; Goitein was an observant Jew, Horovitz and Baneth were not.

Horovitz at the Founding

It was Horovitz who first made his imprint. The Hebrew University opened its gates officially to its first forty-nine regular students in 1925. By then, it was composed of three "Institutes": Natural Sciences (chemistry and microbiology), the teaching of which started even earlier; Jewish Studies, instruction in which commenced at the end of 1924; and the School of Oriental Studies which opened to students only in 1926. This School of Oriental Studies was supposed to be part of Jewish Studies, following the practice of European and especially German universities, where Hebrew, Arabic and other languages were taught together under the rubric of Semitic languages. (Non-Semitic languages such as Persian and Turkish were also part of the curriculum for students who chose Semitic languages.) Many of the teachers of these languages at German universities were Jewish, and almost all of the early faculty of the Hebrew University had studied under them, especially in Berlin and Frankfurt.

One of the most famous Jewish professors in Frankfurt was Josef Horovitz, scion of a well-known family of Orthodox rabbis, born in 1874 in Lauenberg. His father was Markus Horovitz (1844–1910), one of the leaders of German Jewish orthodoxy, and an anti-Zionist. Horovitz grew up in Frankfurt, where his father officiated as a rabbi, and later studied in Berlin under Eduard Sachau (1845–1930), the general editor of Ibn Sa'd's *Kitāb al-Ṭabaqāt*. Horovitz wrote his doctoral thesis (under Sachau's supervision) on early Muslim historiography (especially Wāqidī's *Kitāb al-Maghāzī*). But from the outset, he was very interested in other fields as well: early Arabic poetry, *adab* literature, and Qur'anic studies. According to Goitein, Horovitz had hoped all his life to write a scholarly commentary on the Qur'an, but died just before embarking on the project, having first published several important monographs on Qur'anic themes (such as his *Koranische Untersuchungen* and his *Jewish Proper Names and Derivatives in the Koran*).[1] His Jewish Orthodox upbringing and his studies prepared him well for the comparative study of Judaism and Islam, which fascinated him.

He was not an observant Jew, and his attitude towards Zionism is not altogether clear. According to Magnes, he was not a Zionist, but gladly accepted Magnes' invitation, in the early 1920s, to assist the Hebrew University as its first director of oriental studies.[2] Yet according to family and other sources, he was close to Zionism (as was his brother, Jacob Horovitz, a Frankfurt rabbi), and to the small group known as Brit Shalom, a circle founded by German-Jewish Zionist intellectuals who tried to find a political solution in Palestine acceptable to both Jews and Arabs.[3] In any case, Horovitz did not move to Jerusalem. He took part in the opening of the university in 1925 as a member of the first board of governors, and then came to Jerusalem once more in 1926 to teach a six-week seminar. But for the next five years, until his death in 1931, he directed the School of Oriental Studies of the Hebrew University from abroad—and in a most authoritarian way.

At the outset, he demanded that there be established a separate School of Oriental Studies, and that Arabic and Islamic studies should not be taught within a department at the Institute of Jewish Studies, as had been originally planned. He explained his reasons for this demand in a memorandum sent to Magnes on 14 May 1925.[4] He may have had perfectly good reasons to insist on this point, for he probably feared that the new Institute of Jewish Studies would constrain the development of oriental studies or transform them into a subordinate branch of Jewish studies. But this demand, which was accepted by Magnes and then implemented, deeply influenced not only the course of academic studies of Arabic and

Islam in Israel, but also the trajectory of Jewish medieval studies, an influence felt until this very day. Both disciplines flourished in the Yishuv—and still do so in Israel—but both fields also paid a very high price for their separation. For there is no point in studying medieval Judaism without Arabic, or teaching the history of early Islam without a solid knowledge of Judaism and Semitic languages. Fortunately, the university's first teachers combined both in their own formation, and thus compensated, through the first generations at least, for the absence of institutional ties between the two disciplines.

As for Horovitz, he was involved in every detail of administering the new School of Oriental Studies. In a typical German fashion of university management, he was the one who decided who would teach what and when, and how every administrative issue was to be resolved. The Jerusalem faculty accepted his chairmanship unreservedly. Once, for example, Max Schloessinger (1877–1944), vice chancellor of the university and an orientalist himself, wrote to him:

> I wish to point out to you that when the protocol says that it has been decided here to do this or that, we do not mean that this should be the last word, but we only mean that this has been the attitude of the men [!] of the department...The final word is yours—not ours.[5]

Horovitz even used the Jerusalem school as an appendage of his own personal scholarly projects, and thus determined—one might well say mortgaged—the scholarly agenda of the institute in Jerusalem to this very day. He was involved in two huge projects. One was an edition of *Futūḥ al-Buldān,* the great history by the early Muslim historiographer Balādhurī (d. 892). This project was started in Germany by Carl Heinrich Becker (1876–1933), and handed over to Horovitz when Becker entered politics. The other project was a massive concordance of early Arabic poetry, from the pre-Islamic era until the end of the Umayyad period, with the help of which Horovitz planned to write the definitive history of early Arabic poetry. Johann Fück, in his book on the development of Arabic studies in Europe, writes:

> Bei seinen koranischen Untersuchungen berücksichtigte Horovitz sorgsam den Sprachgebrauch der vorislamischen Dichter und trug sich mit dem Plan eines Wörterbuchs zur altarabischen Poesie, wozu er im Orientalischen Institut der 1925 eröffneten Hebräischen Universität die

> gedruckt vorliegenden Diwane (bis zum Ende der Umaiyadenzeit) verzetteln ließ.[6]

In other words, Horovitz used the staff at the new Hebrew University to collect items of early Arabic poetry, for a lexicon or book which he intended to write in the future. It is important to stress here that the German word used by Fück—*verzetteln*, the writing down on small pieces of papers (of Arabic words as items for the concordance)—is not a very nice word, and well reflects a paternalism which Horovitz seems to have shown toward the new school in Jerusalem. Horovitz was going to do the scholarly work and write the history of early Arabic poetry; the "local" people in Jerusalem—his research assistants—were only tasked with collecting the raw material on pieces of paper. These pieces, and the monthly payment for them, are often mentioned in the university archives, and most of the faculty (not the students!) took part in the project—only after being deemed competent for the job by Horovitz.

But things turned out differently. Horovitz died at the age of fifty-six in 1931, and never wrote the book about Arabic poetry. But Horovitz's concordance lives on in Jerusalem and has became one of the hallmarks of the Jerusalem school. Today, under the chairmanship of Albert Arazi, it contains about one and a half million items, and scholars from all over the world make good use of it. For decades, no plans were made for publication, because of the immense expenditure such a project would involve. But even without publication, the concordance cut deeply into the funds which became available to the school for research projects, and continues to do so up to this very day.

After the death of Horovitz, Gotthold Weil (1882–1960) of Frankfurt University was appointed his successor as director of the School of Oriental Studies. From 1931 to 1935, he too served in this capacity *in absentia*. After he was dismissed by the Nazis from his chair, in 1934, he left Frankfurt for Jerusalem, where he served on the faculty and as the university librarian until his retirement in 1952.

Only in 1935 was a Jerusalem-based director appointed. Leo Ary Mayer (1895–1959) served as the third director of the school from 1935 to 1949. An archeologist and great art historian, he also belonged to the same group of Jewish orientalists who received a twofold education: he studied both at the University of Vienna and at Vienna's rabbinical seminary. Coming from a very Zionist family, he emigrated from Germany and settled in the Yishuv in 1921. (In the 1950s, I had the good fortune to be one of his students, but his fields of interests were very remote from mine. I remember him above all as an extremely impressive and handsome man—certainly the most handsome of all my teachers.)

Goitein in Jerusalem

In 1949, Goitein became the director of the school, which he headed until 1956. Goitein, born in 1900 in Burgkunstadt in Bavaria into a family of Hungarian rabbis, had studied under Horovitz in Frankfurt, and wrote his doctoral thesis under his guidance. The scholarly link between the two was the Qur'an. Horovitz had a deep understanding of the religious issues involved, and this may have been one reason why the young Goitein chose to write his thesis under Horovitz's supervision (to which, according to Goitein's autobiography, Horovitz devoted no more than ten minutes). Goitein wrote about prayer in the Qur'an—an important work which has never been published in full, but which anticipates Goitein's approach in many of his subsequent studies. He read every text for its linguistic and religious aspect—in this case for the Christian sources of Qur'anic prayer—and was always deeply concerned with religious issues himself. He precisely fit the description of the "pro-Islamic Jew" given by Bernard Lewis: he was an "emancipated, liberal, West European Jew who achieved an immediate and intuitive understanding of Islam,"[7] based on the great affinity between the two religious cultures, Jewish and Muslim.

Goitein was an observant Jew (though far from orthodox), and remained a practicing Jew even in his later years, when he could no longer maintain his faith. He had an excellent grounding in Jewish studies, acquired with great Frankfurtian personalities like Rabbi Nehemiah Anton Nobel (1871–1922) and Franz Rosenzweig (1886–1929), and the lesser-known *dayyan,* Jacob Posen (1857–1924).[8] He published biblical studies and was even asked to teach the subject at the Hebrew University shortly before he left for the United States in the 1950s. He was also very concerned about the state of contemporary Judaism. I was lucky to have been close enough to him in the 1950s to hold many conversations with him about the stagnant orthodoxy in Israel, and we discussed the ways in which the Jewish heritage could be revived so that young Israelis could accept or at least identify with parts of it.

This religious feeling and understanding served Goitein well in later life, when he was no longer what he called "a thoroughly medieval man, that is, one for whom religion is the overriding concern in life," but had become "an ordinary participant in the modern, scientific-technological civilization." In his famous Geniza studies, to which he devoted the last thirty years of his life, his modern attitude provided "an Archimedean point of vantage from which the medieval scene might be observed objectively from the outside, while the inner experience gained by me in a previous life might serve as a corrective, a Socratic *daimon,* a restraining inner voice."[9]

This understanding of the religiosity of the medieval other—whether Muslim or Jew—also helped Goitein understand the problems of modernity for religious Jews and Muslims. He was always interested in contemporary developments, perhaps under the early influence of Horovitz, who for several years had been a professor at the Muhammadan Anglo-Oriental College in Aligarh and was—in addition to his interest in classical Islam—also an authority on contemporary issues, especially Indian Islam. The interest Goitein took in the modern Middle East was quite unusual among scholars of classical Islam before the Second World War. There was a feeling, shared even today by some old-fashioned scholars, that the study of the modern Middle East was somehow a less scholarly endeavor than the study of classical Islam. Magnes, for example, could not convince the faculty of the School of Oriental Studies to consider the modern problematics of the Arab population of Palestine. Even many years later—when the modern Middle East was introduced as a legitimate field of study—scholars of classical Islam still looked down upon it, and upon the social sciences which provided disciplinary tools for contemporary research. This may be traced to the way classical Islam had been taught at the university (and is still taught by some scholars even today). This approach, following the German (as opposed to the French) model, embraced the philological tradition of classical studies: reading the text and translating it, then explaining and analyzing it, without any reference to modern equivalents or to the disciplines of the social sciences.

Goitein was one of the first to include historical surveys and lectures in his teaching, pointing out modern evolutions of classical antecedents, or analyzing new developments in modern times. Thus, for example, at the end of his well-known article on the origins of the fast of Ramadan,[10] he describes the fast in modern times in Saudi Arabia in 1918, and in Cairo in 1836, 1956 and 1963. His conclusion:

> Ramadan was more generally kept than prayer...prayer requires a personal relationship to God to a far higher degree than abstention from food, which may be motivated and rationalized in many different ways. Therefore in a period in which religious fervor has been on the wane, the Ramadan, which is mentioned only in one single passage in the Koran, has remained far more popular with modern Muslims than prayer—although the latter pervades the holy Scripture of Islam from beginning to end.[11]

In addition to Horovitz and Goitein, there were, of course, many others who took part in transmitting European Arabic and Islamic studies to Jerusalem. They included Joseph Joel Rivlin (1889–1971), who, although born in Jerusalem, also studied with Horovitz in Frankfurt in the 1920s; Walter Joseph Fischel (1902–73); Eliyahu Ashtor (1914–1984); Martin Plessner (1900–73) and many others. They were very different from one another but all shared a broad education and vast erudition, which we—the generations raised in Israel—do not possess. They were schooled in Greek and Latin in the German *gymnasium*, and later mastered an array of European and Semitic languages. They all had a solid grounding in Jewish studies, having studied not just in the university but in the rabbinic seminary or its equivalent. And they were widely read in history, literature, and philosophy. These are points worth remembering when we, their Israeli students, still employ their philological methods of teaching. We lack their vast erudition and rich sources for comparison, and so do our students. Indeed, the so-called "introductory courses" introduced very late at the School of Oriental Studies (in part at Goitein's instance) were virtually unknown in European universities at the beginning of this century. They were not necessary then; they are essential now.

Bashful Baneth

I come now to Baneth, who was not only a close friend of Goitein, but also related to him. They used to call themselves "cousins," although their actual family tie seems to have been further removed. In their character, they showed no signs of a common ancestry whatsoever, for they were radically different from one another.

Baneth was born in 1893 in Krotoszyn in Poland, but grew up in Berlin. His father was Rabbi Eduard Ezekiel Baneth (1855–1930) who taught Midrash and Talmud at the Jüdische Hochschule in Berlin. Baneth himself studied there, and at the universities of Berlin and Frankfurt. In 1920 he received his doctoral degree for his important study of the letters of Muhammad, which was never published. Unlike Goitein, Baneth hesitated to publish his work. He was shy and insecure to an incredible degree, and held himself in very low esteem. (His students well remember how he would never pass through any door before anybody else, including his students—a fact which often caused considerable traffic jams at doors and exits. But Baneth, who was also very stubborn, always won the battle to pass through a door last.)

At the same time, he was revered by all his colleagues, and the high standard of his scholarly demands was feared by all the students. Goitein used to say that for decades, everything that was published in Jerusalem in the field of Arabic and Islam was influenced, if not written, by Baneth, even if it appeared under the names of others. As Baneth's only doctoral student, I can testify from personal experience to his unrelenting demands from his students, and indeed from himself. The topic he chose for my thesis was "The Literary Character of Al-Ghazālī's Writings"—a subject so vast that a lifetime would not have been long enough to finish it, certainly not in the way Baneth expected me to finish it. In fact, at one point Baneth advised me to take a couple of years of leave from the thesis, as I seemed tired of it, and then to return to it with double vigor. He could not understand that this would not have been the best solution to my prospects of an academic career. It was the late Uriel Heyd (1913–68) who advised me to write my thesis on the basis of the material I had collected up to that point, and submit it to the senate of the Hebrew University (as was the custom then), without ever showing it to Baneth, my supervisor—a most unusual procedure, to be sure. So I did just that, and Baneth, instead of being furious with me, wrote at the beginning of his extremely generous evaluation of my thesis something like: "Indeed the candidate did not accept my advice, but as things turned out, it was very good that she did not heed me."

Baneth had immigrated in 1924, and began by working in the National and University Library, like many other scholars at that time. (In those days, the oriental section of the library was much enriched by the acquisition of the private library of Ignaz Goldziher, consisting of some 6,000 volumes. On the margins of some of these books, one can still find

Goldziher's own remarks, on others Baneth's corrections and remarks.) In 1926 Baneth began to teach at the new School of Oriental Studies, almost against his own wishes. He remained so insecure and skeptical of his own abilities that many years later, when he was promoted to the rank of professor, he asked that the promotion—which to his mind was apparently undeserved—not be made official and public until he decided whether to accept it.[12]

Goitein joined him two years later, in 1928, after having first taught for four years at the Reali School in Haifa, and after returning once more to Berlin for several months to renew his contact with academic research. Both constituted the first link between European Arabic and Islamic studies and the new university in Palestine, and both taught for many years at the Hebrew University: Baneth for forty years until his retirement in the mid-1960s, and Goitein for thirty years until he left for the United States at the end of the 1950s. The curriculum they instituted was very much the same as in Frankfurt: reading classical texts in Islamic philosophy, history, and theology, much in the same way Horovitz and his colleagues had done in Frankfurt, except perhaps for the much greater emphasis laid in Jerusalem on Judeo-Arabic texts. Baneth was in fact the founder of what came to be known the study of Judeo-Arabic. He spent many years on a new edition of the Judeo-Arabic text of the *Kuzari* (correcting the nineteenth-century edition of Hirschfeld), and on Judeo-Arabic texts by Maimonides. He also studied the characteristics of medieval translations from Arabic into Hebrew. His knowledge of both languages was the closest one could come to perfection, and he was for many years an active member of the Academy of the Hebrew Language.

Unlike Goitein, Baneth was a convinced atheist, but he had an unusual reverence for religion and a profound understanding of religious texts, both Jewish and Islamic. This was due, to a certain extent at least, to his upbringing in a family of noted rabbis and scholars. (Indeed, he never paraded his atheism, out of respect for his late father.) But it was also certainly due to his teachers and the higher education he had received in Berlin and Frankfurt. Nevertheless, his sincerity and integrity induced him to doubt religious motives, in ancient texts and modern actions. He often drew our attention to the many ways of religious deceit, and taught us to search for the worldly ambitions hiding behind ostensibly religious motives, as an integral part of any true understanding of religion, where the highest motives often combine with the lowest. Again, we Israeli scholars tend to misunderstand this paradox, and see everything in black or white, perhaps because we lack the personal experience of growing up in the European liberal scholarly tradition.

Baneth, like Goitein, also took part in the many debates about contemporary Jewish identity and thought. In a review of a book by Yitzhak Heinemann (1876–1957) on the mission of man in late antiquity and in Jewish medieval literature, Baneth wrote: "The question about the origins and development of our culture is a question which these times have raised. It was never thus asked before us and may never be asked again. If our scholarship makes no attempt to answer this question as best as it can, it will become an atrophied, wasted member of contemporary culture."[13]

Baneth died in 1973 after a long illness which affected his mind and sanity. Goitein died in 1985 in the United States, after finishing his monumental series *A Mediterranean Society*. Both scholars, with the help of Josef Horovitz and many others, constituted the vital connecting link between European, especially German, Islamic scholarship and the newly-founded School of Oriental Studies at the Hebrew University. Their students carried the torch onward to other newer universities in Israel, and created an independent school of Middle Eastern studies in Israel, in the reputation of which all of us can take pride. But let us not forget the main characteristics of our first teachers: a deep and intimate knowledge of our Jewish heritage, which opened the door to a profound understanding of Arabic and Islam; and a broad erudition in the classics, which made them humanists in the widest sense of the word. Theirs was a path we would do well to follow.

Notes

1. See S.D. Goitein, "Josef Horovitz," *Der Islam* 22 (1935): 122–27. This item is missing from Goitein's published bibliography.
2. See the eulogy of Horovitz by Magnes, 27 November 1931, in the archives of the Hebrew University.
3. On Brit Shalom see Hagit Lavsky, "German Zionists and the Emergence of Brit Shalom," in *Essential Papers on Zionism,* eds. Jehuda Reinharz and Anita Shapira (New York: New York University Press, 1996), 648–70; Aharon Kedar, "Le-toldoteha shel Brit Shalom be-shanim 1925–1928," in *Pirkei Mehkar be-Toldot ha-Zionut,* ed. Yehuda Bauer (Jerusalem: Ha-Sifriya Ha-Zionit, 1976), 224–85. The relationship between Horovitz and Brit Shalom is not altogether clear. While some regard him as one of Brit

Shalom's founders, and even as the one who pushed Arthur Ruppin into founding it, others minimize his role; see Kedar, "Le-toldoteha shel Brit Shalom," 229–30. Cf. also Menahem Milson, "The Beginnings of Arabic and Islamic Studies at the Hebrew University of Jerusalem," *Judaism* 45 (1996): 171.

4. See Milson, "Beginnings," 172.
5. See Schloessinger's letter in the archives of the Hebrew University. It must have been written in the late 1920s.
6. Johann Fück, *Die arabischen Studien in Europa bis in den Anfang des 20. Jahrhunderts* (Leipzig: Otto Harrassowitz, 1955), 314.
7. Bernard Lewis, "The Pro-Islamic Jews," in his *Islam in History: Ideas, People, and Events in the Middle East*, new rev. ed. (Chicago: Open Court, 1993), 150.
8. Goitein described this *dayyan* in a lengthy footnote in his *A Mediterranean Society*, 6 vols. (Berkeley: University of California Press, 1967–93), 2:546–547 n. 20.
9. S.D. Goitein, "Religion in Everyday Life as Reflected in the Documents of the Cairo Geniza," in *Religion in a Religious Age*, ed. S. D. Goitein (Cambridge, Mass.: Association for Jewish Studies, 1974), 3–4.
10. S.D. Goitein, "Ramadan, the Muslim Month of Fasting: Its Early Development and Religious Meaning," in his *Studies in Islamic History and Institutions* (Leiden: E.J. Brill, 1966), 90–110.
11. Ibid., 109–10.
12. See his letter of 10 September 1946 in the archives of the Hebrew University.
13. Baneth's review of Isaak Heinemann, *Die Lehre von der Zweckbestimmung des Menschen im griechisch-römischen Altertum und im jüdischen Mittelalter* (Breslau: M. & H. Marcus, 1926), in *Qiryat Sefer* 3 (1927): 135–37. A bibliography of Baneth's writings compiled by R. Attal was published in *Studia Orientalia, Memoriae D. H. Baneth Dedicata* (Jerusalem: Magnes, 1979), 175–79 (Hebrew section).

9

The Interaction of Judaic and Islamic Studies in the Scholarship of S.M. Stern

Shulamit Sela

Fortunately we are able to draw upon a first-class witness.
—S.M. Stern

A person undertaking a research project may be compared to someone packing their bags in preparation for a journey. But there is one major difference between taking a journey in physical space and in scholarship. A person embarking on an earthbound trip will prefer to keep baggage to a minimum, excluding any superfluous item that might prove a burden. In contrast, a person embarking on the pursuit of intellectual knowledge, *fī ṭalab al-'ilm,* prefers to fill suitcase after suitcase, in preparation for any intellectual eventuality along the route.

A student of Islamic civilization obviously should be outfitted with the basic tools for the study of the heritage of Muslim peoples. However, since Islam inherited the science of the ancients, and recognized the two monotheistic religions that came before it, a well-equipped scholar must have the basic tools for researching the civilizations which predated Islam. A scholar embarking on Islamicist research has an advantage if he or she is familiar with Judaism, classical cultures and Christianity. Particularly well-equipped were those Jews born and raised in Christian Europe, steeped in Jewish tradition, and graduated from the classic *gymnasium*. Success in scholarship depends mainly on ability and hard work.

Nevertheless, fortunate accidents of birth can make a decisive difference, as they did for the many European Jews who embarked on Islamic studies. Samuel Miklos Stern (1920–69) was an outstanding member of this group, whose work represents the ultimate example of mutual enrichment between Jewish and Islamic scholarship.

The Making of a Polymath

From a chronological point of view, Stern cannot be considered one of the pioneers of Islamic studies. But he does represent one of its pinnacles, as one of his eulogists later emphasized: "In a period of topical and disciplinary specialization, Stern was a polymath, and his part in the continuing progress of our studies may be likened to that of the pioneers and founders of *Islamkunde* in the nineteenth century."[1]

Indeed, from the very beginning of his scholarly career, Stern was obviously a polymath. This can be discerned from a close look at his first article, published under the title: "Miniatures: Two New Data about Ḥasdai B. Shaprut."[2] The different genres of Muslim literature contain very little information about Jews. Nevertheless, the young Stern was able to track down references to the senior Jewish minister who served the rulers of Muslim Spain in the mid-tenth century in two very different works by two Muslim writers. He found the first reference to Hasdai in a philosophical work, the Epitome of Aristotle's *Poetica* by Ibn Rushd.[3] He located the second in a map drawn by the Muslim geographer Ibn Ḥawqal.[4] Stern's first article was an early indication of his interdisciplinary command of the study of the medieval Eastern world, and his thorough familiarity with its varied cultural components.

Stern's extensive scholarly achievements are all the more impressive given that he died young.[5] He was born in 1920 in the small town of Tab in Hungary. His father died when he was three. His mother was his first teacher, and she taught him the Hebrew alphabet even before he learned the Latin one. Like all the other Jewish children in his milieu, he received a traditional Jewish education. But he also received a classical education at a Benedictine school where he studied Greek and Latin at an early age. For his post-elementary education he attended the *gymnasium* affiliated with the rabbinical seminary in Budapest. When he was sixteen he started to learn Arabic on his own. In 1939, when the winds of war began to be felt in Europe, his mother prudently sent him to the Hebrew

University in Jerusalem. Thus was he saved from the massacre of the Jews of Budapest.[6]

The Hungarian-born students attending the Hebrew University at that time made a strong impression on their fellow students,[7] and Stern stood out in this group.[8] One of his most important teachers was the Arabist David Zvi Baneth (1893–1973).[9] Other important Hebrew University instructors in the fields which Stern was to master included the Semiticist and linguist Hans Jacob Polotsky (1905–91) and the philosophers Leon Roth (1896–1963) and Julius Guttman (1880–1950). The study of Romance languages and literature under the guidance of Hiram Peri (Heinz Pflaum; 1900–62) figured very significantly in Stern's future work on Hispano-Arabic poetry. In Jerusalem, he also met Shlomo Dov Goitein (1900–85), who may have been responsible for stimulating his interest in Islamic history, and with whom he remained in close contact. During the Second World War, Stern served in the British censorship department for three years, first in Baghdad, and later in Port Sudan. During his service, while on a visit to Egypt, he made the acquaintance of Paul Kraus (1904–44), and this meeting inspired his interest in the study of Ismā'īlism. When the war was over, Stern returned to Jerusalem and completed his final examinations.

This concluded what may be termed Stern's formative period. The foundations of his scientific scholarship were laid during these years, and in his subsequent career he continued to expand his work on the basis of that foundation, although he was always prepared to meet other scholarly challenges. This formative period was marked by an integration of Jewish and oriental studies (although, according to the evidence available, until the end of the 1940s Stern had only come into contact with Jewish scholars). In 1948, Stern left Israel (as an asthmatic, he had been exempted from Israeli military service), and proceeded to Oxford, to prepare his thesis under the supervision of Hamilton A.R. Gibb (1895–1971). In 1950 he completed his dissertation on the old Andalusian *muwashshaḥ*, which was entitled "Hispano-Arabic Strophic Poetry." In 1951 he was appointed secretary-general for the new edition of the *Encyclopaedia of Islam,* and was responsible for organizing its first 320 pages. In 1956 he began his career at Oxford, first in the Coin Room of the Ashmolean Museum and later as a research fellow at All Souls College. In 1965 he was given official teaching duties in the Faculty of Oriental Studies. In the last year of his life, Stern had twelve research students (two from Israel).[10] Stern died as a result of a severe asthmatic attack in 1969. Although he had not yet reached the age of forty-nine, the magnitude of his scholarly work is remarkable and the list of his publications includes 261 items.[11] These books and articles deal with various topics connected with the medieval Islamic world: literature (especially Spanish poetry), art, history (especially early Ismā'īlism), philosophy, diplomatics (the study of Muslim royal documents) and numismatics.

Stern's private life at Oxford illustrates additional aspects of his Jewish identity. Stern never married and his main companions were Richard Walzer (1900–75) and his gifted wife, Sofie.[12] Walzer was a Jewish scholar of Greek and Arab philosophy. He was born in Germany, but when the Nazis came to power he was forced to leave, arriving first in Italy and finally settling in Oxford, where he received a fellowship.[13] Stern and the Walzers shared a two-story home in the university town for twenty years, and the couple took the place of his lost family.[14] Apparently, their common fate as Jewish refugees brought them together and forged this unique family—although neither Stern nor Walzer dwelt in public on their shared circumstances.

In Walzer's eulogy for Stern, he described the course of his friend's life and scientific work in detail, but made no mention whatsoever of the fate they shared as Jews. In general, Walzer belittled the importance of Jewish studies in Stern's scholarship, and declared his opinion that "Hebrew studies remained, on the whole, a side issue." This perspective is also apparent in the style of Walzer's eulogy; when he described Stern's transformation into a secular Jew, he chose to use an Arabic word: "a boy...who had just... abandoned the *taqlīd* of his childhood." And when he was lamenting Stern's untimely death, he turned to Greek: "Those whom the gods love die young."[15] Walzer omitted the mourner's Kaddish or any other words of commemoration from the Jewish tradition in his eulogy. In contrast, his non-Jewish colleagues did not ignore the tribulations of his life as a refugee or the traditions of his fathers. As the historian Albert Hourani (1915–93) put it: "He came to us as a stranger twenty years ago: he rarely spoke about his early life, although he may have thought about it more than he spoke (he liked to eat food which brought back memories of some lost world of central Europe). In a way he remained a stranger, not quite at home in the world, carrying inside him some pain which lay too deep for words."[16] Another non-Jewish orientalist who paid homage to Stern concluded his eulogy with a suitable quotation from the Ethics of the Fathers.[17]

As noted by his eulogizers, Stern was not given to sharing his innermost feelings with others; nevertheless, he left behind a confirmation of his awareness that he was an exiled Jew in the prestigious university. Deliberations were being held at All Souls College on the question of whether to admit women as readers to the Codrington Library, and an opponent, referring back to the founders, asked: "What would Archbishop Chichele have thought of such an idea?" Stern did not hesitate to side with the weak minority, despite the fact that his candidacy for a fellowship then stood at a critical stage. His retort: "What would Archbishop Chichele have thought of the election to his college of a Hungarian Jew?"[18]

In the end, Stern was elected, and he became a full-fledged fellow of the college. Yet in this scholarly community, he saw himself as a member of the Jewish people, and his colleagues acknowledged him as such.[19] He maintained a connection with the scientific community in Israel and he bequeathed his house, library and writings to the Hebrew University.[20]

Jewish Sources on Islam

These were the intellectual sources which nourished Stern.[21] They infused his research, which constituted an important contribution to the integrated study of Judaism and Islam.

Stern's dissertation dealt with Hispano-Arabic strophic poetry. He was particularly interested in the development of the old Andalusian *muwashshaḥ* (in Hebrew, *shir ezor*). This type of poetry was preserved in Arabic and in Hebrew, and Stern carried out a comparative study of the genre in both languages. One of the characteristics of the *muwashshaḥ* is its ending, which is known by its Arabic name *kharja*. According to the theory of the *muwashshaḥ*, the endings of some of these Arabic poems were written in a Romance language, or to be more specific Mozarabic, the Spanish dialect that absorbed Arabic words. Nonetheless, until Stern made his discoveries, no one had found these Romance-language endings in Arabic poetry. He discovered Spanish endings in the contemporary (medieval) Hebrew poetry of al-Andalus. Hebrew poets such as Yehuda Halevi would conclude their Hebrew *muwashshaḥs* with an Arabic or Mozarabic ending written in Hebrew letters.[22] Stern deciphered these difficult endings, which were preserved in the Hebrew poetry of Spain,[23] and afterwards he even succeeded in finding an Arabic *muwashshaḥ* with a Spanish ending.[24] He also proposed a theory to explain the origin of this special phenomenon. Today these stanzas are considered the earliest examples of Spanish poetry, and modern anthologies of Spanish poetry begin with *kharja*s that Stern published.[25] In short, this ancient Romance-language poetry was discovered as a component of an Arabic literary genre adopted by Hebrew poets. The reconstruction and study of this literary style required a scholar who was very well-versed in both Arabic- and Hebrew-Spanish literature.

The literary form of poetry was shared by Muslims and Jews, but Stern also approached more explicitly Islamic subjects through Judaic doors. He became interested in early Ismāʻīlism and was one of the most important students of this Islamic sect. The main difficulty in the study of Ismāʻīlism is the fact that most of the material pertaining to it is found in the writings of the sect's opponents. Hence, these sources are inherently unreliable and must be thoroughly examined. Stern set out to investigate the claim made by the opponents of Ismāʻīlism that "the sect sought to make the different religions their dupes by pretending to sympathize with their different doctrines, while in their hearts they scoffed at all religions."[26]

Stern searched for unbiased evidence that described Ismāʻīlism's relations with other religions and was "free from that odium theologicum in the testimony of orthodox Muslim writers." Stern managed to locate a contemporary witness in the person of Yefet b. ʻAli, the Karaite, whose commentary on the Book of Daniel includes a description of the relationship between Ismāʻīlism and the Jews. Medieval commentators, and particularly the Karaites, liked to interpret the apocalyptic verses in Daniel as relevant to their generation. In his commentary, Yefet includes information about Jews who converted to Islam and about the religious persecutions of al-Ḥākim. The unique aspect of the commentary is its description of the methods which the Ismāʻīlīs employed in the Fatimid propaganda to proselytize the Jews. Yefet gives examples of these Ismāʻīlī *ta'wīl* techniques which were applied to the Hebrew Bible and to Jewish religious practices. Stern's mastery of medieval Arab and Arab-Jewish theological literature provided unique "inside" information about the sect, and he proclaims: "Fortunately we are able to draw upon a first-class witness."[27] After Stern juxtaposed Yefet's testimony about Ismāʻīlism's relations with the Jews and the biased accounts written by orthodox Islam against the sect, he came to the following conclusion: "The so-called latitude of official Ismāʻīlism, when examined on the basis of authentic texts, seems to be reduced to the fact that, in propagating Ismā'īlism among the believers of other religions, weapons taken from the holy texts of those very religions were freely used. But this was only the practice of Islam as a whole."[28]

Stern worked in the Coin Room of the Ashmolean Museum at the beginning of his career at Oxford. His interest in numismatics continued throughout his life and his studies in this field were always related to his philological endeavors. In this discipline as well, his knowledge of Arab-Jewish culture enriched his Arabist research. In his comprehensive study on the quarter-dinar (*rubā'ī*) of southern Italy, Stern attempted to find out why this coin became know as *tari* in southern Italian Christian sources.[29] His philological study on the origins and meaning of the name indicated that the word was derived from the Arabic adjective *ṭarī*, which means "fresh." Initially the coin was called "fresh quarter-dinar" and, finally, the adjective alone was used as the coin's appellation. Stern discovered concrete evidence for the Arabic origins of the coin's name in Geniza sources (documents found in the lumber room of the Cairo synagogue). There he discovered Hebrew letters written by Sicilian Jewish merchants in which the coin was called *ṭārī* in the singular and *ṭeriyyīm* in the plural. Since the authors of these letters were undoubtedly Arabic-speaking, Stern made the assumption that they borrowed the word from the Arabic vernacular.

Stern was at home in the world of the Geniza, and he used its treasures frequently for his research on Jewish and Arab culture. Furthermore, one area of Geniza research owes its existence to Stern: the royal decrees which the Egyptian authorities granted to their Jewish subjects. Stern analyzed these documents and compared them to others which had been granted to Christians, who were also protected subjects. Stern explained that these decrees, which were issued by the caliphs, were constructed according to a pattern which included fixed formulas for preliminary matter, expositio, dispositio, final injunctions, date, final eulogies, signature and registration.[30] Stern's diplomatic research remains the basis for new studies of letters of appointment for the heads of the Jewish communities, recently discovered in the Geniza.[31]

Did this "stern" philologist ever make any personal references to his Jewish heritage? Personal reflections did not figure in Stern's work: trained in the rigors of philology, he saw himself as a scientist. An exception (which may hint at the rule) regarding Stern's empathy towards the heritage of his people appears at the end of his article, "'The First in

Thought is the Last in Action': The History of a Saying Attributed to Aristotle."[32] Stern followed this philosophical saying from its first appearance in Greek sources, through its representation in Arabic literature, and up to its appearance in Jewish medieval philosophy. The last quote in the article is taken from the famous hymn *Lekhah Dodi* ("Come, my beloved") by Solomon Alkabeẓ (ca. 1505–76), which occupies a prominent place in the Friday evening service of the synagogue. The kabbalist poet describes the Sabbath as "the end of action, the first in thought." After quoting the hymn, Stern abandons his usually terse academic style and gives himself license to include the following nostalgic epilogue:

> With this hymn we have reached the end of our study, our "action." Not that the wish to trace its sources was the "first in our thought"; what originally provided the impetus for following up the history of the saying was the desire to explain its occurrence in some early Islamic texts, more especially in the Isma'ili passage quoted by al-Busti. When reading it in those texts, the author was, however, immediately reminded of the hymn, long familiar to him, and was curious to find out the ways leading from early Islamic authors to the Hebrew hymnographer; so that the hymn, last in action, was definitely in his mind at the beginning of his thought.

Notes

1. J. Wansbrough, "Obituary: Samuel Miklos Stern," *Bulletin School of Oriental and African Studies* 33, pt. 3 (1970): 600–2. I thank Prof. M.J. Kister, who sent me reprints of the eulogies for Stern.
2. *Zion* 11(1945–46): 141–46.
3. Ibid., 141. In a passage dedicated to the art of conversation, Ibn Rushd declares that there is no need for rhetorical embellishment when truth is obvious. He then demonstrates his case with a story about a *faqīh* who wanted to discredit the Jew Hasdai in the eyes of the Caliph, 'Abd al-Raḥmān.
4. Ibid., 143. Ibn Ḥawqal wrote a remark concerning Hasdai's relationship with Khazaria on one of his maps.
5. Unless designated otherwise, the biographical material is based on R. Walzer, "S.M. Stern, In Memoriam," *Israel Oriental Studies* 2 (Tel Aviv: Tel Aviv University, 1972): 1–14.
6. I was informed by a relative of Stern's, Mrs. Ruth Elon, that his mother

died in the ghetto.

7. The outstanding work of the Hungarian students is repeatedly mentioned and documented in the memoirs of other members of their class. Edward Ullendorff, *The Two Zions* (Oxford: Oxford University Press, 1988), 52, claims that among his fellow students, the Hungarians were the cleverest.
8. Ibid. "Stern... was, I think by general consent, the most gifted among us. Already as a student he stood out in his single-minded devotion to his studies, constantly reading and working and never engaging in idle student chat." Prof. Joshua Blau, too, told me that Stern was the most serious of them all, and that he achieved scholarly maturity at an early age.
9. According to Baneth, quoted by Walzer, "In Memoriam," 3: "Stern had no need to be taught anything any more."
10. Prof. Tova Rozen of Tel Aviv University and Prof. Etan Kohlberg of the Hebrew University. I thank both of them for sharing their memories with me, and I thank Prof. Rozen for referring me to her book, mentioned in n. 25 below.
11. The most up-to-date list of Stern's articles, compiled by J.D. Latham and H.W. Mitchell, was appended to the collection of his work on Spanish poetry, which was published posthumously: *Hispano-Arabic Strophic Poetry*, ed. L.P. Harvey (Oxford: Clarendon Press, 1974), 231–45. This list does not yet include the three collections of articles which were edited and published by Variorum, or the anthology on Ismā'īlism published by the Hebrew University; see references below.
12. Along with R. Ostle, she translated (from German into English) J. Wellhausen's *Religious Opposition Parties in Islam,* which Stern launched in 1969.
13. For the biography of Walzer, see "Richard Walzer," in *Islamic Philosophy and the Classical Tradition*, eds. S.M. Stern, Albert Hourani, and Vivian Brown (Columbia, South Carolina: University of South Carolina Press, 1973), 1–3.
14. These family ties, which were described to me by Stern's friends and acquaintances, even received official recognition at Oxford. According to the rule in the statutes of All Souls College—a rule intended to keep the college family together, so far as possible—any bachelor Fellow who lives in Oxford must reside within the college walls. Attached to the rule is a provision enabling it to be relaxed in case of need. Stern's case was recognized as unusual according to the testimony of the Warden: "To have torn him from the bosom of what I cannot but call his family would have been an act of cruelty to them and would have crippled him, both as a scholar and a human being." I have quoted the above from a collection of eulogies: *All Souls College, S.M. Stern, Fellow 1957–1969* (Oxford: Oxford University Press), 12.
15. Walzer, "In Memoriam," 6, 14 (consecutively).

16. Albert Hourani at Stern's funeral on 31 October 1969, *All Souls College*, 3. R.W. Southern, in *The Oxford Magazine*, 28 November 1969: "Although he later lost his early religious beliefs, he remained, in all his sympathies firmly attached to the Jewish community. He would never consent to set foot on German soil and I do not think he could ever feel comfortable with anyone who had abandoned the Jewish faith for another."
17. Wansbrough, "Obituary," 602. Avot 2:8: *bor sud she-'eno me'abbed tippa.*
18. Stern himself told various people about this incident. Written documentation of this anecdote is found in the collection of eulogies, *All Souls College*, 10.
19. Prof. Mark R. Cohen told me that, when he was a student in London in 1965, he was invited to the Passover Seder conducted by Prof. J. Weis, a boyhood friend of Stern's. Weis and Stern, who was also present, conducted an intellectual Seder, which was based on Jewish lore such as that of Sa'adia Gaon. The Warden of All Souls referred to the nature of Stern's Jewishness at the memorial service held in honor of Stern at the chapel of the college: "Samuel Stern was of the Jewish faith; but his beliefs—I am assured by those who knew him best—were not so strict that he would have thought it improper for us to mourn his death with some formality on the Sabbath day, in a building consecrated to Christian uses." *All Souls College*, 7.
20. Ullendorff, *Two Zions*, 53. But his relationship with the Hebrew University and with Israel was complex. According to his family, he had been very much attached to Jerusalem in his youth and would often spend time touring in the Old City. In the early 1950s he had sought a position at the Hebrew University, but was refused. Apparently he never forgave the Hebrew University for this; see the letter written by J. Weis to S.O. Heller Willensky, published in *Igra* 3 (1990): 45, 79. At a later stage in his life Jerusalem was one of the many cities where he had been offered positions he declined to accept, according to Walzer, "In Memoriam," 4: "He refused calls to fill chairs in Leiden, Manchester, Jerusalem, Harvard and Philadelphia." His Israeli students describe with enthusiasm his relations with them; nevertheless, he refused to talk with them about subjects connected with Israel.
21. For the interaction between his biography and choices made during his career, see Walzer, "In Memoriam," 2; cf. Stern in his preface to *Isaac Israeli: A Neoplatonic Philosopher of the Early Tenth Century*, Scripta Judaica, no. 1 (Oxford: Oxford University Press, 1958), xxiii.
22. Stern, *Hispano-Arabic Strophic Poetry*, 133 n. 22, mentions several scholars who preceded him in their initial attempts to understand Yehuda Halevi's Spanish verses.
23. "Indeed, there are stories, current among members of his family, of the young student wandering bemusedly through the streets of the Holy City,

bumping into lamp-posts and quite unaware of his surroundings as he evolved his first hypotheses with regard to the interpretation of these enigmatic lines." Foreword by L.P. Harvey to Stern's *Hispano-Arabic Strophic Poetry*, v.

24. Stern, *Hispano-Arabic Strophic Poetry*, 161–65.
25. Tova Rozen, *Le-ezor Shir* (Haifa: Haifa University, 1985), 83 n. 22.
26. S.M. Stern, *Studies in Early Ismā'īlism* (Leiden: E.J. Brill, 1983), 85.
27. Ibid.
28. Ibid., xviii, 95.
29. S.M. Stern, *"Tari,"* in his *History and Culture in the Medieval Muslim World* (London: Variorum Reprints, 1984), ch. 12. For additional information about the coin, see Moshe Gil, "Sicily 827–1072, in the Light of the Geniza Documents and Parallel Sources," *Italia Judaica* 5 (1995): 139–42.
30. S.M. Stern, *Fāṭimid Decrees* (London: Faber and Faber, 1964).
31. *Arabic Legal and Administrative Documents in the Cambridge Geniza Collections*, ed. Geoffrey Khan (Cambridge: Cambridge University Press, 1993); Shulamit Sela, "The Head of the Rabbanite, Karaite and Samaritan Jews, on the History of a Title," *Bulletin School of Oriental and African Studies* 57 (1994): 254–67.
32. S.M. Stern, *Medieval and Hebrew Thought*, ed. F.W. Zimmermann (London: Variorum Reprints 1983), ch. 4.

10

Evariste Lévi-Provençal and the Historiography of Iberian Islam

David J. Wasserstein

In 1934, when he was just forty years old, and in the middle of his adult life, Evariste Lévi-Provençal published, or caused to be published, an eight-page "Note sur les titres et travaux scientifiques de M. E. Lévi-Provençal."[1] It is an interesting document. In a two-page introduction, it tells us when (4 January 1894), but not where, the author was born; it lists his academic degrees and honors up to 1934 (he obtained the *doctorat d'état* in 1923, at the early age of twenty-nine), but it does not mention where he carried out his studies. It tells us that he began teaching Arabic language and literature in 1913; that he was wounded in the Dardanelles campaign and in 1917 began working in Morocco, "to which country he thenceforth devoted the greater part of his scientific activity." It reports that he taught in Rabat until 1927, when he was called to Algiers, to a chair in the history of the Arabs and of Islamic civilization. And finally, it reports that for the previous four years, since 1930, he had offered various courses at the Sorbonne as well as in Morocco. In addition to all this, he had also edited the journal *Hespéris* since its foundation in 1921; and from 1926 he had been one of the editors of the French edition of the *Encyclopaedia of Islam*. The following six pages list his publications up to the end of 1934. According to this inventory, they numbered, apart from book reviews and encyclopaedia articles, some forty-seven published items, as well as another three or four in the press.

By any measure, the record is impressive: the *doctorat d'état* at the age of twenty-nine; the level of his academic rank by well before the date of this "Note," and the publications themselves. Some of the items listed in this bibliography remain standard works to this day (for example, his corpus of the Arabic inscriptions of Spain, which appeared in 1931);[2] there are over a dozen editions and/or translations of texts, virtually all of them discovered by Lévi-Provençal himself;[3] and there is his re-edition of the great *Histoire des Musulmans d'Espagne* of Dozy, produced in 1932. Lévi-Provençal was active and energetic in the profession more broadly conceived too: as an editor of a journal and as one of the animators of the *Encyclopaedia of Islam*; as a teacher; and so on. By the time he entered his fifth decade, Lévi-Provençal had already stamped his name indelibly on the field of the study of western Islam.

Nevertheless, one is impelled to ask why he, if it really was he, felt the need to publish this "Note."[4] Most of us do not publish such items. At the most we leave it to others to do so for us. It is tempting to try to associate the date of the work's appearance, December 1934, with political developments in Germany the year before—but it is difficult to see what kind of association there might be. It is a trifle easier to sense a link with that watershed age of forty which the scholar had just passed. But there is in fact no reference to this in the publication, and since his exact birth date is given, 4 January 1894, and the work itself is dated very clearly to December 1934, the apparent precision of four decades becomes less than elegant. Even if there were some link with his age, it is, once again, hard to see what that link might be.

There is another possibility: perhaps the scholar hoped, through publication of a document not overtly linked with his name as author, to establish his credentials, to advertise himself, possibly with a view to a job then about to become vacant. The introduction does have rather the ring of a(n unsolicited?) testimonial; and the list of his publications is cast in an unusual form (one which recurs, interestingly, in some of the later bibliographies published after his death): the publications are arranged chronologically, but they are also grouped within certain categories:

I. Editions et traductions de textes arabes
II. Histoire littéraire et bibliographie
III. Monographie linguistique

IV. Paléographie, épigraphie, archéologie
V. Histoire politique, religieuse et sociale de l'Occident musulman

and a reference to miscellaneous reviews and editorial work for the *Encyclopaedia of Islam.*

It is almost as though the scholar were looking for a job, and thought he could demonstrate his suitability for employment across a wide range of fields by arranging his publications thematically. We all know the technique. And indeed, in 1935, according to Régis Blachère (1900–72), Lévi-Provençal was appointed to a chair in the Faculty of Letters in Algiers, although he seems to have moved there only in 1936.[5] Might there be a connection between the "Note" and the move?

This is but one of several puzzles in the life and career of this scholar. For example, this publication imparts some facts, but not others: we do not learn from this where he was born; we do not find out where he pursued his studies; we do not even find a complete list of his publications;[6] and there is that curious, and unjustified, emphasis on Morocco—as distinct from Islamic Spain.

The puzzles do not end here. According to the late Eliyahu Ashtor (1914–1984), in his *Encyclopaedia Judaica* article on Lévi-Provençal, this scholar's name was actually Mabkhush.[7] Although Ashtor does not say so, it looks as though this name may be an Algerian form of one of the diminutives of the Hebrew name Mordechai.[8] Where the name Evariste came from it is impossible to say. Its Greek linguistic origin is clear, but its use as a name in French is uncommon, at best. The name Lévi-Provençal, if it is the scholar's original surname, would tend to confirm his identity as a North African Jew, and not a Jew of European immigrant stock in North Africa; but it would do no more than *tend* to confirm it (see below). The use of the name Mabkhush, on the other hand, seems to offer solid confirmation of a North African background, as no such onomastic form would have been in use among European Jews settled in Algeria. "Evariste," perhaps because of its Greek source, might suggest a particularly strong gallicizing tendency, of a piece with the rest of our knowledge of the man (and might also point to a similar tendency in his background).

What is more interesting in this connection is that one of Lévi-Provençal's closest friends, the Spanish scholar Emilio García Gómez (1905–95), points out that Lévi-Provençal himself never liked to use the full name Evariste, but limited himself to the initial, "E"; and that his friends, for want of any other intimate name by which to address him, always called him "Don Julián."[9] This is also the name, in the form "D. Julian," under which Lévi-Provençal published, in 1953, a translation of a romantic novel by García Gómez.[10] There is a very obvious puzzle here.

As to the name Lévi-Provençal itself, this too offers a little oddity: its very Jewish sound conceals its very great rarity. The name Provençal occurs among Jews in France, although with less frequency than might be expected.[11] The name Lévi-Provençal is found from time to time among Moroccan Jews, but there seem to be no examples later than the eighteenth century (and the single one known from that century is actually from Alexandria, while all the rest are of the sixteenth century or earlier).[12] But the scholar was (so far as we know) from Algeria. There are lists of names of Algerian Jews from the late nineteenth century, just before the time of his birth: for example, a petition from the Jews of Algeria addressed to the emperor at the end of 1869, concerning the naturalization of Algerian Jews as French citizens. This is signed by hundreds of Jews of that city (at a time when there were some five thousand Jews there). The name Lévi-Provençal is not among them. Another list is to be found in a document of August 1874, a collective request, formulated by the Chief Rabbi of Constantine on behalf of 94 Jewish families, 512 individuals in all, to be settled at a single place. Here too the name does not occur at all.[13]

(While preparing this paper, I discussed Lévi-Provençal with a number of Israeli Islamicist colleagues. Three of them reacted in ways of particular relevance here: one said that "despite the name," Lévi-Provençal was not a Jew at all; another claimed that the scholar "had changed his name because of his wife," who was Jewish, although he was not sure what the name had been before; and a third reported that Ashtor, the author of the entry on Lévi-Provençal in the *Encyclopaedia Judaica* mentioned earlier, "used to deny his Jewishness." Such testimonies scarcely constitute evidence, but they add to the general fog surrounding the image of the man.)

All this semi-detail about the biographical puzzles of a scholar is offered by way of introduction to a genuine mystery. García Gómez, in the same obituary just referred to, mentions that Lévi-Provençal never spoke about his youth: "Nada sobre sus primeros años." It is remarkably difficult to probe behind this reticence. And this raises a question. But there is another fact which endows the question with some little significance, especially in the present context. Throughout his works, those listed in 1934, when he was just in mid-career, and those listed after his death, in March 1956, and in such places as the *Index Islamicus*, we find no evidence whatsoever of any interest in the Jews. It seems to me that it would be normal to expect such interest. I shall return to this point in a moment.

The Understanding of Iberian Islam

Evariste Lévi-Provençal was one of a tiny handful of scholars who in the last century and a half have dominated the serious scholarly study of Islam in the Iberian peninsula. The two principal figures in this enterprise were both non-Spaniards: the first, Reinhart Dozy (1820–83), a Dutchman, and the second, Lévi-Provençal, an Algerian Jew. Each of them made the field peculiarly his own, not least through the production of major histories of the subject as a whole.

That of Dozy, *Histoire des Musulmans d'Espagne*, appeared first in 1861; it was translated into English just before the First World War, and appeared (as already mentioned) in an edition revised by Lévi-Provençal himself in 1932. Dozy's work was marked by literary and scholarly qualities alike. He had delved more than anyone into the manuscript resources for Islamic Spanish history; many of his works are either editions of texts or major works of primary research based on texts still in manuscript; he produced dictionaries which are still on the desks of scholars today; he edited (with others) the text of the *Nafḥ al-Ṭīb* of al-Maqqarī, an important seventeenth-century source for Islamic Spanish history and literature of all periods; and he produced a heavily annotated collection of texts dealing with one of the major dynasties of eleventh-century al-Andalus, the Abbadids of Seville.[14] His *Histoire des Musulmans d'Espagne* has all the hallmarks of its writer and of its period: it is a monument both of modern, nineteenth-century erudition and of the liberal sentiments of its Dutch author.

More than this, however, it was a reaction against the romanticism of earlier writers, shy of scholarship, who had produced a picture of Islamic history in Spain which owed much to Christian Spanish attitudes derived from the Reconquista and from literary images of the distant past, and very little to exact reading, or even understanding, of the sources.[15] The outstanding exponent of this trend, at least in Dozy's view, was José

Antonio Conde (1766–1820), whose *Historia de la Dominación de los árabes en España*, first published in 1820–21, enjoyed great popularity for a time (it was also translated, with considerable commercial success, into several languages, including English, by Mrs. Jonathan Foster, in 1854). Not the smallest part of Dozy's achievement lay in his demonstration of Conde's ignorance of Arabic and of Islamic history, of his lack of paleographical skills, and of the manifold errors, resulting from these faults, which were scattered throughout the pages of his work.[16] Dozy was the first to treat the subject with a scientific method and an encyclopaedic acquaintance with the sources, and his *Histoire* served unchallenged for three quarters of a century and more.

The second of the great scholars of Ibero-Muslim history was Lévi-Provençal. The "Note" to which I have already referred, produced when Lévi-Provençal was just in mid-career, demonstrates a man of great energy and productive capacity. As has been seen, it lists editions of texts, linguistic, historical and literary studies, as well as catalogues of manuscripts, and much besides. Almost single-handedly, Lévi-Provençal laid down many of the essential foundations for the field of study offered by al-Andalus. All of his many-sided productivity is associated with the world of the Islamic west, North Africa and Islamic Spain, al-Andalus; Lévi-Provençal almost never, in his academic writing, ventured outside the geographical confines of the Islamic west. Nevertheless, despite the new edition of Dozy's *Histoire*, and, in the same year, his production of an important volume on institutions and social life in tenth-century Islamic Spain,[17] there was no indication in all of this that Lévi-Provençal would soon embark on the major enterprise of a new synthesis of the history of Islam in Spain.

Six years after the appearance of that "Note," in 1940, political developments in Germany did have an effect after all on the career pattern of Lévi-Provençal. With the fall of France, he was, in the words of Régis Blachère, "hit like so many others by the stupid and ignominious racial laws,"[18] and deprived of his post. He was able for a time to enjoy a nominal appointment in Toulouse, and he spent the next two years (in this "enforced leisure," as he described it)[19] composing the first volume of his new *Histoire de l'Espagne Musulmane*. This was far more than an updating of Dozy. It was a totally new work, designed to fill six volumes, and to cover the whole eight-centuries-long presence of Islam in the Iberian Peninsula in all its aspects. It was a major enterprise. It was also, perhaps, a slightly quixotic one. Lévi-Provençal never completed it—

the first volume alone took him two years to complete, in the enforced leisure of Toulouse—and it has stood as an incomplete monument to his life's work ever since, both in remaining incomplete and in remaining, so far, unrivalled by any later production.

In this new work Lévi-Provençal took full advantage, in particular, of the new sources which he had done so much in the preceding two decades to bring to the attention of modern scholarship. One of the most impressive features of this work, indeed, is the range of the sources deployed by the author, who not only knew all the Arabic and Latin, as well as other western European, materials for the subject, but who drew upon some even more obscure sources on occasion. I shall return to this point below.

The incorporation of Lévi-Provençal's work into the multi-volume, authoritative *Historia de España* of Ramón Menéndez Pidal (1869–1968), founded by that scholar just over sixty years ago on the eve of the outbreak of the Spanish Civil War, effectively closed off the production of parallel Spanish works. The greatest histories of Islam in Spain have been the product of outsiders. Part of the reason for this is that the Spaniards have, until very recently, tended to view the Islamic element in the history of the peninsula in terms of the general debate about the nature of Iberian, Spanish identity. Even when they have not rejected the Muslims and all their works outright, even when they have gone far over towards the opposite extreme, their arguments over identity have made their writings on the broader history of Islam in Spain an integral part of the debate itself, and in doing so have led often to attempts to present that Islamic history in ways which suit present political and social Iberian needs. It is only since the death of Franco that it has become possible for Spanish scholars to engage in a genuinely disinterested historical investigation of their own past.[20]

The Jewish Absence

I said a moment ago that we find no evidence anywhere in his writings of interest by Lévi-Provençal in the Jews. This was not quite exact. If we look at his new, comprehensive *Histoire*, we do of course find sections devoted to religious minorities, in the manner which used to be fashionable (and perhaps still is). Here he spends a couple of pages in the first volume, and some six pages in the third, on the Jews of al-Andalus up to the end of the caliphate, in the early eleventh century.[21] It is noteworthy here that he depends wholly on materials in Latin and in Arabic, not on material in Hebrew (other than in translation). He recognizes the existence of sources and of scholarly work in this language, but, as he writes, this important scholarly work, produced by philologists and historians at the Hebrew University, is practically inaccessible to the majority of hispanists and medievalists.[22] This is a truth which has changed but little since his time. But it provides a link with what I was saying earlier.

Bernard Lewis has reminded us that "like most powerful myths," that of the golden age of the Jews in Spain "contains an element of historic truth."[23] Here not the mythic but the historic element is of interest. The real historic achievement—real in a Rankean sense—of the Jewish diaspora in Muslim Spain compares easily with those of the other great exile communities of the Jews—Babylon and Ashkenaz—and places it above Hellenistic Alexandria and most of the rest of the Jewish dispersion in Islamic lands. Lévi-Provençal seems not to have appreciated or understood this at all. The manner in which he treats the Jews in his *Histoire* suggests that, like most of those who treat of *dhimmī* communities in Islamic societies in the Middle Ages, he thought of them as merely quaint remnants of a pre-Islamic society which was on the way out. True, they might produce a vizier or two, and a couple of poets writing verses, but the viziers were transient individuals, they would disappear, and they would be less than likely to be succeeded by other Jews; and the verses served purely internal needs and were not necessary reading for the modern student of an Islamic society. Lévi-Provençal totally ignores the significance of the tenth century for those developments in the eleventh century and later, in Spain, which are of such enormous importance for subsequent Jewish history. It is true, of course, that Lévi-Provençal's primary concern was with Muslims, not with Jews, in al-Andalus, but the Jews there formed part of an Islamic society, and the brilliance of Jewish life in al-Andalus was at root inseparable from the brilliance of that Islamic society.

It is difficult to square the disregard for the significance of Jewish history in al-Andalus revealed in this work with the overall reality which the work seeks to uncover. In part, Lévi-Provençal's concern with a positivist history of an *événementiel* type explains this, and in part, too, a somewhat atomistic approach to the *événements* themselves. Further, while the sources for this exile bulk large, they are mainly, although not entirely, in Hebrew. Lévi-Provençal apparently never learned Hebrew. It seems worth enquiring why he did not—and why, as a member of an Algerian Jewish community which saw itself at least in part as a successor to that Spanish Jewry that was exiled in 1492, he took so little interest in the Jewish aspect of Islamic Spain, so important both for Islamic and for Jewish history.

The answer to the first question is more or less mechanical: Lévi-Provençal never acquired a proper knowledge of Hebrew in his youth probably because he grew up in a more than usually assimilated household in Algeria. If we cannot know this as a definite fact, we can infer it from its effect: Lévi-Provençal never quotes anywhere in his voluminous writings, so far as I am aware, any source written in Hebrew that is not available in another language, one known to him. This is particularly striking when we consider the fact that Lévi-Provençal was the discoverer and publisher of the memoirs of the last Zirid king of Granada, 'Abd Allāh; this text, which deals *inter alia* with the early history of the Zirid state, includes much on the most famous Jewish vizier of the Middle Ages, Samuel ha-Nagid, whose poems, along with other texts in Hebrew, provide much material illuminative of the ruler's memoirs.[24] And Samuel ha-Nagid in his person and in his career offers a prime example of the Jew between two worlds.[25] But this fact should not surprise: Algerian Jewry, unlike that of Morocco, was going through a process of enormous gallicization just at the time when Lévi-Provençal was a boy; one aspect of such a process was the loss of important cultural features specific to Jews.[26]

But it is the second question which is of greater interest. On the one hand it raises an issue which is still in search of adequate solutions: how are we to write the history of the Jews, and indeed of Christians too, in such medieval Islamic societies as those of Spain and Egypt? Is the ghettoization of a chapter on the Jews in more general works a useful way of looking at them? Must we deal with them via larger works on them as separate groups? Lévi-Provençal did not attempt to address this issue directly. Yet this question is of greater interest precisely because of the scholar himself. Lévi-Provençal seems, at least from the perspective of those with a special interest in Jews, to have had an almost ostentatious lack of interest in them. Islamic Spain, it is worth repeating, is the home to one of the greatest exiles of the Jews: the value of this for Jewish history is huge; the significance of the Iberian example of Jews in Islamic society is also of striking interest as part of Islamic history. If we ask why the scholar Lévi-Provençal took so little interest in these Jews, the answer may well lie less in the Jews than in the scholar.

Lévi-Provençal was extremely reticent about his background; we know too little about it. But we are not completely ignorant of it. We do know a little more than what he tells us in that possible job application of 1934. We are told by his obituarists that he was born in Algiers, and pursued secondary studies with brilliant results in Constantine, before studying at the university in Algiers. There, he studied particularly closely with two scholars of renown. One was René Basset (1855–1924) and the other Jérôme Carcopino (1881–1970). René Basset, who died young, was a famous Islamicist;[27] and Jérôme Carcopino, an ancient historian and author of an influential history of social life in ancient Rome, who served Vichy as French minister of education during the Second World War. He was elected a member of the Académie Française in the year of Lévi-Provençal's death.[28] Like Levi Della Vida (1886–1967)—and other orientalists—Lévi-Provençal came to orientalia after a start in ancient history and related studies. His earliest publications, indeed, include work in that area.[29]

René Basset was also the teacher of another Algerian Islamicist, Mohammed ben Cheneb (1869–1929). He was twenty-five years older than Lévi-Provençal, and cooperated with him in the preparation of an *Essai de répertoire chronologique des éditions de Fès*.[30] Carcopino, his teacher, and Ben Cheneb, his older colleague and like him a student of Basset's, offer us two very different angles from which to look at Lévi-Provençal. The one was a traitor honored by his own country only a decade after the event of his treachery, the other an almost completely gallicized Algerian Muslim, but both offer similar integrating visions of France.

This is not the place to look at Carcopino: both the field of his activity as an ancient historian and the nature of his activity in French political life during the Second World War take him too far from his fellow-citizen of France, Lévi-Provençal. But Ben Cheneb, that other Algerian, comes closer to Lévi-Provençal. In an obituary of Ben Cheneb which is itself a remarkable human document and historical testimony, Alfred Bel (1873–1945), another member of a distinguished generation of French scholars who worked on North Africa in the first half of the twentieth century, wrote the following:

> Loyal to his religion, and even to the habits of his fathers, Ben Cheneb, in order not to deny the traditions of Islam, had not judged it necessary

> to have himself naturalized as a French citizen, an action which would have obliged him to give up [his subjection to the jurisdiction of] Islamic law and his personal status. But for all that he was profoundly French at heart. He had understood that the future of his Algerian co-religionists did not lie in a premature political assimilation, so long as this was not preceded by a material, intellectual and moral evolution which might raise the natives (*indigènes*) to the level of the family and social ideas of modern Europe.... he thought it more useful to show his attachment to France and to his teachers in different ways [from his colleagues] by employing his fertile activity and his learning in the enterprise of French science in Islamic studies in North Africa.

Bel goes on to quote a French colleague of Ben Cheneb's about him: "He did not try to flatter by facile words the France which gave him so fine a welcome, and we should have been angry had he done so. He did not think to offer empty concessions and we never asked him for them. His innate delicacy guessed, without much difficulty, at our intimate thoughts and our deepest sensibilities; he was grateful that we understood and respected his."[31]

These are extraordinary words, and they say much about the intellectual, social and political atmosphere of French Algeria at the time when Lévi-Provençal was a young man there. He was born in a period marked by *émeutes* against Jews by Christian *pieds noirs* arising out of the granting of French nationality to the bulk of Algerian Jews by the Decret Crémieux of 1870.[32] The Jewish Algeria in which he grew up was observed by Nahum Slouschz (1871–1966), who visited North Africa in 1910: he tells us that while the Jews there at that time were "prosperous and well educated," nonetheless, "the young people [Lévi-Provençal was at this time 16 years old] are very little given to Jewish studies and, had it not been for the outburst of anti-Semitism in 1900, they would by this time, no doubt, have completely forgotten that they are Jews."[33]

Lévi-Provençal grew from this stock, and he breathed this atmosphere, and the result was to make him a scholar and a man of whose identity as a Jew even his close colleagues and friends were scarcely aware. Régis Blachère, as quoted above, referred to Lévi-Provençal's suffering from the "stupid and ignominious racial laws" of Vichy; and another friend of Lévi-Provençal's, Emilio García Gómez, similarly speaks of Lévi-Provençal's exclusion from his university chair "for no other reason than that of his racial origins." García Gómez is particularly interesting here. He died in 1995 at great age, one of the last of those giants that Spanish historiography used to produce in abundance. He saw himself as a sort of latter-day Spanish grandee, both in Spanish society and in Iberian Islamic scholarship, acquiring a minor title of nobility and writing right-wing columns in the daily press in Madrid.[34] He also held rather old-fashioned ideas about Jews. He wrote in unpleasant racist terms about Samuel Stern (whom he also professed to admire greatly), and dispensed anti-Semitic abuse even about non-Jews.[35] He almost never did so about his close friend Lévi-Provençal; he translated Lévi-Provençal's great *Histoire de l'Espagne Musulmane* into Spanish, where it provided, until a few years ago, the only volumes devoted to Islamic Spain in the multi-volume, authoritative history of Spain created by and bearing the name of Ramón Menéndez Pidal.[36] García Gómez went out of his way, in one of the obituaries which he wrote about Lévi-Provençal, to let us know that he, García Goméz, "always chose [his] friends from the heart and not on the basis of their race."[37] Yet even here, in the eulogies offered to their dead colleague by Spanish and French orientalists, we do not find any *explicit* recognition that he was a Jew.[38] He suffered under Vichy, "stupidly"; he was excluded from his post for a while, according to a man who likes to let us know that some of his best friends were not Christians. But the word Jew does not appear here at all, any more than it appears anywhere in Lévi-Provençal's own identity. It is an absent presence at the heart of his work.

Yet it is that very absent presence that lies at the root of the work by which he is most remembered, the *Histoire de l'Espagne Musulmane*, for this book was a product of the loss of his job and his deprivation of an identity as a Frenchman. Published in Cairo in 1944, it carried the following somewhat pathetic dedication: "to Charles de Gaulle and Georges Catroux I offer this book written in the shadows"; and Lévi-Provençal goes on to say of the book: "The preparation [of it] was begun in the autumn of 1940, when, scarcely demobbed, I had been excluded, for a time, from my University chair. It was completed in 1942. The two glorious names which I have inscribed [in the dedication] evoke with sufficient eloquence the moral climate, the faith, undamaged, in the future, despite the humiliations of the present, which at that time surrounded and kept me going." All of this is missing in the second edition of 1950, following victory by the Allies, and Lévi-Provençal's reinstatement as a French university professor, now at the Sorbonne; and the omission too is very revealing of the man.[39] Of course, Lévi-Provençal was not really a Frenchman, as Vichy had sought to proclaim. He was an Algerian French

Jew, neither quite French, because Algerian; nor fully Algerian, because Jewish; nor yet really Jewish because so fully assimilated into France.[40] The slogan "Ici, c'est la France" had meaning for a man like Lévi-Provençal largely because it had to. There was nothing else. It is perhaps in this mixture of exclusions, rather than of positive identities, that we should look for Lévi-Provençal the Jew.[41]

Notes

1. Paris: Larose, Editeurs.
2. *Inscriptions arabes d'Espagne*, 2 vols. (Paris: Larose; Leiden: E.J. Brill, 1931).
3. It is worth mentioning here the edition of the *Musnad* of Ibn Marzūq, the third volume of the *Bayān* of Ibn 'Idhārī, the fragmentary texts on the Almohads and the *Mafākhir al-Barbar*, as well as the *A'māl al-A'lām* of Ibn al-Khaṭīb and the treatise on *Ḥisba* of Ibn 'Abdūn.
4. It is odd, and perhaps significant, that this little work does not figure among the publications of this scholar in any of the bibliographies devoted to him.
5. Régis Blachère, "Evariste Lévi-Provençal (1894–1956)," *Arabica* 3 (1956): 133–35, at 134; see also "E. Lévi-Provençal 1894–1956" (unsigned), *Cahiers de Tunisie* 4 (1956): 7. There is a curious, and unexplained, puzzle here, for according to the "Note," as has been seen, Lévi-Provençal had held the chair in Algiers since 1927.
6. Later bibliographies of the publications of Lévi-Provençal, as has been mentioned, do not include this little work itself. Cf. the "Bibliographie analytique de l'œuvre d'E. Lévi-Provençal," in *Etudes d'orientalisme dédiées à la mémoire de Lévi-Provençal*, 2 vols. (Paris: Maisonneuve et Larose, 1962), 1:xvii–xxx; J. and D. Sourdel, "Liste des travaux du Professeur E. Lévi-Provençal," *Arabica* 3 (1956): 136–46; "Travaux de E. Lévi-Provençal," *Cahiers de Tunisie* 4 (1956): 7–15; and see further below, n. 29.
7. *Encyclopaedia Judaica*, s.v. "Lévi-Provençal, Evariste." (It is not wholly clear from the text whether Ashtor intends to refer here to Lévi-Provençal's first name or his surname, but the question is of little significance here.)
8. Cf. D. Corcos, "Quelques aspects de la société juive marocaine dans le Vieux Maroc—Les Prénoms des Juifs marocains," *Folklore Research Center Studies* (Hebrew University of Jerusalem) 3 (1972): 143–229, at 175, no. 162; repr. in idem, *Studies in the History of the Jews of Morocco*, (Jerusalem: Rubin Mass, 1976), 191, no. 162, for other diminutives of the name Mordechai, all from Morocco: Bakhay, Bakha, Bakka, B'khash, B'khass, Mourdokh, M'rdokh, M'rd'kho, Bedoukh, Dokho, Dakho, Mikhayo, Mikayou, Okha.

9. E. García Gómez, "E. Lévi-Provençal (4 enero 1894–23 marzo 1956)," *Al-Andalus* 21 (1956): i–xxiii, at iii. García Gómez suggests a connection with D. Julián Ribera (1858–1934), the great Spanish orientalist, but does not explain very clearly why he thinks there might be such a link. Another possibility, this too not the clearest, might lie in the well-known Count Julian, who controlled Ceuta at the time of the arrival of the Muslims there on their way to the conquest of the Iberian peninsula.
10. Emilio García Gómez, *Une Française à l'Alhambra —Grenade romantique,* trans. D. Julian [E. Lévi-Provençal] (Paris: Maisonneuve, 1953); originally published as *La Silla del Moro* (Madrid: Revista de Occidente, 1948).
11. Paul Lévy, *Les Noms des Israélites en France, Histoire et Dictionnaire* (Paris: Presses Universitaires de France, 1980), 79 f., from the years 1207, 1317, 1370, 1425, 1756, 1875; the number of occurrences, six, in the context of the number of years covered, some seven hundred, is telling.
12. Cf. Abraham I. Laredo, *Les Noms des Juifs du Maroc. Essai d'onomastique Judéo-Marocaine* (Madrid: CSIC, Instituto B. Arias Montano, 1978), 761–62, no. 694. There are none of this name now in the telephone directory of the Tel Aviv area; and in that for the Jerusalem area there is only one, living in Beit Shemesh.
13. Both documents are in the Archives in Aix; they are respectively Inv. 7169 F80/2043 R10/I–37/F80 (5 December 1869), and Inv. 7245 R10/I–37l Fonds GGA série L sous-série 51L, 50L, 50L5 Dossier 662 (August 1874). I examined copies of them in the Central Archives for the History of the Jewish People in Jerusalem. I wish to thank the staff of this institution for their help when I worked there.
14. See the entry on Dozy (by Wensinck) in *Nieuw Nederlandsch Biografisch Woordenboek,* vol. 1 (Leiden: A.W. Sijthoff's Uitgevers-Maatschappij, 1911), col. 749, with references.
15. See James T. Monroe, *Islam and the Arabs in Spanish Scholarship (sixteenth century to the present)* (Leiden: E.J. Brill, 1970).
16. Richard Hitchcock, "Hispano-Arabic Historiography: The Legacy of J.A. Conde," in *Arabia and the Gulf: From Traditional Society to Modern States. Essays in Honour of M.A. Shaban's 60th Birthday (16th November 1986),* ed. Ian Richard Netton (London: Croom Helm, 1986), 57–71, attempts to salvage Conde's reputation from the devastation wrought by Dozy, but with little success.
17. *L'Espagne musulmane au Xe siècle: Institutions et vie sociale* (Paris: Larose 1932).
18. Blachère, "Evariste Lévi-Provençal," 134: "Frappé comme tant d'autres par les stupides et ignominieuses lois raciales..." It is worth recalling, in the context of this phraseology, that the French government responsible for what this distinguished French scholar describes, only a decade after the end of the Second World War, as these "stupides et ignominieuses lois

raciales," also sent more than seventy thousand Jews, most of them French citizens, to their deaths at German hands; see Michael Marrus and Robert Paxton, *Vichy France and the Jews* (New York: Basic Books, 1981). Understatement is not an English monopoly.

19. In the "Avertissement pour la nouvelle édition" of the *Histoire de l'Espagne Musulmane*, of 1950, at p. vii: "pour utiliser les loisirs qui venaient de m'être imposés."
20. See now the valuable article of Manuela Marín, "Arabistas en España: Un Asunto de Familia," *Al-Qantara* 13 (1992): 379–93.
21. *Histoire de l'Espagne Musulmane*, vol. 1, *La conquête et l'émirat hispano-umaiyade (710–912)* (Paris-Leiden: Maisonneuve-Brill, 1950), 77–81 (devoted in fact to "Les communautés chrétiennes et juives d'al-Andalus"; the Jews receive very limited attention here); vol. 3, *Le siècle du califat de Cordoue* (Paris: Maisonneuve et Larose, 1967), 226–32.
22. *Histoire de l'Espagne Musulmane*, 3:227, n. 5.
23. Bernard Lewis, "The Pro-Islamic Jews," in his *Islam in History: Ideas, People, and Events in the Middle East*, new rev. ed. (Chicago: Open Court, 1993), 148.
24. Evariste Lévi-Provençal, "Les 'Mémoires' de 'Abd Allāh, dernier roi Zīride de Grenade," *Al-Andalus* 3 (1935): 233–344; 4 (1936–39): 29–143; 6 (1941): 1–63. These articles provide the Arabic text, together with a French translation and notes. The Arabic text was published in a corrected and revised edition as *Mudhakkirāt al-amīr 'Abd Allāh, al-musammāt bi-kitāb al-Tibyān* (Cairo: Dār al-Ma'ārif, n.d. [1955]). For translations into Spanish and English, see E. Lévi-Provençal and E. García Gómez, trans., *El Siglo XI en I[a] Persona: La "Memorias" de 'Abd Allāh, último rey Zīrí de Granada, destronado por los Almorávides (1090)* (Madrid: Alianza, 1981); Amin T. Tibi, trans., *The Tibyān, memoirs of 'Abd Allāh b. Buluggīn Last Zīrid amīr of Granada*, Medieval Iberian Peninsula Texts and Studies, vol. 5 (Leiden: E.J. Brill, 1986).
25. Cf. D.J. Wasserstein, "Samuel Ibn Naghrila Ha-Nagid and Islamic Historiography in al-Andalus," *Al-Qantara* 14 (1993): 109–25.
26. See, *inter multa alia*, Michel Abitbol, "The Encounter between French Jewry and the Jews of North Africa: Analysis of a Discourse (1830–1914)," in *The Jews in Modern France*, eds. Frances Malino and Bernard Wasserstein (Hanover, N.H.: University Press of New England, 1985), 31–53.
27. See necrologies by A. Bel, *Revue Africaine* 65 (1924): 12–19; V. Gordlevsky, *Vostok* 5 (1925): 275–77 (non vidi), and, by Lévi–Provençal himself, in *Hespéris* 4 (1924): 1–8.
28. See the dry comment of Henry Rousso, *Le syndrome de Vichy de 1944 à nos jours*, 2d ed. (Paris: Seuil, 1990), 83.
29. "Mars africain?" *Revue Africaine* 57 (1913): 63–69; "Note sur un fragment de *cursus* sénatorial relevé à Constantine," *Revue Africaine* 58 (1914):

21–28; "Deux nouvelles inscriptions de Timgad," *Revue Africaine* 61 (1920): 14–18. None of these figures in the "Note" referred to above. All three, it should be noted, belong to the very earliest phase of Lévi-Provençal's career. Thereafter Lévi-Provençal devoted himself exclusively and in some sense narrowly to the study of Islam.

30. *Revue Africaine* (1921): 158–73, 275–90; (1922): 171–85, 333–47.
31. A. Bel, "Mohammed Ben Cheneb," *Journal Asiatique* 214 (1929): 359–65; the French colleague whom Bel quotes here on Ben Cheneb is P. Martino, then dean of the Faculté des Lettres in Algiers.
32. See Michel Abitbol, *From Crémieux to Pétain. Antisemitism in Colonial Algeria (1870–1970)* (Jerusalem: Zalman Shazar Center for Jewish History, Jewish Historical Society of Israel/Vidal Sassoon International Center for the Study of Antisemitism, Hebrew University of Jerusalem, 1993); and Geneviève Dermenjian, *Juifs et Européens d'Algérie, l'antisémitisme oranais 1892–1905* (Jerusalem: Institut Ben-Zvi, 1983).
33. Nahum Slouschz, *Travels in North Africa* (Philadelphia: Jewish Publication Society of America, 1927), 321. We should not depend blindly on what Slouschz says here; he may have found what he expected to see in North Africa, by contrast to what he knew at home in the Jewries of eastern and western Europe. For a somewhat different view of Jewish life in Algeria at this time, see for example André N. Chouraqui, *Between East and West: A History of the Jews of North Africa* (Philadelphia: Jewish Publication Society of America, 1968; reprint, New York: Athenaeum, 1973).
34. See Joaquín Vallvé Bermejo, "Don Emilio García Gómez, Conde de los Alixares (Madrid, 4 junio 1905–31 mayo 1995) In memoriam," *Boletín de la Real Academia de la Historia* 192 (1995): 185–202.
35. See, for example, "El escándalo de las jarchas en Oxford," *Boletín de la Real Academia de la Historia* 188 (1991): 1–104 (by García Gómez); "Jarchas, moaxajas, zéjeles I," *Al-Andalus* 39 (1974): 273–99 (by "Angel Ramírez Calvente"; it seems a peculiar kind of cowardice to hide behind a transparent pseudonym in making anti-Semitic attacks, in what pretends to be a work of scholarship, both on a dead Jew [Stern] and on a live non-Jew [L.P. Harvey]).
36. Lévi-Provençal's work is vols. 4–5 in that series: *España Musulmana (711–1031), La Conquista, el Emirato, el Califato* and *España Musulmana (711–1031), Instituciones, Sociedad, Cultura*; it has now been joined by a distinguished vol. 8: *Los Reinos de Taifas, Al-Andalus en el Siglo XI*, ed. M. J. Viguera Molins (Madrid: Espasa Calpe, 1994). García Gómez was well-known for his racy, and racist, style. It was so easily recognized that even when he attempted to conceal the real identity of the writer of some of his nastier pieces, as he did occasionally towards the end of his long life, when he used for example the pseudonym Ramírez Calvente in the pages of the journal *Al-Andalus*, no one even pretended to be taken in.

37. Emilio García G6mez, "E. Lévi-Provençal," *Al-Andalus* 21 (1956): i–xxiii, at iii.
38. For the case of the Frenchman Blachère, see Eugen Weber, "Reflections on the Jews in France," in *The Jews in Modern France*, eds. Frances Malino and Bernard Wasserstein (Hanover, N.H.: University Press of New England, 1985), 8–27, at p. 25, who writes, "what strikes me... is not the imbecile and understandable politics of Vichy, which I do not regard as specially representative of modern France; but the high degree of public indifference to the plight of the Jews."
39. An anecdote told by Bernard Lewis at the conference in his honor at which this paper was presented seems worth preserving, and repeating here. Lewis reported that Lévi-Provençal was "aggressively French" at meetings of the editorial board of the *Encyclopaedia of Islam* after the Second World War. He reported also that at a meeting where it was proposed that the next international orientalists' congress should be held in Munich, in Germany, Lévi-Provençal announced belligerently that if it were to be held there, "Je ne marche pas!"—to which a voice from behind Lewis was heard to reply, "Qui ne marche pas, Lévi ou Provençal?" The story is not unamusing, but it reminds one of the remark of Weber cited in the previous note.
40. See now Gérard Noiriel, *Population, immigration et identité nationale en France, XIXe–XXe siècle* (Paris: Hachette, 1992); and Michel Abitbol, "The Integration of North African Jews in France," *Discourses of Jewish Identity in Twentieth-Century France*, Yale French Studies, no. 85 (New Haven, 1994), 248–61.
41. I am grateful to Camilla Adang and Ursula Wokoeck for valuable comments and criticisms in discussions on drafts of this essay.

Contributors

Benjamin Braude
Associate Professor of History, Boston College

Lawrence I. Conrad
Lecturer in the History of Medicine, The Wellcome Institute for the History of Medicine, London

Joel L. Kraemer
Professor of Jewish Studies, The University of Chicago

Martin Kramer
Senior Research Associate, The Moshe Dayan Center, Tel Aviv University

Jacob M. Landau
Professor of Political Science Emeritus, The Hebrew University of Jerusalem

Jacob Lassner
Philip M. and Ethel Klutznick Professor of Jewish Civilization, Northwestern University

Hava Lazarus-Yafeh ז״ל
Professor of Islamic Studies, The Hebrew University of Jerusalem

Minna Rozen
Professor of Jewish History, Haifa University

Shulamith Sela
Research Associate, The Ben-Zvi Institute, Jerusalem

David J. Wasserstein
Professor of Islamic History, Tel Aviv University

Index

MANSFIELD COLLEGE
LIBRARY
WITHDRAWN
OXFORD